Old Towpaths

Also from Westphalia Press
westphaliapress.org

The Idea of the Digital University

Earthworms, Horses, and Living Things

Bulwarks Against Poverty in America

Gems of Song for the Eastern Star

Treasures of London

Avate Garde Politician

Anti-Masonry and the Murder of Morgan

L'Enfant and the Freemasons

Understanding Art

Baronial Bedrooms

Spies I Knew

Making Trouble for Muslims

Ancient Masonic Mysteries

Material History and Ritual Objects

Collecting Old Books

Masonic Secret Signs and Passwords

Paddle Your Own Canoe

Opportunity and Horatio Alger

The Thomas Starr King Dispute

Careers in the Face of Challenge

Earl Warren's Masonic Lodge

Bookplates of the Kings

Lariats and Lassos

The Boy Chums Cruising in Florida Waters

Mr. Garfield of Ohio

The Wisdom of Thomas Starr King

Freemasonry in Old Buffalo

Original Cables from the Pearl Harbor Attack

The French Foreign Legion

War in Syria

Social Satire and the Modern Novel

Naturism Comes to the United States

The Essence of Harvard

New Sources on Women and Freemasonry

The Genius of Freemasonry

A Definitive Commentary on Bookplates

Designing, Adapting, Strategizing in Online Education

James Martineau and Rebuilding Theology

Gunboat and Gun-runner

Meeting Minutes of Naval Lodge No. 4 F.A.A.M

No Bird Lacks Feathers

Old Towpaths

The Story of the American Canal Era

by Alvin F. Harlow

WESTPHALIA PRESS
An imprint of Policy Studies Organization

Old Towpaths: The Story of the American Canal Era
All Rights Reserved © 2014 by Policy Studies Organization

Westphalia Press
An imprint of Policy Studies Organization
1527 New Hampshire Ave., NW
Washington, D.C. 20036
info@ipsonet.org

**ISBN-13: 978-1-63391-140-6
ISBN-10: 1633911403**

Cover design by Taillefer Long at Illuminated Stories:
www.illuminatedstories.com

Daniel Gutierrez-Sandoval, Executive Director
PSO and Westphalia Press

Rahima Schwenkbeck, Director of Media and Publications
PSO and Westphalia Press

Updated material and comments on this edition
can be found at the Westphalia Press website:
www.westphaliapress.org

OLD TOWPATHS

Courtesy Dr. B. F. Fackenthal, Jr., Riegelsville, Pennsylvania

THE DELAWARE DIVISION CANAL AT THE NARROWS OF NOCKAMIXON

OLD TOWPATHS

The Story of
THE AMERICAN CANAL ERA

By Alvin F. Harlow

TO
DORA

ACKNOWLEDGMENT

NO book of this sort can be written without much kindly assistance from persons other than the one known as the writer. Many have not the time nor in some cases the inclination to extend this assistance even when asked; and it is therefore with peculiar pleasure that I mention the following who have supplied me with data or pictures or have told me where I could find such things: —the Historical Societies of New York, New Jersey and Pennsylvania, of Buffalo, Worcester, Massachusetts, Easton, Pennsylvania, and Bucks County, Pennsylvania; the Western Reserve Historical Society of Cleveland; the Wyoming Historical and Geological Society of Wilkes Barre, Pennsylvania; the Department of Indiana State History and Archives, Indiana State Library, Indianapolis; the New York State Library; Boyd P. Rothrock, Curator, Pennsylvania State Museum, Harrisburg; H. H. She:.x, Archivist, Pennsylvania State Library, Harrisburg; Mrs. Sam R. Taylor, Curator, Allen County Historical Museum, Fort Wayne, Indiana; Dr. H. R. McIlwaine, State Librarian, Richmond, Virginia; William D. Goddard, City Librarian, Woburn, Massachusetts; Mrs. Sallie C. Hughes, City Librarian, Terre Haute, Indiana; American Numismatic Society, New York City; *The Numismatist*, Frank G. Duffield, Proprietor, Baltimore; Maine State Library, Augusta; Roy G. Finch, State Engineer, New York, Albany; R. T. Wisda, Assistant Superintendent Division of Public Works, Columbus, Ohio; Otto A. Rothert, Secretary Filson Club, Louisville, Kentucky; the Pennsylvania, Delaware and Hudson, Lehigh Valley and Baltimore & Ohio

Acknowledgment

Railroad Companies; the Chambers of Commerce of Columbus, Piqua, Dayton, Chillicothe, Portsmouth, Akron and Springfield, Ohio (and especially Mr. R. A. Warfel, Publicity Manager of the Chamber of Commerce at Columbus), of Norfolk-Portsmouth, Virginia and of Joliet and Ottawa, Illinois; National Cash Register Company, Dayton; Eastman Kodak Company, Rochester; *The Explosives Engineer*, Wilmington, Delaware; I. M. Church, Canal Superintendent, Lehigh Coal and Navigation Company, Mauch Chunk, Pennsylvania; Jay V. Hare, Secretary Reading Company, Philadelphia; Wilfred H. Schoff, Secretary The Commercial Museum, Philadelphia; Harry Marks, City Librarian, Easton, Pennsylvania; Dr. B. F. Fackenthal, Jr., Riegelsville, Pennsylvania; A. P. Walton, Schenectady, New York; R. B. Walton, Oswego, New York; John M. Schuler and Son, Oswego, New York; Bert J. Griswold, Fort Wayne, Indiana; J. F. Hubbard and John H. Rayner, Piqua, Ohio; E. W. Drinker, Bethlehem, Pennsylvania; Hal C. Phelps, Peru, Indiana; Ellis C. Soper, New York City; Charles R. Arnold, Ivyland, Pennsylvania; Charles M. Fish, Joliet, Illinois; Horace Hull, Ottawa, Illinois; Mrs. Laura Nash Griggs, Ottawa, Illinois; Moses Whitcher Mann, West Medford, Massachusetts; Edwin Charles, Middleburg, Pennsylvania; Harvey C. Morgenstern, Easton, Pennsylvania; John J. Baird, Honesdale, Pennsylvania; Jesse J. Mallory, Jr., New Haven, Connecticut.

ALVIN F. HARLOW.

CONTENTS

CHAPTER		PAGE
	ACKNOWLEDGMENT	vii
I.	THE ANCESTRY OF OUR CANALS	1
II.	THE BEGINNINGS OF OUR CANALS	5
III.	MORE AMBITIOUS CANALS—THE SANTEE AND MIDDLESEX	17
IV.	THE GENESIS OF THE ERIE	26
V.	OLD BOATING DAYS—THE NEED FOR BETTER TRANSPORTATION	33
VI.	THE BUILDING OF THE ERIE CANAL	44
VII.	THE CONSUMMATION OF A GREAT WORK	56
VIII.	THE PEAK OF CANAL-BUILDING ENTHUSIASM	66
IX.	CANAL OR RAILROAD?	76
X.	THE OPENING OF THE SCHUYLKILL AND UNION CANALS	86
XI.	THE BUILDING OF THE PENNSYLVANIA STATE CANALS	92
XII.	FLUSH TIMES AND THE CANAL MANIA OF THE THIRTIES	104
XIII.	WESTWARD HO!	117
XIV.	THE DECLINE OF THE PENNSYLVANIA CANALS AND THE END OF THE CANAL-BUILDING ERA	127
XV.	THE NEW YORK BRANCH CANALS—THE TRIUMPHAL PROGRESS OF THE ERIE	141
XVI.	THE RISE AND FALL OF THE NEW ENGLAND CANALS	158
XVII.	THE SUSQUEHANNA AND TIDEWATER AND ITS EFFECT ON THE UNION CANAL	169
XVIII.	THE LEHIGH AND DELAWARE DIVISION CANALS	177
XIX.	THE DELAWARE AND HUDSON CANAL	185
XX.	THE MORRIS CANAL	195
XXI.	THE LINKED FORTUNES OF THE SCHUYLKILL AND DELAWARE AND RARITAN CANALS	203
XXII.	THE JAMES RIVER AND KANAWHA CANAL	213
XXIII.	THE CHESAPEAKE AND DELAWARE CANAL	223
XXIV.	THE CHESAPEAKE AND OHIO CANAL	230
XXV.	THE OHIO CANALS	241
XXVI.	THE INDIANA CANALS	263
XXVII.	THE ILLINOIS AND MICHIGAN CANAL	279
XXVIII.	SHORTER CANALS	289
XXIX.	CANAL ENGINEERING	295
XXX.	CANAL OPERATION	308
XXXI.	LIFE ON THE CANAL	327
XXXII.	TRAVELING BY CANAL	342
XXXIII.	CANAL LOTTERIES	369
XXXIV.	THE LAST OF THEIR RACE	379
	BIBLIOGRAPHY	391

ILLUSTRATIONS

The Delaware Division Canal at the Narrows of Nockamixon *Frontispiece*

	PAGE
Many New Hampshire Flatboats Floated down the Merrimac and Were then Drawn through the Middlesex Canal............	20
Balance-Beam Lock Gates on Middlesex Canal..................	21
De Witt Clinton, Builder of the Erie Canal............... *Facing*	28
The Old and the New: Flatboats on the Susquehanna and the Canal alongside It, about 1835......................... *Facing*	40
Erie Canal Aqueduct over the Genesee River at Rochester... *Facing*	50
Invitation to the Celebration at New York in 1825 on the Completion of the Erie Canal............................. *Facing*	58
Invitation to the Canal Celebration Ball at New York City, November 7, 1825..................................... *Facing*	58
The Lock-Tender's Home............................. *Facing*	62
The Erie Canal at Frankfort, New York, about 1876........ *Facing*	62
Easton, Pennsylvania, a Prominent Canal Center, in 1831... *Facing*	70
The Canal Still Struggling Feebly against the Giant Force Which Destroyed It.................................. *Facing*	80
Loading Coal Boats on the Schuylkill Canal.............. *Facing*	88
A Schuylkill Canal Boat............................... *Facing*	88
Hollidaysburg about 1835...............................	94
Hotel at the Summit of the Allegheny Portage Railway...... *Facing*	100
Canal Packet Boat in Sections Being Carried up the Allegheny Portage Railway..................................... *Facing*	100
Richmond in 1833—The James River and Kanawha Canal in the Foreground.................................... *Facing*	110
Looking Down on the Erie Canal from the Head of the Locks at Lockport, about 1835........................... *Facing*	120
The Canals of Pennsylvania and New Jersey, Showing Connections with Adjoining States................................	129
Double Canal Boats Used on the Pennsylvania Canals along the Susquehanna....................................... *Facing*	134

Illustrations

	PAGE
Old Stone Sleepers of the Portage Railroad................Facing	138
Map of the New York Canals..................................	143
Oswego and the Oswego Canal about 1840......................	147
Clinton Square, Syracuse, and the Erie Canal in 1878.......Facing	150
The Amoskeag Canal and Blodgett Mansion.....................	161
The Only Steamboat Ever Tried on the Middlesex Canal....Facing	162
Worcester and the Blackstone Canal in 1828...............Facing	166
Burning by Confederate Troops on June 28, 1863, of the Combination Railroad Bridge by Which the Canal Towpath Crossed the Susquehanna......................................Facing	170
Ruins of Tunnel on the Union Canal—The Second Tunnel Built in the United States................................Facing	174
Ruins of Entrance Lock of Susquehanna and Tidewater Canal at Wrightsville, Pennsylvania, 1900..................Facing	174
A Weigh Lock on the Lehigh Canal about 1870...........Facing	178
The Lehigh Canal between Easton and Bethlehem.........Facing	182
Suspension Aqueduct of the Delaware and Hudson Canal across the Delaware River................................Facing	190
Canal Paper Money......................................Facing	196
A Loaded Boat Starting up One of the Inclined Planes on the Morris Canal...Facing	200
Aqueduct of the Morris Canal over the Passaic River at Little Falls as It Appeared in 1924..........................Facing	200
The Last Remaining Horse Boat on the Delaware and Raritan Canal Facing	208
The James River and the Canal near Balcony Falls.........Facing	214
Confederate Troops in 1861 Going via the James River and Kanawha Canal from Lynchburg to Buchanan on Their Way to the Front in Western Virginia........................Facing	220
The Old Drawbridge on the Chesapeake and Delaware Canal..Facing	224
The Deep Cut on the Chesapeake and Delaware Canal, One of America's Early Great Engineering Works................Facing	224
Aqueduct of the Chesapeake and Ohio Canal across the Monocacy River..Facing	234
Type of Freight Boats in Use on the Chesapeake and Ohio Canal in Its Last Days, 1923..................................Facing	238
The Ohio Canals...	243
Corn Being Shipped by the Ohio and Erie Canal from Chillicothe Facing	244
A Canal Shipping Agent's Advertisement, 1837.................	246
The Miami and Erie Canal in Cincinnati in the Seventies....Facing	250
Akron and the Pennsylvania and Ohio Canal in 1865........Facing	250

Illustrations

	PAGE
Outlet Lock at St. Mary's, Ohio, from Grand Reservoir into Feeder of the Miami and Erie Canal.......................	Facing 258
Indiana's Great Scheme of Internal Improvements...............	264
Wabash and Erie Canal Aqueduct across St. Mary's River at Fort Wayne...	269
Bill of Lading from New York to Peru, Indiana, 1843, via Erie and Wabash and Erie Canals................................	272
Winter View of the Aqueduct of the Illinois and Michigan across Fox River at Ottawa	Facing 280
The Final Trip of the Last Illinois and Michigan Canal Packet Carrying a Picnic Party in 1885.......................	Facing 280
Certificate of Land Sale for the Benefit of the Illinois and Michigan Canal...	282
Modern Lock on the Louisville and Portland (Ohio Falls) Canal	Facing 290
Cable Anchorage of the Remarkable Suspension Aqueduct of the Delaware and Hudson Canal across the Delaware River...	Facing 296
The "Drop" or "Fall" Gate for Locks....................	Facing 296
Aqueduct of Miami and Erie Canal across Great Miami River near Dayton, Collapsed in 1903.........................	Facing 298
A Lock for Weighing Boats and Cargoes, Shown Empty of Water, Harrisburg, Pennsylvania........................	Facing 302
Ingenious Water Wheels at New Hope, by Which the Delaware River Was Made to Pump Its Own Water into a Feeder of the Delaware Division Canal...........................	Facing 304
Testing Electric Traction on the Lehigh Canal.............	Facing 310
For Canals with Earthen Banks, No Tractive Power Superior to the Mule Has Yet Been Found.....................	Facing 310
Handbill of the Middlesex Canal, Offering a Reward for Muskrat and Mink...	317
Canal Boats Wrecked by Flood in the Adjacent River and Piled in the Bed of the Ruined Canal; Delaware Division, near New Hope, Pennsylvania, 1903....................	Facing 320
Repairing a Canal Whose Banks Have Been Broken by a Flood	Facing 320
A "Shot" or "Crib" or Timber Going through a Lock...........	322
John I. Weeks's Design for a Canal Towboat...................	323
Propeller Invented by Benjamin D. Beecher on the New Haven and Northampton Canal, Claimed to Antedate Ericsson's by Several Years..	324
More or Less Permanent Houseboat Life on the Canal......	Facing 328
Boy Overboard!...	Facing 328

Illustrations

	PAGE
A Morris Canal Captain of 1860.	331
A Floating Circus of Ante-Bellum Days Which Once Toured for Some Distance along the Wabash and Erie Canal.	Facing 334
A Driver, and Team of 1860.	Facing 334
Poster Advertising Ohio Canal Packets.	344
Type of Cargo Boats in Use on the Ohio Canals.	Facing 346
The Old Packet Boat "John Marshall" on the James River and Kanawha Canal, on Which "Stonewall" Jackson's Body Was Carried from Lynchburg to His Home.	Facing 346
One of Leech & Company's Fast Pennsylvania Packets.	Facing 352
Sectional Packet Boat Leaving Stock Exchange Corner, Philadelphia, for Pittsburgh about 1840.	Facing 356
Packet Boat "St. Louis" on the Miami and Erie Canal.	Facing 366
Lottery Advertisement in an Easton, Pennsylvania, Newspaper, 1831	371
Lehigh Navigation Lottery Ticket.	373
Union Canal Lottery Ticket.	373
A Modern Canal Ship, 258 Feet Long.	Facing 382
The Old and the New at Lockport—Five Locks of the Old Erie Canal and the New Barge Canal.	Facing 382

OLD TOWPATHS

OLD TOWPATHS

CHAPTER I

THE ANCESTRY OF OUR CANALS

HERE and there in Ohio, Indiana and the Eastern States the pedestrian—for nobody else would be apt to see such inconspicuous remains—may sometimes notice the faint indication of an embankment or a shallow depression, weed-grown but stretching away with such regularity of line as to rouse his belief that it may be an artificial work. He may even find a bit of crumbling stone wall, and—what is less probable—shreds of decaying timber still weakly attached to the wall by bits of rusty iron. Surely it is of human origin; perhaps prehistoric! But if he will inquire in the neighborhood he may find some white-bearded ancient who remembers that these poor ruins are all that is left of what was once a great internal improvement, the pride of the locality and the State—a canal.

The old canals are passing away rapidly. The year 1924 witnessed the death of two of the great ones among them—the Chesapeake and Ohio and the Morris. The Chesapeake and Ohio went as did several of its fellows, through the agency of an ugly spring flood which tore its banks in so many places and so cruelly that repairs were declared too expensive to be thought of. The Morris was already suffering from anemia, but its death was immediately induced by thirst; it died because water could no longer be spared to keep it alive. For the problem of water in

Old Towpaths

upper New Jersey, as around all great cities, is becoming a serious one.

These two canals were survivors of a system of transportation lines, most of which have long since vanished from the land. Some of them passed away even as far back as sixty to eighty years ago. But most middle-aged folk who lived east of the Mississippi River in their youth—and some even later—can remember the time when the canal-boat mule still plodded his long, long trail along an occasional waterway in New York, New Jersey, Pennsylvania, Maryland, Ohio and Illinois. He may still be seen in a small section of eastern Pennsylvania and on one short canal in New Jersey. Only very, very elderly persons can recall the canal boats in Massachusetts and Connecticut and Virginia and Indiana.

The history of our canals is a significant commentary upon American life and character—restless as it is, eager for speed, yearning for change, tearing down as soon as we have built, tossing away an almost new tool simply because another has been invented which is a split second faster. Of the more than forty-four hundred miles of artificial waterways constructed during our youthful expansion period, barely seven hundred remain in operation—even if we count the big New York State Barge Canal as being the old Erie, which to a considerable extent it is not.

Canals have been known in America but little more than a century, but they are by many thousands of years the oldest artificial avenues of transportation on our earth. Undoubtedly the first channels dug by man were those for irrigation purposes; but the human mind grasped the fact that they might be made large enough for navigation as far back as the meridian days of ancient Egypt, Assyria and Babylonia. In fact, Egypt had canals, though possibly not for navigation, ten thousand years ago. Babylon's glory and power were due in no small measure to her canals, which were built fully sixteen or seventeen centuries before Christ, and were restored about 600 B.C. by Nebuchadnezzar.

The Ancestry of Our Canals

Her greatest canal is said to have been over seven hundred miles long, or twice the length of the Erie.

An ancient predecessor of the Suez Canal brought the waters of the Mediterranean and the Red Sea together about 1380 B.C. and continued in operation for fifteen hundred years. The Romans did not a little canal building. The Fossa Marianna, from the Rhone to the Mediterranean was completed in 102 B.C. and the Emperor Claudius dug a canal from the Tiber to the sea. The lords of the world also built canals in Lombardy and Britain. One may still see in England the Foss Dyke, by which they connected Lincoln with the River Trent. This canal was a continuation of the Caer Dyke, now filled up, which ran from Lincoln to Peterborough. The Foss Dyke was said to have been deepened and made navigable about 1121, during the reign of Henry I. Even Odoacer, the barbarian ruler of Rome in the latter part of the Fifth Century A.D., constructed a canal from Mentone, near Ravenna, to the sea.

The Moors built canals in the vicinity of Granada during their occupation of Spain; but these works fell into disrepair after Ferdinand V reconquered that territory at the end of the Fifteenth Century. Meanwhile the Chinese had built their Grand Canal from the Yangtze-kiang to the Pei-Ho in the Thirteenth and Fourteenth Centuries. This colossal work, nearly a thousand miles long, was in part a series of canalized rivers with artificial channels connecting them. It was there that the lock or the inclined plane—possibly both—were first used, if we are to accept Marco Polo's report that the Chinese had a method of raising vessels from one level to another. Some students believe that they used locks of modern design. During the known history of the lock, from its first recorded appearance in Europe to the making of the great electrically operated gates of the Panama Canal, it has changed but little in design and not at all in principle.

The two brothers Domenico of Viterbo, Italy, have often been given credit for inventing the lock. They con-

Old Towpaths

structed a lock chamber with gates in 1481, but the Chinese were probably ahead of them, and many contend that locks were in use in Holland nearly a century before their appearance in Italy. The versatile Leonardo da Vinci was, among other things, a canal engineer. He built six locks in the canals of Milan in 1487, and he probably did the first canal work done in France. The Low Countries, with their numerous natural waterways, their flat terrain and their easily excavated alluvial soil, were natural breeding grounds for canals. Artificial channels existed in those parts in very early times, and as centuries passed, more and more were dug and the population became more amphibious, even aquatic. The canal system of Holland and Belgium is to-day the most efficient and valuable in the world.

Old Charlemagne dreamed of connecting the Rhine and the Main with the Danube, but his idea was not carried out until hundreds of years had elapsed after his death. Sweden completed a short canal with locks in 1606, and France dug her first canal of any importance, the Braire, between 1605 and 1642. But her greatest canal and one of the most important ever constructed in Europe was the Languedoc, which connected the Bay of Biscay with the Mediterranean. It was 148 miles in length, had over hundred locks and fifty aqueducts. Baron Paul Riquet de Bonrepos was its designer and it was completed in 1681. France's interest in waterways persisted until she had 3,000 miles of canals and 4,600 miles of navigable rivers.

It is a curious and not altogether explicable fact that England did not build canals until after the middle of the Eighteenth Century. It was in 1759 that the Duke of Bridgewater began the construction of a channel between Manchester and his collieries at Worsley, the first in England really independent of a natural stream. The thinly-settled, financially feeble American colonies began tinkering with the idea of canals almost or quite as early as did the mother country.

CHAPTER II

THE BEGINNINGS OF OUR CANALS

REMEMBERING that almost all of our really important old canals were dug during the first half of the Nineteenth Century, it may be surprising to the average American to learn that some of them were suggested one hundred or even one hundred and fifty years before they were built. And it is still more astonishing to discover that the first artificial waterway suggested on the continent was that which afterwards became the Illinois and Michigan, the farthest west of any of the old canals, and one of the last to be constructed.

Louis Joliet, exploring the great interior wilderness with Father Marquette in 1673, pointed out that a water connection between Lake Michigan and the Illinois River might easily be achieved. Father Dablon wrote in 1674:

"According to the researches and explorations of Joliet, we can easily go to Florida in boats and by a very good navigation with slight improvements. There will be but one canal to make—and that by cutting only one-half a league of prairie from the lake of the Illinois (Michigan) into the St. Louis River (Illinois), which empties into the Mississippi. . . ." La Salle also mentioned the desirability of such a canal; and as early as 1795 the Indians were induced to grant a right of way through their land for it.

The next suggestion of which we have any knowledge proposed a canal whose building actually did not take place for more than two hundred years thereafter. The seafaring colony of Massachusetts Bay began very early to consider the matter of cutting through the narrow neck near the base of Cape Cod, where it is less than eight miles wide and no more than thirty feet above sea level, in order to shorten and make safer their navigation between Boston and New Amsterdam. In Samuel Sewell's diary, October 26, 1676, is the following entry:

"Mr. Smith of Sandwich, rode with me and showed me the place which some had thought to cut, for to make a passage from the south sea to the north."

We do not know how much earlier this channel was thought of; in fact, it may have been the first canal suggested in America. In 1697 and again in 1776 the General Court of Massachusetts appointed committees to view the ground, but nothing of consequence was done on either occasion. In 1824 the National Government made surveys and estimates, but once more inertia overcame the project, and nothing more was heard of it until the '70's. A ship canal across Cape Cod was finally opened in 1914—which makes it too modern a thing to be considered in this history.

The third documented canal suggestion is that for a connection between Chesapeake and Delaware bays. Danker and Sluyter's *Journal of a Tour in Maryland*, written in 1679–80, remarks upon the short distance between the navigable parts of Apoquemene and Bohemia Rivers, the first-named flowing into the Chesapeake and the latter into Delaware Bay. The connection of the two bays through this portage was thought by the writers to be so important as to merit the attention of "higher authorities than particular governors."

The second canal *survey* made in the colonies was that of a route for this canal in 1764. Another line was run in 1769, this time under the auspices of the American Philosophical Society of Philadelphia, business men of that city contributing £200 to pay the expenses of the survey. But the route then chosen was thought to be too far down the coast to be of benefit to Philadelphia; and presently the

The Beginnings of Our Canals

Revolution came on and the idea was dropped for the time. Thirty-five years elapsed after the second survey before work was begun on the job, and sixty years before the canal was finally completed! Of that, more hereafter.

The next recorded suggestion comes from William Penn. Having laid out Philadelphia in 1682, in 1690 he issued proposals for another city in the Province of Pennsylvania. In his announcement he alludes to the feasibility of connecting the waters of the Delaware and Susquehanna:

"It is now my purpose to make another settlement upon the river *Susquehanagh*, that runs into the bay of Chesapeake and bears about fifty miles west from the Delaware. . . . There I design to lay out a Plan for building another city in the most convenient place for the communication with the former plantations in the east . . . which will not be hard to do by water, by benefit of the river *Scoulkill*, for a Branch * of that river lies near a Branch † that runs in the *Susquehannagh* river, and is the common course of the Indians with their skins and furrs into our parts . . . from the west and northwest parts of the continent."

This canal connection was discussed for many years before anything definite was done. In 1762 two men, David Rittenhouse, the astronomer, and Dr. William Smith, Provost of the University of Pennsylvania, made surveys over Penn's route from the Susquehanna at Middletown to the Schuylkill at Reading—the route afterwards covered by the Union Canal. This was the first canal *surveying* done in America. These men were dreaming ambitiously of nothing less than a water route from the Delaware River to the Ohio at Fort Pitt and to Lake Erie at Presque Isle. They proposed only the improvement of rivers, a short canal or two and a turnpike across the Allegheny backbone, which they found no way of passing by water.

But the population of the colony was as yet too small

---
* Probably Tulpehocken Creek.
† Probably Swatara Creek.

Old Towpaths

to enable such an undertaking to be financed; then the Revolution came on, and to shorten the story, thirty years passed after the surveys of Rittenhouse and Smith before any organized effort was made to build the canals. In 1791-92 two companies were chartered by the State of Pennsylvania, one to build the line between the Susquehanna and the Schuylkill, the other to improve the Schuylkill from Reading down to Norristown and to build a canal 17 miles long from Norristown to the Delaware. The intention of connecting the eastern and western parts of the State was definitely expressed in the acts incorporating these two companies.

In 1793 President Washington, that ardent friend of internal improvements, accompanied by David Rittenhouse, Robert Morris, and Tench Francis, made a horseback tour of inspection over the line of the Schuylkill and Susquehanna. A year later, when troops set out from Philadelphia to suppress the Whisky Insurrection, Washington accompanied them; but one of his objects in doing so was to give himself another look at the work on the proposed canal in which he took so much interest. In his diary we read under date of October 2, 1794:

"An accident happening to one of my horses occasioned my setting out later than was intended. I got off in time, however, to . . . view the canal from Myerstown towards Lebanon, and the locks between the two places; which (four adjoining each other in the descent from the summit ground along the Tulpehocken, built of brick) appeared admirably constructed."

By 1794 the two companies had nearly completed 15 miles of work, some of it difficult—rock excavation, heavy embankments and several locks. They had spent $440,000, which exhausted their funds; and here the work halted again, this time for a siesta of twenty-seven years. Its stoppage had a discouraging effect upon other efforts at public improvement.

The Beginnings of Our Canals

The fourth canal suggestion in America came again from a Frenchman—Antoine de la Mothe Cadillac, pioneer and commandant in Canada, who in 1707 communicated to Louis XIV a scheme for connecting Lakes Erie and Ontario by canal, to avoid the great portage at Niagara Falls. The Government admitted the desirability of the work, but feared the expense. The French continued to think of the canal as a desirable military link between Detroit and Montreal in case of war; but in the end, it was the English who built it.

Another one of our very old canal projects was that which sought to connect the Atlantic seaboard with the Mississippi Valley through the medium of the James and Kanawha Rivers. Tradition has persistently credited Governor Spotswood of Virginia with having conceived this idea during his tour through the Blue idge and the Alleghenies in 1716; but no valid evidence of this has been discovered.

A few Virginians had doubtless thought vaguely of this east and west connection, but the man who first made a definite campaign in favor of linking the Atlantic coast with the Mississippi Valley—and a vigorous campaign it was, too—was that most practical and far-seeing man of the Eighteenth Century, George Washington. He was not only first in war, in peace and in the hearts of his countrymen, but he has also been called our first expansionist. We find no public man previous to the Revolution who so keenly appreciated the enormous potential value of the western territory. Very early in life he became a traveler on horseback and on foot through the Appalachian passes, beginning in 1748 at the age of sixteen as a surveyor of Lord Fairfax's great mountain valley estates; and wherever he went he saw with a photographic eye, he analyzed and he remembered.

In 1749 a group of Virginian men organized the Ohio Company, a trading concern which, among other operations, acquired a considerable tract of land in southern Ohio. To reach these new possessions the company blazed a trail up the Potomac and down the Monongahela in 1749–50. Washington helped to survey a road over that route in 1750–51. He followed it in part on his mission to the French forts as an envoy of Governor Dinwiddie in 1753; and he went over it again with the unfortunate Braddock on his last march in 1755. Upon his return from the French mission Washington tried to convince Governor Dinwiddie and the council of the value and importance to England of the western territory, and the necessity of public highways if she expected to retain it. But such improvements would have been very expensive, and the solons seem to have paid scant attention to the visionary ideas of the enthusiastic young chap of twenty-two.

Washington, however, was not disposed to let the matter rest. He talked of it everywhere, wrote letters about it to friends and public men and published articles in the colonial newspapers. In 1770, 1772 and 1774 he made journeys through the mountains to westward, by both the James and the Potomac routes, and his ardor redoubled. He was astounded to find how greatly the number of settlers in the upper Ohio Valley had increased. He brought the matter before the House of Burgesses in 1774, but could get no action. Then he introduced a bill for the improvement of the navigation of the Potomac for 150 miles above tidewater. This was opposed by the burgesses from the central and southern portions of the colony on the ground that it would benefit only the northern section. To conciliate them Washington amended his bill to include the improvement of the James, though he regarded that stream as much less important in the matter of western communication than the Potomac. The amended bill might have passed, but while it was being discussed, the war came on and all matters of internal improvement were forgotten.

But Washington's arduous military labors during the Revolution did not make him forget the subject. When he

The Beginnings of Our Canals

returned to Virginia after the war he again took up his propaganda in favor of westbound highways. On September 1, 1784, he left Mount Vernon for a trans-mountain tour, further to satisfy himself as to conditions and requirements. He traveled 650 miles, mostly on horseback, though partly on foot. Upon his return he handed a report with recommendations to Governor Harrison, which was the first general outline of a system of public improvements in our history. He urged the importance of the western territory and hinted that as matters stood, the settlers in those parts were apt to throw their allegiance either to the British to the north of them or to the Spaniards in the south, unless they were brought more closely in touch with their brethren of the thirteen states. He urged actual surveys and mapping of middle western rivers and made many other practical suggestions.

"The great object," he wrote to Edmund Randolph in 1785, "for which I wish to see the navigation of the Rivers James and Patowmack extended is to connect the Western Territory with the Atlantic States; all others with me are secondary."

In sharp contrast to his standing with Dinwiddie in 1754, Washington was now become a man of such overwhelming importance that a word from him was given the profoundest attention. Harrison strongly approved his report and laid it before the Assembly. Action upon it was immediate. Bills incorporating the James River Company and the Patowmack Company were passed in 1785. The Patowmack Company was organized in May of that year and the James River Company in August. Washington was present at the Patowmack meeting and was made President. Considering the impoverished condition of the country so soon after the Revolution, it is remarkable that 403 shares of stock were subscribed for at that meeting, which meant in cash £40,300. The corporation insisted on presenting Washington with fifty shares of stock in recognition of his

Old Towpaths

services, and the Virginia Legislature for the same reason tendered him one hundred shares of James River stock. He at first objected to both gifts on the broad ground that he had never accepted any pay for his public services, and did not wish to begin the practice now. He finally accepted the shares with the proviso that if he were permitted to appropriate them to public use, he "would receive them on those terms with due sensibility."

He bequeathed the James River stock to Liberty Hall Academy in Rockbridge, which later became Washington College in Lexington and, finally, Washington and Lee University. His stock in the Patowmack Company he desired to be made the nucleus of a great national university in the city of Washington—a project never realized.

Work began that summer on the canal around the Great Falls, just above Washington—the first corporate work in America on an improvement of navigation for public use. It is probably true that Cadwallader Colden, afterwards Lieutenant-Governor of New York, had dug a short, crude waterway in Orange County of that State in 1750 for the transportation of stone, but it was a private one and without any remarkable engineering features, though Colden deserves credit for having been the pioneer.

In 1786 two hundred men were employed on the Patowmack Company's work at Great Falls and other points farther up the river. The struggle against inexperience, lack of money, floods and other difficulties was a terrific one, and the canal around Great Falls was not completed until 1802. Washington did not live to see it opened. By 1808 there were five short canals between Washington and a point above Harpers Ferry, the longest being the one around Little Falls, 3,814 yards, which carried the navigation to tidewater.

The James River Company was also organized in 1785, and they, too, insisted on making Washington President, though he urged that he could not be active in the position.

The Beginnings of Our Canals

They were content to have him merely as honorary President, because of the value of his name, and so he continued until 1795. Edmund Randolph was made active President. The chartered purpose of the company was that of making the river navigable by damming, dredging or any other means necessary "from the highest point practicable to the great falls beginning at Westham," and to cut a canal around the said falls. The improvement of the upper portion of the river was done mostly by dredging and opening sluices; the canal around the rapids above Richmond was a harder nut to crack.

Progress was slow, and by 1790 the company was out of funds; but in the meantime, it had achieved something. On December 29, 1789, its canal was completed around the rapids from Richmond to Westham, seven miles, in such fashion that the water was turned on and a party of jubilant citizens went through it in a small boat. The James River Canal has thus been claimed to be the first of any consequence completed in America. But to tell the truth about it, it was not yet in practicable condition for the bringing of freight boats into Richmond. Not until 1795 was this accomplished. In the meantime three other canals had been completed and put into practical use, and the honor of having been the first in America probably lies among those three. These three were respectively at New Orleans, at South Hadley Falls in Massachusetts and on the border line between Virginia and North Carolina.

The conditioning of their canal brought the James River Company to the verge of bankruptcy again, and shrinking from the idea of trying to sell any more stock, they began borrowing money. Thus runs the pitiful story of all those earlier attempts at internal improvement! The country was so dreadfully poor! "The Proprietors of the Upper Locks and Canals on the Connecticut River in the County of Hampshire" (for such was the impressive official title of the South Hadley Falls corporation) were forced to go to Holland,

Old Towpaths

then a great world money center, for funds with which to dig their little ditch, though it costs less than $100,000. A half million dollars in those days was a sum such as people in America only read about in books like the *Arabian Nights*.

The question as to the oldest canal in America is one that has often been debated. The three mentioned above all came into use during the same year—1794. The honor of having been the first on the continent to be really completed probably belongs to one or the other of the first two —the Carondelet and the South Hadley Falls.

During the Spanish régime in Louisiana in the Eighteenth Century, one of the Governors, Baron François Louis Hector de Carondelet, saw that New Orleans needed a water connection with the great Lake Pontchartrain, four miles back of the town, and that via Lake Pontchartrain's mouth, lay a shorter way to the Gulf coast than by the Mississippi River. With this in mind, he ordered a canal dug from the border of the town northward two miles to Bayou St. John, which led into Pontchartrain.

This ditch—dug with slave labor loaned by loyal citizens —was only 15 feet wide, but through it to the basin just outside the ramparts for many years came batteaux and schooners from the other side of Pontchartrain and from the Gulf Coast, even as far as the Floridas, bringing cattle, fish, farm products, lumber, charcoal and firewood.

The canal at South Hadley Falls, only two miles long but very important to the navigation of the Connecticut River, was begun in 1793 and opened for traffic in the following year. The Dismal Swamp Canal, begun in 1787, was in use in 1794, but only for small boats, as it had not reached its originally contemplated width of 32 feet nor depth of 8 feet. This canal connected the lower end of Chesapeake Bay with the Pasquotank River, a small stream emptying into the North Carolina sounds. Washington visited the location, thought the plan feasible and subscribed $500. Patrick Henry also invested in the stock. The original estimate of

The Beginnings of Our Canals

cost was too low, and by 1807, it had expended $100,000 and was navigable only by flats 6 feet wide, drawing 2 feet of water. These flats were mostly engaged in bringing hand-split juniper shingles out to the little port of Deep Creek, where they were bought by the captains of coasting schooners. The canal then had a perhaps unique distinction in that the company owned six slaves who were keeping the works in order. It was afterwards enlarged. It and the Carondelet or Old Basin Canal can claim another distinction, that of being the two oldest canals in America *still in use*.

A canal now almost forgotten by historians was that one nine miles in length along the lower Susquehanna River in Maryland from Port Deposit around some shallows in the river to tidewater near Havre de Grace. The company was chartered by Maryland in 1783. The stockholders, prominent citizens of Maryland, promised to complete the waterway in seven years and with an expenditure of £20,000. But by 1802 they had spent £80,000, and needed fully £40,000 more to finish the job. Thence the project (although an important one to the commerce of Pennsylvania) limped along until 1817, when a forced sale put it into the hands of a few individuals, and it shortly faded out of the national scene.

Farther up the Susquehanna a serious obstacle to navigation was Conewago Falls or rapids, just below Columbia, Pennsylvania. They were so rough that not many keel boats attempted to pass them, but stopped—most of them—at Middletown. Between 1792 and 1798 a company of men, most of whom were stockholders in the Schuylkill and Susquehanna Canal Company, dug a canal one mile long around Conewago Falls and improved the river by sluices for seventeen miles below that point. The canal was opened on November 15, 1797—the first canal completed in the State of Pennsylvania. It had cost $102,000. Governor Mifflin and other prominent men came to the opening celebration, riding horseback. Notwithstanding snow and sleet, hun-

Old Towpaths

dreds of people were present and the newspapers said that but for the bad weather there would have been thousands. The Governor and other notables went aboard a boat, were drawn into a lock at the lower level, and in a few minutes, to their intense astonishment, the water had raised them nine feet! Cannon firing was always necessary at an affair of this kind, and we learn that the workmen, "having no artillery of brass or iron," had drilled holes in some of the big rocks to serve as cannon barrels, whence they fired several salutes. This canal continued in use until the building of the Susquehanna and Tidewater Canal, forty years later.

There were some small early canals in New England which were a bit more successful financially than some others we have mentioned. One of these, a mile and a half in length, made an avenue around Pawtucket or Patopwick Falls in the Merrimac River, at the spot where the city of Lowell now stands. It was begun in 1792 and completed in 1797. The canal around Montague Falls in the Connecticut River, completed in 1800, was three miles long, had eight locks and two dams. It saved twice its length in land carriage and was unique in that it paid a 4 per cent dividend for twenty years. The Bellows Falls Canal in Vermont was less than a mile long, but it overcame a fall of fifty feet by means of nine locks, and opened navigation for 120 miles.

CHAPTER III

MORE AMBITIOUS CANALS—THE SANTEE AND MIDDLESEX

OUR canal builders were now growing bolder in conception. As the Eighteenth Century closed, two waterways, the longest yet attempted, were being dug contemporaneously, one in New England and one in the South. These were the Middlesex Canal, which connected Boston Harbor with the Merrimac River, and the Santee and Cooper Canal, which extended from the Cooper River just above Charleston to the Santee, a distance of 22 miles.

The latter canal was built primarily to give the agricultural products of central South Carolina a better outlet. Charleston was the most important city on the south Atlantic coast, while the Santee drained the largest and one of the most productive watersheds in the Carolinas. But that river enters the ocean through a labyrinthine swamp, fifty miles northeast of Charleston, and navigation through its mouth was almost out of the question. After the Revolution, when the indigo and rice trade lay almost dead, it was believed that if the Santee could be connected directly with Charleston, the condition of all parties concerned would be greatly improved; the farmers in the interior could get their products to market more economically, while Charleston's trade would be bettered and yet her food supply would be cheaper.

In 1786 the Legislature granted a charter for a company to dig a canal between the Santee and the Cooper; but work did not begin until 1792. A route was chosen between favorable points where the lower reaches of the two rivers approached each other closely. Agriculture was at a low ebb in the State at the time. Slaves were cheap, and their owners found it more profitable to lease them to the canal company as navvies than to keep them on the plantations.

The canal had to contend against many hindrances. The plantation owners through whose property it passed almost unanimously opposed it. To say nothing of its slashing through their acreage, they feared that it would damage the irrigation of their rice fields, and that the passing boats would demoralize their negroes and perhaps give them opportunities to run away. Furthermore, there were no native engineers in South Carolina, and the job of building the canal was therefore entrusted to Colonel John Christian Senf, a man of Swedish birth and chief engineer of the State. Senf was a vain and jealous man, and permitted his professional judgment often to be warped by personal considerations, to the great detriment of his product.

The slave labor, too, was stupid and inefficient at this unusual sort of work. By the end of 1795 not more than five miles of the ditch had been dug and a few locks were being built; but now a new complication appeared. Cotton had begun to be successfully grown in South Carolina, and threatened to take the place of indigo as the staple crop. Agriculture was looking up and labor was therefore higher and harder to get. It became evident (as was the case with almost every other canal built in America) that the job was going to cost far more than had been expected. The directors in their extremity fell back upon the favorite expedient of those days, and induced the Legislature to grant them a lottery privilege. But this did not produce sufficient cash, and numerous assessments were made on the stock. In July, 1800, the canal was declared complete. It had been eight years in building and had cost $750,000—an unprecedented amount for a public work in those days and one which made dividends impossible for a long period.

The idea for the Middlesex Canal is said to have origi-

The Santee and Middlesex

nated in the mind of James Sullivan, judge of the Superior Court of Massachusetts for six years and later governor. The conception seemed a clever and logical one. The Merrimac River was the chief outlet for New Hampshire's great store of raw materials, principally timber and granite, and Boston and vicinity furnished an excellent market for them. But to reach Boston the merchandise had to pursue a roundabout course and come down to the city from the Merrimac either by wagon or by sea. Boston was therefore receiving practically all its supplies by wagon, even timber, firewood and building stone, which increased costs enormously.

The new canal was accordingly surveyed from Boston northward to tap the Merrimac just above Lowell. The principal fault in the plan was that the Middlesex, like several other of the earlier canals, was built when its territory was too young and scantly settled to give it adequate support. But an enormous optimism was now springing up in America, and canal promoters were unterrified by any such slight drawback as sparse population. The projectors of the Middlesex even envisioned Boston as connected with Quebec and Montreal by canals from the Merrimac to the Connecticut and from the Connecticut to streams flowing into the St. Lawrence.

Governor John Hancock of Massachusetts signed the charter of "The Proprietors of the Middlesex Canal" in 1793. Colonel Loammi Baldwin, who was scarcely second to Sullivan among the promoters in either ability or enthusiasm, turned the first spadeful of earth in September, 1794. "I consider the prospects before us," said he, "more flattering than any I have seen in the Southern States, the Washington Canal alone excepted."

But amateur estimates as to costs often prove fallacious, and though laborers received only $8.00 per month in Massachusetts in those days and carpenters $10 to $15, expenditures mounted alarmingly and many assessments were necessary. By the time the canal was completed in 1803 it had

Old Towpaths

cost $528,000—a staggering sum for a young nation just making its start in the world. Boston at the time was a town of 20,000 inhabitants, and its whole assessed valuation was only $15,000,000. Medford, Woburn and Chelmsford were tiny villages. Lowell did not as yet exist. But public confidence was great. The stock had sold at $25 per share in 1794. In 1803 when full navigation was established the stock reached $473, and in the following year $500.

The canal was 27 ¼ miles in length, 30 feet wide at the water surface, and accommodated boats drawing 3 feet of

From Old Residents' Historical Association Publications, Lowell, Massachusetts
MANY NEW HAMPSHIRE FLATBOATS FLOATED DOWN THE MERRIMAC AND WERE THEN DRAWN THROUGH THE MIDDLESEX CANAL

water. It had nineteen locks, some built of wood and some of stone. At its highest level it passed through the Concord River, its chief feeder, at grade, the mules crossing by a floating towpath. Boats operating on the canal carried from 10 to 25 tons cargo. Much timber also came through in rafts. New Hampshire's supply of oak and pine was believed to be practically inexhaustible, and Daniel Webster guessed that this had been enhanced in value full $5,000,000 by the canal. Much ship timber was brought to the yards at Medford, and New Hampshire's granite, firewood and farm products found in it a short route to Boston.

But confidence was soon shaken. For years the canal

The Santee and Middlesex

was not profitable. Its value to the territory it served was great, but that territory was too small and too thinly settled to yield it adequate returns. In 1810 it vainly petitioned Congress for financial assistance. The Embargo and the War of 1812 brought more hardship, and it was not until 1819 that it paid its first dividend. By that time the long-suffering stockholders had paid exactly one hundred assessments, and each share of stock had cost them, including interest, $1,455.25, making the whole cost of the canal to them actually more than a million dollars.

From Old Residents' Historical Association Publications, Lowell, Massachusetts
BALANCE-BEAM LOCK GATES ON MIDDLESEX CANAL

It is impossible today to form an adequate conception of the difficulties under which early American canal builders labored. That they achieved such notable construction as they did is high testimony to their daring, originality and persistence. To be sure, some of the canal engineering of those days was accomplished, as rustic humor used to put it, "by main strength and awk'ardness," but in other cases genius of a high order seems to have been developed to meet the emergency. The builders not only created works which were equal to those in Europe, but they did things which had never been done with canals before.

But when the Middlesex Canal project was begun, "the

Old Towpaths

science of engineering," wrote Caleb Eddy, manager of that waterway, in after years, "was almost unknown to anyone in this part of the country." He might have added, "or in any other part of the country." There were few men in America who had even seen a canal lock (for one must go to Europe to see such a thing) and fewer still who understood the principles involved.

No engineer being available in New England, the Middlesex directors appointed a builder named Thompson to lay out a line for the canal. Thompson knew nothing of surveying and could not have used a theodolite if he had had one, but he did his best by rule of thumb. After laborious calculation and much squinting along carpenters' levels, he decided that the ascent from the Medford River to the Concord amounted to 68½ feet. When the line was afterwards surveyed by a practical engineer, the rise was found to be in reality 104 feet! Thompson also figured a further ascent from the Concord at Billerica to the Merrimac at Chelmsford of 16½ feet; but an accurate survey later showed the Merrimac to be in reality 25 feet *lower* than the Concord at the points designated. Fortunately, Thompson was not permitted to build the canal. The directors sensed the fact that better calculations would have to be made, and so engaged an English engineer named Weston, who built the canal, and made a good job of it.

The personal peculiarities of Senf, the engineer of the Santee Canal, have already been mentioned. Doubtless the company would have been glad to replace him with another man, but they knew not where to find another. Due to his jealous vanity and to his favoring certain property owners, he so located the canal that the greater part of its course had to be fed by artificial reservoirs instead of by natural flow, as should always be the case when possible; and the time came when fourteen miles of the channel lay absolutely dry.

When the directors of the Patowmack Company had completed their organization and the question of an engineer

The Santee and Middlesex

to plan the work arose, no one had a single name to suggest. Advertisements were inserted in the Philadelphia, Baltimore and Alexandria papers for months for a skillful person to conduct the work, but there were no applicants. The Board finally offered the job to James Rumsey, believed to be the cleverest mechanician in either Maryland or Virginia, and he accepted.

Rumsey had never seen a canal; but he, his fellow workers and the men who eventually succeeded him proved fully equal to their task. The locks at the Great Falls were considered as among the great engineering feats of the Eighteenth Century, and were commented upon by every scientific publication in Europe and the Americas. The descent was 76 feet in 1,250 yards. High cliffs rose directly from the water below the falls, which made the return to the river very difficult; and the last two locks were cut in solid rock.

Remember that they had no means but hand drilling by which to make powder holes in the stone, and nothing but old-fashioned black powder to do the blasting, or "blowing," as it was usually called then. There were no pneumatic drills, steam shovels, steam loaders, clamshell or orange-peel buckets, skidders or tramways for removing débris. All earth must be hand dug with plow, pick and shovel, and both it and the stone moved away in wheelbarrows or horse-drawn wagons. When the Erie Canal was building, the Buffalo *Patriot* printed a paragraph upon the remarkable record made by 8 men who removed 203 cubic yards of earth in 11 hours. A steam shovel would do that job now in a few minutes.

Even for decades after the Patowmack job the method of blasting was the same. After the powder hole had been toilsomely drilled, it was poured nearly full of coarse blasting powder, and the mouth was then tamped with clay, leaving a small orifice into which some fine powder was poured for priming. The fuse was a strip of brown wrapping paper soaked in saltpeter.

Old Towpaths

Blasting powder in the hands of Tom, Dick and Harry often proved a serious worry to the boss, as is shown by a report of Rumsey to the treasurer of the company in 1786, in which he says that they had lost two blowers, "One Run off, the other Blown up; we therefore was Obliged to have two new Hands put to Blowing and there was much attention gave to them least Axedents should happen."

Such were the difficulties of blasting that a cutting was always regarded with wonder. The cleft 40 feet deep and 300 feet long on the South Hadley Falls Canal was regarded in its day as a distinct achievement. Captain Basil Hall, the English traveler, spoke with high admiration of the heavy cutting on the Erie Canal at Lockport as "a magnificent excavation," "a work of great expense and labor and highly creditable to all parties concerned." Later the Deep Cut on the Chesapeake and Delaware, which clove for a mile through solid rock, at one place 76 feet deep, was spoken of as one of the wonders of the world.

The little South Hadley ditch was noteworthy also because it built the first inclined plane in America—230 feet long and with a vertical lift of 53 feet. The face of the plane was of stone, covered with heavy plank. The body of the car was a water-tight box with folding gates at each end. Two water wheels 16 feet in diameter on either side of the channel at the head of the plane were operated by water from the canal, and pulled the car up or let it down, according as the gears were shifted. Boats floated directly into the car; the gates were then closed behind it and the car emptied of water through sluices in the sides. The carriage was then pulled up or let down the plane on three sets of wheels, like big wagon wheels, graduated in size so as to hold the car exactly level.

The inclined planes on the Morris Canal in after years received much greater notice and praise, but they were built by an English engineer, and were merely adaptations of an instrument which he had known in Europe. The South Had-

The Santee and Middlesex

ley Falls plane was a far greater achievement because it was of purely native design and construction, it was built by men who were not engineers and had never seen anything of the kind in their lives—and it worked!

So rare was engineering skill in America in those days that even as late as 1823 we find the editor of a magazine called *The Portfolio* gravely listing the qualifications of a canal engineer:

"The engineer should be well acquainted with the principles and use of the several instruments in geodesic operations. . . . He should be qualified to survey with the utmost accuracy, embracing not only horizontal but vertical sections and lines, and to level with minute precision, making accurate allowance for the earth's curvature. . . . In prosecuting the duties of his profession, he should be so familiar with the several mechanical powers, as to be able to apply them to the best advantage, as he will have a constant variety of occasions for resorting to their aid."

CHAPTER IV

THE GENESIS OF THE ERIE

FOR the better part of a century—at least, for more than half a century—the question as to who originated the idea of the Erie Canal was of sufficient importance to engender no little rancor every time it was stirred up. Books, pamphlets and magazine articles were written about it, orations were delivered upon the subject, and "Spartacus," "Pro Bono Publico," "Justitia" and "Constant Reader" belabored each other through newspaper columns over it.

The truth of the matter is that the idea was not born, full-formed, from any one's brain, but was a gradual development. It was well-nigh inevitable that a canal would be built along the line of the Erie when the age of canals had arrived. From New England to Georgia the Appalachian Mountain chain formed a great barrier to westward travel and communication; and the line of the Hudson and Mohawk Rivers was the only place where it was broken so that travel might pass conveniently to and from the western territories without climbing a thousand feet or more above sea level. From the upper Hudson to the two nearest of the Great Lakes was a natural trade route. The old Iroquois trail led up the Mohawk River, thence past the site of Utica and so away to the Genesee Valley and on to Niagara. A branch of it led down the Oswego to Lake Ontario.

Eventually this became the white man's route—though a somewhat difficult one—from the Hudson to Ontario.

The Genesis of the Erie

The Cohoes or falls of the Mohawk were impassable at any season, making a portage necessary from Albany to Schenectady; and the portage from the Mohawk to the upper waters of the Oswego was an awkward one. There were also the Little Falls of the Mohawk, where there was a portage of one mile; in early days the Dutch farmers in the neighborhood carried passengers, baggage and freight over that distance in sleds. Later they devised ingenious, broad-wheeled vehicles upon which the entire boat was carried (of course the boats were small—about one and a half tons) around the falls.

Some investigators see in a memorial of Cadwallader Colden, the elder, to the Captain-General and Governor of New York Province in 1724, concerning the fur trade in America, the germ of the idea of the Erie Canal. But Cadwallader D., his grandson, wrote, "It is vain to inquire who first thought of connecting these western, northern and southern waters. Could we pursue the inquiry with success, it would be a futile labor."

Gradually the idea began to take form. The traveler, Jonathan Carver, wrote in 1766 that the Mohawk River and Wood Creek, a tributary of the Oswego, had been joined by sluices at Fort Stanwix. Two years later we find the first recommendation for improvement of waterways in New York in the suggestion of Sir Henry Moore, the Governor, to the Assembly, that the Mohawk be made navigable at the falls of Canajoharie. From that time on it is evident that the matter of a connection between the Hudson and the lakes was continually on the minds of thoughtful men. Christopher Colles, an Irish-born citizen of New York, gave a series of lectures in that city in 1773 on the improvement of waterways. Governor Tryon in his Report for 1774 recommended a system of locks and canals along the Mohawk and upper Hudson. Then the Revolution came on and stopped all possibility of such improvement for several years.

It was during the war that Gouverneur Morris, patriot

and statesman, is said to have prophesied the building of the Erie Canal. Morgan Lewis, then Quarter-master, later Governor of New York, relates that one evening in camp in 1777, Morris in conversation with him "announced in language highly poetic and to which I cannot do justice, that at no very distant day the waters of the great western inland sea would by the aid of man break their barriers and mingle with those of the Hudson."

But in the only documentary evidence to be found, a letter written by Morris to General Lee, he merely says, "As far as I can judge from observation and information, the communication between Lake Ontario and the Hudson is not only practicable but easy, though expensive." Not a word about direct communication between the Hudson and Lake Erie.

When Washington visited central New York in 1783 he commented upon the wonderful possibilities there for western and northern travel, but he did not suggest any definite canal route. Jefferson, with a touch of characteristic selfishness, feared that a New York waterway to westward might become a competitor of the Potomac route; but Washington, the greater minded, though seeing this possibility quite as clearly, was yet in favor of the Hudson–Great Lakes thoroughfare because his chief aim was the consolidation of the country, and the more links there were between East and West, the better could this be accomplished.

Joel Barlow, the poet, might very well have laid claim to the honor of having been one of the first prophets of the Erie Canal. In his poem, "The Vision of Columbus," published in 1787, he makes the discoverer of America foresee its internal improvements:

He saw, as widely spreads the unchannell'd plain
Where inland realms for ages bloom'd in vain,
Canals, long winding, ope a watery flight,
And distant streams, and seas and lakes unite.

De Witt Clinton, Builder of the Erie Canal, and Regarded as the Leading Exponent of Canals in America

The Genesis of the Erie

From fair Albania, tow'rd the falling sun,
Back through the midland lengthening channels run;
Meet the far lakes, the beauteous towns that lave,
And Hudson joined to broad Ohio's wave.

In 1784-85 Christopher Colles asked the Legislature for aid and permission to remove obstacles from the Mohawk. He was given permission and the princely sum of $125, which he expended in making a survey. He published the results of his investigation in a small pamphlet, but accomplished nothing more.

Bills were introduced in the Legislature in 1786, aiming to improve the navigation of the Mohawk, Wood Creek and the Onondaga (or Oswego) River, but the measures failed. A more persistent man now took up the fight.

During the Revolution a young New Yorker named Elkanah Watson had been sent by Congress with dispatches to Benjamin Franklin, then in Paris. Watson remained five years in Europe. He became interested in canals and studied those in France, Belgium, Holland and England, meanwhile thinking of the benefits such waterways would bring to his own country. When he returned to America in 1785 he visited Washington and was deeply impressed by the General's ideas and enthusiasm regarding inland navigation.

Starting in 1788, Watson made a westward journey by way of the Mohawk to the lakes, keeping a journal by the way which shows that he had a pretty clear idea of the needs of the country and the probable results of better transportation. In 1791 he prepared a pamphlet embodying his views and presented it to General Schuyler. Thenceforward he carried on a campaign of publicity for his idea, determined to make the New York westward route a rival to Washington's Potomac project.

The powerful influence of Schuyler and Governor George Clinton was now brought into play, and general public interest was aroused not only in favor of a better water

Old Towpaths

route to westward but also northward through Lakes George and Champlain to Canada. The result was that in 1792 the Legislature granted charters to two companies, the Western Inland Lock Navigation and the Northern Inland Lock Navigation; the first to open a navigation via the Mohawk from the Hudson to Lakes Ontario and Seneca; the second to construct similar works from the "boatable waters" of the Hudson to Lake Champlain. General Schuyler was elected President of both companies. The State was to aid both financially.

The Western Company began work at Fort Stanwix and Little Falls in the spring of 1793 and soon had 500 men employed. But money troubles developed early. It had been difficult to interest investors and now some of those who had subscribed failed to pay for their stock. Workmen were laid off and the job stopped twice for lack of funds. The State came to the rescue by buying all told, $57,500 worth of the company's stock. With this aid the canal around Little Falls was so nearly complete in November, 1795, that boats began to pass through it. It was a trifle less than a mile in length and had five locks. More than half the canal was cut out of solid rock.

This little canal alone was of great assistance to the commerce of the State. Before it was built batteaux of no more than one and a half tons' capacity could be carried around the falls by the portage. These boats required a crew of three men to pole them, and a trip from Fort Schuyler (Utica) to Schenectady and back occupied not less than nine days. As they usually came back empty, the cost of transporting a ton of goods from one place to the other was about $14.00. Likewise it cost $75 to $100 to haul a ton from Albany to Seneca Lake.

With the completion of the canal, however, flatboats, arks, or as they had come to be called, Durham boats, of ten or eleven tons' capacity could pass the falls, and the cost of carrying a ton down to Schenectady was reduced to about $5.

The Genesis of the Erie

Traffic immediately began to increase, and the company collected about $400 in tolls during the month before its canal closed for the winter.

Immigration to central and western New York and beyond was stimulated by the canal. Formerly, an emigrant's family and goods made, as a rule, a full load for one batteau. Now several families could be carried on one boat, and the fare was therefore lower.

Meanwhile the company had been carrying on work—intermittently—at other points. The portage at Rome between the upper Mohawk and Wood Creek had been cut through, thus opening up a waterway, crude though it was, from the Hudson into the wide-spreading chain of lakes and streams, large and small, in central and western New York, extending almost to the Genesee Valley and the Pennsylvania line. Another small canal on the Mohawk was completed and one was surveyed around the Cohoes or Great Falls, but was not built for lack of funds; so travel still passed between Albany and Schenectady by coach and wagon.

The Northern Inland Lock Navigation, which was practically identical with the Western Company, surveyed and partly completed some work in the direction of Lake Champlain, but never finished a real waterway. The corporation spent $100,000 in this work, which was almost totally lost, because, it is said, of the inexperience and poor judgment of General Schuyler and others of the directorate. The bad example of this company was a powerful deterrent to the promotion of the Erie Canal. Many people argued that if a comparatively small navigation enterprise were such a failure, to attempt a canal more than 350 miles long would be a colossal folly.

The Western Inland Lock Navigation had facilitated travel; in fact, its benefits to the State were said to be large; but the increasing needs of the new territory were beyond its power to meet. Dr. Timothy Dwight, traveling through central New York in 1820, observed that the State was being

Old Towpaths

held back by its lack of transportation facilities. If you wished to go from New York City to Buffalo, even as late as 1808, you waited perhaps several days until there was a sailing vessel leaving for Albany, and then, after striking a bargain with the captain as to fare and accommodations, you spent from two to five days on the trip, according to the caprices of the wind. From Albany you rode overland to Schenectady, 17 miles; then took a boat on the Mohawk, operated variously by sails, long oars and poles, for the 104-mile journey to Utica. The speed limit was fifteen or twenty miles per day, so that you might be a week on this part of the trip. From Utica you went partly overland and partly by water to Oswego, 114 miles, which occupied eight or ten days more, according to the weather. At Oswego you might occasionally get a boat for Lewiston, at the mouth of the Niagara River; and thence you must go overland again to Buffalo. Think of the transfers that freight must undergo! You paid about $50 to get it hauled over this route from New York to Oswego, and $100 to Buffalo. Much freight was actually wagoned all the way between these points at a lower cost than by water.

The difficulties of water transportation were diverting travel to land and leading to the improvement of roads and building of bridges. The Navigation Company found it necessary to lower the toll rates to meet wagon competition. In 1810 it petitioned the State for relief. It had spent all the money received from stockholders, from the State and from tolls, and still owed $10,000. It had not paid a dividend in eighteen years. And now the rising tide of agitation for a great canal from Lake Erie to the Hudson smothered its appeal for help. The Legislature decided to build the new waterway upon an independent route, and eventually took over the Western Inland Lock Navigation property, paying therefor a trifle over $150,000. The face value of the capital stock then outstanding was $232,000.

CHAPTER V

OLD BOATING DAYS—THE NEED FOR BETTER TRANSPORTATION

MOST American canals completed before 1805 (which means all those we have discussed save the Dismal Swamp, Middlesex and Santee) were merely short stretches of lockage around rapids or waterfalls in the larger rivers, and were used by the clumsy craft which floated down those rivers loaded with products of the interior country and were rowed or poled back upstream, if they went up at all. The Middlesex and Santee were the only canals to use horse-drawn boats regularly, but even on the Middlesex, hundreds of arks and flatboats which yearly floated down the Merrimac were towed by horses through the canal to Boston.

The first pioneers who boated down the streams with their merchandise used canoes or dugouts. Then as the needs of commerce grew, batteaux—squared-toed, flat-bottomed craft with a capacity of a ton or so—were built; and then came the Durham boats, which were the forerunners of the arks and keel boats. Durham boats were the product of the Delaware River, where they were first used about 1723. So widespread did the name and pattern become that we hear of them in later years on the New England rivers, on the Mohawk, and even on the St. Lawrence.

The Durham boat was a great step forward from the old batteau, for it was a more shapely, more commodious and more manageable craft. Its ordinary length was about sixty feet, its width about eight feet. It tapered to a cutwater at the bow and stern. It had a slight rake fore and aft. Going downstream it carried fifteen to eighteen tons and sometimes twenty. A mast could be stepped in the deck and a sail erected, but the boat had no keel, so it could sail only when the wind was astern. The ark and the keel boat were more or less modified forms of the Durham boat, the latter having, as its name indicates, a keel which aided in steering.

As the Eighteenth Century drew to a close and the Nineteenth began, the volume of this primitive traffic increased enormously. Farmers, stock raisers, timbermen and artisans in the more thinly settled districts could get little or nothing for their products in their home neighborhoods, and boats were built to float the merchandise down to market either by the producer himself or by a neighbor. Some of the most picturesque and heroic scenes in American annals were those of the old boating days—though one finds little mention of them now in books of history.

No one to-day can have any conception of the daring, heroism and soul-trying bodily toil that made up that old river boating and rafting. If one excepts the placid course of the Hudson from Albany to New York City, there was not a river in the eastern half of the country, not even excepting the Ohio, which was not beset with shoals and rapids; and some, even of the largest, were further tormented by sheer waterfalls, vicious ledges and snags, to say nothing of trees which fell across them every year. Down some of them boats could travel only in spring and early summer, when the water was high enough to carry them over the roughs. Frequently a boatman starting hopefully to market was wrecked and perhaps lost the fruit of his whole season's toil, if not his life.

The batteau or small flatboats, as used on the Mohawk, was the first craft to have a plank along each gunwale on which the polemen walked while propelling the boat. Going downstream the task was not so hard. The current did a part of the work, long sweep-oars were sometimes used, some boats hoisted a sail when the wind was fair, and when

Old Boating Days

the water was shallow, the speed was hastened by poling. But upstream—ah, there was where men were tested!

In the shallower, more turbulent streams, poling was necessary all the way. The butt end of the pole was enlarged to a knob called a "button"; this was set against the boatman's shoulder, the other, iron-shod, end against a rock or the bed of the stream, and with back to the prow the man slowly walked aft, pushing with all his might. On some rough streams such as the Mohawk or the Connecticut, his shoulder would often be fearfully bruised and lacerated after a few hours' toil up through the rapids.

Batteaux had from three to six men in their crews, or from one to three polemen on a side. The Durham boat, ark or keel boat might have a crew of from six to twelve men. Both large and small boats played an important though not always a spectacular part in the Revolution by carrying munitions and supplies. Captains even of the smaller batteaux which did such work were entitled to the same pensions as captains in the Continental army. Durham boats carried Washington's force across the Delaware when he was retreating before Howe into Pennsylvania, and it was a fleet of sturdy Durham boats which ferried him back through the ice on that Christmas night in 1776 to smite the British and Hessians at Trenton. Again in the War of 1812 the Durham boats, arks and keel boats were indispensable.

The Connecticut was an important avenue of commerce in early times. Down it in spring and early summer came thousands of boats loaded with lumber, grain, home manufactures and agricultural products. In the vicinity of its numerous rapids there were men who earned their living by piloting boats down through the perils of the stream. At the foot of the rapids were "fallsmen" who assisted in poling boats on their return up through the swift water. At Willimansett Falls was old Captain Ingraham, who would hitch a team of six oxen and two horses to a boat by a one-hundred-foot chain and draw it up through the sluiceway around the

Old Towpaths

rapids. In rocks along the shores of the Delaware may still be seen some large iron rings which the early boatmen used in pulling themselves up against the current. Windlasses on shore were also used, and sometimes the boatmen just hugged the bank and pulled on bushes and boughs of trees.

The rafting of timber began on the Delaware in 1764, and in the century and a half following that date the quantity taken down the Pennsylvania rivers was enormous. Hazard's Register stated in 1828 that 1,000 rafts had descended the Delaware that spring, containing 50,000,000 feet of lumber. From the heights along that river in spring in the '40's and '50's sometimes fifteen to twenty rafts could be counted in view at once. There were raft pilots at the rapids, and a fee of $5 was often paid for taking a long raft through Wells Falls.

A faint idea of the heartbreaking toil and waste of time incurred in the boating operations of those days may be derived from the statement in 1798 of the projectors of the canal at the Conewago Falls on the Susquehanna that "at the Falls of *Schuylkill,* which are about 3½ feet fall in 30 perches, it is commonly an hour's hard work of 12 or 15 men to draw up an empty or light-loaded boat; and an expence of $2 or $3 in drink, and loss of time. It is seldom that boats of any weight have been attempted to be towed up either shore of the Conewago Falls, and then it has required 30 or 40 men a great part of a day, and an expence of £5 or £6 at least, to accomplish the work; for the men are obliged to perch and scatter themselves (as it has been humorously expressed) like *black-birds* on the rocks and to drag their burden, shifting from rock to rock, through the fall."

Such conditions could not be tolerated as commerce increased in volume and greater efficiency was demanded. Boatmen on the more incorrigible rivers and those who came from far up towards headwaters now began selling their boats as well as the cargo when they reached port—the boat

Old Boating Days

to be broken up and used as lumber. Then the boatman would walk back home, picking up a ride on a wagon by the way whenever he could. For some years wagons were operated from Philadelphia to the upper Lehigh to carry returning boatmen and the few iron parts of their boats. West of the Alleghenies, where manufactured iron was a scarce commodity, the boats were apt to be put together entirely with wood—even having wooden pins instead of nails.

For several decades, even after the steamboats came, thousands of these homemade craft went down the rivers every year. As early as 1790, 150,000 bushels of grain came down the Susquehanna from Pennsylvania and south central New York to Middletown, destined for Philadelphia and the export trade. Niles's Register said that from February 28 to June 23, 1827, a count was made at Harrisburg, which showed that 1,631 rafts, 1,370 arks and 300 keel boats had passed down the river, estimated to contain, among other things, 40,000,000 feet of lumber, 468,000 barrels of flour and whisky, 244,000 bushels of wheat and 11,000 tons of coal. At Catawissa, far up the river above Harrisburg, from 100 to 200 craft passed downstream daily in spring and early summer. Even at Towanda, almost up to the New York state line, where the river was little more than a brawling creek, 1,099 rafts and 236 arks, requiring more than 3,000 men in their crews, passed down on the high tide between April 6 and 19, 1829.

In the thinly settled Middle West as early as 1817 it was said that 1,500 flatboats and 500 barges went down the Mississippi in one season to New Orleans, which was the great market for the central valley. When the steamboats came to western waters in the twenties this traffic did not stop, but rather increased. It may be found hard to believe that on the little Wabash River in the spring of 1826, 152 flatboats passed Vincennes, carrying 250,000 bushels of corn, 100,000 barrels of pork, 10,000 hams, 3,600 venison hams, 10,000

Old Towpaths

pounds of beeswax and 2,500 live cattle, besides hogs, meal, oats, chickens, etc., all from upper Indiana and eastern Illinois. Apples, potatoes, dried fruit, lumber, horses and liquors were other products that went southward, and certain States sent their own peculiar products, as Kentucky her tobacco, hemp, bagging and rope and Missouri her lead. At New Madrid, just below the mouth of the Ohio, it was no uncommon thing for a hundred boats per day to arrive in spring. From there they often floated the rest of the way to New Orleans lashed together in groups of eight or ten. Of course New Orleans could not absorb all this merchandise, and much of it was reshipped to New York and foreign ports. Sometimes the boatmen found the market glutted, and had to wait several weeks for better prices or sell at starvation figures. After the steamboats came, some of the boatmen worked their way back upstream as deckhands; but others walked the seven or eight hundred miles back home. You may see old houses in the French Quarter to-day partly built of stout planking taken from those western arks and flatboats.

The Great Seal of the State of Ohio very appropriately displays an "ark" as one of the instruments upon which the State's commerce, indeed, its very life, was founded. The name of the craft has even stamped itself upon geography. Far up the Pepacton, the eastern branch of the Delaware, is a town significantly named Arkville. And a new participial adjective is discovered when we read in the Mifflin, Pennsylvania *Eagle* one February that "the Juniata has been in good arking order all winter."

"People nowadays," said Dr. Samuel C. Busey in his *Pictures of the City of Washington in the Past,* "talk about push and enterprise as if it were a new invention and they the only discoverers of it. . . . I assure you I have seen evidences of a 'get-there' spirit among the grandfathers of the business men of today that surpassed much of their so-called push. Those ark-owners had goods to sell, and though they

Old Boating Days

did not come with lightning speed, they got down to market just the same."

It is not to be wondered at that people in the interior in 1800 to 1810 were longing for canals or some other more efficacious method of transportation. The roads of the period were little better than a series of rocks and mudholes. The President's inauguration was set for four months after his election in order that he might be sure to reach the capital on time. The desperate need for better communication was felt in every quarter of the land.

For now the signs of a new era were in the sky. The Louisiana Territory, with its marvelous resources, had been added to our domain in 1803. Pennsylvanians were discovering that anthracite coal would really burn; the first ark loaded with it left Mauch Chunk in 1806. The cotton industry had been developed in the South. Only 138,000 pounds were exported in 1792—in 1897 we shipped no less than 64,000,000 pounds; and Whitney's invention of the cotton-gin had decreased the cost of production to one-fifth of its former figure. Our exports of all kinds had increased remarkably. In 1791 they amounted to but little more than $19,000,000; in 1807 they were $108,000,000. In 1789 nearly half our exports were carried in foreign ships; but the wars in Europe drove much of the foreign shipping from the seas, to the great advantage of Yankee tars. By 1796 only six per cent of our exports was being shipped in foreign vessels, and by 1807 we were using homemade craft almost exclusively.

Grain was becoming a profitable commodity in the North, and would have been more so if it could have had better transportation. England was now buying breadstuffs from us, and the price of flour rose in a few years from $5 to $9 a barrel. This accelerated immigration to the level land west of the Alleghenies, so well adapted to grain-growing, but the new settlers in those parts soon found that the cost of sending grain to market cut them off from all hope of

Old Towpaths

profit. Even western New York, Pennsylvania, Maryland and Virginia found little profit in agriculture when it cost ten dollars to haul a ton of low-priced grain a hundred miles; while the Ohio Valley could not send its grain to market at all save by the long, roundabout way down the Mississippi to New Orleans.

The demand for public improvements grew so great that the Federal Government was urged to take up the matter. The harassed directors of the still prospective Chesapeake and Delaware Canal brought the question to a focus by asking Congress for help early in 1807. The Senate in turn passed a resolution asking the Secretary of the Treasury to investigate and make a report on the subject of internal improvements in general. Secretary Gallatin spent a full year in study of the subject and on April 4, 1808, presented his famous Report on Roads, Canals, Harbors and Rivers. It is one of the most admirable of his official papers, and embodies a remarkably complete summary of all information available at the time regarding canals.

Gallatin displayed rare political acumen as well as sound business judgment in preparing the document. He approved the leading projects then under consideration and suggested others which would extend certain measures of benefit to every state in the nation. His transportation route proposals were classified roughly in four groups.

One of these was a series of intracoastal canals extending from New England to the southern states; a system which even to-day is regarded as highly desirable for both commercial and military reasons. At the time of Gallatin's report, one canal of the four he listed as comprising the system—the Dismal Swamp—had been completed. Two others—the cut across Cape Cod neck and the canal between the Delaware and Chesapeake Bay—had been projected long before but were still unbuilt; while the fourth, the channel across New Jersey, had only begun to be talked of, but later was built as the Delaware and Raritan.

From an engraving by W. H. Bartlett

THE OLD AND THE NEW: FLATBOATS ON THE SUSQUEHANNA AND THE CANAL ALONGSIDE IT, ABOUT 1835

Old Boating Days

The second need which the Secretary pointed out was that of communication between the Atlantic coast and the rivers of the Mississippi Valley. Under this head he mentioned the Santee Canal and the improvement of the James, the Tennessee, the Potomac and the Susquehanna. East and west traffic was to be further aided by four great roads, leading from the Susquehanna or Juniata, the Potomac, the James and the Santee or Savannah to the Allegheny, the Monongahela, the Kanawha and the Tennessee respectively.

Thirdly, he urged better communication between the Atlantic, the Great Lakes and the St. Lawrence River by means of two canals (with parallel roads) connecting the upper Hudson with Lakes Champlain and Ontario. A canal around Niagara Falls was also a necessary part of this scheme.

Fourthly, he listed a number of miscellaneous interior improvements, a few of them entirely or partly completed; but most of them as yet only in the prospective stage. Among these were the Middlesex, the Schuylkill and Susquehanna, Schuylkill and Delaware, several small canals in North Carolina and one at New Orleans, also the improvement of the Merrimac River.

Gallatin estimated that all the works mentioned which were not yet completed could probably be constructed for $20,000,000—a vast sum for those days, but he was confident that the country could afford it; which indicates a wonderful advance over fifteen years before, when no canal company in America could raise as much as $100,000 in cash for the carrying on of its work. Now the United States Treasury was comfortably filled and a surplus of $5,000,000 per year was accumulating. Using $2,000,000 yearly for internal improvements, as the Secretary suggested, the whole vast scheme could be paid for in ten years.

States and canal corporations were immensely cheered by the report, and most of them immediately began preparing memorials, setting forth their claims to shares of the money. But the report had come at an unfortunate moment. The

Old Towpaths

Embargo had already begun to injure commerce and decrease the revenue. Under the circumstances, Congress did not think it advisable to authorize so large an expenditure of money. Then came the War of 1812, which made any national project impossible for at least another three or four years.

But that war showed us even more vividly the crying need for better avenues of communication. During its progress the Government spent many futile millions for haulage over our terrible roads. We paid $400 for the making of a certain type of cannon and from $1,500 to $1,800 more to haul it to Lake Erie. Flour delivered at Fort Meigs during the northwestern campaign cost the Government $100 a barrel and oats $60 a bushel. Louisiana sugar at one time sold in the East at $30 per 112 pounds. Even after the war the Government was expending $127 per barrel on pork required to feed the western garrisons. In the American State Papers on Military Affairs it is estimated that the expenses of transportation during the war would have paid the cost of every road and canal opened in New York and all those planned in Ohio and Pennsylvania.

By way of contrast to these shocking figures Robert Fulton, a lifelong enthusiast for water transportation, declared in a Congressional report that a bushel of salt, which it was then costing $2.50 to haul 300 miles, could be carried that distance by canal (including handling) for 7½ cents. He calculated that one man, one boy and one horse could move a boat carrying 25 tons 20 miles per day at the following cost:

1 Man	$1.00
1 Boy	.50
1 Horse	1.00
Tolls	2.00
Interest on the Wear of the Boat	.50
	$5.00

Old Boating Days

Or one cent per ton per mile!

But the War of 1812 had other effects also. It stimulated domestic commerce, introduced us more thoroughly to our western wilderness and gave us a feeling of confidence in ourselves. Hordes of new citizens were coming to us from the British Isles and there was a corresponding movement into the new territories of the Middle West. Traders and trappers pushed still farther on, across the mountains and even to the shores of the Pacific. The awakening of the American nation may be said to have come with the advent of the Nineteenth Century. In the first three or four decades after 1800 the young giant stretched his limbs, discovered something of his power and began to grow. It was during those decades that practically all of our greater canals were built. And it was within the span of those few brief years that the railroad came in turn and dealt the death blow to the canals.

CHAPTER VI

THE BUILDING OF THE ERIE CANAL

THERE were men in New York State who had never ceased to ponder and keep alive the topic of a better water connection between the Hudson and the Great Lakes. The Western Inland Lock Navigation had proved a great disappointment. It was woefully inadequate to the needs of the growing state and nation.

In 1797 General Schuyler and William Weston, the English engineer, made a tour of exploration through central New York, and "talked of water communication by means of canals as far as Lake Erie, keeping the interior, provided the face of the country would admit of it; but they considered the period remote when it could be done, and their whole views were continued towards perfecting the navigation from the Hudson to the Seneca Lake and to Oswego."

A corporation was formed in 1798 to construct a canal around Niagara from Lake Erie to Ontario; but money was of course lacking at that early date for so tremendous an undertaking, and nothing was done.

Jesse Hawley, a prominent citizen of New York, can claim the credit of having been the first to set forth in print and in coherent form the proposition for a canal from the Hudson to Lake Erie. This he did in a series of fifteen letters printed in newspapers in 1807. These struck an able and telling blow for the project. But even he was still unable to break away from the idea of using canalized streams, such as the Mohawk, as considerable parts of the scheme, largely from motives of economy.

The Building of the Erie Canal

But notwithstanding the impression created by these letters, when Judge Forman offered a resolution in the Assembly in February, 1808, favoring the building of such a canal, the proposal was received by many members of the House "with such expressions of surprise and ridicule as are due to a very wild or foolish project." It might well have seemed too stupendous for consideration. It would be nearly twenty times as long as any canal yet completed in the country. We had as yet no engineers in America and no contractors, there were no excavating tools, and the way of the proposed canal lay through a vast wilderness of forest and swamp.

But there were men of much influence in the Legislature who thought the matter worth looking into; and after much debate, a tentative survey of the proposed line was ordered, and $600 was appropriated to pay the cost of it. This sum proved insufficient by $75, and Judge James Geddes, who did the surveying, paid the balance out of his own pocket.

Geddes was a lawyer who had done some surveying, but could by no means be called an engineer. Using the theodolite (made by David Rittenhouse) which had been used by Weston when surveying the Western Inland Lock Navigation, he surveyed routes from Albany to both Lakes Erie and Ontario; but he too planned to follow and use the natural waterways as much as possible. In the following year he made his report. Both he and others shrewdly argued that if commerce from the West were taken past the Falls of Niagara into Lake Ontario, it would be more apt to go on down the St. Lawrence River than to turn aside on a canal into the United States. Building a canal from Albany to Lake Erie and leaving Niagara still as a barrier would result in turning commerce from the western Great Lakes inevitably into the State of New York. In later years the Canadians essayed to meet this competition by building the Welland Canal.

Gallatin's report had now been made public, and New York moved to get her share of the $20,000,000 supposedly

Old Towpaths

soon to be distributed. Judge Forman and William Kirkpatrick, New York legislators, called on President Jefferson to urge their claims; but when they had laid their data before him and declared the advantages that would accrue not only to New York but to the whole country from the canal, Jefferson again revealed his jealousy as to this supposed rival of the Potomac navigation by replying coldly:

"It is a splendid project and may be executed a century hence. Why, sir, here is a canal of a few miles projected by General Washington, which, if completed, would render this a fine commercial city, which has languished for many years because the small sum of $200,000 necessary to complete it cannot be obtained from the general government or from individuals. And you talk of making a canal *three hundred and fifty miles long through a wilderness!* It is little short of madness to think of it at this day!"

Congress failed to act on Gallatin's suggestions for internal improvements, but New York continued her preparations. It is a bit astonishing to find that De Witt Clinton, the man who may be called the "builder" of the canal, had displayed little or no interest in the project up to 1810, when he was brought into it by others for political reasons. General Jonas Platt, a Federalist member of the State Senate, says that he suggested to some of the canal promoters that if they could enlist the aid of Clinton, one of the most prominent of the Democratic leaders in the State, they might put measures favorable to their project through the Legislature; but if Clinton opposed it, it would certainly fail. The matter was laid before Clinton at length, and his support asked for a resolution appointing a commission to study the situation. He would not move the resolution but he agreed to second it. Through his influence the act was passed, and Clinton was named as one of the committee, along with Gouverneur Morris and five others. From that time forward his lukewarmness vanished and he speedily assumed a foremost position among the protagonists of the canal.

The Building of the Erie Canal

The committee journeyed over the proposed routes to Oswego and to Buffalo, and in 1811 declared strongly in favor of a canal through to Lake Erie, and recommended for use no natural watercourses save the Mohawk up to Utica. From Lake Erie to that point the canal was to be a long inclined plane with a descent of six inches to the mile—Morris's pet idea. Many persons at once branded this as impracticable. But there were also other daring features. The canal was to be carried over the mouth of Cayuga Lake on an embankment one mile long and 130 feet high; and at Schoharie Creek it was to run along the crest of an embankment 150 feet high! The cost of such a canal was estimated at from five to six million dollars.

Aid was sought from the Federal Government, but Congress was too deeply engrossed just then in the growing quarrel with England to think of internal improvements. But Clinton was now pushing the project with all his tremendous enthusiasm and energy. He and others recommended in 1812 that New York cease trying to get help from Congress and build the canal herself. In June of that year the Legislature authorized the purchase of the Western Inland Lock Navigation Company's rights, the borrowing of moneys and the procuring of voluntary cessions of land for the benefit of the proposed canal, if the project should still be deemed expedient after examination by a competent engineer.

The war with Great Britain had come on by this time, and little could be done in the Legislature. The commissioners were working busily elsewhere, however. They tried to borrow $5,000,000 abroad, but our precarious position because of the war nullified their efforts in that direction. In the meantime they gradually divested themselves of the idea of making the canal a long inclined plane, as well as certain other of the more extravagant engineering caprices.

As the project assumed more definite shape, it was compelled to contend more fiercely against innumerable crosscurrents of jealousy, skepticism, selfish interest and disagreement as to practicality. Eastern New York was jealous of western New York. New York City was stupidly opposed to the whole project—at least, her politicians were. The counties around the eastern end of Lake Ontario who had been compelled to do their trading (at much disadvantage to themselves) with Montreal, clamorously demanded that the canal come to Lake Ontario at Oswego. Rochester thought it ought to connect with Ontario via the Genesee River. The southern-tier counties along the Pennsylvania border were opposed to the canal because, as they said, they would not derive any benefit from it, and would have to continue floating their products at great hazard and expense down the Pennsylvania rivers. To appease them Clinton promised to work for the building of a road through the southern tier from the Hudson to Lake Erie. He also labored to secure for them some branch canals leading from the Erie.

In 1814 opponents of the canal in the Legislature triumphed momentarily, and the authority given the commissioners to borrow $5,000,000 for construction purposes was rescinded on the ground that the times were unpropitious. But this temporary halt was probably after all the best thing that could have happened to the project, for it enabled the promoters to get a better start after the war was out of the way, and to build the canal with American engineers and American money.

On December 3, 1815, a party of prominent citizens met at a hotel in New York with the object of reopening the canal question. The tall, dignified presence of De Witt Clinton dominated the gathering. With the exception of two years' time, he had been mayor of the city continuously since 1803.

The war had now been over for nearly a year. Opportunities for greatly increased business were knocking at our doors, and the meeting was agreed that we were being held

The Building of the Erie Canal

back more and more by our poor transportation. The principal action taken by this gathering was the appointment of a committee consisting of Clinton, Cadwallader D. Colden, John Swartwout and Thomas Eddy to set forth its views in writing. This committee produced a memorial which, says one writer, "was the foundation of the present system of internal navigation. . . . It effectively exploded the Ontario route and silenced forever its advocates."

The memorial was signed by a majority of the responsible citizens of New York City. Copies of it were sent through the State, which brought about canal mass meetings in almost every town and village in the counties through which the waterway would pass. The Legislature in its next session was confronted by appeals signed by more than 100,000 petitoners, urging that the canal work be set in motion. Governor Daniel D. Tompkins supported the appeal in his speech to the Legislature in February, 1816, though he was believed to have done so only from political expediency, being at heart opposed to the project.

In April of that year, an "Act for improving the Internal Navigation of this State" was passed, under whose provisions a board of five commissioners, of whom Clinton was one, was empowered to scheme a communication by canal between the Hudson and Lakes Erie and Champlain. The commissioners were given $20,000 for surveying expenses, but they were not given power to raise other moneys or to begin actual building.

Governor Tompkins was elected to the vice-presidency of the United States that year, and so large a place in public opinion had Clinton made for himself, not only as Mayor of New York City and as a leader of his party, but principally by his achievements for the canal, that he was at once proposed for the Governorship and was elected thereto in the spring of 1817.

But meanwhile the commissioners had appointed engineers for resurveying the Erie and Champlain routes and

Old Towpaths

had brought in their reports. A final bill, giving them power to proceed, was then brought into the Assembly. Some of the money was to arise from donations of land already made or soon to be made by individuals or companies who would be benefited by the improvement. Then there were the tolls to be collected after the canal was built. As these were not expected to be sufficient, taxes were laid upon all lotteries, auction sales, salt manufactured, and others of one dollar on each person who traveled more than one hundred miles, and fifty cents on everyone traveling more than thirty miles by Hudson River steamboats; and finally, at some future time, if necessary, $250,000 more could be raised by a land tax.

There was a bitter struggle of a month's duration over the bill. The State was just then in the throes of another disappointment. John C. Calhoun in the previous December had introduced a bill in Congress, proposing to devote the bonus and net proceeds of the Government's interest in the National Bank to internal improvements. It was voted to apportion the money on a pro rata basis, under which arrangement New York's share would have been about $90,000 annually. She and other States might almost be said to have had their hands extended for the money, when President Madison vetoed the bill, and New York was thrown back upon her own resources again.

The opponents of the great western canal in the New York Legislature were now making their last stand. Every member from New York City was in opposition—that city whose present preëminence in America is largely due to the impetus it received during the first twenty years' functioning of the Erie Canal. But there were some men in the Legislature bigger than party or faction. The most powerful speech in its favor in the Senate was that made by Martin Van Buren, who was laboring to defeat Clinton in his gubernatorial campaign, but who—however much of an "offensive partisan" he may have been at other times in his

Erie Canal Aqueduct over the Genesee River at Rochester

From an old print

The Building of the Erie Canal

life—on this occasion nobly placed the public interest above partisanship. On the day of adjournment the measure passed both Houses by comfortable majorities, the members from New York City, however, voting against it to a man.

The commissioners wasted little time in getting to work. It had been decreed that excavation should begin in the middle section of the job. On July 4, 1817, at Rome, the president of the village, Joshua Hathaway, with an appropriate speech handed a spade to Mr. Young, the only one of the commissioners present, and he in turn passed it to Judge Richardson, the first contractor, who plunged it into the sod and lifted the first shovelful of earth—and America's biggest job was begun. Thereafter it became almost an ironclad custom to begin internal improvements and especially canal jobs on the nation's birthday. The canal project which did not turn its first earth on the Fourth was considered to have made a bad start.

To gain even a partial understanding of the courage and vision that went into the planning and building of the Erie and Champlain Canals, one must remember that the entire population of the State of New York in 1817 was less than a million and a half, and that it was assuming the burden of two pieces of construction which were expected to cost at least $6,000,000, and in the final balancing actually cost $7,944,770. It must be remembered that so thinly settled was the State west of the Mohawk Valley that there was not even a stage line from Albany to Buffalo. Canandaigua and Batavia were the only villages of any size throughout that entire region. Buffalo was a mere village, and in fact, its neighbor and rival, Black Rock, was seriously considered as the western terminus of the great waterway.

For the final survey Benjamin Wright was assigned to the Erie and James Geddes to the Champlain Canal. Wright had first done some surveying on the Erie route in 1812. Like Geddes, he could not lay claim to the title of engineer. Yet these two assumed the technical direction

Old Towpaths

of the biggest job yet attempted in America, and with some able assistance carried it through to success.

The real genius developed by the building of the Erie Canal was Canvass White. When Wright was forming a surveying corps in 1816 White, then a young man of twenty-six, sought and obtained a position with the crew. He had studied surveying along with mathematics, astronomy and other subjects, at an academy. He was set to taking levels west of Rome and soon won the approbation of Wright and later the notice and friendship of Clinton, who, with his usual keen judgment, saw rare possibilities in the young man. At Clinton's solicitation White went to Europe in the fall of 1817 to inspect the canals of the Old World and to get some up-to-date surveying instruments. He walked two thousand miles on the towpaths of the canals of Great Britain, studying their every feature. He returned the following year with new instruments and many careful drawings of various canal works.

He came back to find engineers and contractors sadly puzzled over the question whether to build the canal locks of wood or stone. Cement could be procured only from Europe and at great expense; but wood was too perishable a material for locks. So it was decided to build of stone, putting the blocks together with quicklime mortar and merely pointing the joints with the costly imported cement. They could afford no more; but most of them feared in their hearts that the work would not stand up.

With this makeshift stonework throughout its course, the early years of the canal would probably have been full of trouble; but within a few months after his return White (with the assistance, it must be admitted, of one or two others) discovered near Chittenango, on the line of the canal, a stone from which hydraulic cement equal to the best European could be made—the first cement produced in America. From that time forward the Erie stonework was of the best.

The Building of the Erie Canal

By the end of 1817 the equivalent of fifteen miles of canal channel had been completed. During 1818 the work was pushed forward vigorously, though weather conditions during the spring were very unfavorable. By August "the whole line became a scene of the most animated and laborious exertions." "From that time to the 10th of December, between 2,000 and 3,000 men, with half as many horses and cattle, and a considerable variety of mechanical inventions" were constantly employed upon the work.

Some of these "mechanical inventions" were remarkable examples of Yankee ingenuity. Here the plow and scraper were for the first time extensively used in excavation. A plow with an additional cutting blade was devised for use among small roots. An ingenious dumping wheelbarrow and a sharp-edged shovel for use in cutting roots in swamp muck were other clever ideas. A cable attached to the top of a tree and wound on a wheel worked by an endless screw enabled one man to fell the largest trees single-handed. A stump-puller was invented, consisting of an axle twenty inches in diameter and thirty feet long, supported on wheels sixteen feet in diameter. Midway on the axle was mounted a drum fourteen feet in diameter. When the outer wheels were chocked, a chain wound around the axle and fastened to the stump, and a team of horses or oxen hitched to a rope which encircled the central drum several times, the stump was easily pulled. The outer wheels were then released and the same machine hauled the stump away. One of these machines operated by seven men and a team could pull and move thirty to forty stumps per day.

In the Montezuma marshes near Syracuse, some of the ground was so saturated with water that the experiment was tried of excavating it in winter when it was frozen. This swamp country gave the builders much trouble. In the summer of 1819 a thousand men were incapacitated in that district between July and October by malaria, ague and bilious and typhus fevers, and many of them died.

Old Towpaths

The Erie was the second big job in America on which we find large numbers of Irish laborers employed. Thenceforward, they were indispensable. In fact, with the exception of the early southern works, practically all the canals constructed in America prior to the Civil War may be said to have been dug by Irishmen. That they were working on the abortive Schuylkill and Susquehanna canal in 1783 is proven by the records of a clash which they had with the Pennsylvania German citizens of Myerstown. Dr. O. P. Hubbard, an old citizen of Rome, wrote to the historian of Oneida County that in the Montezuma marshes in summer, "Wild Irish bog trotters from the West of Ireland, cutting out the trees the width of the canal track, were set to work knee deep in the wet muck; they could wear no clothing but a flannel shirt and a slouch cap."

That was a memorable day in October, 1819, when water was first turned into the completed section of the canal between Rome and Utica. A citizen of Utica who witnessed it wrote to a friend that "I consider it one of the privileges of my life to have been present to witness it." He tells how he took position on a bridge crossing the canal, and therefrom "had a sight which could not but exhilarate and elevate the mind. The waters were rushing in from the westward and coming down their untried channel towards the sea. . . . The interest manifested by the whole country as this internal river rolled its first waves through the state, can not be described. You might see the people running across the fields, climbing on trees and crowding the banks of the canal to gaze upon the welcome sight. A boat had been prepared at Rome, and as the waters came down the canal, this new Argo floated triumphantly along the Hellespont of the West."

This boat, the first on the canal, was named *Chief Engineer of Rome*. Drawn by a single horse, it carried Clinton and the commissioners, "attended by many respectable gentlemen and ladies," from Rome to Utica, and back

The Building of the Erie Canal

again the next day. "The Scene," says a reporter, "was extremely interesting and highly grateful. The embarkation took place amid the ringing of bells, the roaring of cannon and the loud acclamations of thousands of exhilarated spectators, male and female, who lined the banks of the newly created river. The scene was truly sublime."

At that time 96 miles of channel had been completed. The Erie Canal was becoming a reality. The Champlain Canal was in a navigable state a month later, though it was so overshadowed by its great neighbor that due notice was not given it. It had cost a trifle over a million dollars.

CHAPTER VII

THE CONSUMMATION OF A GREAT WORK

THERE were many people in New York City and State who, like Jefferson, did not believe that the Western Canal could ever become a reality. Thurlow Weed says that the idea of connecting the Hudson with a lake more than five hundred feet higher than itself was by most persons considered preposterous. All united in saying that the generation which began the work would not witness its completion. Not even its most sanguine advocates guessed less than twenty years as the time required. The Holland Company, a great land-holding corporation originally financed mostly by Dutch capital, gave 100,632 acres of land for the benefit of the canal on condition that it be completed by 1842—which some considered a not-too-great allowance for overenthusiasm and unforeseen hindrances. A common remark was, "We shall never see it finished, but our children may."

Many of the doubters carried their disbelief to the point of striving with tooth and nail to block the work. But there were others whose opposition was less honest and more political—a not uncommon proportional coincidence. Chief among their motives was the desire to injure Clinton. The Governor was a hard fighter and a bit haughty in manner and had made many enemies thereby; but the greatest objection to him was that he was acquiring too much glory. As soon as he became Governor in 1817 the Republicans proceeded to harass him in every way possible. Among the numerous accusations brought against him was one to the effect that he had opposed and hindered the prosecution of

The Consummation of a Great Work

the recent war. They even tried to deny him the credit of having furthered the cause of the canal.

Daniel D. Tompkins, then still Vice President, was induced to run against Clinton for Governor in 1820. This device failed, though Clinton was reëlected by less than 2,000 votes in a total of 180,000. The petty warfare against him was then continued with more virulence than ever. His opponents had a majority in both Houses, and they now proceeded to remove all his friends and supporters from State offices and put opponents in their places. In 1821 they even made a change in the State constitution by which his power was lessened.

Meanwhile the canal project itself was harried and embarrassed by all manner of jealous, spiteful and petty partisans. It had been under way for months and thousands of dollars had been expended when Tammany Hall headed an effort to stop it. As it was being built westward towards the Genesee a movement arose (in which Rochester was not uninterested) to end it there and connect it via that river with Lake Ontario. The Legislature in 1820 was induced to appoint a committee to consider the question of "stopping the canal west of the Seneca River" until the Champlain Canal should be entirely completed and the Western (Erie) Canal completed to the Hudson. This was merely a pretext for halting the work altogether, and the Legislature was either too wise or feared public opinion too much to fall into the trap. Clinton was constantly warning the people against the folly of such suggestions. He and his confrères had acted shrewdly in beginning the work on the middle section, where the excavation was easiest. They afterwards admitted that if in their inexperience they had begun first on the eastern section, where the difficult descent past the falls of the Mohawk was to be negotiated, or on the western portion, where the difficult rock cutting at Lockport was necessary, the discouragement resulting from the heavy expense and from probable blunders might have ruined the

Old Towpaths

whole project or delayed its completion for years—which would have meant forever.

As already related, it was late in 1819 that the first boat navigated its waters. By the time the canal opened again in the spring, a passenger packet boat 76 feet long and 14 feet wide had been built and came into Syracuse April 21, 1820. When Syracuse held her great Fourth of July celebration that year, 73 boats took part, many delegations from other counties arriving by water. Clinton himself was among the guests.

Within the year 1822 boats were operating over the canal for a distance of 220 miles. Already a speed limit was found necessary. Brought about by fast passenger boats operating at breakneck velocity, possibly 5 miles per hour, a law was passed forbidding any boat to move faster than 4 miles per hour without permission in writing signed by a majority of the canal commissioners.

A correspondent wrote from Utica on June 26, 1823: "Our village on Friday, twenty-fifth inst., presented a scene of bustle and stir never before witnessed here. . . . On Saturday the packet boat for Rochester left here with 84 passengers on her first trip. A boat will leave this place every morning, Sundays excepted, during the season and continue through to the Genesee River. . . . The new boats are built in the best manner and fitted up in a style of magnificence that could hardly be anticipated in the infancy of canal navigation in this country."

Another correspondent wrote from Rochester at about the same time that "On Wednesday last a boat was launched from the yard of H. Goodman & Co., and though we may not announce the event in as lofty language as is used in city prints on like occasions, yet perhaps it was an occurrence equally interesting as the launching of the proudest ship from a seaport. To behold a vessel committed to the water 400 miles inland, and in a place which ten years ago was a wilderness . . . excites emotions of no common kind."

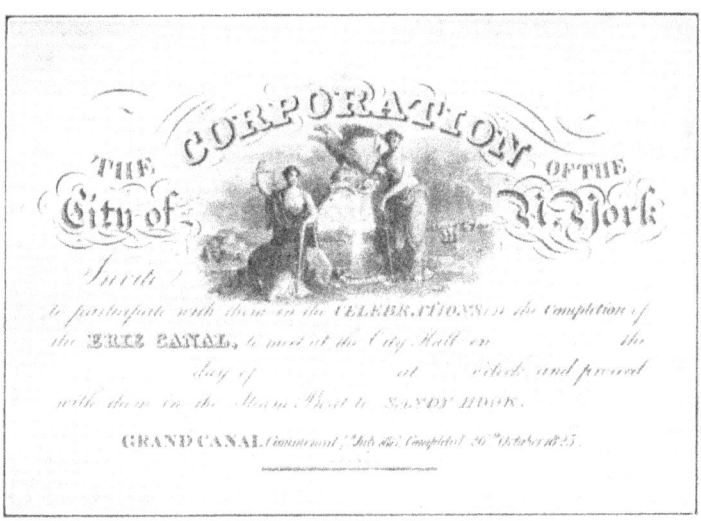

INVITATION TO THE CELEBRATION AT NEW YORK IN 1825 ON THE COMPLETION OF THE ERIE CANAL.

INVITATION TO THE CANAL CELEBRATION BALL AT NEW YORK CITY, NOVEMBER 7, 1825

The Consummation of a Great Work

The Erie and Champlain Canals formed a junction at Watervliet, eight miles north of Albany. On October 8, 1823, the first boats passed from the west and north through the junction canal into the Hudson and down to Albany, where the event was celebrated with a great military demonstration and pageant, salutes, fireworks, a grand ball and a banquet at which thirty-nine toasts were drunk!

Meanwhile a side cut had been extended to Onondaga Lake and a southern arm had been thrown out to Seneca and Cayuga Lakes. Thus began the system of branch canals which afterwards grew so large. A vessel of 60 tons arrived at New York City in 1823 which had come from the farther end of Seneca Lake, 70 miles from the Erie Canal and after a trip of 350 miles over a very roundabout route, reached her destination.

Work did not begin on the western end of the canal at Buffalo until 1823. For a long time it was uncertain whether the terminus would be at Buffalo or Black Rock; and bitter were the discussions between the two villages, the recriminations, the appeals to the good sense of the public, the protests against the shameless lobbying of the other fellows. Each claimed the better lake harbor and denounced the other's as worthless. For months—even years—the decision hung in doubt. Now the news would come that Black Rock had been designated, and the citizens of that village would bring forth their old Revolutionary cannon and fire a few joyous salutes by way of celebration. A few days later Buffalo would hear (in strict confidence) that she was to be the chosen point, and her townsmen would wheel out her cannon and set up a great bombilation by way of depressing Black Rock's spirits. The selection of Buffalo condemned Black Rock forever to a minor rôle in history and geography—first as a mere way station and later as a suburb of the fortunate town.

Ground was broken at Buffalo in August, 1823. Several yoke of oxen pulled a big plow which did the first excavating. So primitive were conditions there at the time that they

Old Towpaths

had no scrapers nor even wheelbarrows to move the dirt. Swiftly the heavy cutting from Buffalo to Lockport—which Captain Basil Hall and other foreign travelers and engineers admired so much—was pushed through. It became increasingly apparent that Clinton's remarkable prediction, made in 1820, that the canal would be completed in five years, was about to be verified. This was the last straw for those numerous politicians even of his own party who were eaten by the canker of envy. Angered by the constitutional amendment which took away much of his prerogative, he had refused to run again for Governor in 1822. Now, early in 1824, by an overwhelming vote of both Houses of the Legislature, he was deposed from his position as canal commissioner. Only men unbalanced by envy could have failed to foresee the inevitable result of such an act. That being election year, there was an instant popular demand that Clinton again be made Governor; and he was accordingly swept into office by a majority of 16,000, the largest that had ever been given a candidate in the State.

The great task was now drawing to a close. Early in 1825 three hydrostatic weigh locks—ingenious devices by which the weight of a boat and cargo could be ascertained for toll purposes, and the first of their kind in America—were installed at Troy, Utica and Syracuse. The locks were in use day and night, and it was not unusual to see sixty or seventy boats awaiting their turn. The capacity of the short section of the canal between its junction with the Champlain Canal and Albany was already being tested. It was estimated that 10,000 boats had passed the junction within the season. Nearly $300,000 in tolls had been collected on the great canal in 1824, and it was apparent that in 1825 the amount would be enormously greater. Albany, then a city of 16,000 population, reported that her wholesale business had quadrupled since the canal reached her port two years before.

In June, 1825, the gates at Black Rock were opened and

The Consummation of a Great Work

the water of Lake Erie admitted for the first time into the western section. That month also the capstone of that remarkable double chain of locks at Lockport—five for ascending and five for descending traffic—was laid with Masonic ceremonies. But not until autumn was this section ready for any traffic; tolls were first collected at Buffalo and Black Rock on October 1. By October 26 the channel at the mountain ridge just west of Lockport was ready for use, and though there were many finishing touches to be put to the work throughout this entire district, yet the canal was declared open to the public. "It was considered an object of primary importance," says Captain Hall, "to open the canal from end to end and bring it into actual use as soon as possible, even though some parts of it might not have been completed with the utmost degree of perfection. The result showed the wisdom of this proceeding, as receipts from tolls have greatly exceeded the anticipated amount; and accordingly have furnished the canal commissioners with adequate means for bringing the whole into proper condition."

Preparations had been going forward for months to signalize the opening of the canal by the greatest celebration that America had even seen. By this time the tremendous volume of business developed for her by the waterway had thoroughly convinced New York City (where 3,500 new buildings had been erected in 1824) of the value of the improvement, and she prepared to surpass all others in the magnificence of her display. The pageant was scheduled to begin at Buffalo on October 26.

On that date Governor Clinton, all the canal commissioners and many other notables were assembled at Buffalo. There was much oratory, of course, there was the singing of an original ode composed for the occasion by a journeyman mechanic of the town, and after certain other formalities, the citizens and militia escorted the distinguished guests to the fleet of gayly decorated canal boats waiting in the basin. The Governor took up his quarters in the

Old Towpaths

Seneca Chief, which headed the line. Behind it were the *Superior, Commodore Perry, Buffalo, Lion of the West* and others. On the last-named boat was a sort of menagerie containing a bear, two eagles, two fawns, two Indian boys and many birds and fish, all typical natural products of the West before the advent of the white man. In the cabin of the *Seneca Chief* were "two elegant kegs," painted with patriotic designs and filled with water from Lake Erie.

As the boats moved away from the bank at Buffalo, the *Seneca Chief,* drawn by four gray horses, in the lead, the news was carried thence to New York by the voices of a row of cannon within hearing distance of each other—from eight to twelve miles, according to the lay of the land and the caliber of the guns—all the way from Buffalo to Albany and down the Hudson to New York. Many of the cannon had been brought from the Presque Isle navy yard, and were from Commodore Perry's former ships and from the British vessels he captured on Lake Erie in 1813. At least one of them—perhaps there were others—was fired by a veteran of the Revolution, Goshen Van Alstine. The news is said to have been carried thus to New York in eighty minutes; and when the last gun was fired at the Battery, the forts in the harbor returned the salute, and the news that New York had heard the tidings was then carried back to Buffalo in a similar manner.

As the little fleet moved eastward along the canal it was saluted by rattling salvos of musketry, the blare of bands of music and the ecstatic cheers of crowds at every village along the way—for even Rome, Utica and Schenectady, the largest settlements on the route, were little more than villages. At Albany there was a great demonstration, and the cavalcade, now augmented by many gayly dressed steamboats, moved down the river to New York. There it was greeted by the entire population plus thirty thousand out-of-town visitors, many thousands of whom boarded all manner of craft and followed the steam-towed canal boats down to

Courtesy of the Baltimore & Ohio Railroad Company
THE LOCK-TENDER'S HOME

THE ERIE CANAL AT FRANKFORT, NEW YORK, ABOUT 1876

The Consummation of a Great Work

Sandy Hook, where the final function was to be performed. There the "elegant" and patriotically painted kegs were opened, and Governor Clinton, with an appropriate speech, poured their contents into the sea, thus symbolizing the union of Lake Erie with the Atlantic. Vials containing water from the Mississippi, Columbia, Thames, Seine, Rhine, Danube, Amazon, La Plata, Orinoco, Ganges, Indus, Gambia and Nile Rivers were also emptied into the ocean. To some other less fortunate cities in the East, especially Philadelphia, this ceremony appeared very absurd.

A grand salute was now fired and the celebrants returned to the city, where a great industrial parade was the next event. "Persons abroad may judge of the splendor of the celebration," says a contemporary newspaper account, "when it is stated that there were displayed among the different societies, upwards of two hundred banners and standards—many of them extremely splendid and a large number painted expressly for the occasion." There were the Agricultural and Horticultural Societies; the Butchers, mounted and wearing aprons, with floats carrying animals; numerous fire companies; the Tanners, Cordwainers, Hatters, Bakers and many other guilds, nearly all with floats which advertised their industries.

At night there were balls, parties, theatrical entertainments, banquets and illuminations. "A large transparency was exhibited at the City Hall, representing the introduction of Neptune to the Lady of the Lake by the Genius of America"; and if we are to judge by a contemporary engraving, the fireworks from the City Hall must have been well worth seeing.

Handsome official souvenir medals were struck and were presented to President John Quincy Adams, to former Presidents John Adams, Jefferson, Madison and Monroe, to General Andrew Jackson, Marquis de Lafayette and many other prominent personages in the United States and Europe. These medals were enclosed in boxes of cedar said to have

Old Towpaths

been brought to New York on Clinton's official canal boat, *Seneca Chief*—or perhaps made from the hull of the boat itself.

"The completion of the Erie Canal," grumbled an envious writer in a neighboring city, "has been celebrated with greater éclat, pompous show and parade, not unlike those triumphal games and processions that were given to some of the Roman Emperors. . . ." And the enthusiasm continued to manifest itself in various ways. Sketches of canal scenery were stamped on pottery, wall paper and various implements in commemoration of the event; and the name of De Witt Clinton was bestowed upon babies, boats, locomotives and everything else that would bear christening.

Clinton's Big Ditch, as its detractors called it before it was completed, seems a small affair now—hardly worth making so much pother about. It was only 4 feet deep, 40 feet wide at top and 28 at bottom; but it was the longest in existence—364 miles; it directed the movements of populations, fixed the destinies of cities, States and whole sections of America and left traces, still visible, of its handiwork upon the nation. Even its most ardent advocates did not dream of the results so quickly to flow from it. Before it was fully completed its tolls had begun to exceed the interest charges. In 1825 the tolls collected on the Erie and Champlain Canals were $566,000, of which the Erie contributed nearly $500,000; and 13,110 boats and rafts passed to and fro that year on the junction canal between Watervliet and Albany. Forty thousand persons passed Utica on freight and packet boats during that season; a daily average of forty-two boats, arks and cribs passed the town throughout that year's period of navigation. So near were the times to the old boating days that many of the old Durham boats which had formerly shot the rapids of the Mohawk and been so laboriously poled back were still in use, being pulled tamely through the canal by horses.

So much space has been devoted to the Erie Canal be-

The Consummation of a Great Work

cause it was the greatest and most successful of all the earlier American canals; because it was the most audacious venture in American history to be pushed through to successful accomplishment; because it gave the forward signal to many other canal projects and spurred other States on to making internal improvements—some of them, ill-timed and rash, to be sure, but most of them of enormous value. Taking into consideration the times and conditions, the Erie Canal was a more daring project and its building was a greater achievement than was the building of the first railroad through the western mountains to the Pacific coast in the '60's.

CHAPTER VIII

THE PEAK OF CANAL-BUILDING ENTHUSIASM

THE story of the early years of the Erie Canal constitutes the first of those romances of expansion and progress which later came to be regarded as synonymous with the word America. Although the Atlantic seaboard was not uncomfortably crowded, yet even before 1800 the composite American race was straining against its mountain barriers, yearning towards the open spaces, the freer air and the difficulties to be conquered beyond. Now the Erie Canal offered the first great highway for travel and commerce through the barrier, and its business grew by leaps and bounds.

In 1826 the tolls of the Erie and Champlain Canals amounted to $765,000. It was no unusual thing for fifty boats to start westward from Albany in a day. For many years the Albany newspapers recorded daily the arrivals and departures of canal boats by name, as modern New York journals do of ocean vessels in the shipping news. During 1826, 19,000 boats and rafts passed West Troy on the junction canal. New England ordered lumber from Buffalo. The Middle (then called Western) States sent their grain, timber, fur and other products to the Eastern markets and in turn, manufactured goods flowed back from New York and New England and even from Philadelphia to the West and South.

In 1826 a boat passed east through the canal bearing a cargo of fur valued at $100,000; and a boat cleared from Albany for Buffalo with merchandise principally for Ohio and Michigan, on which the tolls alone were over $300—

The Peak of Canal-Building Enthusiasm

tolls being charged partly on valuation. In 1828 we read of nine tons of merchandise shipped from New York up the Hudson and through the Erie to a firm in Little Rock, Arkansas Territory, via Lake Erie and Sandusky, thence overland to the Ohio River. Even Nashville, Tennessee, received its goods from New York via the Canal. And in 1830 Niles's Register tells us of travelers passing between New York City and New Orleans through the Hudson River and Erie Canal, crossing overland from Erie, Pennsylvania, to Pittsburgh and there taking the Ohio River steamboats. The distance by that route was 2,995 miles and the fare was $73, including meals.

Far from being called a ditch, the Erie was now known in the uttermost parts of the land as The Grand Canal. Not only do Rochester and Syracuse owe their existence to it, but also dozens of smaller towns along its route, many of whose names indicate their origin—Lockport, for example, to say nothing of Middleport, Eagle Harbor, Shelby Basin, Port Byron and others. America had never before seen what came to be known in after years as a boom; now she saw one, or rather several of them, in central and western New York.

Colonel William Leete Stone, editor, politician and writer, traveling over the canal in 1829, was astounded by the growth of Utica, which he had known but recently as a hamlet; and Syracuse seemed to him like a city risen by enchantment where nine years before, when he had visited the site, there had been only "some five or six scattered tenements . . . the whole being surrounded by a desolate, poverty-stricken country, enough to make an owl weep to fly over it." A projected branch canal at Utica in the early '30's caused such a speculation in real estate that eleven acres of wharf lots brought one million dollars.

Rochester was one of the most remarkable of the boom towns. In 1812 its site was a wilderness. In 1822 its population was 2,700—a remarkable growth for those days. In

Old Towpaths

1825 it had 4,274 inhabitants and the following year 7,669. By 1828 its population had almost reached 11,000. From the very first, it was a flour manufacturing city. On October 29, 1822, the first canal boat left Rochester, destined for Little Falls, where canal navigation then ended—and the boat was loaded with flour. Rochester boats loaded with flour were first to enter Albany when the canal was opened to that city in 1823. Rochester sent 10,000 barrels of flour to Albany that year. In 1826 the little city produced 150,169 barrels of flour. It had also a cotton factory, three iron furnaces, breweries, distilleries, tanneries and other industries. Three years later Colonel Stone saw there a flour mill which produced 500 barrels per day.

Captain Hall's description of Rochester as he saw it in 1827 sounds like a pen picture of a western mining camp in the '70's. "Everything in this bustling place," he wrote, "appears to be in motion. The very streets seemed to be starting up of their own accord, ready made and looking as fresh and new as if they had been turned out of the workman's hands but an hour before. . . . The canal banks were at some places still unturfed; the lime seemed hardly dry in the masonry of the aqueduct, in the bridges and in the numberless great saw mills and manufactories. In many of these buildings the people were at work below stairs, while at the top the carpenters were busy nailing on the planks of the roof. . . . I cannot say how many churches, court houses, jails, and hotels I counted creeping upward. Here and there we saw great warehouses without window sashes but half filled with goods and furnished with hoisting cranes, ready to fish up the huge pyramids of flour, barrels, bales and boxes lying in the streets. I need not say that these half-finished, whole finished and embryo streets were crowded with people, carts, stages, cattle, pigs, far beyond the reach of numbers, and as all these were lifting up their voices together, in keeping with the clatter of hammers, the ringing of axes and the creaking of machinery, there was a fine concert."

The Peak of Canal-Building Enthusiasm

But not only to New York State but to people in the West the opening of the canal was productive of incalculable benefit. "It takes thirty days," said a Columbus, Ohio, newspaper, "and costs $5.00 a hundred pounds to transport goods from Philadelphia to this city; but the same articles may be brought in twenty days from New York by the Hudson and the Canal at a cost of $2.50 a hundred. Supposing our merchants to import on an average five tons twice a year; this means a saving to each of $560." It meant far more than this; it mean lower costs to the western consumer for eastern manufactured goods, and higher selling price for the merchandise of the western producer. It meant greater comfort of living in all the newly settled States; it meant more internal improvements and the opening up of vast areas of territory as yet a wilderness.

Philadelphia and other eastern cities were not unmindful of the threat to their commerce suggested by the Ohio newspaper. In fact, they were mightily perturbed about it. Early in American history, Boston and Philadelphia had been our leading cities. At the close of the Eighteenth Century, Philadelphia bade fair to be the American metropolis. Now both of these saw their supremacy snatched from them by the upstart village of New York.

Boston straightway fell a-dreaming of a canal connection with the Hudson. She had already been talking of a canal to Worcester and possibly to the Connecticut River. Said a writer in the *Patriot*, "A canal from Springfield to Boston will make our harbor the mouth of the Connecticut." But with the building of the Erie, Boston's vision suddenly widened. Her canal enthusiasts now pictured a waterway to tap the Hudson and the Erie Canal at Albany. Such a canal, they believed, should draw off towards Boston at least half of the business coming from the West via the Erie. A commission was appointed by the Legislature to ascertain the practicability of the idea. Surveys were made by the younger Loammi Baldwin. A southern route to the Con-

Old Towpaths

necticut via Worcester was considered, also a northern via Fitchburg. The latter was recommended because it was feared that if boats got any farther down the river, they might just continue on to Hartford instead of coming to Boston.

The great obstacle to the scheme lay west of the Connecticut. Baldwin found only one practicable point to cross the Berkshire range, and that was at the place where the Hoosac railroad tunnel was later built. A canal tunnel was recommended as the only alternative to a long system of locks. He calculated that to cross the mountain there would have to be 220 locks in 18 miles of canal, requiring two days for the passage and costing $2,090,000 to construct. The tunnel could be passed in one hour and twenty minutes.

Baldwin figured the cost of a tunnel 4 miles long and found it to be, at the highest possible estimate, $920,832; at the lowest, $370,000. When one remembers that the thing would have to be done by hand drilling and gunpowder, one marvels at his optimism. An interesting comment on his estimate is found in the fact that when the Hoosac railroad tunnel was constructed a number of years later, it cost $10,000,000.

The entire cost of a canal from Boston to the Hudson was guessed at $6,023,172. When the report of the canal commissioners was laid before the Legislature in 1826, that body was so frightened by the figures that the canal was never even begun.

Philadelphia was menaced not only by New York and the Erie Canal, but in other quarters as well. As early as 1817 commissioners appointed by Pennsylvania and Maryland had urged legislative action for making the Susquehanna navigable to headwaters. Now the Susquehanna was a direct feeder for Baltimore, and Philadelphia saw much of the internal trade of Pennsylvania being drawn to that city instead of herself. Philadelphia's only means of reaching the Susquehanna was by wagon to Middletown, the nearest

From an old lithograph. Courtesy of the Easton Historical Society

EASTON, PENNSYLVANIA, A PROMINENT CANAL CENTER, IN 1831.

The Morris Canal is in the foreground, the Lehigh Canal and Delaware division across the river.

The Peak of Canal-Building Enthusiasm

practicable port on that river. The attempted Schuylkill and Susquehanna Canal, lying unfinished since 1794, had been an attempt to divert the Susquehanna River business over the cheaper and easier water route to Philadelphia via the Schuylkill River.

In unpleasant dreams Philadelphia saw in the near future her own manufactures compelled to go around by sloop or steamboat to Albany and thence west by canal. That meant that because of distance, she could not compete with New York or even Albany, Rochester and Buffalo. Furthermore, the contemplated Chesapeake and Ohio Canal, connecting the Potomac River with the Ohio Valley, and thereby destined to bring Western trade to Washington and possibly Baltimore, now arose as another threat to Philadelphia.

"Geographically considered," her citizens would argue, "no city is so favorably situated as Philadelphia for commanding the whole inland trade of the continent. Seventy-five miles of canal are all that is needed to give us full water communication with the Pacific Ocean via the mouth of the Columbia River." They reached this startling conclusion by projecting a canal to connect the upper waters of the Susquehanna with Seneca Lake and thence with the Erie Canal and the Great Lakes. Beyond there, their geography was a bit hazy.

It was in part the threatened competition of the Erie Canal that put new life into the old Schuylkill and Susquehanna projects and brought them to completion almost simultaneously with the Erie.

But while the State of Pennsylvania pondered plans for a great system of State-owned waterways which should not only serve her own interior but should also fix the great east-and-west highway across her territory, other canals were springing into being in all quarters of the land. As section after section of the Erie was completed, and as the tolls collected thereon began mounting into astonishing figures, a wild enthusiasm for internal improvements swept over the

Old Towpaths

land. New schemes were brought into being and old ones which had been hopefully discussed for years were put into corporate form and work begun on them. The record of accomplishment of that third decade of the Nineteenth Century is astounding.

In 1821, while work was starting again on the rejuvenated Union Canal, Maine incorporated the Cumberland and Oxford Canal, to build from Fore River to Sebago Lake. In 1822 an old project to unite Providence and Worcester by a canal along the Blackstone River was revived and set in motion. In 1823 the long-delayed Chesapeake and Delaware Canal got under way again and two new companies were incorporated—the Hampshire and Hampden, to build from Northampton, Massachusetts to New Haven, Connecticut, and the Delaware and Hudson, to give an outlet for the Lackawanna anthracite coal. In 1824 the Susquehanna and Tidewater Company was chartered to build a canal down the Susquehanna from Middletown to the mouth of the river; and in the same year the Morris Canal and Banking Company was organized, to build another anthracite-carrying canal across the State of New Jersey, from the Delaware River to New York harbor.

Eighteen hundred and twenty-five was an eventful year. Ohio had caught the infection and had planned an extensive system of canals, including two between Lake Erie and the Ohio River, for which she broke ground in July of that year. In the same month the Delaware and Hudson began its excavation. That year also saw the Erie completed and its branch to Oswego begun; a company chartered to build a canal from the Illinois River to Lake Michigan (although it did no work); a company organized and work begun on a canal around the falls of the Ohio at Louisville; and the James River and Kanawha Canal reaching a point twenty-seven miles above Richmond.

Eighteen hundred and twenty-six saw the Schuylkill

The Peak of Canal-Building Enthusiasm

Navigation thrown open for business and the Seneca and Cayuga branch of the Erie begun; and on July 4 the State of Pennsylvania broke ground for her great system of canals, the most pretentious and costly scheme yet attempted. "We trust the time is not far distant," wrote an editor, "when the whole territory of Pennsylvania, to adopt the figure of one of our representatives in Congress, will present nothing but a congregation of islands."

In 1827 the Lehigh Canal was begun and the Union Canal completed. In 1828 work began on the Chesapeake and Ohio. Meanwhile, other and smaller canals, such as the Conestoga in Pennsylvania, were being built. And so the story ran. It really seemed in those stirring '20's as if the wish of Robert Fulton—expressed in a letter to Governor Mifflin—for the coming of the day when "canals should pass through every vale and wind 'round every hill," might soon be gratified.

Canal construction was solving the labor problem—if there had ever been one. Before the end of 1825, 1,200 men were working on the Delaware and Hudson. In 1826 there were 1,100 working on the Morris, 1,500 on the Chesapeake and Delaware and 1,000 even on the little 2-mile channel at the falls of the Ohio. In 1828, 5,000 were working on the Pennsylvania canals, and in the following year, when 46 miles of the Chesapeake and Ohio were under way, there were 1,800 laborers, masons. carpenters and stonecutters employed. And each and all of these jobs were in progress for several years. Between 1820 and 1830 over 800 miles of canals were opened to navigation in New York, Pennsylvania, Delaware and Maryland—namely, the Erie, Champlain, Oswego, Seneca, Delaware and Hudson, Chesapeake and Delaware, Schuylkill, Union and some shorter ones. In 1830 full 1,300 miles more were well under way and most of it nearing completion. This included the Morris, the Pennsylvania State canals, the Miami and Erie, Ohio and Erie, James River and Kanawha, Chesapeake and

Old Towpaths

Ohio, Lehigh and others. Meanwhile, other canals had been projected, such as the Delaware and Raritan, and Indiana and Illinois were entering the canal-building epoch.

The whole land was aflame with the fever of progress. Even today we do not advance as rapidly in a decade as we did then. "Freight could now be moved," says the historian McMaster, "from New York to Buffalo through the Erie Canal for four cents a ton per mile, tolls included. These rates revolutionized business. The merchant's and the manufacturer's field seemed boundless. West as well as east became his market, and transportation companies for the handling of freight had been established in order to enable him to reach that market. Banks were multiplying. Insurance companies, steamboat, pike and canal companies, mills and factories were springing up on every hand. The whole course of life was changed.

"Tens of thousands of men who under the old conditions would have been doomed to eke out a scanty livelihood by farming or by cobbling or by toiling in the crowded ranks of unskilled labor, now found new occupations opening before them. They became mill hands and operatives; they turned machinists and mechanics; they served as engineers and firemen on the steamboats, as clerks and bookkeepers in banks and insurance companies; they handled freight, tended the gates on the turnpike or the bridges on the canals; drove the horses that dragged the canal boats or found employment in some of the older industries which, such as tailoring and printing, shoemaking, stage-driving, hatmaking and carpentry, had been greatly expanded since the war."

In the last piece of writing of his life Joseph Conrad said of the old sailing days that "The pathos of that era lies in the fact that when the sailing ships and the art of sailing them reached their perfection, they were already doomed." Even so with the canals; when work on the Erie Canal began, George Stephenson, away over in England, was toiling away at his first locomotive engine; and even

The Peak of Canal-Building Enthusiasm

While the completion of the Erie was being celebrated with such rapturous joy, Stephenson's Stockton and Darlington Railway, the first apparatus in history to haul passengers and freight on land by steam, was being put in operation. The little cloud, no larger than a man's hand, had appeared in the sunlit sky of the American canals' prosperity; but few people comprehended it, and many refused, against all evidence, to believe it for many years.

CHAPTER IX

CANAL OR RAILROAD?

THE Erie Canal had not yet been completed when the railroad specter loomed, though unseen by most Americans. The Pennsylvania Society for the Promotion of Internal Improvements in the Commonwealth, organized in 1824, exhibited from its inception a keen interest in the new invention. The State of Pennsylvania was then planning its great system of canals, and the society, espousing the cause of railroads in a cautious way, sent William Strickland to England to study the transportation system of that country. The reports which he presented upon his return made a considerable impression upon the popular mind. One of them, published in June, 1825—just as the Erie Canal was being finished—contained this significant remark:

"In fact, the introduction of the locomotive has greatly changed the relative value of railways and canals; and where a communication is to be made between places of commercial or manufacturing character, which maintain a constant intercourse and where rapidity of transit becomes important, it cannot be doubted that railways will receive a preference because of this very powerful auxiliary."

Another paragraph in Strickland's report in which he predicted that railways were destined to supersede canals was stricken out by the society for fear of its appearing too radical. It will be noted from the above paragraph that railways were already in use in Europe in a small way before

Canal or Railroad?

the locomotive was invented, horses being the motive power. Three or four small tramways for hauling stone were built in this country between 1800 and 1825, but no one ever seems to have thought seriously of the railway as a method of long-distance transportation. With the invention of the locomotive, however, such men as Strickland and John Stevens, who has been called the "father of American railroads," were able to comprehend the enormous possibilities therein. When Pennsylvania was planning her great system of canals, Stevens and some associates whose enthusiasm he had aroused, offered to build, if given permission, a railroad across the State from Harrisburg to Pittsburgh.

But Philadelphia cried this proposition down. The public mind was not yet ready for the railroad. In fact, so little was known of its nature that when a citizen wrote to his newspaper, asking "What is a railroad? What does this plan mean?" the editor was fain to reply, "Perhaps some other correspondent can tell us." A long article in the Williamsport *Gazette* declared that railways were inexpedient in Pennsylvania and their construction was a visionary scheme, whereas canals were much more available and economical. This opinion prevailed, and Pennsylvania decided to build her canals.

In 1827 Baltimore took a radical step. Her western trade was menaced on the one side by the Pennsylvania canals, now under construction, and on the other by the projected Chesapeake and Ohio Canal. In desperate determination to have her share of the great interior business, Baltimore threw down the gauntlet to her neighbors by boldly adopting the new invention. On July 4, 1828, the "cornerstone" of the Baltimore and Ohio Railroad was laid —a railroad whose cars most of its promoters expected would be pulled by horses all the way to the Ohio River. Ridiculous enough it seems now; but Baltimore had builded better, far better than she knew.

Old Towpaths

Strangely enough, it was a canal company, the Delaware and Hudson, which first brought the locomotive to America, to pull its coal cars over a ridge from the mines to Honesdale, where the canal began. The locomotive when tried out proved so heavy that they were afraid the track wouldn't sustain it, so it was discarded—but the damage had been done. The canal had taken to its bosom the serpent which later was to sting it to death.

The Erie Canal had scarcely been completed when a Pennsylvania opponent of canals predicted that it would soon be superseded by a railway. And in 1829 a Connecticut editor, after describing the recently completed Morris Canal with its numerous locks and inclined planes, remarked, "For ourselves, we believe that a railway might as well have been constructed along the whole route." Niles's Register declared in 1829 that "the public mind is every day more and more settling into a belief that railroads will supersede canals"; but then he immediately mars his reputation as a prophet by adding that "we rather think that from improvements now presented, locomotives will never come into general use." "The ascent of considerable heights," he continues, "over which railroads shall pass will possibly be assisted by stationary engines or the use of additional horse power."

The speed mania, the principal factor in the downfall of canals, was becoming evident in American character even a hundred years ago. Steamboats, stage coaches, all lines of travel were making an effort to shorten their schedules. The New York *Daily Advertiser,* speaking in 1827 of "the mania of steamboat passengers to make the trip between New York and Albany *a few minutes* quicker than any others have ever done," said, "An old gentleman in New England conveyed a just idea of the character of those who were so fond of travelling at such a wondrous rate, when he said he believed that his son John, if he was riding on a streak of lightning, *would whip up!*"

Canal or Railroad?

Competition between fast transportation lines was of course very keen. A Pennsylvania stage line proprietor openly exults over his competitor in the following advertisement:

COMMUNICATION

The Easton Mail Stage left Philadelphia at 5 o'clock A.M. and arrived at Easton 30 minutes after 1 o'clock P.M., and on the same day left Easton at 5 o'clock A.M. and arrived in the city of Philadelphia 45 minutes after 12 o'clock besides changing the mail at 20 different post offices going and coming. ☞ *Smoke that, neighbor Spriggins!*
Easton, June 16, 1829
W. WHITE, *Proprietor.*

I. Daniel Rupp, a humorous old historian of Pennsylvania, records that "two daily lines of stages run from Philadelphia (to Pottsville)—Reeside against Coleman—and they merit a eulogium for the vigor with which they crack their whips, the matchless fury of their driving and their exquisite skill in upsetting." Another chronicler speaks with high admiration of the coolness of Mr. Henry Clay, when the stagecoach in which he was riding was upset in the mountains between Pittsburgh and Washington—Mr. Clay continuing to smoke his cigar imperturbably even while the coach was going over.

But all accidents were not so innocuous. Steamboat boilers began to blow up and stagecoaches were not infrequently wrecked with loss of life. Two four-horse coaches racing into Wilmington, Delaware, locked wheels and had a terrific smash-up in which several were killed and injured.

Niles declared that "it has become necessary that travellers should take a decided stand on the subject," and prosecute those public carriers whose recklessness was responsible for such havoc. He believed that pitiless publicity in the newspapers would aid in restraining the speed fiends.

Old Towpaths

But in spite of the danger, speed was demanded. With such a temper in the people, it is not to be wondered at that they looked with interest upon the newly invented locomotive which, as had been proved, was capable of the unheard-of velocity of fifteen miles per hour—though the controversy still raged as to whether locomotives or horses were the best all-around motive power for railroads. Horses had certain superiorities, even furnishing a good argument in favor of canals; for it was shown that a horse could pull thirty tons of cargo in a boat weighing fifteen tons, while on the first railroads built he could draw only fifteen tons, all told. Improved tracks enabled a single horse to move thirty tons gross, but still the water had the advantage. On the rails the horse did not emit smoke and sparks and required only a small quantity of fuel, which he carried with him; but he had a tendency to stray off the track or fall down, which caused wrecks.

During the latter twenties, when canal building was at its height, the debate between canal and railroad protagonists was prosecuted with great vigor and no little acrimony. McMaster has collected and condensed the canal arguments so nicely that one cannot do better than quote him:

"Canals, said one faction, are facts; railroads are theories, and are opposed to the habits and feelings of our people, for they create monopolies in transportation. A farmer cannot own railroad wagons. But for a hundred dollars he can buy a boat, or with the help of his hands can build one to carry twenty-five tons. To move such a load by railroad would require eight carriages and a locomotive, costing $4,000. Into his boat the farmer can put an assorted cargo of flour, bacon, hemp, plank, lumber and vegetables, draw it to market with his own horses, sell at any village on the way, and bring it back loaded with what he pleases. Does anybody suppose railroads will take on loads offered anywhere along the line? No, indeed! The farmers must haul them to the stopping places. Canals will carry live

Courtesy of the Baltimore & Ohio Railroad Company

THE CANAL STILL STRUGGLING FEEBLY AGAINST THE GIANT FORCE WHICH DESTROYED IT

Canal or Railroad?

stock, hay, firewood, large timber for ship-building, boards and planks. Railroads cannot do this. What would be thought of a load of hay coming along a railroad? The sparks from the locomotive would set it afire before the journey began. Canals are adapted for military purposes; railroads are not. Imagine a regiment of troops with baggage, provisions, ammunition and camp equipage transported by railroad! By canal this can be done and the soldiers live and cook comfortably on the way. The boat will carry tents, food, baggage and ammunition, and may be drawn by the horses or by the men as they walk along the towpath. Canal-boats will carry artillery, which cannot be transported by rail unless the guns are dismounted and the caissons taken apart. Snow will make a three-hundred mile railroad impassable for weeks; rain will wash earth over the rails in quantities which, in deep cuts, will take weeks to remove. Railroads for long distances are wholly untried in any country and for short distances are yet in the experimental stage. The longest in existence, the Manchester and Liverpool, is but forty miles in length, passes through the heart of a populous country and may anywhere get aid to repair cars, wagons and engine. But that such a railroad as the Baltimore and Ohio, ten times as long, running through a rough, wild and sparsely inhabited country, with great difficulties of construction to overcome, should ever compete with a canal of the same length as the Chesapeake and Ohio surpasses probability.

"If locomotives were used it would be necessary to have water-boiling stations every six or seven miles to furnish the engines with tanks of boiling water, for a supply of cold water would check the generation of steam and stop the train.

"Rails would be broken by passing teamsters wantonly, as they did milestones and copings of bridges, or from spite towards a means of transportation likely to injure their business. In the mountains the cold in winter is often so severe that an axe will break when struck against a tree. Would

Old Towpaths

not rails snap under these conditions as a train passed over them? Admit that the railroad can be made a success; would it not monopolize transportation, and would farmers and teamsters submit to this?"

Even as late as 1832 Governor Throop of New York declared that "railroads are not so well adapted to general use as either roads or canals, because they will admit upon their tracks none but public vehicles of a peculiar construction."

"We are not inimical to railroads," asserted the editor of *The Portfolio* with fine disinterestedness, "but we consider every invention as having a limit of utility beyond which it will always prove disadvantageous to extend it. We also think that the present feeling on this subject has more of zeal than discretion, and that a few cautionary remarks may excite a more critical investigation before this feeling shall have extended itself into ruinous and costly experiments."

The Boston *Transcript* on September 1, 1830, in speaking of a projected railroad which would compete with the Middlesex Canal, said editorially, "It is not astonishing that so much reluctance exists against plunging into doubtful speculation"; while in the Legislature Mr. Cogswell of Ipswich asserted, "Railways, Mr. Speaker, may be well enough in old countries, but will never be the thing for so young a country as this. When you can make the rivers run backward, it will be time enough to make a railway."

But the railroad enthusiasts had some powerful arguments on their side. They pointed out that canals in a northern climate could not be used more than eight months in the year, whereas railroads could be used at least eleven months; and it was even proposed to avoid obstruction by snow in winter and thereby make the railroads available for use the year round by "building the rails two feet, eight inches above the earth, which, with our great command of wood, can easily be accomplished." Furthermore, said they, "it requires a number of years to complete a canal and

Canal or Railroad?

get it in order, the owners losing the interest of their capital during the time; but a rail-way of considerable length may be completed in a single year."

It could not be denied that canals, in spite of low costs of labor and material, were very expensive. Sweet's "Documentary Sketch of the New York State Canals" gives the following construction costs per mile:

Erie Canal	$19,255.49
All New York State Canals, average	17,367.57
Delaware and Hudson	20,655.00
Lehigh	33,610.00
Pennsylvania State Canals	22,113.44
Schuylkill	16,741.26
Union	18,518.51
All New England Canals	12,838.71

From other sources these figures are derived:

Middlesex Canal	$19,000.00
Ohio and Erie	10,000.00
Miami and Erie	12,000.00
Chesapeake and Delaware variously estimated at from $150,000 to	161,000.00

But as against these figures it was asserted that railroads never cost over $15,000 per mile and seldom that much; while branch lines could be constructed for as little as $600. "Branches will be run to every village contiguous to the main line," said one booster, "and goods will come in on those lines and proceed without obstruction on the main line." One man predicted that locomotives weighing about two tons would be most practical.

"News was received in one day this season," sneered a railroad advocate, "of the stoppage of three canals in Pennsylvania, viz., the Schuylkill, the Susquehanna and the Allegheny, by breaks in the banks." After speaking of the delays of many days, even weeks, caused by such disasters, he points out that "railways will rarely be interrupted, as in case of any accident to one track the carriage can turn on to the other track and pass the imperfect place."

To these generalizations the canal men retorted vigorously, quoting quite different figures and pointing out other supposed fallacies also. "A single track," said one, "is of such limited utility that it is idle to propose it as a means of intercourse—the least number is a double track, or a going and returning track. Taking the surface of the earth as we find it, we have no estimate less than £5,000, or $22,000 per mile.

"It is also agreed by all writers upon these subjects that one set of rails admits of but one kind of traveling, and that for stage coaches and mails a second set would have to be laid. This would increase the expense about one-half, making it $33,000 per mile. A canal fifty feet wide and six feet deep could haul boats at six miles per hour, which is the limit also on railroads—a greater speed being at the expense of the horse. . . . A canal is a road of innumerable tracks and offers comparatively no impediment to boats passing and repassing each other. But this cannot be permitted on railroads; a carriage must maintain its relative position to the end of the journey."

Another expert said that because of the greater effort to overcome friction and gravity, the railroad was handicapped in comparison with the canal. The single track railroad in particular could not compare with the canal. Horses only could be used on it. "If asked why, I answer that a locomotive engine and train of seventy tons, hurling along at twenty miles an hour cannot be stopped at will; and when stopped, it must have room to get agoing again. . . . Then if a locomotive carriage has the even chance of meeting another every mile, she will be continually whipping up or holding in. . . .

"These remarks, however, will not apply to short rail-

Canal or Railroad?

roads, where the carriages can all pass one way for a certain period, and all return during another period; there can be no meeting or turning out in this case."

Notwithstanding all logic and ridicule, railroad sentiment continued to grow and railroads to be built and planned. The Charleston and Hamburg line was built in South Carolina in the latter '20's, and bought the first locomotive built in America for regular and practical use. New York chartered the Mohawk and Hudson Railroad, to be built from Schenectady to Albany, which enterprise, with unconscious irony, christened its first locomotive "De Witt Clinton." Massachusetts projected two or three railroads and Pennsylvania chartered five. So strongly did railroad enthusiasts believe in the future of the new invention that when the books were opened for subscriptions to the stock of the Camden and Amboy Railroad in the spring of 1830, the whole issue of $4,000,000 was taken in ten minutes, and $5 cash paid down on each share.

CHAPTER X

THE OPENING OF THE SCHUYLKILL AND UNION CANALS

THE early efforts (and the failure of the same) to connect the Schuylkill with the Susquehanna and to make the Schuylkill navigable to the Delaware have already been described. When work on these two projects lapsed in 1795 for lack of money, the Legislature granted the two companies the right to raise $400,000 by means of a lottery—the Schuylkill and Susquehanna to receive two-thirds of the proceeds and the Delaware and Susquehanna one-third. But after fifteen years of the lottery the entire net proceeds had amounted to no more than $60,000, which was of course far below the companies' needs. A stock subscription of $300,000 was offered by the state, but the incorporators could not raise the additional funds necessary.

In 1811 the two companies were united under the name of the Union Canal Company, and the lottery privilege was renewed, but for several years the new corporation was able to advance no faster than the old ones. The failure of early projects had destroyed public confidence.

But Philadelphia business men had never ceased to cherish the design of connecting the city with the Susquehanna and thence with the waters of the West. When the Union Canal was incorporated, it was authorized to extend its line to Lake Erie and to build such other waterways within the State as might be desirable. Its canal, if built to Middletown, would deflect to Philadelphia the trade of the Susquehanna above the Conewago Falls—the chief obstacle to navi-

The Schuylkill and Union Canals

gation in that river—thereby injuring Baltimore and bringing to Philadelphia not only the trade of the Susquehanna Valley in Pennsylvania, but also of the lakes in central New York, of the region contiguous to Lake Erie and even of the tributaries of the upper Ohio. Some of the early theorists had traced what they believed to be a practicable line 582 miles long from Philadelphia to Lake Erie at Presque Isle via the junction of the Allegheny and Monongahela at Pittsburgh. The gradual crystallization of the Erie Canal scheme now stirred the Philadelphians to action. In 1815 a new company was organized to take over the Schuylkill improvement and work was begun in 1816.

The Schuylkill Navigation, as it is frequently called, was partly canal and partly slack-water pools created by dams in the river. As originally constructed, there were 50½ miles of slack-water navigation and 57¾ miles of canals. Later the canals were lengthened to 62 miles and the pools reduced to 46. The navigation extended from Philadelphia to Mount Carbon, a short distance above Pottsville. The report of 1820 shows that there were 38 dams, 32 short canals, one tunnel and 116 locks, the fall in the canal being 588 feet. The dams consisted entirely of timber fastened together with iron bolts and anchored with iron rods to the rocky bed of the river.

In spite of much conflicting evidence, it seems certain that the Schuylkill Canal can claim the honor of having completed the first tunnel ever built in the United States. It was located just above Pottsville. Its story reveals some amusing sidelights on human character. Its existence was wholly unnecessary. It was dug through the end of a small, diminishing ridge, and could have been avoided entirely had the canal been located no more than a hundred feet to westward. But the promoters were eager to have the first tunnel in America, and they had it, regardless of expense. The contractors who built it were three brothers named Job, Samson and Solomon Fudge. It was 400 feet in length and was probably com-

Old Towpaths

pleted about 1820-21. It was regarded as one of the engineering wonders of the country; people came long distances to see it. When the canal was enlarged a few years later the tunnel was shortened to 175 feet in length, and in 1857 it was reduced to an open cutting.

The canal was regarded as fully completed in 1825. The first real canal boat is said to have been built on a vacant lot at Orwigsburg and hauled on a Conestoga wagon drawn by mules decorated with red, white and blue rosettes and ribbons and attended by the entire population to Schuylkill Haven, where it was launched with vociferous rejoicing. The multitude then adjourned to the "Seven Stars" tavern near by, where many libations were poured, perhaps to Jerry and Moses, the patron saints of boat builders.

The first boats on the canal carried only eighteen tons cargo, but larger ones were soon built, carrying twenty-three tons. The canal had not been in existence a year when it became evident that the channel was not large enough. It was accordingly enlarged in 1829.

It is a curious fact that horse power was not used on the canal for fully two years after water was first turned into it. Few people to-day are aware that the herculean labor of the Volga boatmen was once reproduced here in America. A boat was towed by two men walking side by side along the bank like a team of horses, straining with their breasts against a cross stick attached to the end of the towline. In this laborious fashion the trip from Mount Carbon to Philadelphia and return, 216 miles, often consumed six weeks.

The story of those early days is full of quaint surprises. In later years one of the greatest of the anthracite canals, the Schuylkill when it was building was not thought of as a coal carrier, for the reason that most people did not yet know that anthracite coal would burn. As with all the other canals, it was supposed that timber, agricultural products, fur and the like would furnish most of its business. So when Abraham Potts—doubtless one of the Pottses of Pottsville

Courtesy of Jay V. Hare, Secretary Reading Company
LOADING COAL BOATS ON THE SCHUYLKILL CANAL

Courtesy of Jay V. Hare, Secretary Reading Company
A SCHUYLKILL CANAL BOAT

The Schuylkill and Union Canals

—came down the canal in 1824 with the first boatload of anthracite and reached the toll office at Reading, the collector was in a quandary. He had a schedule of toll rates on every known commodity of the region, even to a bushel of hickory nuts, but none on coal. Yet so rapidly did the coal business increase that in 1826, 16,767 tons came down the canal and in 1830, 89,984 tons.

For ten years and more after the reorganization of the two old companies into the Union Canal Company in 1811, the new corporation did nothing because of its inability to lay hands on any funds. In 1819, in order to attract investors, the State guaranteed 6 per cent interest on any stock sold. This interest was to be raised if possible from the proceeds of the company's lottery, and if the lottery failed to produce the required amount, the State was pledged to supply the balance. The new subscriptions attracted by this inducement and by the encouraging reports that came from the Erie Canal enabled the company to begin work on its ditch in 1821, and to carry the job through to completion in 1827.

A new line was surveyed and the old works of the Schuylkill and Susquehanna were abandoned. Loammi Baldwin the younger was the first engineer, but he and the directors fell into disagreement in 1824, and Canvass White came from the Erie to take the position of chief engineer. The great problem of this canal lay in the fact that because of the topography of its territory, it was perhaps the most difficult to supply with water of any of the country's canals. This deficiency led to the canal's being made at first entirely too small. The locks were only 8½ feet wide and 75 feet long, whereas the Schuylkill Canal locks were twice as wide and 90 feet long. Some of the first Union boats built at Schaefferstown, six miles from the canal, were said to have been hauled to the water on hay wagons. None of the boats was able to carry more than 28 tons until the canal was enlarged, more than twenty years later.

Old Towpaths

It was soon evident that more water would be needed, even for the narrow canal. Serious leakage through the limestone bed near Reading was increasing the drain, already too rapid for the feeble supply. A plan was conceived of building a dam across upper Swatara Creek and thus creating a reservoir from which water might be pumped. Work was begun on this improvement in 1828 and it was completed about two years later. A navigable feeder channel 22 miles long was dug to Pine Grove.

The Union Canal was 77 miles long, exclusive of pools and navigable feeders, and had 91 locks. The great reservoir, formed by the 45-foot-high Swatara Dam and containing over 700 acres of water, together with the giant pumping engines and the long aqueduct which supplied the summit level with water made this an engineering wonder for all the country roundabout; and a greater wonder still was the tunnel, the second to be constructed in America, and at that date the longest.

In this case there was a better reason for the tunnel than for the one on the Schuylkill Canal; in fact, it could hardly have been avoided save by a long series of locks to carry the canal over the watershed ridge through which it was bored. This has frequently been referred to as "the first tunnel in America," and even the date of its completion has been garbled. The newspaper, *Der Pennsylvanische Beobachter,* of Lebanon, said on February 16, 1827:

"The work of tunnelling the hill for the Canal is proceeding rapidly, and will, in a few weeks, be completed. The working men at both sides of the hill have so far advanced their work that they can hear each other working. According to this, we shall soon have the privilege of seeing boats pass through."

On June 15, 1827, the same newspaper said:

"Last Monday evening the citizens of this town and vicinity had the privilege of seeing a boat, the Alpha, come up from Tulpehocken on the Union Canal and remain all

The Schuylkill and Union Canals

night at North Lebanon. The following morning it started on its journey westward, and passed through the tunnel. This was the first boat of its kind to pass through a piece of ground over which corn and potatoes were growing, and hay was being made."

The fact that hay, corn and potatoes were growing on the hill seems to have given the tunnel a noteworthy distinction. The little ridge through which the Schuylkill tunnel passed was probably clad in nothing but scrub timber! The Union Canal tunnel was 729 feet long, 18 feet wide and 16 high. When the canal was enlarged in 1850 its length was reduced to 600 feet. It had handsome cut stone arched portals which still endure with remarkably little deterioration.

The waterway was not in a finished condition in 1827, but the Schuylkill Canal received a thousand tons of freight from it that year. On January 1, 1828, the work was announced to be practically complete—sixty-five years after it had been first surveyed! It had cost $6,000,000. When the canal opened in the spring the first boat, the *Fair Trader*, went through from Philadelphia to Middletown in about five days. There were few boats in service that first season—only seventeen in July; the locks were so small that Schuylkill boats could not pass through them, and special boats must therefore be built; but such was the enthusiasm along the line that by the end of the year nearly two hundred boats were ready.

CHAPTER XI

THE BUILDING OF THE PENNSYLVANIA STATE CANALS

THE advice of Washington had not received the attention it merited. Pennsylvania, like most of the other eastern States, did not realize the importance of a more intimate connection with the West until De Witt Clinton and his coworkers pointed the way. Then she and other easterners began to comprehend the tremendously growing importance of the Northwest Territory; she began to discover that the farmers and trappers of the great Mississippi Valley were getting into closer touch with New Orleans and Mobile than with the East; that their seacoast threatened to be that of the Gulf rather than that of the Atlantic.

The Erie Canal was the first great bid for this commerce. Other westward canals were projected along the Potomac and the James; and Philadelphia and eastern Pennsylvania were aroused to the need for action. Scarcely had work on the Erie Canal begun when newspaper articles and pamphlets began to circulate in Pennsylvania, stirring up public interest in favor of highways of commerce. A state senator wrote a pamphlet in which he set forth the dogma that Philadelphia was best situated geographically of all eastern cities to handle the trade of the West. He estimated the distance of Pittsburgh from New York (by water, evidently) at 766½ miles; of Pittsburgh from Philadelphia, 423 miles. He compared the resources of the two States and found Pennsylvania's unquestionably superior. He quoted the statement of the New York canal commissioners that they expected

The Pennsylvania State Canals

from their great waterway an income from which "the whole expense of this magnificent operation would be defrayed in a few years, and an immense revenue would be secured to the State. This would enable it to patronize literature and science, to promote education, morality and religion; to encourage agriculture, manufactures and commerce." If New York could do this, Pennsylvania with her superior resources could do more. It behooved her to take immediate action, however, lest the alacrity of New York give her an advantage which might not be overcome.

On the other side the threat of Baltimore was disquieting. That city, by way of the New National Road, was 90 miles nearer the Ohio River than Philadelphia and her road was largely toll-free, whereas heavy tolls must be paid along the whole route from Philadelphia to Pittsburgh. Moreover, a canal was talked of, running up the Potomac and thence to the Ohio. Water communication with the West seemed so necessary to Philadelphia's welfare that there were not wanting those who urged that she finance it herself if the State would not do so.

In December, 1823, a special committee was appointed by the Legislature to look into the question. Two weeks later the committee reported, recommending that surveys be made at once for a route between the Allegheny and the Susquehanna. They mentioned the Erie and the proposed Chesapeake and Ohio Canals and commented upon them thus:

"These improvements, so honorable to the enterprise of the respective States and so useful to our common country as permanent sources of national riches and aggrandizement, should excite a spirit of emulation and induce Pennsylvania to create improvements of a similar character. . . . Noiseless and modest she may continue to move, but unless she awakes to a true sense of her situation, she will be deprived of the sources of public prosperity . . . and instead of regaining the high commercial rank she once held, she will be

Old Towpaths

driven even from her present station in the system of the Confederacy."

A board of three canal commissioners was appointed April 1, 1824. Ten months later two of them reported (the third one dissenting) that a canal from Philadelphia to Pittsburgh was "perfectly practicable." Their scheme contained one startling item. The route suggested led from Philadelphia to the Susquehanna near Harrisburg, thence followed

HOLLIDAYSBURG ABOUT 1835
At the left, passengers are seen transferring from a packet boat to cars of the Portage Railroad

the Susquehanna and Juniata to a point near Hollidaysburg and on the slope of the main range of the Alleghenies; it then passed through that ridge by a tunnel four miles long, reaching the forks of the Little Conemaugh River—and therefrom followed the Conemaugh and Allegheny Rivers to Pittsburgh. As many people in Pennsylvania and presumably some members of the Legislature even in 1825 had doubtless not yet seen or heard of the little tunnel on the Schuylkill Canal, the commissioners explained to the Assembly that a tunnel was "a hole like a well dug horizontally through a hill or mountain."

The Pennsylvania State Canals

The cost of that portion of the canal from the Susquehanna to Pittsburgh was estimated at $3,000,000. They would have been apt to spend that much on their four-mile tunnel alone. It was predicted that the tolls collected would "support the Government and educate every child in the Commonwealth"; and furthermore, that with a canal to the West, Philadelphia would become the metropolis of the United States.

No immediate action was taken on the report, but it provoked much discussion throughout the State. The canal scheme was unpopular in some parts of the State, and as a means of spreading information, "The Pennsylvania Society for the Promotion of Internal Improvements in the Commonwealth" was formed. This was the organization which sent Strickland to England to investigate, where he became much more impressed with the value of railroads than canals.

The Society was instrumental in getting up a mass meeting of the citizens of Philadelphia in January, 1825, at which a resolution was passed to the effect that "water communication ought to be opened with all practical expedition between the Susquehanna and Allegheny Rivers, and between the Allegheny and Lake Erie." A memorial to the Legislature was prepared and circulated in every county in the State for signatures; and public meetings were held in many places. The signed memorials began to bombard the Legislature in great numbers and that body was moved to further action. Early in 1825 a new board of five canal commissioners was appointed and instructed to prepare for "the establishment of communication between the eastern and western waters of the State and Lake Erie." Power was given them to employ engineers and draftsmen and they were also directed to devise a scheme for financing the work.

Meanwhile there was no little opposition in many quarters of the State. "It will break up the bell-teams and ruin the taverns! It will put the turnpikes out of business!"—these were the wails that arose. No farther back than 1800

Old Towpaths

it had been a common sight to see as many as 500 pack mules crossing on the ferry at Harrisburg, bound westward, loaded with iron, salt, merchandise, etc. When wagons began to be used, the horse carriers were outraged and couldn't imagine what the country was coming to. Now the wagoners and other folks with a rooted dislike for change opposed the canals.

Neither did the railroad advocates, though few in numbers, fail to let themselves be heard. John Stevens, the most persistent of all early railroad promoters, had, after long travail, secured for himself and associates a charter for a railroad (horse-operated, of course) from the Legislature in 1822. With the usual object of diverting the trade of the Susquehanna to Philadelphia, the Legislature had specified that the railroad must run from Philadelphia to Columbia, a town on the Susquehanna 27 miles below Harrisburg. Stevens was unable to raise the capital necessary and the road was not constructed.

Now the railroad backers became vocal again. An anonymous pamphlet put forth in 1825 declared that a railroad could be built from Philadelphia to Pittsburgh in one-third the time required to build a canal, and at one-third the cost. It would, moreover, be available for use throughout almost the entire year, whereas the Erie Canal (for example) was navigable only about 220 days in the year. If a railway, or even a canal, existed between Philadelphia and Pittsburgh, the competition of New Orleans as a seaport would be eliminated; and as for Baltimore, she would be unable to compete with the enormous capital of Philadelphia. Even if she built a canal or railway, little apprehension need be felt, as the length and cost of building them would be far greater than those contemplated by Pennsylvania. "New York is the third rival . . . but the communication between New York and Pittsburgh must be effected by a long, tedious and expensive voyage, *requiring four changes of vessels. The route of nearly 800 miles will be very circuitous and will*

The Pennsylvania State Canals

be impracticable five months every year. . . . It does not require the voice of prophecy to predict that *the period is not far distant when the New York canal will be superseded by a railroad."*

One of the answers of the canal party to these arguments was the assertion that because of a more favorable climate the Pennsylvania Canal would be able to operate ten months out of the twelve; that it would always close at least a month later than the Erie and open at least six weeks earlier.

There were other and very bitter objections raised to the project because of sectional jealousies and belief that a favored portion of the state was about to be benefited at the expense of other parts. But some well-balanced men in Pennsylvania saw clearly the real weakness in the proposition. An editorial in the Erie *Gazette,* published that summer when canal enthusiasm was at its peak, analyzes the situation as soundly as a historian might have done fifty years after the event:

"The advocates of a grand canal in this State have, in taking the New York canal as the basis of their calculations, entirely overlooked its peculiar advantages. The Clinton Canal traverses a country so level that the amount of its lockage does not much exceed the height of Lake Erie above tidewater—passes at right angles to the course of numerous rivers that flow from the south, is consequently easily and abundantly supplied with water—possesses along its whole extent a fine wheat country—terminates in Lake Erie, and thus connects an immense inland navigation with the ocean at the city of New York, the commercial depot of America. A canal through Pennsylvania would have nothing in common with this, excepting its termination in Lake Erie. Before it could advance 15 miles from the lake it would require a lockage almost equal to the whole of that of the New York canal. The amount of the whole lockage required can only be known when surveys are completed, probably four or five times that of New York. The expense of constructing such

Old Towpaths

a canal ought to be estimated, not from the average of the other, but from the most expensive part of it. . . . We will certainly fail to compete with the State of New York for the trade of the West. Nature has given her advantages which we cannot overcome."

Delegates from every county in the State save two met at Harrisburg in a great canal convention on August 4, and as an opening move a committee framed resolutions favoring the building of a State canal from the Susquehanna to the Ohio and Lake Erie. A violent opposition at once arose. The scheme was impracticable, premature, beyond the reach of the State's finances! It would require oppressive taxation; Philadelphia and other favored districts which fostered the proposition would receive all the benefit, while other sections would help to pay the cost and receive nothing. The leaders in the opposition were a tier of counties along the southern border and another group in the extreme northeastern corner of the State. The former did most of their trading either with Baltimore or with their immediate neighbors in Maryland and Virginia; the latter carried on their limited trade with New York City and State.

But there was a very substantial majority in the meeting in favor of the canal; and the three resolutions supporting the project were passed. When the Legislature convened in December, the wishes of the people, thus recorded, were brought to its notice; and the Governor's message also mildly favored the canal. A bill to provide for the construction of the waterway was introduced and passed both Houses in February, 1826.

It was evident from the terms of the bill that the Schuylkill and Union Canals were to be regarded as the eastern section of the great east-and-west waterway. All the agitation so far, as well as the act just passed, contemplated the building only of a single great water highway from east to west. Lateral canals were mentioned casually as being desirable and necessary in future; but the building and even the discus-

The Pennsylvania State Canals

sion regarding them was postponed—or was supposed to be —until after the main line should be an accomplished fact.

Ground was broken with much ceremony at Harrisburg on July 4, 1826. Pennsylvania (and in fact, all America) being now much farther advanced than was central New York when the Erie Canal was begun nine years before, the work did not suffer so greatly from lack of tools and equipment and from human inexperience as did the Erie in its earlier days. From the Erie school of canal engineering came James Geddes and Nathan Roberts to direct the building of large sections of the Pennsylvania Canals. Canvass White gave advice regarding the Portage Railway.

The work proceeded with a fair degree of speed. Two years' study had convinced the engineers that there was no feasible all-water route. By far the shortest and best line was that via the Juniata and the Conemaugh, and on that route the problem of conquering 2,291 feet of elevation in less than 320 miles had to be faced. The only practical plan seemed to be to build the canal along these rivers as far as possible, and link the sections together where the Allegheny backbone blocked the way, by means of a railroad which should consist largely of inclined planes.

Plans for the section east of the Susquehanna were also changed. The narrow Union Canal was pronounced too small to give adequate service as a link in the great western waterway. The State must build its own route from Philadelphia to the Susquehanna. But the intervening hilly territory promised to make a canal a difficult and expensive piece of work, and it was therefore determined to make the eastern terminus of the canal at Columbia on the Susquehanna and to build a railroad from there to Philadelphia, 81.6 miles.

The Legislature authorized the building of this line in 1828 and it was completed in 1834—one of the earliest railroads in America and the first in the world built by a government. At the beginning it was horse-operated, like most of the others of its period. It was also regarded in the same

Old Towpaths

light as a canal—*i.e.*, that it was a public highway upon which any one might put his own vehicle and operate it on payment of the tolls. Individuals and firms therefore placed cars upon this single-track line, provided their own teams and drivers, and either hauled their own products or did a public transportation business. The resulting confusion, brawling and ill feeling were indescribable. The State double-tracked the line, then in 1834 introduced locomotives, and finally eliminated all horses and itself took over the operation of all cars.

The western section of the canal from Pittsburgh to Johnstown was partly open in 1829, but was not in a completed condition until the following year. The Juniata Division was so far advanced in the fall of 1829 that on November 5 a new packet boat, gayly decorated and loaded with prominent citizens, members of the Legislature and a brass band, reached Lewistown from Mifflin. This division was completed from Columbia almost to Hollidaysburg, at the foot of the Allegheny divide, in 1832. Work on the Portage Railroad across the divide was begun in 1831, but it was not completed until 1834. Meanwhile, passengers were carried over the mountain in stages and freight in wagons.

The matter of building branch canals had not been long postponed. In fact, the main line had scarcely gotten well under way when the northern and northeastern portions of the State began to demand canals for their own territory. Lines along the North and West Branches of the Susquehanna and another along the Delaware were the ones most vociferously called for. In vain did Philadelphia and the central counties urge that the main and most important canal ought to be completed before heavy expense was incurred on side issues. The northeastern quarter was well organized for the fight and it had some adherents in other sections, too; and it was able to prevent the passage of any appropriation bills for the main line which did not include the branch canals also.

Reproduced by permission of the Philadelphia Commercial Museum
HOTEL AT THE SUMMIT OF THE ALLEGHENY PORTAGE RAILWAY, WHERE MANY THROUGH TRAVELERS SPENT THE NIGHT

Reproduced by permission of the Philadelphia Commercial Museum
CANAL PACKET BOAT IN SECTIONS BEING CARRIED UP THE ALLEGHENY PORTAGE RAILWAY

The Pennsylvania State Canals

What could the other legislators do? It was out of the question to abandon the main line, the State's chief hope, when so much money had already been expended on it. They could only yield to the bludgeons of the district politicians; and thus an enormous additional debt was saddled upon the State. The branch canals were surveyed in 1827 and excavation on them began in 1828. There were four principal ones. The Susquehanna Division left the main line at the junction of the Juniata and Susquehanna and ran up the latter river to Northumberland, 40 miles. There it forked. One line followed the north branch of the Susquehanna past Bloomsburg and Wilkes-Barre, aiming for the New York State line, where it was expected to connect with the Chemung and Chenango canals of the New York system and thereby draw a considerable amount of business from the central part of that State. The other fork followed the West Branch of the Susquehanna from Northumberland up past Lewisburg and Williamsport. The Delaware Division followed the Delaware River from Easton, at the mouth of the Lehigh, down to tidewater at Bristol, a distance of 60 miles. This line was in reality built for the benefit of the Lehigh Coal and Navigation Company, which had just completed a costly canal along the Lehigh; the Delaware Division was in effect a continuation of that canal. A small line called the Wiconisco Canal, 12 miles in length, was also constructed at a cost of $1,500,000. So high did enthusiasm arise in 1829 that a canal was even planned across the mountains from the Susquehanna to the upper Lehigh—a canal with dozens of locks and no less than five tunnels, from 800 to 1,800 feet in length. But the Legislature finally drew the line at such a costly venture as that.

A traveler when ready to leave Philadelphia over the Pennsylvania Canal in the '30's, gave his name and address to the agent of a transportation line on the day before departure, so that the "bus" might call for him and his baggage next morning. Arrived at the railway station, he en-

Old Towpaths

tered one of two little cars coupled together, his baggage was put upon the roof, and he was drawn by two horses to a point just outside the city, where he reached the first inclined plane. This was 2,800 feet in length, with a rise of 187 feet. Several cars were pulled up the grade at once by an immense hawser, a stationary engine at the top being the motive power. At the summit horses were attached again or, after 1834, a steam engine. The trip was somewhat speedier after steam began to be used. The locomotive hurried the train along at the rate of nine or ten miles an hour, deluging the passengers with smoke and red-hot cinders, until Lancaster was reached, where they spent the night, starting again at four o'clock next morning for Columbia, the railroad terminus.

There the canal began. Every week day about 4 P.M. a few blasts on a horn announced that the packet was ready to start. The canal meandered along the east bank of the Susquehanna through Middletown and Harrisburg to a point opposite the junction of the Susquehanna and the Juniata. Here a dam 9 feet high created a pool, across which extended a bridge 2,231 feet long which carried a sort of two-story towpath—one story for teams going in each direction, so that there would be no interference as the boats were being towed across the pool. On the west bank, at the junction of the Juniata, the canal forked, the Susquehanna Division turning to the right or northward along the bank of that stream. The main line crossed the Juniata by an aqueduct 700 feet long and continued westward up that river. In places the Juniata was dammed and the boat entered the river for short distances.

At Hollidaysburg, far up towards the headwaters of the Juniata and 172 miles from Columbia, the canal ended and the most famous but least practical feature of the Pennsylvania internal improvements began—the remarkable Allegheny Portage Railroad. The crest of the mountain ridge was 1,398 feet above Hollidaysburg—which grade was as-

The Pennsylvania State Canals

cended in 10.1 miles of track. On the western slope the grade was easier, the descent to Johnstown being only 1,171 feet in 26½ miles.

The passenger spent the third night out from Lancaster at Hollidaysburg, and began his journey over the mountain at five o'clock in the morning. Several cars carrying 100 passengers each followed each other closely. The horses carried them at a trot along an almost level but slightly ascending plane for 3¾ miles, which brought them to the foot of the first incline. The inclined planes were operated by stationary engines, one car descending as another went upward. The horses were unhitched, the cable hooked on, and the car rose nearly 300 feet in less than a mile. Reaching the top, horses drew the car again for two miles, then another incline was passed; and so on until five inclines and five levels had been negotiated, one of the levels being less than 800 feet in length. The final climb landed the passengers on the summit in time for an eight o'clock breakfast at one of the two taverns there.

Going down the west slope there were five inclined planes and five levels. The longest level on that side was 13½ miles in extent. All the levels had grades of from 14 to 20 feet to the mile. At the Staple Bend of the Conemaugh, four miles east of Johnstown, was a tunnel 901 feet in length —the third in America and the longest that had yet been constructed. Several worthy historians have mistakenly declared this tunnel to be the earliest in America; but the Schuylkill and Union Canal tunnels were both completed before the Portage Railroad was even authorized by the Legislature.

At Johnstown the canal began again and continued along the banks of the Conemaugh, the Kiskiminetas and the Allegheny Rivers to Pittsburgh, 104 miles. The extension which was to connect Pittsburgh with Lake Erie was one of the last begun, and was never completed.

CHAPTER XII

FLUSH TIMES AND THE CANAL MANIA OF THE THIRTIES

AS early as 1828 Captain Basil Hall, an honest and tolerably shrewd observer, remarked in commenting upon the Erie Canal, "The example of this successful experiment has, I suspect, done some mischief in the rest of the American States; for it has set agoing a multitude of projects many of which, I am convinced, can never answer any good purpose, except to such speculators as may have sold their original shares at a premium and then backed out of the scrape." These words become profoundly prophetic in the light of what happened after 1830.

Beginning soon after the close of the war with England in 1815 and continuing until 1837, there was a rising swell of prosperity in the United States, culminating in a period of flush times in the middle '30's such as the people had never known before. Such a wave carried with it its inevitable curses—speculations, inflation, loss of mental balance, financial legerdemain and thievery, and finally, the disastrous reaction.

One of the first phases of this growing prosperity is seen in the enthusiasm over canals just as the Erie was being completed. The entire stock issue of a new canal corporation, let it be one or two millions or what not, was sometimes fully subscribed and more within a few minutes or hours after the books were opened. To be sure, many of the subscribers made only small payments down and then failed to pay the balance; but many others eagerly invested large sums, often

Canal Mania of the Thirties

their all, in canal enterprises which sometimes prospered, but which in many cases made small returns or none at all.

About 1831 the canal fever was succeeded in the popular mind by a railroad mania. Locomotives had been tried in several places and found to be really practicable. Some men saw or fancied they saw that the railroad was destined to revolutionize transportation and commerce and to supply a new means of building up the wilderness. Stock of the Mohawk and Hudson Railroad, which at first could hardly be given away, now jumped to 162. When the books of the Paterson and Hudson Railroad were opened, three times the amount of stock available could have been sold, and the price quickly went up to 126. All the shares of the new Catskill Railroad were taken in a few minutes.

There was a comparatively mild depression in 1834, but the country quickly recovered from this, and by 1836 the peak of prosperity, high prices and speculation was reached. That was a memorable year in American history. Cotton had risen rapidly in price; emigrants were pouring into the Middle West and even across the Mississippi; scores of new banks were started and older ones increased their capital stock, all of them sending forth floods of paper money; thirty-five State banks had large Government deposits formerly in the Bank of the United States, and all were anxious to loan money to any one who wanted it. Some of the new banks were organized by sharpers merely to speculate with the public's money; and in other banking organizations, honest men were frequently led into ruinous ventures and crime by the gambling spirit which pervaded the air.

One of the phases of the aberration was a craze for land speculation, especially in Government lands, which could be bought for $1.25 per acre. Millions of acres were bought and held for a rise in value. Paper towns were laid out in prairie and wilderness, and land just bought from the Government was at once valued at $10 or $15 per acre, or in the newly platted towns often at $20 per lot. The village of

Old Towpaths

Chicago was the center of the land mania in the Middle West, and salesmen went from there back to New York and Boston to sell lots in the new metropolis as well as other even more imaginary cities. Never prior to 1834 had the sale of public lands amounted to $4,000,000; but they rose to $4,887,000 in 1834, to $14,757,000 in 1835 and to $24,000,000 in 1836.

These great sales were made not for cash but mostly for credit on the books of the thirty-five banks which held the Government deposits. Their notes—which were legal tender for Government land—were borrowed by the professional speculators, exchanged for land, deposited as public revenue in some deposit bank, loaned again to speculators, used again to buy land, came back once more to the Government banks, and so went around and around again, transferring hundreds of thousands of acres from the Goverment to the land sharks, but without adding one dollar of cash to its available funds.

One of the cruel results of such a system was that the speculator, with his pockets stuffed with this inflated bank currency, could outbid genuine settlers and then hold the land at a higher price, which he demanded in real money. And most of this speculation had to do with land in the Middle West, which as yet had no railroads, almost no wagon roads, and canals only in Ohio.

There was the rub! The farther one got away from the Atlantic coast, the less benefit the average citizen derived from the wealth which the country was said to possess. Prosperity might be rampant in the East, but the people in the backwoods of Indiana, Illinois, Michigan and neighboring States couldn't seem to feel themselves any the better off for it. They owned some of the most fertile land in the world—could produce farm crops, meat, timber, leather and other things in enormous quantities, but they had no means of getting their merchandise to market. The vast majority of the citizens of those States, in spite of the fact that some

Canal Mania of the Thirties

of them owned hundreds of acres of land, were in desperate poverty. Transportation seemed absolutely necessary to save them.

Ohio had begun to build canals in 1825. Her position then had been much like that of the territory just west of her in 1835—many settlers but no money and no markets. "Within my memory," wrote Henry Howe, the Ohio historian, "the farming folks used to start to church Sundays barefoot, carrying their shoes and stockings in a handkerchief until they got to the foot of South Hill . . . where they would stop and put them on. At that time wheat brought but 25 cents a bushel and had no outlet except by wagon to Cleveland or Pittsburgh. Whisky sold for two cents a dram or eighteen cents a gallon.

"The only things that would bring cash were beeswax and ginseng. Store coffee then cost 50 cents a pound; and of course it could not be bought without ginseng, beeswax or cash. Most well-to-do families made it a point to have store coffee on Sundays; on other days they used coffee made from burnt rye or wheat."

The opening of the Erie Canal, followed by the building of Ohio's canals, brought about a great change in this situation. Home-produced flour, which had sold for only $3.00 a barrel in Cincinnati in 1826 brought double that figure in 1835. Corn had risen from twelve to twenty cents per bushel, and other products were proportionately higher. And yet some citizens of the State, especially those who had received no great benefits from the canals, were pointing to their tax bills and to the distressed financial situation of the State government, and wailing that they had exchanged the frying pan for the fire.

The lamentable feature of the internal improvement policy of the fourth decade was that States continued to build canals when it was becoming evident to discerning people that canals, if not obsolete, were at least outmoded. It is a significant fact that after 1830 very few canals were built by private enterprise; and that those which were built were comparatively short ones, and in almost every case more or less profitable. States, on the other hand, built hundreds of miles of new canals, spending enormous sums and receiving no visible profit in return—though it must be admitted that there was scarcely a one of these waterways which did not confer certain incalculable benefits, sometimes great benefits, on its surrounding territory.

One of the curses of the times was a surplus in the national treasury, which Congress had decided to distribute among the States, to do with as they saw fit. Every State politician at once began planning how his Commonwealth would spend its share of that money; and the mere existence of such a surplus served to strengthen the popular belief that a sort of millennium had arrived, when nothing untoward could happen.

In 1835–36 the chief topics of the day were banking, real estate and internal improvements. The national debt had been paid, foreign capital was flowing towards us in large quantities and money was dirt cheap. Banks sprang up like mushrooms, and all began to issue paper money and urge people to accept loans. At the beginning of 1830 there were 330 State banks in existence in the country, with a banking capital of something like $110,000,000. The loans and discounts for that year were $200,000,000, and note circulation $61,000,000. The refusal to recharter the United States Bank brought about a scramble for a share of its business, and more than 170 new banks sprang into existence at once. Then the removal of the deposits and the ensuing speculative craze caused as many more to be organized, and by the end of 1836 there were 677, with a capital of $378,000,000; loans and discounts were $457,000,000 and notes in circulation $140,000,000.

Meanwhile the mania of land speculation continued in crescendo. Lotteries had but recently been eliminated, but this new form of gambling filled its place acceptably and

Canal Mania of the Thirties

furnished even greater thrills. Prices were paid for certain pieces of real estate then which were not realized again for half a century or more afterwards. Farmers, shopkeepers, clerks, mill workers and laboring men mingled with the wealthier gamblers at the auction sales, exchanges, banks and real estate offices. Many forsook their normal pursuits and gave their whole time to get-rich-quick schemes. Wild and inaccessible forest tracts in Maine, prairie lands in the far West, city lots in New York, Philadelphia, Chicago and elsewhere, all were meat and drink to the high-rollers. A township in Maine, purchased seven years before at 25 cents an acre, now sold at $12 an acre. Farm land on Long Island brought $1,000 an acre. One hundred and fifteen acres near Louisville which in 1815 had cost $675 sold in 1835 for $275,000. Some of the prices in Chicago, whose population was 4,000, were almost comic. Water-front lots, for example, 45 by 200 feet, sold for $7,000. Auction sales were taking place daily somewhere in the country, and it was no uncommon thing for two or three hundred thousand dollars' worth to be sold in an afternoon.

The inflation of the currency caused prices of labor, fuel, clothing and all commodities of life to rise to figures previously unheard-of save occasionally in war times. Grain became so high in the East that cargoes of wheat, rye and oats began coming from Europe early in 1836 and sold at good prices. Flour, which had been $6.00 a barrel in Cincinnati in 1835 brought $15 early in 1836. Late in the year it sold at $8.62 in New York. Salt was $10 a bag in Cincinnati, and New York was paying eighteenpence a pound for beef and $2.00 for a good turkey. Oak firewood cost $16.50 a cord in New York in March and $20 in Philadelphia.

It was a tragic thing that grain should have been imported from Europe when the Middle Western States could have grown all that the country then needed, and more. The principal reason why they did not was that even if they had, very little of the grain could have been hauled to market at a

Old Towpaths

cost to compete with the European product. This goes far towards explaining the internal improvement madness which seized the Midwestern States in the '30's. Their citizens have been sharply criticized for their ambitious attempt at sudden expansion, but when all the facts are known, their desperate strivings for a transportation system were not so blamable as might at first appear.

Even in the '20's dwellers on the upper Wabash were begging for relief. Salt could then be gotten only by wagon and ox team from Michigan City, at a cost of $12 a barrel. Their neighbor to eastward, Ohio, was enthusiastically building an extensive system of canals, and was thought to be on the high road to prosperity. Indiana, Illinois and Michigan heard wistfully of the rejoicings in Ohio as this and that section of the canals was completed. Stirring news came also of the wonderful progress of the Erie—more than a million dollars in tolls in 1831!—fifty millions added to the value of property along its course—cities springing up on its banks as if by a magician's touch! The stocks of the leading corporation canals—Schuylkill, Lehigh, Morris, Delaware and Hudson—were all above par; Schuylkill, par at 50, reached 145 in 1832.

All this could not fail to unsettle States whose land was sweating richness, yet whose citizens and whose State Governments were in poverty largely for lack of transportation. "We are apt to judge leaders of this period hastily," says Logan Esarey, the Indiana historian, "and accuse them of losing their heads. They did make a gigantic mistake but there are some mitigating conditions. This venture (the Wabash and Erie Canal) was considered and held before the public ten years before the work was commenced. Then it was undertaken only in despair of any better means of reaching a market. A bushel of corn at Indianapolis was worth twelve to twenty cents. On the river board it was worth fifty cents. An ordinary acre of farm land would produce sixty bushels—a loss on each acre, due to lack of trans-

From an old painting

RICHMOND IN 1833—THE JAMES RIVER AND KANAWHA CANAL IN THE FOREGROUND

Canal Mania of the Thirties

portation facilities, of $18. On such a basis, fabulous arguments can be reared. The loss on 100 acres was $1,800 annually. The State had within its boundaries millions of such acres whose value and usefulness to the State depended on commercial communication with the world."

Borrow money and build canals, was the popular cry. Canals would not only build cities and commerce in the wilderness, but they would soon pay for themselves and eventually take care of most of the expenses of the State government—some said all! Look at the Erie—a million dollars revenue in a year, and still growing! And though the Erie had threatened the well-being of Pennsylvania and Maryland, yet those States were now back on the path to fortune again with their series of canals, destined to search out every corner of their respective commonwealths.

When a bill was introduced in the Illinois Legislature in 1825 authorizing a corporation to build a canal between the Illinois River and Lake Michigan, Daniel P. Cook, member of Congress from Illinois, vehemently opposed the measure, insisting that "the rich harvest which it (the canal) was destined to yield should go into the treasury of the State." He declared that "in less than twenty years it would relieve the people from the payment of taxes and even leave a surplus to be applied to other works of public utility." The same arguments were heard in Indiana and Michigan in 1836.

Indiana had begun the Wabash and Erie Canal in 1832. By 1835 some 25 miles of channel was in operation, but its tolls were not even paying for its maintenance. Not yet comprehending that the State was too sparsely settled to support a canal, the people were swept off their feet by the ecstasy of 1835–36, and the Legislature authorized the construction of more than 1,200 miles of canals, to say nothing of one, perhaps two long railroads and many miles of macadamized road. The cost of this system was vaguely guessed at $20,000,000. As a partial payment the State

Old Towpaths

blithely bonded itself for $10,000,000. As Indiana's population that year was about 500,000, this meant a debt of $20 a head for every man, woman and child in a State where a goodly percentage of the people were so "land-poor" that they lacked the common necessities of life.

The insistence upon canals was the most deplorable feature of the Indiana program. Every day news was coming from the East of the rapid building of railroads and of their gain in popular favor. Already some of the Eastern canals were feeling the effect of their competition. But whenever a canal enthusiast was reminded of these facts, he replied by pointing to the Erie. If other canals did not succeed, they were wrongly located or poorly managed. The routes of the Wabash and Erie and the Illinois and Michigan, so ran the arguments of their partisans, were strategically just as sound, just as inevitable as that of the Erie.

But Illinois, though rushing into an infatuation wilder than that of Indiana, still retained sufficient balance to plan only one short canal. With a population of less than 400,000 and a much larger territory to improve, the people themselves nevertheless held a convention in 1836 and planned a great improvement system, which the Legislature promptly adopted. The Illinois and Michigan Canal was to be built and no less than nine railroads, aggregating 1,300 miles in length, were to crisscross the State. In addition to this, five rivers were to be improved, and to every county not touched by a railroad or a navigable river, $200,000 in cash was to be handed by way of compensation. In the prevailing land boom so many cities were planned that some of the best thinkers were gravely concerned lest the State become crowded with cities and leave no room for agriculture.

And all this in the face of the fact that the State was heavily in debt, that its school fund had been borrowed by the Legislature and spent, and that its territory was in even more of a frontier condition than Indiana's. Twelve million

Canal Mania of the Thirties

dollars was to be raised by a loan—a debt of thirty-five dollars for every man, woman and child in the Commonwealth. Eight millions were intended for railroads and four millions for the canal. Just why eight million was specified for the railroads it is difficult to say, for there had been no preliminary survey of the routes, no estimate of the cost. The crowning absurdity was the specification that work should begin on all the railroads at each end and from the crossings of the rivers simultaneously. Large brick depots were built at many places in advance of the track, and sometimes the railroad never reached them, or passed several miles away from them.

Michigan was perhaps the most insane of all. With a population of only a few more than a hundred thousand, she bonded herself for $5,000,000 and planned three railroads across the State and several canal routes. Remember that all three of these Midwestern States did not contain more than a million people; they were still mostly forest and prairie, a goodly percentage of their population lived in log cabins and millions of acres of land within their boundaries were still owned by the Federal Government.

In the East the greater States did not escape a touch of the midsummer madness. New York's million and a half yearly revenue from the Erie was partly responsible for her venture into two of her greatest errors (to say nothing of some minor ones), namely, the building of the Chenango and the Genesee Valley Canals, at a combined cost of about $8,000,000.

Pennsylvania meanwhile had built up a canal system which was bringing in $700,000 a year in tolls, but she had likewise accumulated a debt of $24,000,000, on which the tolls did not even pay the interest. Maryland, again alarmed for the prosperity of Baltimore and the State, now planned to borrow $8,000,000 and therewith to give financial aid to a great system of internal improvements, the main east-and-west line of which consisted of the Chesapeake and

Old Towpaths

Ohio Canal, the Baltimore and Ohio Railway and three other short rail lines. The Chesapeake and Ohio Canal was to be extended to Baltimore, and another canal was to be built from Baltimore to the Susquehanna and up that stream. Still another canal was to connect Baltimore and Annapolis, and there were to be north-and-south railroads reaching into Pennsylvania and to the remotest counties at the southern point of the State.

Boom conditions and the cheapness of money caused materials and labor to be higher than ever before. Particularly was this true in the Western States, where some manufactured materials must be carried farther, and where the scarcity of labor caused them to offer unusually high wages—$20 to $30 a month!—which drew many men away from the works in New York and Pennsylvania.

The panic of 1837, which followed hard upon this year of delirium, upset a great many calculations, and caused the relinquishing of many contracts; but most of the public work continued until another stringency in the autumn of 1839 dealt State projects the severest blow they had yet received. The hardest hit were those three Western States which had risked so much. All three of them had allowed large blocks of their bonds to get into the hands of banking or brokerage concerns who sold or hypothecated the securities and then went bankrupt without paying the States for them. The Morris Canal and Banking Company failed, owing Indiana two and a half millions; and it, with its sister concern, the United States Bank of Pennsylvania, had gotten possession of Michigan's entire bond issue of five millions, but had paid the State very little cash. Illinois had suffered heavily from the suspension of the same United States Bank and of a London firm of brokers. Her own State bank failed, and added to the general distress. She owed $14,000,000, her treasury was empty, and at one time there was not even sufficient cash to buy postage stamps for the State's letters.

All work was necessarily brought to a halt. Fortunately,

Canal Mania of the Thirties

Michigan had not begun work on her canals, and never did begin it. Neither Illinois nor Indiana had much to show for their expenditures. Illinois was strewn with short bits of partly constructed railroad track, Indiana mostly with unfinished canals. Isolated and useless bridges, culverts, aqueducts, locks, dry canal channel, rails, ties, timber, tools were scattered everywhere, and already were beginning to decay.

Michigan simply repudiated her debts. Indiana compromised with her creditors, forcing them to accept much less than was due them. Fortunately for Illinois, in this crisis she had a wise Governor who by abandoning the greater part of the State program of improvement and by extra taxation and general retrenchment, finally steered the State into calmer water. The details of these episodes will be more fully discussed in the chapters devoted to the two States.

Ohio had completed her two main canals long before the panic, but was still saddled with their debts. The net earnings of the canals were not half the amount of the annual interest on the State debt, and she was compelled to assess heavy taxes at a time when farm products, owing to the depression, were selling at very low prices. Maryland, too, was in trouble. The canal and railroad companies who had borrowed heavily from the State had not (with the exception of one railroad) even kept up the payment of their annual interest. The State was therefore compelled to resort to drastic retrenchment and taxation.

Pennsylvania was in perhaps the worst case of the Eastern States. The suspension of specie payments in 1837 forced her to pay her interest for that year and the two succeeding ones in paper money, and her bonds, which had hitherto stood well in the market, now fell below par. The State owed $34,000,000, and her yearly expense was a million dollars greater than her income. On February 1, 1840, Pennsylvania was for the first time compelled to default in

Old Towpaths

the payment of interest. Thereupon special taxes were laid; after much pleading, some bank loans were obtained, the interest was paid and the crisis was past.

But for several years afterwards all those States left keenly the evil effects of that period of wild inflation, and paid for it in increased taxes. Those four disastrous years from 1836 to 1840 mark the beginning of the end of the age of canals in America.

CHAPTER XIII

WESTWARD HO!

THE Erie Canal was barely completed when on July 23, 1826, the newspapers recorded a "novel scene" at Albany—that of a boatload of Swiss immigrants, still in their native costume, on th 'r way to Ohio via the Hudson River and the Erie Canal. They had with their wagons, plows and other farming tools, said by the reporters to be "rude" in construction. This became a common sight in later years, the Swiss for a long time continuing to bring their implements with them.

Even this was not the first migration by canal. Before the Erie was half done, native Americans from New York and New England and Irish and English immigrants were following the canal as far as it went and then continuing by wagon to some likely-looking new town or pushing far into the interior.

Similar scenes were common when the Pennsylvania main canal was opened. "Almost every summer day in the latter '30's and '40's," says another item, "groups of merry German immigrants in wooden shoes might be seen on the decks of line boats going west from Harrisburg towards Ohio, Indiana and Illinois." Cincinnati, Chicago, St. Louis, Milwaukee and other western cities, to say nothing of the country, owe their large German populations in considerable degree to the Erie and Pennsylvania waterways. Switzerland County, Indiana, with its county seat of Vevay and its numerous French-Swiss family names, is a typical creation of the old canals.

The completion of the Erie and Pennsylvania Canals

Old Towpaths

(not to deprecate the assistance of several others) did more to populate all that vast territory lying beyond the Alleghenies than any other agency in our history. The old waterways deserve to be gratefully remembered for that, if for nothing else. Westward through all the westbound canals in the three decades preceding the Civil War poured a ceaseless, eager yet patient, dogged yet fiery and enthusiastic throng of pioneers, with eyes straining towards the new lands beyond the horizon. And as they went they sang the wistfully humorous songs which the great hegira had brought forth—"Ah, ha! Bound away—for the wild Mis-sou-ree!" and

>   *Oh, Susanna!*
>   *Don't you cry for me;*
>   *I'm a-going out to Oregon*
>   *With my banjo on my knee.*

The last two lines had several variants.

And then there was that Michigan classic, first heard in 1837, two stanzas of which ran thus:

Then there's old Varmount, well, what d'ye think of that?
To be sure the gals are handsome and the cattle very fat.
But who among the mountains 'mid cloud and snow would stay
When he can buy a prairie in Michigamia?
  Yes, yea, yea, in Michigamia.

Then there's the State of New York where some are very rich.
Themselves and a few others have dug a mighty ditch,
To render it more easy for us to find the way
And sail upon the waters to Michigamia.
  Yes, yea, yea, to Michigamia.

Silas Farmer in his *History of Detroit and Michigan* says that this song is "known to have been largely influential in

Westward Ho!

promoting emigration." The reference to New York indicates what was thought of the Erie Canal's part in the great westward movement.

Many of the emigrants who reached Buffalo by the canal took lake boats thence to Detroit and from there pursued their journey westward by wagon or in whatever manner they could. During the year 1830, 15,000 arrived at Detroit from the East—a few stopping there, but most of them going on. The Detroit *Free Press* of May 19, 1831, chronicles the arrival of lake steamers from the East during the past week carrying more than 2,000, "and nearly all in the prime of life." "Such was the tide of immigration during the entire season of navigation," says Farmer, "that both steam and sail vessels were crowded to their utmost capacity. On October 7, 1834, four steamboats brought nearly 900 passengers. . . . On May 23, 1836, 700 passengers arrived, and during the month there were ninety steamboat arrivals, each boat loaded with passengers. The roads to the interior were literally thronged with wagons. A careful estimate made in June by a citizen showed that one wagon left the city every five minutes during the twelve hours of daylight. In 1837 the immigration was fully as large; there was an average of three steamboats a day, with from 200 to 300 passengers each, and on one occasion in May, 2,400 passengers landed in a single day. The larger part of these immigrants were from New York, and the rest mostly from New England."

New York and New England! Through the vast artery of the Erie poured so much of the sturdiest, most vigorous, most restless blood of the northeast that Michigan, southern Wisconsin, northern Illinois and northern Ohio were largely peopled with pioneers from New England and New York —especially New England. Lois Kimball Mathews, in an interesting study of this subject, points out that of the first fourteen Governors of Michigan, six were from New York and six from New England; she points to the preponderance

Old Towpaths

of Congregational churches in Michigan, and also to the fact that the township system of Michigan is more like that of Massachusetts than is any other local government outside of New England. And Herbert Quick in *Vandemark's Folly* shows vividly how the Dutch and Yankee flood which rushed through the Erie rolled on, on, across the Mississippi into Iowa and Minnesota, into Missouri and Kansas, sending its wavelets even to the shores of the Pacific.

The canals of the Middle West, too, played a part in the populating of the States of that section of which few people have any conception to-day. The canals of Ohio, for example, distributed new settlers throughout the length and breadth of the State. Many turned aside from the lake at Cleveland and went down into the central portion, or came down the Ohio River and turned north on the main canal from Portsmouth. Others left the lake at Toledo and went up the Miami Canal. But from Toledo one of the great western avenues was that via the Miami and Wabash and Erie Canals into Indiana and Illinois; for the Wabash and Erie, after it passed Lafayette, ran southward so closely along the Illinois line that it benefited eastern Illinois almost as much as its own State.

Work on the Wabash and Erie was shrewdly begun at Fort Wayne, the point farthest east and nearest the Ohio line. The result was that the first sections completed (from 1835 on) were a valuable aid to westbound immigrants. When the canal was begun in 1832 Indiana had probably a little more than 350,000 inhabitants. By 1840 she had 684,000 and in 1850, 988,000. The growth of Illinois was even more phenomenal—157,000 in 1830, 476,000 in 1840 and 851,000 in 1850.

An early settler in upper Indiana said in later years, "All the immigrants from the East came in by the canal. The boats would take grain to Toledo and bring back immigrants and their goods by the hundred." The Indiana counties bordering on the section of the canal opened in 1835 had at that

From an engraving by W. H. Bartlett

LOOKING DOWN THE ERIE CANAL FROM THE HEAD OF THE LOCKS AT LOCKPORT, ABOUT 1835

Westward Ho!

time 12,000 inhabitants; in 1850 they had 150,000. In the three years following the opening of the first section from Fort Wayne to Huntington, five new counties were created along the route. Many people in southern Indiana moved up to the northern part of the State, attracted by the boom created by the canal.

Even though the Illinois and Michigan Canal was not completed until 1848, it had a large part in the great westward movement. Many emigrants, reaching the foot of Lake Michigan, went by canal to the Illinois River, thence down to the Mississippi; and from there via other streams, notably the Missouri and its tributaries, the courses of the pilgrims spread out fanwise to all quarters of the West, Southwest and Northwest.

Not only did the canals distribute the native American settlers, but also the foreign born. During the thirty years following the completion of the Erie Canal, it was estimated that 30 per cent of the foreign immigration entering the port of New York passed into the States served directly by the Erie and its western connections. The census atlas of 1870 showed a much greater density of foreign population along the trade-route waterways, and this was especially true of the Erie and its connections. In the territory along the Wabash and Miami Canals, for example, between Fort Wayne and Toledo, from 8 to 15 per cent of the total population was German. The Pennsylvania Canal, too, carried large numbers westward from Philadelphia and Baltimore, but New York during the first half of the nineteenth century had become preëminently the port of entry for immigration, handling as much as four or five of her nearest rivals combined.

"When I came down from Utica to Schenectady on my way home," wrote Francis Lieber, a traveler on the Erie Canal, "I believe that not two hours passed without our meeting one or several barges laden with Germans."

As this great Caucasian tide pressed forward, it swept

Old Towpaths

the aboriginal inhabitants of the land before it and along with it towards the sunset. A striking and significant picture of the times is that drawn by William Dean Howells of one of the memories of his early childhood along the Miami Canal:

"In 1831 the Senecas ceded their lands, forty thousand acres on the Sandusky, to the United States, and were removed to the southwest of the Missouri. Each of the other reservations was given up in turn for lands in the far West, and in the early forties I myself, when a boy living in Hamilton, saw the last of the Ohio Indians passing through the town in the three canal boats which carried the small remnant of their nation southward and westward, out of the land that was to know them no more forever."

Historians of Ohio admit that the Erie Canal was the making of Cleveland, and it was but slightly less beneficial to Detroit. During the twenty-five years that followed the completion of the Erie, Cleveland's population increased by more than 2,000 per cent and Detroit's by more than 1,000 per cent. Chicago, too, owes its rapid growth before the Civil War in no small degree to the Erie Canal. As for the State of Michigan, it is sufficiently significant to say that its percentage of increase in population between 1820 and 1840 was greater than that of any other State in the Union.

The ever-perspicacious Washington wrote in 1783 that the people west of the Alleghenies "hang upon a pivot. The touch of a feather would turn them any way. They have looked down the Mississippi till the Spaniards . . . threw difficulties in the way; and they looked that way for no other reason than because they could glide quietly down the stream . . . and because they had no other means of coming to us but by land transportation and unimproved roads."

In the early Nineteenth Century there were no longer any Spaniards to throw difficulties in the way, and so the people of the West again looked down the Mississippi. There was their only accessible market. The Mississippi

Westward Ho!

and its tributaries formed a mighty system of trade routes concentrating at New Orleans; a system which—had no east-and-west highways of commerce been developed—might have made that city the greatest port on the continent. With the coming of the steamboat to western waters, this advantage was enormously increased. All the products of the vast Mississippi Basin and the Great Plains were drained towards the Gulf coast. Even as late as 1841 New Orleans still held supremacy as a shipping port, the value of the exports going out from her wharves being $34,000,000, while those through New York were only $33,000,000. Had the east-and-west canals not been built, the Gulf coast cities might have taken the rank now occupied by Boston, New York and Philadelphia.

But this was not the most important thing. The serious matter was that which Washington dreaded—that the Appalachian Mountains were more and more dividing us into two peoples. The West and Northwest, cut off from the East by lack of trade routes, were coming more and more closely in touch with the slave-holding South. What might have been the political effect as the great issues which brought about the Civil War slowly developed—what it would have meant to present-day America—no one can guess. But with the opening of the Erie—and in lesser degree of the Pennsylvania Canal—the coveted trade connection was not only established, but also there poured into the West such a flood of New England Yankee and other anti-slavery eastern blood as cemented the North into a unit from the Atlantic to the Rocky Mountains. John L. Heaton in his *Story of Vermont* says, "It requires no fanciful imagination to conceive that the opening of the Erie Canal was an agency which did more than almost any other to curb the power of slavery."

The rush of westward emigration was largely responsible for the great number of "line" or emigrant boats which were seen on some of the larger east-and-west canals, particularly

Old Towpaths

the Erie and Pennsylvania. These boats furnished much poorer accommodations than the first-class passenger packets and charged a lower rate of fare. At first they carried some merchandise freight as well as passengers; but when emigrant travel became very heavy, all their freight space was devoted to the baggage, bedding and household goods of the movers.

Fare on the line boats was about 1½ cents a mile, as against 3 or 4 cents on the packets; but at that rate the passenger must pay extra for his meals or else carry his own food with him. Horace Greeley spoke of them humorously as "cent and a half a mile, mile and a half an hour." They were much slower than the packets. A line boat had only two horses to the packet's three or four; the teams were poorer stock and went farther without being changed. The packet covered from 80 to 100 miles a day, while the line boat was lucky to do 45 or 50. Emigrants were not supposed to be in as great a hurry as other travelers, and even if they were, they had to accept their slow progress philosophically.

On the steamboats of the western waters a deck passage (which meant that the traveler lived and slept with his goods on the open deck) was even cheaper than on the canal line boats, the rates being usually less than a cent a mile. The through rates westward from Philadelphia via the Pennsylvania Canal to Pittsburgh and steamer beyond that point, as quoted in Peck's Guide Book for 1836 show this to be a fact:

"The following is from an advertisement of the Western Transportation, or Leach's Line, from Philadelphia:

	Miles	Days	
Fare to Pittsburgh	400	6½	$6.00
" " Cincinnati	900	8½	8.50
" " Louisville	1050	9½	9.00
" " Nashville	1650	13½	13.00
" " St. Louis	1750	14	13.00

Westward Ho!

"The above does not include meals."

The guide book estimates that for the journey to Nashville or St. Louis "a deck passage will range between $20 and $25, supposing the person buys his meals at 25 cents and eats twice a day. If he carry his own provisions, the passage, etc., will be from $15 to $18." The book also admits that the boats seldom get through in the time scheduled, but advises travelers for their own sake to be patient and to make allowances for delays.

Emigrants sometimes moved west in their own boats, especially if they went via the Erie Canal. Horses could be hired from the regular lines to pull an ark, housing perhaps two or three families, through the canal. Then a steamboat took them through Lake Erie to the mouth of one of the Ohio canals or to Detroit or some point on Lake Huron, where they landed and set out overland for their new home. Other pioneers going west by the Pennsylvania Canal built or purchased boats at Pittsburgh—several families often combining in one boat—and floated thence down the Ohio.

It was the boat of a westbound emigrant which was the first to be carried bodily on the Portage Railroad over the Allegheny crest. In the autumn of 1834, only a short time after the railroad was opened, a man living on the Lackawanna River started westward with his family and goods in a small keel boat. He floated down the Lackawanna and the Susquehanna, and entering the canal, was towed to Hollidaysburg. Here he expected to sell his boat; but a transportation manager named Dougherty, who had been anxious to try the experiment, suggested hauling the boat bodily over the mountain. The emigrant, highly pleased, gave his consent and waited a few days while Dougherty superintended the rebuilding of a car "calculated to bear the novel burden." Having been completed, the car was run into the water under the boat, and then drawn out with the boat atop.

"At 12 o'clock on the same day," said the Hollidays-

Old Towpaths

burg *Aurora,* "the delighted family began their progress over the rugged Allegheny. It was pleasing to see the comfort and convenience that the ingenuity of man had added to the journey of the emigrant. The whole family were comfortably located in the cabin of the boat, which appeared to glide up the heights of the Alleghenies, unconscious of its being a fish out of water, whilst some of the family were preparing the coming meal, others were lying on their downy pillow.

"And now you may see her safely resting on the summit of the Allegheny mountains—night has overtaken them, and there they await the coming morn. . . . On Tuesday our boat and crew left the sunny summit and smoothly glided down her iron way to Johnstown, astonishing the natives. She was safely deposited in her own element on the same evening amidst the plaudits of the congregated citizens" —and thence continued her unexpected journey "to the wild Mis-sou-ree."

CHAPTER XIV

THE DECLINE OF THE PENNSYLVANIA CANALS AND THE END OF THE CANAL-BUILDING ERA

THE main line of the Pennsylvania Canals had cost $8,403,775, the Portage Railroad $1,634,357, making the total cost of the line from Columbia to Pittsburgh $10,038,133; but the early opinion of Pennsylvania was that the job was worth it. From all sections came reports of lowered costs, quick service and the rapid upbuilding of the territory. When the western division was first opened in 1829, a Pittsburgh newspaper remarked that the distance by wagon road from that city to Blairsville was 43 miles, and the freight rate had never been less than $8.00 per ton; the distance by canal was considerably greater—73 miles; and yet freight was carried thereby for $2.40 per ton. In short, the rate by land was 18¾ cents per ton per mile, by canal, 3⅓ cents per mile.

In 1833, when the Portage Railway was not yet ready for use, but when the canal was complete to the foot of the mountain on either side of it and goods were being transferred over the crest by wagons, Blairsville reported having received goods from New York by canal in eight days, whereas it had formerly required eighteen to twenty days by wagon or pack-horse.

In order to compete with the Erie Canal, toll rates had been made very low, although the canal was more costly to operate than some others; and Pennsylvania was continually insisting that goods were being handled more cheaply over her canal than by the Erie. In 1834, when the main

Old Towpaths

line was just getting under way, *Moore's Philadelphia Price Current* said: "Only last year (1833) the papers of New York boasted in capital letters that goods had been transported to Cincinnati via Albany and the canal for the trifling sum of TWO DOLLARS AND FORTY CENTS per hundred pounds: we give it in capitals, for the whole benefit of the boast shall be prominently repeated. . . . Goods are now delivered from Philadelphia at Cincinnati for ONE DOLLAR AND THIRTY CENTS! Cotton has been brought from Alabama via the Pennsylvania Canal and delivered in Philadelphia at a less cost than it could be sent via New Orleans!"

This would seem to have been a sufficiently telling answer also to the widely heralded announcement of the merchant in Middleburg, Ohio, that he had received goods from New York via the Erie Canal, Lake Erie and the Ohio Canal for $1.37½ per hundredweight.

The career of the Pennsylvania canals may be considered to have fairly begun in 1834, the year of the completion of the main line. During that year the West Branch Canal was completed to Williamsport, and the North Branch was pushing up the other fork of the Susquehanna in the neighborhood of Wilkes-Barre; the Delaware Division was opened in 1832, but its gravelly bed would not hold water, and it could not be used by large boats for several years. Josiah White, head of the Lehigh Coal and Navigation Company, who was expecting the Delaware Division to be a valuable extension of his own Lehigh Canal, became impatient and put the canal into condition himself.

Pennsylvania was cursed as was New York by insistent demands for canals coming from remote and rugged portions of the State, where waterways could be built only at great expense and with little hope of adequate returns; and the main line was not able to carry the expense of building these side canals as the Erie did its branches, because it did not and could not handle as much traffic as was carried on the Erie.

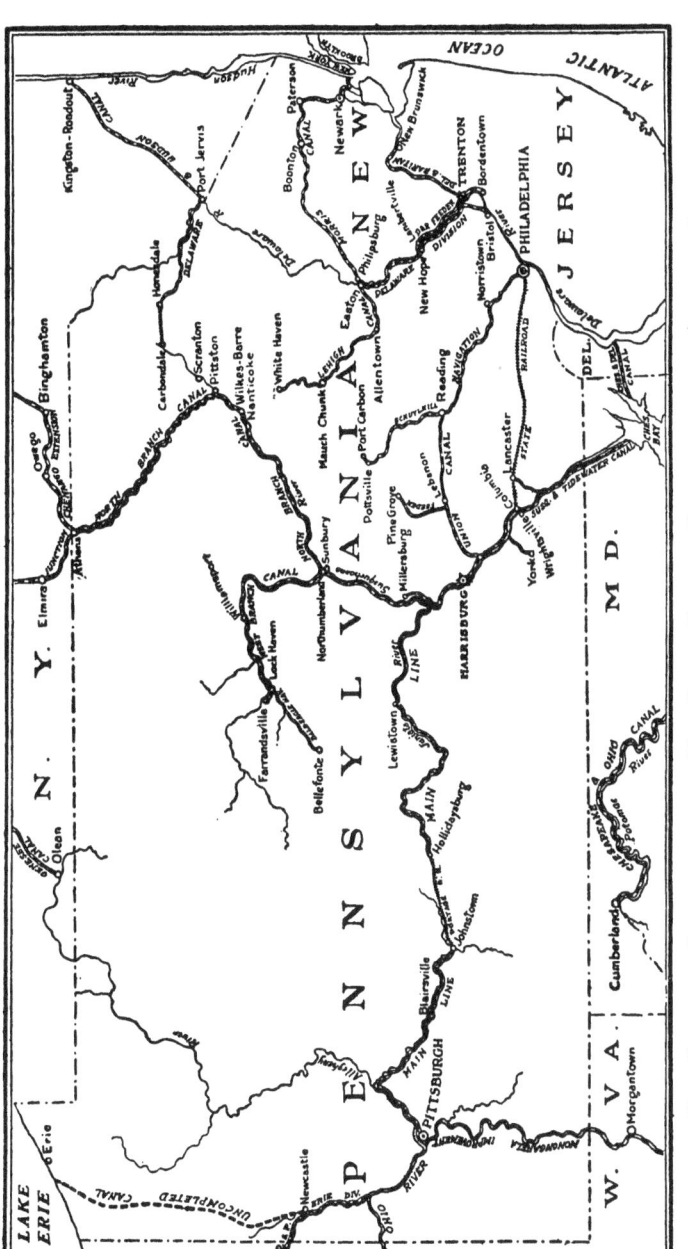

THE CANALS OF PENNSYLVANIA AND NEW JERSEY, SHOWING CONNECTIONS WITH ADJOINING STATES

Old Towpaths

These backwoods districts received a great stimulus when a canal was authorized through their territory. Prices of land began to rise long before work began. Then came the engineers and surveying gangs to increase the enthusiasm; and after them the contractors, sub-contractors, more engineers, foremen, gang bosses and armies of laborers, mostly Irish. Villages of shanties sprang up, blacksmiths' anvils began clinking, public houses and boarding houses were opened, the farmers not only had a good market at their doors for their food products, but they were asked to sell sand, clay, gravel and timber, and those who had good stone suddenly found valuable quarries opened on their farms. Everywhere there was life and bustle, money was plentiful, and it seemed as if permanent prosperity had struck the county at last. To few of those who were so elevated by this temporary affluence did it ever occur that the jovial turmoil was piling up on the back of the State a burden of debt and taxation about which they would grumble ferociously in the years to come; and forgetting the immediate benefits they had received, they would try to seek out the instigators of it and pelt them with hard words and adverse votes, if not, indeed, with criminal prosecution.

On the other hand, they often forgot also when they contemplated their tax bills that the outlet afforded by the canal had been the salvation of their neighborhood—which was true almost everywhere. The majority of the places touched by the old waterways received from them an impetus which was never thereafter entirely lost.

There were several districts which, despairing in their hopes to get canals from the State, finally proceeded to build their own. Lancaster, for example, improved the little Conestoga Creek by dams and short canals down to the Susquehanna, a distance of 18 miles, completing the job in 1828. York, on the other side of the Susquehanna, thereupon bestirred herself and constructed a similar improvement down to the river. Another such canal, the Beech Creek and

The End of the Canal-Building Era

Bald Eagle Navigation, was built from Lock Haven to Bellefonte. The Monongahela River was also improved by locks and dams for a considerable distance and did a very large business for many decades.

During the first six years' operation of the State canals, the receipts averaged about $1,125,000 yearly and the expenses of operation, maintenance, repair, etc., were about $625,000, leaving a balance of $500,000 profit which appeared very large to some citizens; but it was almost infinitesimal as compared with the yearly expenditures for the building of new canal mileage, and in fact, was not even sufficient to pay interest on the debt already existing. The North Branch Canal was being pushed up towards the New York State line and work was going forward on the division which was to connect Pittsburgh with Lake Erie. These ate up enormous quantities of money, and as years went by, more and more of the original works fell into disrepair and must be replaced.

Furthermore, the plain truth was that the Pennsylvania Grand Canal as a freight carrier to the West was not a great success, though it seemed very busy. There were several lines sharply competing for Western business over it. Peter Parley counted forty boats in the basin at Hollidaysburg at once in 1837; but that did not prove it as great a carrier as the Erie, and the very fact that they were halted there hinted at the principal, the irremediable flaw in Pennsylvania's great western canal. The prediction of the Erie, Pennsylvania, editor quoted in Chapter XI had been fulfilled to the letter. Because of its physical limitations, boats and freight could be handled neither as rapidly nor as cheaply by the Pennsylvania Canal as by the Erie.

To begin with, the eastern division alone from Columbia to Hollidaysburg had 108 locks in its 172 miles—25 more than the Erie had in its 364 miles; and adding the western division, there were all told 174 locks on the main line, or more than twice as many as on the Erie. The Port-

Old Towpaths

age Railroad was a veritable bottle neck, constantly clogged with freight, and expensive to operate, climbing and descending a total of 2,569 feet—nearly four times as much as the total lockage of the Erie. Much to their regret and greatly to the scandal of Pennsylvania politicians, the merchants and manufacturers of Philadelphia found it actually to their advantage to pay the freight on their westbound goods to New York and then ship over the Erie Canal.

There had been a great deal of carelessness and inefficiency in the construction of the canals (though the main line was on the whole a remarkably fine work) and costs had been much increased thereby. The costs of building the canals and railroads had, as in so many cases, been enormously greater than the advance estimates. The panics of 1837 and 1839 brought Pennsylvania into desperate straits, and the people became seriously alarmed. For two years the State had been paying the interest on its debt with paper money, which was already depreciating in value. A Philadelphia newspaper editorial of 1839 reflects the feeling that prevailed throughout a goodly portion of the population:

"Our State Debt has been built up through a system of fraud upon the people, and it is attempted to be increased through the same dishonorable means. When our system of internal improvements was commenced, the whole expense was estimated by the Engineer and Canal Commissioners at Five Millions. This was soon falsified by results. Yet estimates equally erroneous and equally deceptive have been made from year to year until now the actual debt of Pennsylvania, either incurred or authorized, amounts to Thirty-Two Million Dollars. And yet the system continues to be prosecuted as wildly as ever, and with as little hope of a speedy termination."

It is difficult to say definitely just how much canal Pennsylvania owned at that time. A great deal of the mileage credited to her in 1840 was only partially completed or in

The End of the Canal-Building Era

such condition that only small boats could traverse it. Possibly 606 miles could be listed, divided as follows:

	Miles		Miles
Main Line, Columbia-Hollidaysburg, Johnstown-Pittsburgh,	276	West Branch Division, Northumberland to Farrandsville,	75
Susquehanna Division, Duncan's Island to Northumberland,	40	Delaware Division, Bristol to Easton,	60
North Branch Division, Northumberland to Wyalsung,	124	Beaver Division, from Ohio River to Newcastle and beyond,	31
		Total	606

On the West Branch Division excavation was proceeding to the mouth of Sinnemahoning Creek, 36 miles beyond Farrandsville. This work was never finished. In 1839 a committee from the Pennsylvania Senate visited Albany to inform the New York government that the North Branch Canal was soon to be completed to the State line and to urge that New York build a connection to it. In the western part of the State were scattered fragments of the division intended to connect Pittsburgh and the Main Line with Lake Erie. The Beaver Division was the only portion in working order; some work had been done between Conneaut Lake and Erie, and a costly feeder and branch aggregating 49 miles had been partially constructed. The State also owned 118 miles of railroad.

On February 1, 1840, for the first time in her history, Pennsylvania defaulted in the payment of interest on her debt; and it was the general opinion that the time had come to stop spending money. Construction work therefore ceased over the whole system, and in some districts it was never begun again.

Gradually the feeling grew that the public works were

Old Towpaths

either a great mistake or else the State could not manage them satisfactorily, and therefore they should be sold. Many legislators favored the idea, and there were investors who were willing to attack the problem from the other side. A group of them in 1844 organized the Pennsylvania Canal and Railroad Company and obtained a charter from the State. The act of incorporation provided for the sale of the railroad from Philadelphia to Columbia and the Main Line of the canal thence to Pittsburgh, including the Portage Railroad, all for the sum of $20,000,000, which was to constitute the capital stock of the new company. The question of making the sale was submitted to the citizens at a special election and a considerable majority voted in favor of it. The difficulty that now arose was that the promoters of the company could not sell their stock; and so the Main Line remained in the hands of the State.

In 1845 the fragments of canal lying between Newcastle and Lake Erie were sold to a corporation which never succeeded in doing anything with them. Meanwhile, the country in general had swung back to such prosperity again that the Pennsylvania canals felt the effects thereof. There were several years of good traffic and revenue. In 1848 Governor Shunk, notwithstanding the fact that Pennsylvania by that time owed $40,000,000 for canals, railroads and improvements on the Susquehanna and Delaware Rivers, notwithstanding the fact that the Pennsylvania Railroad had been chartered in 1846 to build a railroad from Philadelphia to Pittsburgh and had already begun work, declared that the State must never sell its public works. Succeeding Governors echoed this remark with more or less emphasis. The expense account for operation and repairs had mounted in 1847 to $723,000 and in 1848 to $1,008,429. The receipts in the latter year were $1,500,555.

Not only did the new railroad select Philadelphia and Pittsburgh for its terminals, but it actually paralleled the main canal up the Juniata River and down the Conemaugh,

Courtesy of Edwin Charles, Middleburg, Pennsylvania

DOUBLE COAL BOATS USED ON THE PENNSYLVANIA CANALS ALONG THE SUSQUEHANNA, OFTEN CRUISING THENCE TO NEW YORK

The End of the Canal-Building Era

that being the only logical route for such a line. In 1849 the 60 miles between Harrisburg and Lewistown were opened, and in 1850 it had been pushed on from Lewistown to the foot of the mountain. The western division had been built with equal rapidity from Pittsburgh, and on December 10, 1852, communication was established between the two divisions, passengers and freight being transferred over the mountain by stage and wagon. And yet Governor Bigler still had sufficient faith in the canals to proclaim to the people that "The North Branch Canal must be finished, and the Allegheny Mountains must be passed without the use of inclined planes."

The work of altering the Portage Railroad was going on even while he spoke. The Legislature and Canal Commissioners were fighting hard to make the canal a success in spite of railroad rivalry. As early as 1836, when the railroad had been in use only two years, the Legislature had passed a resolution, ordering the Canal Commissioners to ascertain whether the planes could not be discarded. Nothing more was done within the next few years save to substitute locomotives for horses, but the idea of the planeless railway was gradually developed. Routes were surveyed, following in part the original line, though of course some long curves were necessary. Work began on the new line in 1850. The building was going on simultaneously with the building of the Pennsylvania Railroad track over the mountain a little to northward. In 1854 the latter was completed and began immediately to cut heavily into the canal's business.

The Governor was authorized that year to ask for sealed proposals for the purchase of the main canal. But alas! there was not one bid offered. The new Portage Railway was in operation on July 1, 1855, though not entirely completed. Again the Governor was directed to offer the Main Line at public sale. For several months there were no bidders. But in December that dreaded rival, the Pennsyl-

Old Towpaths

vania Railroad, offered $7,500,000. If anything were needed to convince the Legislature of the futility of clinging to the system, it was the balance sheet of the following year, 1856, when the receipts from all the public works were $2,006,000 and the expenditures $1,943,900; leaving a margin of only $62,100, which did not pay enough of the year's interest to be worth mentioning. The deal was accordingly consummated with the Pennsylvania Railroad in 1857.

In 1858 the Delaware Division, the Susquehanna Division and the North and West Branch Canals were sold to the newly organized Sunbury and Erie Railroad Company for $3,500,000. Thus passed, in less than twenty-five years, a great transportation system which had once been Pennsylvania's pride and hope. Such pleasurable emotions as the State Government had ever been able to derive from it were mostly those of hope; for never from 1834, when the Main Line and the larger part of the laterals came into service, had its operations been satisfactory. Its principal merit was that of all the old canals—it had built up the interior of Pennsylvania and given its mineral and agricultural resources an outlet which not only enabled the citizens to pay the heavy taxes laid upon them by the system, but to prosper as well.

The decade between 1850 and 1860 saw the virtual end of the canal-building era in America. On the other hand, it was the greatest railroad-building period that the country had yet known. The two facts are supplementary, one to the other. The Chesapeake and Ohio Canal reached Cumberland in 1850, and never went farther. The James River and Kanawha stopped at Buchanan in 1851, and its subsequent excavations beyond that point were never completed. The Wabash and Erie blundered its way down to the Ohio River in 1855, but as the head advanced, the body was dying behind it. Most of the New England canals had already passed out, and others, such as the Ohio and Pennsylvania, began dropping off the map.

In that decade, also, were built many of the railroads

The End of the Canal-Building Era

which still rank among the greatest in America. One has only to mention such roads as the Pennsylvania, a long western extension of the Baltimore and Ohio, the Erie, the Lehigh Valley, Philadelphia and Reading, Pittsburgh, Fort Wayne and Chicago, Wabash, Rock Island, Ohio and Mississippi, and Louisville and Nashville to indicate the importance of the era. Railroad influence was becoming powerful in legislative lobbies, and the canals could hope for no favors thereafter. Henceforth they were regarded as obsolete. The railroads were also becoming strong enough to wage traffic wars with the waterways. A report of a New York legislative committee in 1855 shows that the railroads entered into agreements with lake steamers, Hudson River and other boats wherever such arrangement was strategically sound, with intent to divert all possible freight from the canals to their roads.

The childish obsession speed!—speed!—more speed! had hastened the downfall of canals. The Congressional Committee on Roads and Canals put its finger upon the crux of the matter in 1834 when, in reporting upon the growth of railroad sentiment in Illinois as against the proposed canal, it said that the public imagination "was led captive by the flying motion of a railroad car, impelled by one of the most powerful agents hitherto discovered by the ingenuity and subject to the control of man."

The latter history of the Pennsylvania Canals may as well be pursued to its sad conclusion. The Pennsylvania Railroad for a short time continued to operate the canal and the Portage Railroad—but kept a sharp eye on costs. In three months' time they discovered that the railroad had lost $7,220. It was therefore closed in October, 1857, and its track torn up. Most of the rails were used on the Pittsburgh, Fort Wayne and Chicago Railroad's line across northern Indiana. Some of the stone sleepers upon which the rails had rested were taken to Altoona and used in building

Old Towpaths

the walls of the railway shops; and some may still be seen to-day, resting in their old places on the mountain slopes.

The east and west sections of the canal were operated in a desultory way for a few years by the railroad company. In 1863 about 30 miles of the western division, extending from Blairsville to Johnstown, was abandoned; and in the following year the remainder of that division was closed.

Meanwhile the Sunbury and Erie Railroad had rather promptly resold the North Branch Canal to the newly organized North Branch Canal Company for $1,600,000; the Susquehanna Division and the West Branch to the West Branch and Susquehanna Canal Company for $500,000; and the Delaware Division to the Delaware Division Company for $1,775,000. The North Branch was extended to its destined terminus, Athens, where another privately owned waterway, the Junction Canal, connected it with New York's Chemung Canal. This line did a considerable business for several years. In 1863 the North Branch Canal Company sold that part of its line between Northumberland and Wilkes-Barre to the Wyoming Canal Company for $1,010,000. In 1865 the portion between Wilkes-Barre and Athens was practically destroyed by a flood, and the half-hearted attempt to repair it was soon dropped. A railroad along its bank was opened in 1869.

In 1866 the Pennsylvania Railroad sold to the Pennsylvania Canal Company, a closely related corporation, that portion of the main line east of Hollidaysburg for a supposed consideration of $2,750,000. The Pennsylvania Canal Company acquired a majority of the stock of the West Branch and Susquehanna Company in 1867 and operated these lines and the Juniata Division in the interest of the Pennsylvania Railroad, for which the branch canals proved rather valuable feeders during several years. In 1869 the Pennsylvania Canal Company absorbed the Wyoming Canal Company. It purchased the scattered fragments in north-

Courtesy of the Pennsylvania Railroad Company

OLD STONE SLEEPERS OF THE PORTAGE RAILROAD STILL IN POSITION ON THE HILLSIDES BETWEEN HOLLIDAYSBURG AND JOHNSTOWN

The End of the Canal-Building Era

western Pennsylvania at a forced sale in 1870, but abandoned them in 1871.

In 1872 the Pennsylvania Canal Company was operating 358 miles of canal. This included the Main Line from Columbia to Williamsburg, near Hollidaysburg; the Susquehanna and North Branch Divisions from Duncan's Island to Wilkes-Barre; the West Branch from Northumberland to Farrandsville, and the little twelve-mile Wiconisco Canal. This system actually carried more than a million tons of freight in its peak year, 1871. The company then raised the tolls, and in 1874 reached its greatest net earnings, $305,665. Thereafter the receipts slowly declined until in the latter 80's the balances began to be written now and then in red ink.

Meanwhile the mileage was also decreasing. In 1875, twenty miles had been eliminated; in 1885 only 324 miles were left; and in 1890 only 144 miles. This sudden drop was caused largely by the terrible rainfall over the Alleghenies in May, 1889, which sent the Juniata and other streams out of their banks and almost completely ruined the eastern division. That portion along the Juniata was partially repaired, but never put into full service again, and soon fell into disuse.

On the west slope of the Allegheny ridge, on the upper waters of the Conemaugh, was a reservoir which had been built sixty years before to impound water for the western division of the canal. After that division was abandoned, this lake had been embellished with a hotel and other attractions and maintained as a pleasure resort. It was the dam of that lake which broke on May 31, 1889, and overwhelmed Johnstown and neighboring villages with a flood which destroyed more than 3,000 lives.

In 1900 only about 100 miles of canal were left, and the net earnings were $1,941. The portion along the main Susquehanna River was abandoned that year. In 1903 only 43 miles remained, and in 1904 the last mile was abandoned.

Old Towpaths

Only the Delaware Division was left. It had not passed into the hands of the Pennsylvania Canal Company, but was leased in 1866 by the Lehigh Coal and Navigation Company. As this book is being written, it is still in operation just as it was ninety years ago—the sole souvenir of Pennsylvania's once great system of canals.

CHAPTER XV

THE NEW YORK BRANCH CANALS—THE TRIUMPHAL PROGRESS OF THE ERIE

WHEN the Erie was first built, it ran through many of the streams it crossed instead of bridging them. Some of the streams were raised to its level by dams. This created some fine water power, and the sale of milling and water rights added to the canal's revenue.

When the channel passed through a river, there must of course be guard locks on either side of the stream to protect the canal from both high and low water. The horses crossed the stream on a special towpath bridge. A freshet was apt to hold up traffic for several days, and long strings of boats would accumulate in the canal on either side, waiting for the water to subside. The congestion and delay often became so serious that boats would attempt to cross after the flood before the stream had fallen to its normal level. The boats first entered the guard lock, the gates were closed, the level changed and then with a strong team, sometimes doubled, the crossing was essayed. There was always danger, especially at Schoharie Creek. If the towline broke, as it sometimes did, with the boat in the middle of the stream, the craft was often swept over the dam and into the Mohawk River—occasionally with loss of life. Once in the Mohawk, even if not wrecked, the boat must go all the way to Schenectady before it could get back into the canal.

The canal had not yet been completed when it became apparent to some that such defects as the above, coupled with its restricted size, were a detriment to its progress. The vol-

Old Towpaths

ume of traffic was increasing far beyond what any one had expected. By 1826 there were 160 freight boats and 882 horses on the canal. The arrivals at Albany in 1824 were 2,687; in 1825, 3,336; in 1826 there were about 7,000.

There were the passenger packets to reckon with, too. No one had ever guessed what a nuisance they were destined to be. They must be given the right of way in passing locks and must be allowed to pass slower-moving freight boats going in the same direction. They and some light freight boats doing a sort of express service moved so rapidly that their waves injured the banks. As early as 1822 it was found necessary to forbid a speed of more than four miles per hour. Even at that rate, the heavy traffic damaged the banks, and they were built higher in places, or else reinforced with stone or wood.

At first appearing as a desirable source of revenue, it was later found that the revenue collected from the packets amounted to no more than one-twentieth of that derived from the freighters. It was even proposed to limit the packets to two a day, and after a time to abolish them entirely; but this was found to be impossible until railroad competition did the work naturally. The public demanded packets and must have them. Their popularity during the first few years of the canal's existence may be guessed from an item in a Schenectady newspaper of April 16, 1831: "This morning the canal became navigable to Schenectady, and the first packet arrived with upwards of 100 passengers." This was more than any packet was built to accommodate, and that on the first trip of the season, whose date was necessarily uncertain.

A magazine writer of 1829 tells of a two-hour delay of his packet at Utica because of a blockade of boats in the canal. An occasional raft of timber two or three hundred yards in length did not improve conditions on the little forty-foot ditch. Records and newspaper reports of those days surprise one by the variety of products carried and by the

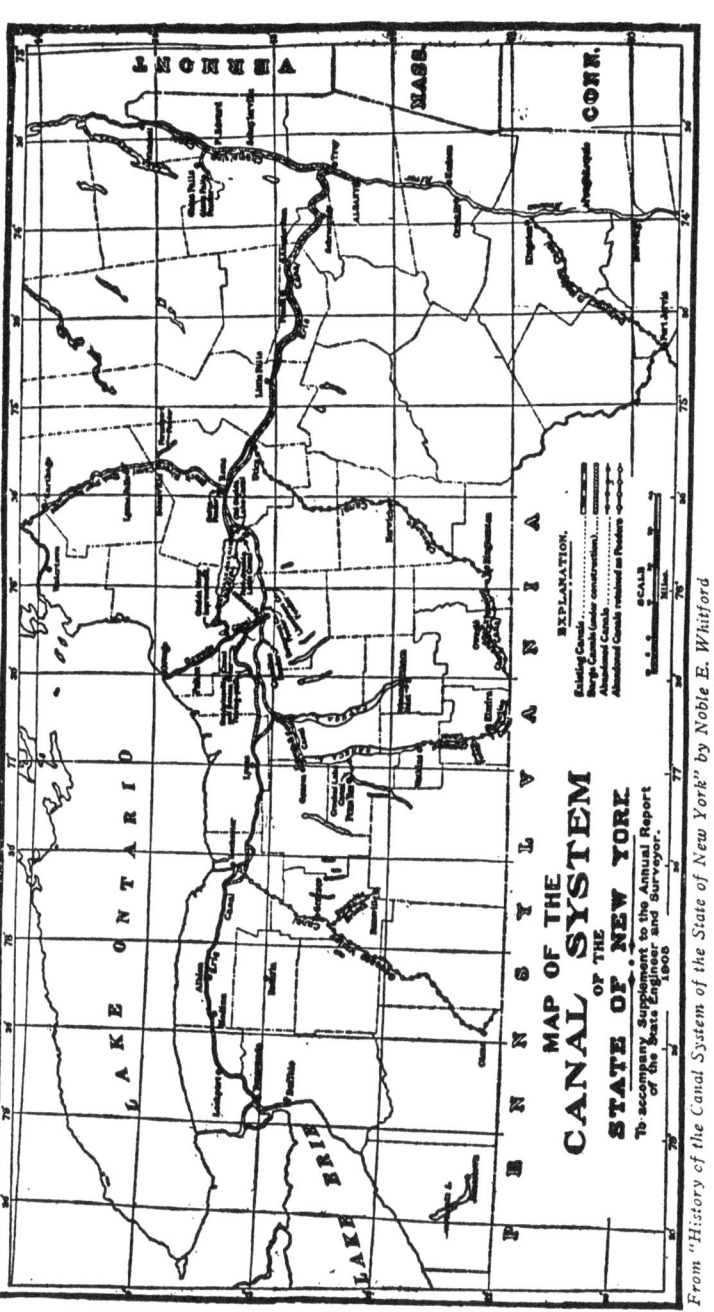

MAP OF THE NEW YORK CANALS

palpable "hustle" already being displayed by American producers and merchants. Not many to-day would suspect, for example, that live poultry were being exported in 1828; yet an item in the Albany *Argus* of that year says: "The canal boat Farmer's Daughter, of Skaneateles, arrived in this city from Jordan, 190 miles in the interior Friday evening with a cargo of 1,000 live turkies, ducks and geese . . . bound for the West Indies."

On March 4, 1825, seven months before the whole canal was thrown open, the Canal Commissioners, in a report to the Legislature, had indicated the need of increased facilities, and suggested that the locks be doubled, so that boats might pass both ways at once. They also hinted at the possible construction of another canal parallel with the eastern section. In the latter '20's the Oswego and the Cayuga and Seneca branches began to add more traffic to the main line. As years passed and a lock now and then fell into disrepair, a new one was frequently built alongside it, thus doubling the capacity of the canal at that point. In 1834 authority was given to double all the locks between Albany and Syracuse; but it was plain that this action would still be inadequate to cope with the rapidly growing business of the canal.

The State, however, had now got itself into something of a pinch. Misled by the generally swelling prosperity of the country and by the enormous increase in tolls on the Erie, the Legislature had authorized the building of one branch canal after another until millions had been spent, millions more were about to be spent, and the State was now threatened with the necessity of either borrowing money or increasing taxes. It is hardly to be wondered at that legislators and populace lost their balance. The triumphal progress of the Erie had been far beyond all expectations. The commissioners had in 1825 made predictions as to the yearly tolls of the canal which were ridiculed by many at the time as extravagant; and yet up to date those predictions had been regularly fulfilled and even exceeded.

The New York Branch Canals

They had prophesied a million dollars tolls in 1836, two millions in 1846, four millions in 1856 and nine millions in fifty years. Incidentally it may be remarked that the tolls surpassed their prediction by $440,000 in 1836 and by $499,000 in 1846. The four-million mark was a few years late in arriving.

The Champlain Canal was doing well, but was not as great a toll-gatherer per mile as the Erie. The Oswego and Cayuga and Seneca branches were so far yielding only small returns. Since 1830 the Chemung, Crooked Lake and Oneida Lake Canals had been completed; the Chenango Canal had been authorized, and citizens of the Genesee and Black River valleys were loudly demanding canals. Even with its tremendous income the Erie was unable to carry the burden of building costly laterals. Specific sources of revenue such as the salt and auction duties had been granted to the canal fund when the Erie was first authorized; they had poured five millions into the fund—and still the canal debt at the end of 1834 was more than seven millions.

It is difficult to realize the gravity of the crisis through which the Erie now passed. Railroads had become so important a factor in social progress that there were many in New York who, unable or unwilling to differentiate between the perplexities of the Erie and those of the other canals, rushed to the extreme of declaring canals obsolete, and urged that the Erie be replaced from end to end by a railroad. Had this foolish suggestion been followed, the story of one of America's greatest enterprises would have been halted almost before it had fairly begun. Successful as the Erie had been up to 1835, it rose to its greatest heights in years thereafter.

The Legislature, however, addressed an inquiry to the Canal Commission on the relative merits of canals and railroads, and the Commission's engineers replied in effect that the expense of transportation on railroads was greater than on canals in the ratio of about $4\frac{1}{3}$ to 1; that canals were common highways, "upon which every man can be the carrier of his own property, and therefore create the most active competition, which serves to reduce the expense of transportation to the lowest rate"; that canals had so far cost less on the average both for construction and maintenance than railroads.

Another project of this period was that of enlarging the channel between Albany and Oswego to ship-canal size, and making that the State's chief dependence. But the friends of the Erie were able to overcome this as well as the railroad; and in May, 1835, the enlargement of the Erie to 70 feet at the water surface, 52½ feet at bottom and 7 feet in depth, was ordered. The State still had no definite financial program, but was trusting to the Erie to take care of everything. It was certainly a marvelous money-getter. Toll rates had been much reduced in 1834, and yet so great was the increase in tonnage that there was only a very slight reduction in income for the following year. By July 1, 1836, the surplus revenue from the Erie and Champlain Canals had become amply sufficient to pay off the remainder of the debt (over $3,500,000) contracted for the building of those canals.

Unfortunately, the work of enlargement had scarcely begun when the panic of 1837, followed closely by that of 1839, reduced revenues and made the problem more difficult. In 1840 the Legislature borrowed $2,750,000 for the various canals, and in 1841 another loan of $3,000,000 was authorized. A slowing up in expenditures was also ordered, but even this did not bring relief, though the tolls of all the canals for 1841 passed the two million mark. In 1842 the Legislature ordered the cessation of all public improvement work save that absolutely necessary for maintenance and repair. Fortunately, much important enlargement had been accomplished on the Erie. The stoppage continued until 1847.

As to the branch canals of the State, some were valuable feeders, some were simply dead weights on the back of the

Oswego and the Oswego Canal about 1840

Old Towpaths

Erie, the State's chief breadwinner. The Oswego was the first real branch to be constructed, the Champlain being in effect a separate waterway. When the route of the Erie was finally agreed upon, the agitation for the connection of the great canal with Lake Ontario was kept up. At one time the citizens of Oswego organized to build the canal themselves. But just as they began work, the State (much to the disgust of Rochester) decided to take over the job. Rochester wished the connection with Ontario to be made via her city and the Genesee, and asserted that the Oswego route "would for many years to come greatly diminish the revenue of the State." On the contrary, the Oswego was a profitable canal.

Excavation was begun in 1825 and completed in 1828. The line was 38 miles in length, 19½ being independent canal and 18½ slack-water navigation in the Oswego River. It had cost a little over half a million dollars. The Assembly Committee on Canals in 1853 remarked that "This canal, although but 38 miles in length . . . is in reality second only to the Erie Canal in revenue. The trade of the Oswego Canal amounts to about 700,000 tons; that of the Champlain Canal 513,000 tons." The Oswego was enlarged along with the Erie and was included in the scheme when the present great Barge Canal was built.

Agitation of a scheme to connect Seneca and Cayuga Lakes with the main canal began early in the Nineteenth Century, and a private company was organized in 1813 which built a canal and some crude locks in the Seneca River; but the work was not satisfactory, and in 1826 the State took over the job and rebuilt it. The navigation was 20 miles in length. Improvements were made from time to time, and the canal was enlarged during the '50's to correspond with the enlarged Erie. It was given a temporarily helpful feeder when the Crooked Lake Canal was constructed in 1832–33. This ran from Dresden, on the western shore of Seneca Lake, to the head of Crooked (now Keuka) Lake, a distance of 8 miles.

During the '60's the business of the Cayuga and Seneca

The New York Branch Canals

Canal increased rapidly, largely due to the fact that it now completed a through line between the Erie Canal and the coal region of Pennsylvania, via Seneca Lake and the Chemung, Junction and North Branch Canals. The tonnage in 1865 was 192,312; in 1869 it was 533,516. But there it paused, and then slowly declined as railroad competition became sharper. When the Chemung and Crooked Lake Canals, its two most important feeders, were abandoned in the '70's, its business suffered heavily. Nevertheless, the canal was kept in operation until the new Barge Canal was built, when it was enlarged to become a part of that system.

Clinton himself was one of those who favored giving the Black River Valley a connection with the Erie Canal. The district was very fertile and rich in iron ore. It was argued also that the proposed canal would aid in making secure the northern frontier. The final argument, which was regarded as a somewhat minor one then, has since proved to be most important of all; namely, that the canal would give the Erie an additional source of water supply. In later years the very existence of the Erie came to depend on that Black River feeder.

The first pretentious plans contemplated extending the waterway on to Ogdensburg—106 miles of canal and 40 miles of navigation in Black River; but this scheme was a bit too ambitious for the Assembly. Two private corporations were organized to build the canal, but both failed to raise the necessary funds. Finally in 1836 the Legislature took up the proposition again and ordered the canal constructed. The final impetus had been given by the disclosure that the enlargement of the Erie, ordered in 1835, would render necessary an increased water supply, which Black River could furnish. The cost of the work was now estimated at $2,431,699, or nearly one-third the construction cost of the Erie. Excavation was begun in 1837, was delayed by the "stop law" of 1842 and other troubles and was not completed until 1855.

Old Towpaths

For several years the canal did a large business; then its traffic declined. But by 1875 it was found that the Erie could not be filled without the aid of the mountain reservoirs of Black River. Thenceforth, even after its commerce vanished, the canal was carefully nurtured as a feeder, even to the days of the Barge Canal.

In the year 1814 the connection of central New York with the Susquehanna Valley began to be talked of, either via Seneca Lake and the Chemung River, or from Utica via the Chenango Valley to the Susquehanna. The people of the Chenango Valley became insistent as the Erie neared completion, and in 1825 the Chenango scheme was among the seventeen proposed laterals whose survey was ordered in "the great canal bill." For several years the Legislature remained cold to the subject, but at length in 1833 the building of the canal was authorized, to run from the Erie to Binghamton.

Work went forward rapidly, but against many handicaps. Prices of labor and supplies rose rapidly as the country became more prosperous. When the canal (97 miles long, with 116 locks) was opened for navigation in the spring of 1837, it had cost $2,316,186—and all the tolls collected on it in the forty years of its life were only $750,251!

An unfortunate feature of the Chenango was that nearly all the locks were built of wood. By 1845 these were in sad need of repairs, but none were made until five years later. Thereafter, the story of the canal consists mostly of records of patching the decaying works.

Complaints were made that the Chenango Canal was not a success because it did not connect with the Pennsylvania system. If this connection had been made early in its history, its business would undoubtedly have been much greater; but the extension was not considered until 1838, when the State was already in deep water financially, and not begun until 1863, years after all thought of building minor canals should have ceased entirely. Prices of material and labor rose tre-

Clinton Square, Syracuse, and the Erie Canal in 1878

The New York Branch Canals

mendously after the Civil War and made the cost of the work far greater than expected. The job dragged on until 1871, when it was halted and the project abandoned. This crowning folly had cost $1,600,889, and not a mile of it was ever used. A record-breaking flood in 1865 inflicted great damage on the original Chenango Canal. Others in 1868 and 1869 added to its dilapidation. The replacing of wooden locks with stone was continued until 1871, but railroads had by that time practically killed its business. It was abandoned in 1876–77.

One of the earliest of the New York canal projects was that of uniting the Ontario and Susquehanna river systems by a canal from the head of Seneca Lake to the Chemung River. General Sullivan conceived this idea during his expedition against the Iroquois in 1779, and wrote to Washington on the subject. Geddes surveyed the route in 1812. The scheme was constantly before the Legislature, and in 1829 the job was authorized, provided it could be done for $300,000. To achieve this the work had to be done cheaply, and the locks were built of wood. Some of them began to bulge and warp when they were first used. The canal was completed in May, 1833. The main line was 23 miles long, with 49 locks, and there was a feeder 16 miles in length.

In 1839 Pennsylvania informed New York that she was about to complete the North Branch Canal to the State line, and suggested that if New York would build a connection to it from the Chenango or the Chemung Canal or both, there might be much commerce thereon between the two States. From Elmira, the southern terminus of the Chemung, a canal of no more than 12 or 18 miles in length would touch the State line on the Susquehanna. But finances were so disturbed at that time that New York for once had the caution to refrain from another costly speculation.

When the stop law of 1842 halted all canal work, the citizens of Elmira grew impatient, and in 1846 organized the Junction Canal Company to build the connection, but

Old Towpaths

found the usual difficulty in raising money and did not begin work until 1853. The canal was put in service in 1858, and was in operation for just thirteen years. During a considerable part of that time it paid good dividends. But the competition of railroads began to tell on it, and in 1865 it suffered a heavy blow in the destruction of the North Branch Canal, its principal connection, by a flood. The North Branch was never rebuilt, and in 1871 the Junction Canal was abandoned.

The Chemung had a very gratifying increase of business in the '60's, but the loss of the North Branch connection and railway competition wore it down rapidly, and it was abandoned in 1877.

The wildest project of all New York's list of canal schemes was that of the Genesee Valley. With every section of the State demanding canals, the claims of this populous and fertile valley would seem to have been as good as any. There was the usual special argument that by way of this valley a connection could be made with the Allegheny River and thereby with the Pennsylvania canals, thus opening a new route to the west and southwest.

The proposed canal made some costly engineering inevitable, for the Genesee had a rapid fall and its upper gorge was precipitous. But western New York was determined to have action, and for several years the Legislature was pestered with petitions. The canal was authorized in 1836 and construction was begun the following year—ominously enough, the year of the panic. In September, 1840, the first packet boat passed up from Rochester to Mount Morris. By 1842 more than 50 miles of channel was in operation.

But that year the stop law was passed, and work on the canal ceased for more than four years. It should have been evident by that time that the project ought to be dropped incontinently. The Erie Railroad was building into western New York, and it needed no prophet to see that further work in the Genesee valley was the height of folly. But when

The New York Branch Canals

money was once more available in 1847, the work went on again. In 1851 the canal reached Oramel, in 1856 Olean and in 1862 it connected directly with the Allegheny River. The Erie Railroad was completed and in operation when the canal reached Olean. The cost (at first estimated at $2,000,000) had been $5,663,183; and all the tolls it ever paid amounted to $852,164. It was always difficult to keep in operation because of scanty water supply and freshets. In the '70's its traffic rapidly declined, and it was closed in 1878. A short section of it was retained as a feeder for the Erie.

Work on the enlargement of the Erie was resumed, along with the branch canals, in 1847. Even with the work at a standstill, traffic had increased amazingly, and when the enlargement began again, there was a great spurt in boat-building. There had been 2,126 boats on the canal in 1843-44. In 1847-48 there were 4,191. Of these 62 were packets, 621 line boats carrying both freight and passengers, and 3,508 were classed variously as lake boats, bullhead boats and scows. Their total value was about a million dollars. At that time the working population of the canal is said to have been 25,000 men, women and boys; and the Black River and Genesee Valley Canals were as yet uncompleted.

In 1846 the tolls on all the canals were $2,756,120. In 1847 they jumped to $3,635,380. For four years thereafter they remained above $3,000,000, though declining slightly each year; then they dropped below $3,000,000. Tonnage was steadily increasing, but the toll rates were being reduced to meet railroad competition.

The railroads chartered in New York in early days, most of which paralleled the Hudson River and Erie Canal, were permitted to carry freight only in winter, when the canals could not operate, and then only upon the payment of canal tolls to the State. These provisions were gradually relaxed. In 1851 the Legislature, while passing appropriation bills to improve the canals so that they might compete with the

Old Towpaths

railroads, at the same time dealt the New York canals the heaviest blow in their history by releasing the railways from the payment of any tolls thereafter. It was declared by the canal commissioners in after years that the two acts constituted a bargain—a very significant hint of the growing power of railroad influence in State affairs.

This act was one of the most potent in the destruction of the branch canals. Within a few years the railroads, waxing fat, improving their freight service to the point where they could haul any article that a canal boat could haul, and bulk material in greater quantity and at greater speed, also began cutting rates in summer and raising them in winter. "Trunk line pools," "differentials" and other ingenious devices were invented, and boatmen were gradually driven off the less profitable routes. The passenger competition of the railroads had driven all the packets off the Erie before 1850, and they disappeared from the branch canals soon after that.

In 1859 the State was in a serious condition financially. The funded debt at the close of the fiscal year 1858 was $24,000,000; the new canal debt was $16,000,000. Three million dollars more was needed to complete the canals, and the treasury was empty. The enlargement scheme was limping along slowly, hampered at every step by lack of funds, while shippers and boat owners crowded each mile of enlargement to its fullest capacity and clamored for more room. Boats were built to the largest size that could possibly be squeezed through the locks.

Canal revenues were decreasing. Many persons, discouraged by canal failures in other States, were in favor of selling the canals. The railroads stood ready to take them over or eliminate them in any way possible. The people at large became alarmed at the seeming menace to the waterways. Many vitriolic editorials and pamphlets were written in protest against the railroad "conspiracy." A great meeting was called in New York "to rescue the canals from the ruin with which they are threatened, by exposing and resist-

The New York Branch Canals

ing the railroad conspiracy for discrediting the canals and diminishing their revenues with a view to bringing them under the hammer." Newspaper editors declared that if the canals were sold, "they would be used as a mighty instrument for the political and pecuniary oppression of the people."

The railroads, somewhat disconcerted by the agitation, became slightly less arrogant. The State borrowed money and assessed taxes to carry on the improvements. Tolls were also raised for 1860 to the rates in force several years before. John Brown's raid on Harpers Ferry in October, 1859, directed public attention to national affairs, and the railroad menace passed into the background.

In 1862 the enlargement of the Erie, which had dragged its slow progress through twenty-five years, was officially declared completed. In making the enlargement, the length of the canal had been reduced from 364 miles to 350½ miles. It had originally had 83 locks, with a total lockage of 675 feet. The locks were now reduced to 72 in number, with a lockage of 655 feet. Boats of 150 tons and more had been using the greater part of the canal for several years, and could now pass through its entire length. As years went by, their size was increased until in the '80's and '90's boats able to carry 250 tons were not uncommon.

The increase in toll rates in 1860 failed to cause a falling off in tonnage as was predicted. Instead, the business was heavier than ever, and the total revenues leaped from $1,723,944 in 1859 to more than $3,000,000 in 1860. The closing of the lower Mississippi River in the early days of the Civil War brought a great increase of business to the Erie and the eastern railroads. Most of the New York canals touched their zenith in earnings in 1862 when the total revenue reached $5,188,943. Of this the Erie contributed nearly fourteen-fifteenths. There were 5,168 boats in service that year. Until and including 1870 the revenue of the canals averaged more than $4,000,000

Old Towpaths

yearly. Then toll-rate reduction and the falling away of the branch canals brought them rapidly down again.

In 1869 there were 6,870 boats on the canals—so many that they were actually crowding each other off the water, and all could not be used. The Erie was still too small! During all this period and even into the '80's, it is said that one standing on a bridge across it might look in either direction and see two continuous lines of boats plodding along, one eastward, one westward, as far as the eye could reach; while at night their headlights gave the appearance of an endless torchlight procession. Other canals were passing out of existence all over the country, but still the Erie went on, and its tonnage actually increased. This reached its greatest figure in 1880—4,608,651 tons. The Champlain Canal's greatest year was 1890, when it carried 1,520,757 tons; while the greatest year for the combined New York system was 1872, when 6,673,370 tons were carried.

During all those stirring days, not only was the Erie Canal jammed, but the Hudson River was perhaps the busiest stream in America. With the Erie and Champlain Canals pouring traffic into it at Albany and the Delaware and Hudson Canal at Rondout, its lower reaches in particular, vast though they were, became almost crowded. Thousands of boats went from the St. Lawrence River, from Buffalo and other lake ports through to New York City. The business of towing fleets of canal boats up and down the river grew to such volume that many former proud passenger liners were pressed into that service. The competition at one time became so keen that a boatman could get a tow all the way from Albany to New York for five dollars. Fleets of 60 to eighty boats towed by one steamer were often seen. Buckman, author of *Old Steamboat Days on the Hudson*, says that the greatest tow ever carried was that of the steamer *Connecticut*, Captain Harvey Temple, which went up the river one day proudly bearing a broom on her jackstaff and towing 108 canal boats. Flotillas are still seen in the river

The New York Branch Canals

to-day, but never as large as in the roaring '70's, '80's and '90's.

Many curious methods of propulsion were given a trial on the Erie. Some of them will be discussed later. Among others the electric mule was tried again and again, but always rejected. Steam-propelled boats became more and more numerous in the canal's latter days, but horses and mules continued to pull hundreds of boats until the very end, when the old waterway was replaced by the new Barge Canal without a towpath. Even in 1900 there were still 2,000 boats on the canal—some of them veterans whose history went back to Civil War days.

By 1882 the toll rates had been so greatly reduced that the year's collections on the four canals still in operation were only a little over $600,000; and that year the Legislature abolished the tolls altogether. The Erie had been more profitable than all the rest of the canals in the country combined. Many a prosperous railroad might have envied it its balance sheet. In its little more than sixty years of toll-gathering, its net profits over all the cost of construction, improvement, superintendence and repairs was $42,599,717. The net loss on all the other New York canals was $34,266,260. Thus the Erie could carry them all and still show more than an eight-million dollar profit. It was not only one of the greatest factors in the building of America, but it made New York the Empire State of the Union and it was the most remarkable success in all the history of American internal improvements.

The canal was deepened in the '90's, but before the work was completed, plans were well under way for its enlargement to accommodate boats of 1,000 tons—the present Barge Canal size. The record of the building of that mighty waterway at a cost of $155,000,000, and the elimination thereby of the old Erie (even to changing the route in many places) is not logically a part of this history.

CHAPTER XVI

THE RISE AND FALL OF THE NEW ENGLAND CANALS

THE Erie Canal was a stimulant and an irritant to all the rest of the country. As section after section of it was completed and began to pile up profits and as its adjacent territory leaped into activity and progress, citizens of other parts began to ask themselves and each other, "Why doesn't somebody around here do something?" Many did proceed to, and not always with happy results.

Some restless souls in New England were thoroughly disgusted because the oldest part of the Union sat passive and let young upstart commonwealths like New York and Pennsylvania and Ohio plan to seize all the commerce of the hemisphere. A picturesque grumbler signing himself "Shadrack" wrote a letter to the *Universal Traveller* in 1825, in which he berated Massachusetts for her inertia, and incidentally flung a sneer at the Middlesex Canal, of which the State had once been so proud:

"Is old Massachusetts in her palsied dotage? Is her sun of prosperity . . . setting to rise no more? This sun with increasing splendor is irradiating the hills of Hudson and fertile vales of New-York. Where are the thousand ships of the Bay State, her accumulated wealth of two centuries? Has the building of a few roads and the cutting of *one* canal or rather *ditch* of inconsiderable distance satisfied her ambition and put her 'at ease in her possessions?'"

The efforts to please Shadrack and his clan by scheming a practicable canal from Boston to the Hudson have already been described. Meanwhile, certain portions of New Eng-

The New England Canals

land had not been inert. Several canals had been planned and some of them built; but all with intent to benefit certain cities only, and not with any broad idea of general improvement. For this reason, these projects were nearly all short-lived, being unable to endure when a railroad was built to compete with them.

One of the earliest of these projects was that of giving Sebago Pond in Maine a navigable outlet to Portland and the sea. It was first proposed in 1791, and two companies were chartered in 1795 to build canals by different routes, but they could not obtain funds, and their projects lapsed. In 1820 a new organization was perfected under the name of the Cumberland and Oxford Canal Company. A lottery privilege to raise $50,000 was granted the promoters, and as a further aid to the plan, the Canal Bank was organized with a capital of $300,000, one-fourth of which capital, according to its charter, was to be invested in stock of the Canal Company.

Excavation was begun in 1828 and the work finished to Portland in 1830. The whole system consisted of a canal 20½ miles long from tidewater near Portland to Sebago Pond. Boats then passed through that lake, and by a single lock in Songo River the navigation was prolonged to Brandy and Long Ponds, an additional 30 miles. Large quantities of timber and agricultural products came down through the canal from the upper lakes. When the Portland and Ogdensburg Railroad was opened in 1870, the canal closed its existence.

Another very early New England project was that of opening navigation between Narragansett Bay and the interior of Massachusetts via the Blackstone River. This idea was first publicly agitated in 1796, Worcester being named as the northern terminus. A corporation charter was obtained from the Rhode Island Legislature, and a petition was also presented in Massachusetts; but opponents promptly brought forward a counter proposition for a canal from

Old Towpaths

Boston to the Connecticut River, which was represented as being of vastly greater importance; and this propaganda had the effect of killing the Blackstone project.

In 1822 the idea was revived, and this time charters were obtained with little difficulty from both States. When subscription books for the Rhode Island corporation were opened in Providence, the total stock issue of $400,000 was subscribed three times over and the shares were soon selling at a premium. The two companies were later merged into one. Ground was broken in Rhode Island in 1824, but work did not begin in Massachusetts until 1826. The first boat passed through the completed canal in the fall of 1828. The total length from Providence to Worcester was 45 miles. There were forty-eight locks of cut granite. The whole cost of the work was $750,000.

The canal did a lively business for a while and conferred great benefit upon its territory. Tolls reached their maximum at $18,907 in 1832; but the building of railroads began to jeopardize it very early in its career. There were other serious hindrances to its prosperity also. New England winters meant that it was always closed four months and sometimes five out of the year. A part of the route consisted of slack-water navigation in the Blackstone River, and here boats were not infrequently delayed by high water, to say nothing of occasional low water. The canal's water supply was shared by several manufacturing plants along the river, and sometimes there was not enough water for both mill and canal. As a result, there was much bad blood between mill owners and boatmen—especially after the mills had begun to be served by railroads. On several occasions the mill men and owners of the water power caused loads of stone to be dumped into the locks at night, which almost precipitated civil war. Threats were made by boatmen to burn the mills, and armed guards were maintained by the manufacturers for long periods.

But after all, the railroads were the chief cause of the

The New England Canals

Blackstone's downfall. Its business steadily declined, and in the early '40's it was operating at a deficit. The building of the Providence and Worcester Railroad was the death-blow. In April, 1846, the company sold all that portion of the canal lying in Massachusetts to the competing railroad. The last toll was collected on November 9, 1848. The life of the canal had been just twenty years.

From Old Residents' Historical Association Publications, Lowell, Massachusetts
THE AMOSKEAG CANAL AND BLODGETT MANSION, ALLEGED TO HAVE BEEN BUILT WITH EMBEZZLED CANAL LOTTERY MONEY

In 1822, the same year that the two Blackstone companies were incorporated, the Farmington Canal Company was granted a charter in Connecticut. This canal was planned as part of a waterway to extend from New Haven to Northampton in Massachusetts. It was strictly a New Haven scheme. That city, jealous of the growing importance of Hartford, plotted to steal all the business coming down the Connecticut River by diverting it in Massachusetts to a canal which should artfully pass several miles to westward of Hartford and terminate at New Haven.

In February, 1823, the project was incorporated in Massachusetts under the name of the Hampshire and

Old Towpaths

Hampden Canal Company. The capital for the whole work, however, was furnished chiefly by Connecticut. The better part of $2,000,000 was spent on the job, of which only about $500,000 came from Massachusetts. The power of the canal party in New Haven is shown by the fact that in 1824 a charter for the Mechanics' Bank in that city was obtained only on condition that it subscribe for $200,000 worth of canal stock. Later another bank and the city of New Haven subscribed for $200,000 more. All these subscriptions made while the work was under way hinted that the canal was (as usual) costing more than had been expected.

The excavation began with much enthusiasm at the State line at Suffield on July 4, 1825, Governor Wolcott of Connecticut turning the first spadeful of earth. The canal route passed through Easthampton, Southampton, Westfield, Southwick, Granbury, Simsbury, Southington and Farmington. In 1828 the channel was open as far as Farmington; in 1829 it reached Westfield, but not until August, 1835, was it completed to the Connecticut River at Northampton so that boats could operate on it.

The passage of the first boat was made the occasion of rapturous demonstration. The boat was drawn by four horses and carried some two hundred men and women, including the Governors of the two commonwealths and "some of the most respectable citizens of both States." At every town it was greeted by cannon fire, cheers, laudatory speeches and other attentions. "It was expected," said the *Democratic Herald* of Westfield, "that the boat would reach Northampton at 10 o'clock A.M., but on arriving at Southampton, it was found that some mean, low-spirited puppy, having nothing of manhood about him except intelligence enough to guide his malice, had let off the water from a half-mile level. This obstacle being overcome by awaiting the arrival of the waters, the boat, passing through Easthampton, was met by a boat at the South Basin in Northampton, where the following address was made by Mr. Bancroft. . . ."

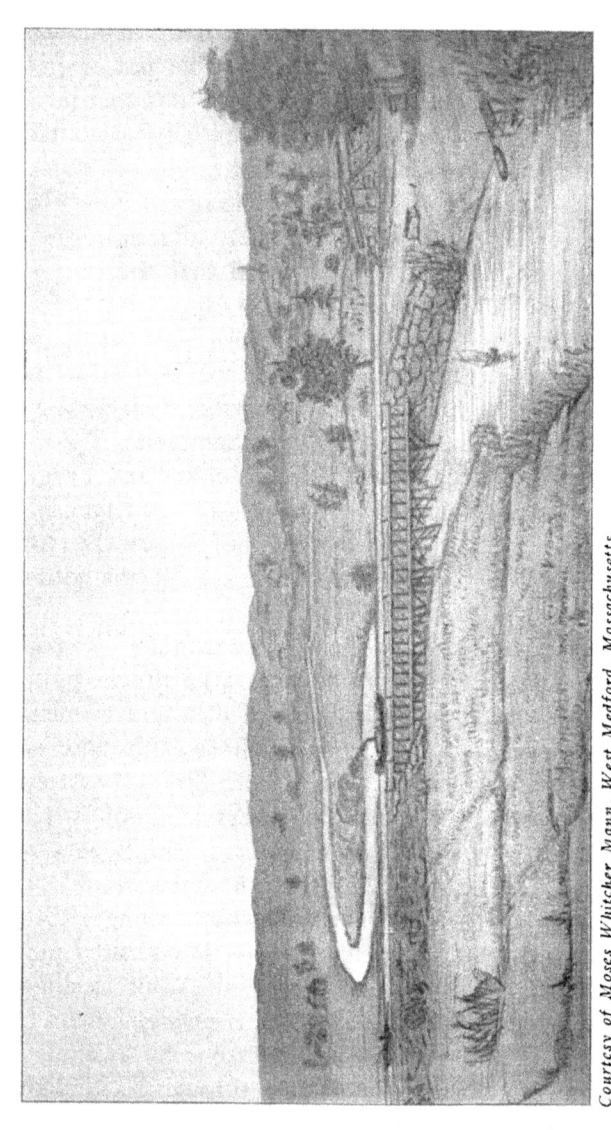

Courtesy of Moses Whitcher Mann, West Medford, Massachusetts.

THE ONLY STEAMBOAT EVER TRIED ON THE MIDDLESEX CANAL

The New England Canals

"Mr. Bancroft" was George Bancroft, the historian, then thirty-five years old. The first volume of his *History of the United States* had appeared during the previous year.

After a great celebration at Northampton, the boat on Thursday morning was locked into the Connecticut River. All this jubilation appears a bit pathetic when one remembers that the canal was already in serious financial difficulties. From the very start it seemed to be under the displeasure of an evil genius. A large stone arch at Granby was washed away twice before the canal was opened. Its boats were small, carrying only twenty to twenty-five tons. Its cost far exceeded the estimates, and for various reasons, its operating expenses and repair bills were exceptionally heavy.

So notwithstanding the fact that it had been doing a considerable business between 1830 and 1836, a flood which assailed it only a few months after its full opening precipitated a crisis; a serious one, as is proven by the fact that a new corporation called the New Haven and Northampton Canal Company was organized to take over the property, agreeing to pay nothing for the capital stock of the old company—only to pay its debts. The stockholders thereby lost $806,195, the total amount of the stock issue.

For five years the new company struggled against increasing railroad competition and all sorts of bad fortune. Freshets frequently inflicted great damage. There were numerous breaks in the banks and towpath, and often heavy damages to pay to farmers whose lands were thereby flooded. Persons with grievances against the canal cut the banks more than once. Another group of men came to the rescue in 1841 and put up more money in an effort to retrieve a losing cause; but their efforts were vain.

Finally the company attempted to compromise with Fate by building a railroad along the lower portion of the canal right of way, but even that could not save the upper portion, which was entirely abandoned in 1847. This canal had one of the shortest and most peculiarly unfortunate careers of

Old Towpaths

any in the country. It is said that the only dividend it ever paid was declared one summer when the grass on its banks was cut and sold and the proceeds distributed among the stockholders. Like many another of the old waterways, it had been a blessing to the territory it served, but a curse to its owners.

The path of the South Hadley Canal, the oldest in New England, was beset with thorns from beginning to end. It was scarcely completed before fishermen on the Connecticut began to complain that its dam prevented shad and salmon from ascending the river. Protests were heard from towns up the river because, as it was claimed, the flooding of the lowlands by the dam caused malaria. Northampton petitioned the Legislature in 1800 for the removal of the canal as a nuisance. But the proprietors made a counter-appeal, setting forth the usefulness of the waterway and asking for a lottery privilege in order that they might improve it. They were given the right to raise $20,000 by a lottery, and with this money they deepened the channel and lowered the dam by several feet, also removing the famous incline and substituting locks therefor.

In a few years another dam became necessary and work on it was begun in 1814. It was only partially completed when a flood swept it away. Another was erected, and nine years later it, too, was destroyed. During these years the toll receipts had been good for so short a canal, but the net profit was small. Then came the railroads and killed the boating business on the Connecticut. In 1848 the property and franchises were sold and the canal became a mere water-power channel.

Finally there remains the Middlesex Canal, whose building was described in a former chapter. Although it was not a financial success, yet the Middlesex paid more dividends than other canals of New England, principally because it began early, years before railroads came into the field. Nevertheless, the stockholders had paid no less than one

The New England Canals

hundred assessments before the company declared its first dividend in 1819.

There were various reasons for this. In the first place, the aqueducts and locks were at first built of wood, and a large sum was required annually for repairs. The replacing of them with stone also cost a pretty penny in later years. Furthermore, the Middlesex, in order to increase its business from the Merrimac River, its chief dependence, subscribed considerable sums towards the building of short canals and locks around the Merrimac's various falls and rapids. The corporation contributed towards the building of the Wicasee Canal, the Union Canal, the little canals at Hookset and Bow Falls a total of $82,797 out of its profits. The stockholders were also interested in the Amoskeag Canal on the same river.

In 1816 the Legislature of Massachusetts granted to the struggling corporation two townships of land in Maine, near Moosehead Lake. The grant was of no immediate value, for the land was in a remote and unknown wilderness, and no purchasers could be found. Lottery schemes and assessments on the stockholders enabled the company to worry along until receipts from tolls, rents and so on increased. The income, which was only $12,600 in 1812, rose to $32,600 in 1816, but never went much higher. By 1819 the directors ventured to appease the stockholders somewhat by the payment of a dividend of $15 a share.

From that date to 1836 were the canal's best years, and dividends were paid continuously. It is surprising to find that sixteen lock-tenders and repair men, three clerks and an "agent" or manager ran the whole canal in the early '30's, at a yearly expense to the company of only $8,000. But the boats were too small and the territory not sufficiently extensive to permit the waterway ever to become greatly profitable. Boats in 1830 were 40 to 75 feet in length and not over 9½ feet wide. Many of them were merely arks or flatboats which floated down the Merrimac, assisted by

Old Towpaths

sails, sculls and poles, and were then towed by horses through the canal to Boston or way stations.

The Boston and Lowell boats could carry twenty tons of coal, but fifteen made a sufficient load for those going up to Concord. When the Merrimac was low, not more than six or seven tons could be hauled. A trip from Concord to Boston and return consumed from seven to ten days.

In 1805 a company was chartered to build a branch from the canal to Medford, which had been left a little off the line. Medford had developed a shipbuilding industry, and needed the canal to bring ship timber down from New Hampshire. The rafts were sometimes drawn through the canal by oxen.

In 1829 a petition was presented to the Legislature, asking for authority to survey a railroad from Boston to Lowell, with a hint that it might be extended even farther. The proprietors of the Middlesex promptly sent in a remonstrance. They set forth the indisputable fact that "no safer or cheaper mode of conveyance can ever be established, nor any so well adapted for carrying bulky or heavy articles." This means of transportation was available "for all but the winter months" (alas, there was the rub!) "as effectually as any that can be provided."

"There is a supposed source of revenue," the remonstrants went on, with a fine touch of sarcasm, "to a railroad *from carrying passengers.* As to this the remonstrants venture no opinion except to say that passengers are now carried at all hours, as rapidly and safely as they are anywhere else in the world. . . ." The petition expressed doubt whether a railroad, as a passenger-carrying agency, would ever gain public confidence and approbation.

"The Remonstrants would add that so far as they know and believe, *there can never be a sufficient inducement to extend a railroad from Lowell westwardly and northwestwardly to the Connecticut, so as to make it the great avenue to and from the interior, but that its termination must be at Lowell . . . and cannot deserve patronage from the sup-*

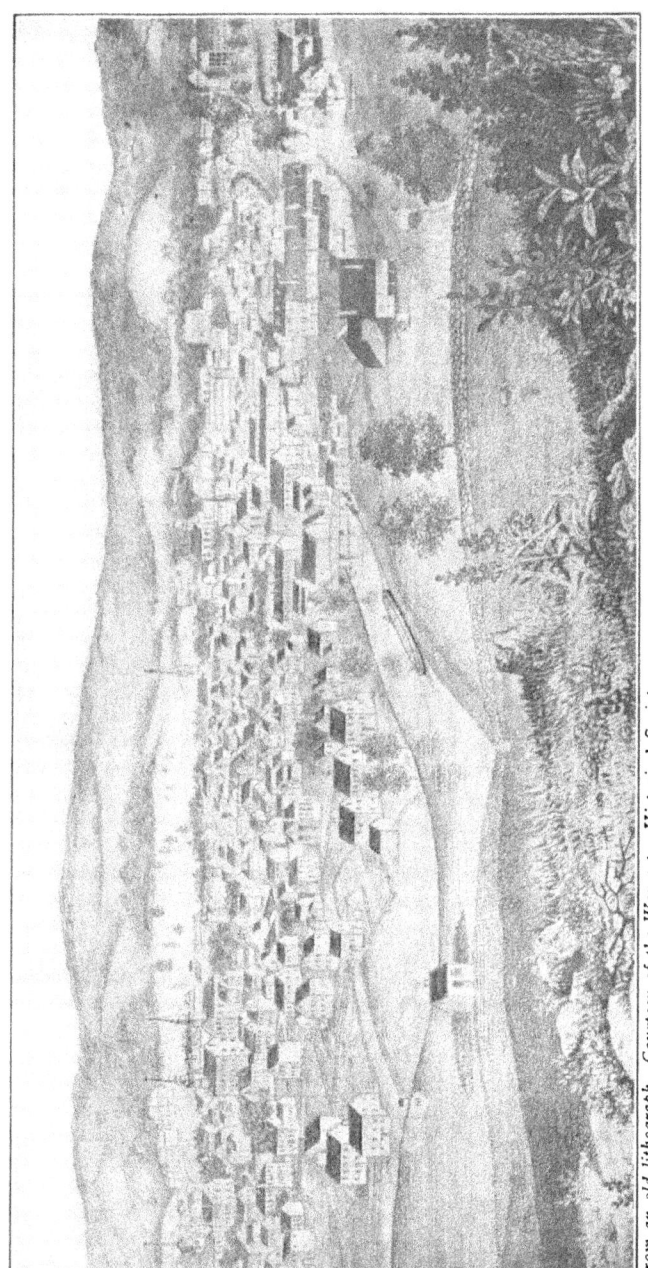

From an old lithograph. Courtesy of the Worcester Historical Society

WORCESTER AND THE BLACKSTONE CANAL IN 1828

The New England Canals

position that it is to be more extensively useful." Therefore, the document urged, a railroad between Boston and Lowell was unnecessary, and should not be authorized; but if it were, the remonstrants felt that they should be indemnified for losses which would thereby be occasioned them.

Not a few editors and legislators agreed with them, but the majority were against them, and after a time the railroad charter was granted. But even while the line was building, the canal directors did not appear to realize the menace in the situation, but continued to pay dividends and to replace wooden work with stone. In 1832 a dividend of $22 a share was paid, and from 1834 to 1837 inclusive, it was $30 a share. The dividends were kept up to this high mark not so much by tolls as by the sale of lands owned by the company in Maine, New Hampshire and Massachusetts.

But meanwhile the railroad was making itself felt. In 1835 the goods carried by the canal from Boston to Lowell paid $11,975 in tolls; in the following year the amount fell to $6,195. The directors vainly strove to outdo the railroad, reducing toll rates on all freight and almost abolishing them on some articles; but all expedients availed naught. The extension of the railroad to Nashua in 1838 killed the Merrimac River business up that far, and reduced the canal's revenues by another third. When the railroad reached Concord in 1842, the river commerce was practically destroyed.

For fifteen years more the dying canal clung to life. "The future has but a gloomy prospect," wrote Caleb Eddy, the manager, in 1843. "What is to be done? Improvements in mechanics and the arts will go on while man has mind; and if the canal cannot put out the fire of the locomotive, it may be made to stop the ravages of that element in the city of Boston, should the proprietors, after mature consideration, deem it to their interest so to devote it."

Eddy was here referring to a proposition which he had made to the city of Boston to sell the canal to it for a water supply. Boston, which had contained only 20,000 inhabitants

Old Towpaths

when the canal was completed in 1803, now boasted 100,000, and still had no public water supply, the inhabitants drinking from cisterns and wells. Eddy proposed to make the canal an aqueduct supplying Boston with wholesome water from the Concord River, whose high quality was vouched for by four able chemists. He found it necessary to combat "an idle story circulated to the effect that the water of Concord River contains some deleterious substance which would cause a wound by contact with it to fester." But all of Eddy's logic did not persuade Boston to utilize the canal, and its stock now fell below par. In 1846 operations on it practically ceased. Even as late as 1852–53 the directors clung to their franchise and went through the formality of electing an agent and collector. On April 14, 1852, the last boat passed through the old waterway. The Medford Branch Canal ceased operations that year; and shortly afterwards the Middlesex directors sold the canal for $130,000 and divided the money among the stockholders. Even after this final dividend, little more than the original assessments had been returned to the shareholders. For many years thereafter, portions of the channel served to convey waterpower to mills along its route, and even to-day bits of the old masonry may be seen by those who know where to look for them.

CHAPTER XVII

THE SUSQUEHANNA AND TIDEWATER AND ITS EFFECT ON THE UNION CANAL

WHEN the Erie Canal was under construction and its already increasing business was beginning to attract attention, Baltimore began to look about for means of extending her commerce, and especially of catching some of the trade of the interior. The little Port Deposit Canal paralleling the Susquehanna for eight miles near its mouth and supposed to open up that river, had proved a disappointment. Conewago Falls, farther up, had also been canalized, but still the river was not a good highway. Only arks or flatboats could come down, and it was difficult for them to get back.

Now that the Union project was being revived for the express purpose of diverting Susquehanna River traffic to Philadelphia, Baltimore again became uneasy. In 1822 a party of Baltimore merchants visited the Erie Canal and consulted and received advice and encouragement from Clinton himself. To study the possibilities of traffic between central New York, Pennsylvania and Baltimore, they returned via Cayuga Lake, portaging from Ithaca to Owego on the North Branch of the Susquehanna, whence they rode on a flatboat down the river to Harrisburg.

Baltimore was in serious need of a better navigation down the Susquehanna, not only as a means of procuring trade, but also to get cheaper transportation from the various Pennsylvania coal fields; for it was actually costing more to bring a ton of coal to Baltimore than to ship it to Europe.

Old Towpaths

The great difficulty was that of inducing Pennsylvania to grant a charter for a canal which would adequately open up the lower Susquehanna. Several years were spent in fencing and negotiating; and had it not been for the help of some of the southern and western counties of Pennsylvania, which were chafing a bit under Philadelphia's dictation of the State's policy, had it not been that the Chesapeake and Delaware Canal project had been revived, the desired charter could not have been obtained. Philadelphia felt certain that with the Chesapeake and Delaware in operation, a goodly portion of the traffic passing down the Susquehanna to its mouth would not go to Baltimore, after all, but would come through the new channel to the Delaware River and so up to Philadelphia—a not unreasonable assumption.

Pennsylvania granted a charter in 1835 to the Susquehanna Canal Company, which was to build along the river from Columbia down to the State line. Maryland had already chartered the Tidewater Canal Company to build that part lying within her own borders. The two companies were united in later years under the name of the Susquehanna and Tidewater Canal Company.

The signing of the charter was a serious blow to the Union Canal. The Susquehanna and Tidewater of course had a copious water supply, and planned to build a large channel and locks, so as to accommodate any possible volume of business. It seemed inevitable that much of the Susquehanna River traffic for Philadelphia, instead of squeezing itself through the narrow Union Canal, would follow the easier route down the river and through the big Chesapeake and Delaware Canal.

Excavation was begun in 1836. Under the new plan the river was dammed at Columbia, and the boats crossed through the pool to Wrightsville, on the west bank, where the canal began and continued down to Havre de Grace, a distance of 45 miles. From Havre de Grace steam towboats took the canal boats to Baltimore or to the entrance of the

From "*Leslie's Weekly*"

Burning by Confederate Troops on June 28, 1863, of the Combination Railroad Bridge by Which the Canal Towpath Crossed the Susquehanna from the Main Line at Columbia to the Susquehanna and Tidewater Canal at Wrightsville

The Susquehanna and Tidewater

Chesapeake and Delaware Canal. The surface width of the S. and T. was 50 feet and the depth of 5 to 6 feet. The locks were 170 feet long and 17 feet wide, permitting in later years some boats of as high as 150 tons capacity to use the canal.

The work was carried forward so rapidly that water was turned into the channel in the fall of 1839. An elaborate celebration of the opening was arranged, and Nicholas Biddle, the great banker of Philadelphia, delivered a memorable address on "Internal Improvements." But alas! scarcely had the guests reached their several homes after the festivity when the rains descended and the floods came and the canal bank suffered a number of serious breaks in places where it had been poorly made. Even a part of a costly aqueduct was destroyed.

After heavy expenditures for repairs the canal was declared open in 1840, but little business was done until the following year. The cost of the work had been more than $3,500,000, or about $80,000 per mile, which places this canal as third among the ante-bellum waterways in point of costliness. High wages during the boom period of the '30's was assigned as one of the principal reasons for the enormous expense.

The business which quickly developed, however, gave promise of future dividends. Four years after the opening, the managers declared that nearly "half of the Western produce shipped from Pittsburgh seeks Baltimore for a market . . . and about a third of the merchandise shipped through the Pennsylvania Canal for the West is also forwarded by this city." A large portion of the other half of the Pennsylvania Canal trade from Pittsburgh and way points went to Philadelphia via the S. and T. and the Chesapeake and Delaware Canal. For fully twenty years, from 1840 to 1860, the trade passing through the C. and D. furnished the Susquehanna and Tidewater more than one-fourth of its business. This trade had formerly been divided

Old Towpaths

between the Union Canal and the Columbia and Philadelphia Railroad. The Union Canal being too small to admit the boats of the Pennsylvania Main Line, could not now compete for this business, because all freight would have to be transshipped at Middletown. The same objection applied also to the railroad, which also was incapable of handling the full volume of the traffic and was compelled to charge higher rates than the canals. It therefore seemed that the Susquehanna and Tidewater (as had been feared by many Keystone legislators) was about to rob Pennsylvania of the fruits of her great effort to build a transportation system between Philadelphia and the West. The State tried to block the private competition by giving a rebate on freight from the West, provided it was shipped from Pittsburgh to Philadelphia entirely over the State's transportation lines. But this law was too unfair to last long, and quickly disappeared from the statute books.

Some of the craft on the canal at this period voyaged to far distant ports. On several occasions boats carried freight from the Susquehanna Valley down through the canal, across the bay, through the Chesapeake and Delaware Canal, and then via Delaware River, Delaware and Raritan Canal, New York Harbor, Hudson River and Champlain Canal, even to Lake Champlain and Montreal. Returning, they frequently brought loads of iron ore to Pennsylvania furnaces.

Meanwhile the Union Canal, which was most seriously affected by the new waterway, had never had a prosperous career. In 1828 it had been compelled to borrow $300,000 to assist in completing the Swatara dam and feeder. The Pennsylvania State canals were now coming into operation, but most of their boats were too large to pass through the Union locks, and so little through traffic was possible. In their report of 1830 the directors confessed that the Pennsylvania canals had not given them much business, but asserted that "they were gratified by the arrival at the city wharves

The Susquehanna and Tidewater

on the Schuylkill of boats from Lewistown and Mifflin on the Juniata, from Berwick and Danville on the East Branch and from Milton on the West Branch of the Susquehanna . . . all having passed through the Union Canal, which now forms a complete line of communication between the waters of the Delaware and Susquehanna." They tried to convince the stockholders and themselves that their narrow boats were preferable, and cited as proof the fact that in 1829 over fifty boats of this size and type had been built on the Juniata and Susquehanna. But other facts were against them.

The Philadelphia and Columbia Railroad, opened in 1835, was the first dangerous competitor for the Union Canal, as it offered a quicker and shorter route between the Delaware and Susquehanna for the lighter kinds of freight; and it at once began taking some of the business. In 1837 the managers of the Union gave in and publicly admitted that their trade was hampered because the Schuylkill and Pennsylvania Canals accommodated boats carrying from fifty to seventy-five tons burden, while the Union locks would admit only boats of twenty-five or at most twenty-eight tons. They had been reluctant to come to this acknowledgment because they knew that enlarging the canal meant enormous expense. They petitioned the Legislature for assistance, but received none. A public convention instigated by them and held at Harrisburg in 1839 unanimously endorsed the company's plea, and a clinching argument in favor of it was presented in 1841, when the Susquehanna and Tidewater Canal was opened. The managers' report of that year says, "The navigation was opened on the 29th of March, but it was soon perceived that without the most vigorous measures the trade would be drawn away by the Tidewater Canal."

Not until 1841 did the Legislature authorize the enlargement of the Union Canal and not until 1851 was this begun. To achieve it, heroic measures had to be taken to insure a water supply. There were now three large dams across

Old Towpaths

Swatara Creek and another a mile long and 40 feet high across Cattail Creek. Three pumping stations and a 4-mile aqueduct were necessary to lift and convey water to the summit level. One of these stations had two big water wheels, 40 feet in diameter, and four pumping engines aggregating 480 horse-power. The leakage from the channel through fissures in the limestone bed on the eastern section made it necessary to keep the canal lined for several miles with timber, at heavy expense for upkeep. The total cost of construction had now reached a point very close to $6,000,000.

Although the enlargement—which permitted boats of 75 to 80 tons to pass through—doubled the volume of traffic, it was, paradoxically enough, the canal's death blow. The company never recovered from the shock of the enormous expense incurred. In 1856 the traffic reached its peak at 267,307 tons, but owing to reductions in rates, the total revenue was only $107,844. During this period, it is an interesting fact that many rafts of huge logs were brought from Clearfield County by way of the West Branch and Susquehanna Canals down to Middletown, thence via the Union to a sawmill near Lebanon, which could cut larger logs than any other nearer the place where the timber grew.

The opening of the Lebanon Valley Railroad from Reading to Harrisburg in 1857 was destined to be another serious blow to the Union. Thereafter revenues declined steadily, and it was plain that the canal was doomed. After 1858 it was operated by trustees for the bondholders. In 1862 a flood almost destroyed the Pine Grove branch, and navigation on it was abandoned. By 1880 a boat was seen only occasionally on the leaky old waterway. In 1884 the traffic totaled just 16,165 tons. In 1885 the directors reported that property and franchise had been sold by the sheriff of Philadelphia. Thus passed out of existence one of the oldest navigation projects on the continent.

But the canal which had done most to destroy the Union

Courtesy of Boyd P. Rothrock, Curator Pennsylvania State Museum
RUINS OF TUNNEL ON THE UNION CANAL—THE SECOND TUNNEL BUILT IN THE UNITED STATES

From "The Canals of Pennsylvania," by Theodore B. Klein. By permission of the State Department of Internal Affairs
RUINS OF ENTRANCE LOCK OF SUSQUEHANNA AND TIDEWATER CANAL AT WRIGHTSVILLE, PENNSYLVANIA, 1900

The Susquehanna and Tidewater

could no more stand up against railroad competition than could the Union. Even before the railroads injured its business, its enormous capitalization and bonded debt prevented its ever being profitable. Its annual receipts sometimes ran to $200,000 and over, but in many seasons they were not sufficient to pay interest charges. In 1864 the traffic reached its high mark at 528,000 tons, the receipts being $278,344. But the managers, even in 1861, had indicated that they foresaw the inevitable. They quoted from the Pennsylvania Railroad report of that year the statement that the recent competition of lines paralleling the Pennsylvania canals had introduced "a serious competition" for the lumber and coal traffic.

The managers pointed out that the canal's only weapon was cheaper rates. They urged that the locks be enlarged so as to admit boats of even greater tonnage. They also suggested the use of double boats, such as were later used on several of the eastern waterways and are now being used on the Lehigh and Delaware Division. Both sections of such a boat, they argued, could be made equal in capacity to the largest of the single boats and towed at but slightly increased expense.

Two steam towboats were introduced in 1861, and the managers were much elated, foreseeing "a new era in the history of our canals" and "a future of continued prosperity." But they learned the bitter lesson, as did other canal men, that America demands speed, and that the ordinary earthen canal bank is not proof against the wash from a boat moving at much greater speed than that of a horse's best walking gait.

Traffic declined with such rapidity after some parallel railroads had been built in the '60's that the company abandoned the struggle for existence, and on January 1, 1870, leased the canal for 999 years to the Philadelphia and Reading Railroad Company. Thereafter no serious effort was made at adequate maintenance of the work, with the result

Old Towpaths

that business fell off still more rapidly. In 1894 a freshet inflicted great damage to the banks, which were never thereafter repaired. The receipts in 1895 were only $2,956.54; and at the end of that season the lock gates were closed for the last time.

CHAPTER XVIII

THE LEHIGH AND DELAWARE DIVISION CANALS

THE Lehigh Coal Mine Company was organized on February 13, 1792, by some of the first men in America to comprehend the value of anthracite coal—Colonel Jacob Weiss, Michael Hillegas, Charles Cist, William Henry and others. They bought and patented about 10,000 acres of land, most of it bearing coal, on the upper Lehigh River in the vicinity of the present town of Mauch Chunk. But during the company's earlier years most people knew nothing about anthracite, and of those who had heard of it, a goodly percentage did not believe that it could be made to burn. As the Eighteenth Century closed, the new fuel was slowly being brought into use in Philadelphia, but now the Lehigh Company was cursed by lack of facilities for getting its coal to market. The Lehigh River seemed almost incorrigible. Furthermore, the average cost of hauling coal from the mines to the river was $4 a ton—and that was more than it sometimes sold for in Philadelphia.

The company secured a lottery privilege for the purpose of improving the Lehigh and raised about $10,000 thereby, but this availed little and the mines remained almost neglected. In 1806 a faint hope was aroused when a daring riverman constructed an ark, put about three hundred bushels of coal aboard at Lausanne, above Mauch Chunk, took it down on the spring freshet to Philadelphia. But this form of navigation could be achieved on the turbulent Lehigh only during high water, and then only at great risk. It appears that not more than one or two per year went through, for each one is mentioned as an almost epochal affair.

Old Towpaths

For twenty-six years after its organization the Lehigh Coal Mine Company was an unsuccessful enterprise. Some of the original promoters died during that time with their faith still unvindicated and their hope still unrealized. Then Josiah White appeared upon the stage.

White was an uneducated but shrewd and energetic man of Quaker stock, with clear vision and a tremendous power of dogged perseverance. Starting as a youth without resources, he had finally gotten into the manufacturing of wire and nails in a small way, but being a little too far ahead of his fellows in imagination, had acquired a white elephant in the form of some dams and water power on the Schuylkill River. Had he been able to raise the capital in 1812, White would probably have built the Schuylkill Canal and developed the great Pottsville coal field. But he was unable to win support for his venture and the Schuylkill Navigation was organized and built by other men.

In 1817, with his affairs almost at a standstill, and longing for a better field of action, White decided to investigate the Lehigh. He had difficulty in borrowing a horse on which to make the trip. His friend Erskine Hazard accompanied him. Upon seeing the Lehigh coal field, the two were so impressed with its possibilities that they decided to take a hand in developing it, if possible.

The Lehigh Coal Mine Company, utterly discouraged, was glad to give anybody a chance at the problem. White and Hazard took in another man, Hauto, and the three were able to get a twenty-year lease on all the company's 10,000 acres for an annual rental of one ear of corn, they undertaking after three years to begin shipping 40,000 bushels of coal annually to Philadelphia. The company hoped thus to popularize its product and get the transportation system in working order by the time the lease should expire. White says that the three lessees did not have among them as much as a thousand dollars; but they hurried off to Harrisburg and obtained the privilege of improving the Lehigh. It was

A WEIGH LOCK ON THE LEHIGH CANAL, ABOUT 1870.
Note the woman cooking on the boat in the foreground

The Lehigh and Delaware Division Canals

freely gossiped that the privilege "gave these gentlemen the opportunity of ruining themselves, as many members of the Legislature predicted would be the result of their undertaking." There was one consolation; even if they were ruined, they wouldn't have far to go.

On the 4th month, 1818 [White records] Erskine and Myself Leveled the River from Stodartsvill to Easton. the Ice had not all disappeared. No House between Lausane and Stoddertsvile we lay out in the woods 6 nights. We borrowed the Levels of Benjn R. Morgan, who had Retained them as the Relics of the Union Canal C^o. We knew of no other Level in Philad^a and if there had been we would have been too poor to buy it.

To finance the job they organized a corporation and after a hard struggle succeeded in selling fifty thousand dollars worth of stock. They were then ready to grapple with the colossal task of harnessing the Lehigh. The work began that summer with thirteen hands; a month later there were seventy and in the following year the number rose to hundreds.

White was the inventive genius and the hardest worker of the crew. "I was in the water as much as out of it for about 3 seasons," he says, "and my cloths dried on my back." He devised a scheme for making the river navigable by what he called "artifitial freshets." Wherever rapids occurred he placed across the stream V-shaped dams, with what were nicknamed "bear-trap gates" in the middle of them. This converted the river into a series of pools. To pass loaded arks down the river, the gates were closed until the natural flow of the stream had filled the pools; then the uppermost gate was opened and the boats passed through it on the artificial flood; then the second gate, and so on down the stream. As soon as the boats had passed Dam No. 1, the gate could be closed again to collect water for another freshet.

Old Towpaths

As this crude but tolerably effective navigation was gradually extended down the Lehigh, the shipments of coal were increased until in 1821, 365 tons were sent to Philadelphia. This glutted the market. A newspaper advertisement in January, 1819, stated that orders would be received for Lehigh coal at 172 Arch Street "in quantities of not less than one Ton between the 1st of April and the 1st of December at 30 cents per Bushel of 80 pounds. The coal may be seen burning at the above place." No. 172 Arch Street was the home of Josiah White. A goodly portion of the coal which he was thus offering to the public had been brought down to the city by wagon, his tireless energy having devoted itself to the improvement of the roads even while he was working on the river.

The first arks which were sent down the improved river were from 16 to 18 feet wide and 25 feet long. It was found that two of these could be hitched together with resulting economy in operation, for thus a doubled capacity was secured with the expense of a single crew. As the men became more expert, more sections were added until the strings were often 180 feet long. As it was impracticable to bring the arks back, their timber was sold at Philadelphia and their iron parts were taken back to the Lehigh on wagons operated by the company, on which the boatmen also returned.

Meanwhile a tramway had been completed from the mines to the river. The volume of coal shipments increased rapidly from year to year, and immense quantities of timber were also rafted. In 1820, two years after White and Hazard had gone to the Lehigh, there was a reorganization, and the Lehigh Coal Company was combined with their Navigation Company to form the Lehigh Coal and Navigation Company. That corporation still operates—one of the oldest in America.

So efficient was the bear-trap method of navigation that in 1824 arks carried out of the Lehigh 31,280 bushels of coal, 6,186 barrels of flour and many tons of other products.

The Lehigh and Delaware Division Canals

But when a knowledge of canals had been promoted by the building of the Erie, White and Hazard decided that they must have one along the Lehigh. With their existing form of navigation, there was the constant trouble and expense of building new boats. The Morris Canal corporation had been organized in 1824 to build a waterway from Easton to New York harbor; and with a canal down the Lehigh, boats could go through to New York and be towed back again with ease and safety to Mauch Chunk or White Haven.

In the summer of 1825, with the versatile White himself as superintendent of construction, the canal was begun at Mauch Chunk, and pushed towards Easton. The company employed Canvass White as chief engineer in 1827, and he completed the canal. Like the Schuylkill, it was a combination of canal and slack-water navigation. Between Easton and Mauch Chunk, 46¾ miles, there were 37 miles of canal, the remainder being a series of pools in the river. Above Mauch Chunk the canal extended 24¾ miles farther, to White Haven. From White Haven on up to Stoddartsville, a more difficult stretch of 13½ miles, the old system of bear-trap dams and artificial freshets was maintained.

The canal was one of the most commodious and efficient in the country. It was 60 feet wide at the surface, 45 at bottom and 5 feet deep. The locks were 100 feet long and 22 wide, built of rough stone laid in cement, the rock for which was found alongside the river. One of the busiest cement manufacturing districts in America to-day is located on that very spot.

Anthracite coal, far from being a drug and a subject of ridicule, was now becoming a necessity. In 1827 the Lehigh Canal, uncompleted though it was, carried down 30,305 tons of coal, while the Schuylkill was hauling 31,364 tons. It was announced in 1828 that anthracite was being sent to the West Indies to be used in the manufacture of sugar. New York City, too, had become a large user of "stone" coal.

Old Towpaths

In July, 1829, the Lehigh Canal was completed to Easton. The Easton *Argus* of July 3 said that "Water through the canal reached Easton last Saturday about 3 o'clock. The packet boat *Swan,* intended to ply between this place and Mauch Chunk, was introduced into the canal the same afternoon. On Monday last several boats laden with coal arrived. Coal immediately fell in price." Anthracite was then selling at Mauch Chunk at $3 per ton, or $2.25 by the boatload. At Easton in boatloads it was $4; at Bethlehem, $3.70; at Allentown, $3.60.

The *Swan* began running regularly to Mauch Chunk and other packets were soon installed. At Mauch Chunk the Easton packet transferred passengers to another line which ran to White Haven. A delightful trip it must have been on the open deck of a canal boat through that wonderful gorge of the upper Lehigh!

The Valley boomed after the completion of the canal. In 1830, 41,750 tons of coal went down the Lehigh. The last of the old arks disappeared from it in 1831. The completion of the Morris Canal to Newark Bay that year and of the Delaware Division, down the Delaware River, a year or two later, opened two mighty outlets for the Lehigh. A boatload of coal managed to get through the Delaware Division in 1832, but because of leakage through the bed and other defects, it was not in good condition for use for a year or two thereafter.

In 1840 the Lehigh carried 225,318 tons of anthracite, delivering some to local points, sending some through the Morris Canal and some through the Delaware Division. In 1850 it hauled 690,456 tons. In 1855 it reached 1,275,050 tons; but in 1857, the year after the Lehigh Valley Railroad was opened, the figure fell to 900,314. The business made a quick, even if temporary recovery, however, and in 1860 reached its peak—1,338,375 tons.

A flood in 1841 came near destroying the canal. The portion below Mauch Chunk was restored the following

Courtesy of the Lehigh Valley Railroad Company

THE LEHIGH CANAL BETWEEN EASTON AND BETHLEHEM

The Lehigh and Delaware Division Canals

year, but that between Mauch Chunk and White Haven did not come into operation again until 1844. The packets were able to resume operations after the restoration, and continued more or less intermittently until after the flood of 1862 put them out of business forever.

That flood was the most terrible ever seen in the Lehigh Valley. To say nothing of damage at other places, it almost completely wrecked the canal from Mauch Chunk to White Haven. As that portion had always been difficult to maintain, anyhow, the company decided to abandon it and build a railroad along its right of way. That railroad, still owned by the company, has for nearly half a century been leased to the Central Railroad of New Jersey.

Notwithstanding the flood and the abandonment of nearly twenty-five miles of its waterway, the period between 1849 and 1868 was the busiest in the canal's history. During that time it carried 19,184,382 tons of coal—an average of 959,219 tons per year. Between 1820 and 1916 no less than 41,000,000 tons of anthracite went down the Lehigh River and Canal.

In 1854 an outlet lock from the Delaware Division Canal to the Delaware River was constructed at New Hope, 35 miles below Easton. There many coal boats would cross the Delaware River, enter the Delaware and Raritan Canal feeder on the other side, continue down to Trenton and either discharge their load there or perhaps enter the main Delaware and Raritan and go on to New Brunswick, Perth Amboy or New York.

In 1860 there were 2,000 boats operating on the Lehigh. One's first thought is that traffic conditions must have been well-nigh intolerable; but it must be remembered that during a part of the time these boats were on other canals, for most of their trips continued on through the Morris, the Delaware Division and Delaware and Raritan Canals. The statement has been made that prior to the flood of 1862 there were from 2,700 to 3,000 boats which operated over the

Old Towpaths

Delaware Division. Beginning with 40 tons, their capacity was gradually increased to 100 tons.

Notwithstanding this heavy business, the State could not make the Delaware Division profitable. It was sold along with the other laterals to the Sunbury and Erie Railroad in 1858. That railroad quickly resold it to the Delaware Division Canal Company; but it was so necessary to the Lehigh Coal and Navigation Company that they leased it in 1866 and have operated it ever since.

The elimination of the Morris Canal and the Delaware and Raritan feeder by the railroads dealt, of course, heavy blows to the traffic on the Lehigh-Delaware Canal; but it still continues to transport 100,000 tons of coal or more per year on its horse-drawn boats. The Lehigh River and Canal for several miles below Mauch Chunk became considerably clogged in recent years with coal dust washed down from the mines and loading places, mostly at flood stages of the river. This led to the partial abandonment of 23 miles of the navigation in 1923, from Mauch Chunk down to Slate Dam or Siegfried's Bridge. Coal is now carried down to that point by rail and loaded into the boats. A few boats are still operating above there, but that portion of the navigation is now given over mostly to dredges which are busily engaged in bringing up slack coal from the river bed, after which it is washed and sold as low-grade furnace coal. Actually more coal was thus salvaged in 1924 than was hauled on the canal. The canal carried 100,000 tons, and the quantity dredged from the river was 175,000 tons.

Electric traction—two varieties—and steel boats have been tried on the Lehigh, both without success; and the old waterway is still operating with mules and wooden boats, just as it did in the beginning—the oldest canal of any importance in America.

CHAPTER XIX

THE DELAWARE AND HUDSON CANAL

ALTHOUGH in the early years of the Nineteenth Century it was demonstrated that under proper conditions the "black stones" of northeastern Pennsylvania would burn and produce intense heat, yet no one, not even those who believed in anthracite, had as yet the faintest conception of what it meant to Pennsylvania and America.

But when one considers the times and the limitations of scientific thought then, it is remarkable how quickly anthracite became a popular fuel and then a necessity. A merchant named William Wurts bought a small quantity, was highly pleased with it and called the attention of his elder brother Maurice to it. The brothers appear to have begun immediately to sense the fact that there were vast possibilities in anthracite. So enthusiastic were they that in 1812 they started on an exploring tour, seeking new coal lands.

The brothers journeyed up the Lehigh, but found that the Lehigh Coal Company had captured all the good territory along that stream. The upper Lehigh and Lackawanna regions were then mountain wildernesses. Night after night these city-bred men slept in the open, day after day they traversed unbroken forest, precipitous gulches and mountain sides. They walked over the sites of the present city of Scranton and other busy towns of the Lackawanna Valley, then almost uninhabited; and they succeeded in getting options—at prices of from fifty cents to three dollars per acre—on several large tracts of land on which they found the stone coal.

Old Towpaths

They next began looking about for transportation routes. Philadelphia seemed their only possible market. The Lackawanna flowed into the North Branch of the Susquehanna, and coal might have been floated down that way; but the Union Canal had not yet been built, and to reach Philadelphia by that route would have been a long, roundabout and costly process. Their best outlet seemed to be eastward into the Lackawaxen, a tributary of the Delaware, or into the Wallenpaupack, which flowed into the Lackawaxen, although by either of these routes they would have to pass over the watershed between Delaware and Susquehanna.

For seven years the indefatigable brothers fought against the most discouraging obstacles; hand-mining small quantities of coal, sledging it over the mountain when there was snow enough, committing it on rafts to the turbulent streams from which they had tried to clear a few of the worst obstacles, sometimes hauling it on wagons still farther down—and then often seeing their craft wrecked and the fruits of weeks' and months' hard labor lost. For a long time Philadelphia was little interested in anthracite, but as it began to be more freely used, new discouragements developed. The Schuylkill and Lehigh fields were much nearer to that city and moreover, their navigation was being so greatly improved that they had a great advantage over the distant Lackawanna field. The Wurts brothers therefore decided to make New York City their market—if possible. They set about finding a highway to that city, and found that the only practicable way was by a canal cut from the Delaware to the Hudson River.

The Erie was at that moment arousing all America to enthusiasm for canals. Money was more plentiful than it had ever been; and it was inevitable that when Maurice and William Wurts, with their unquenchable enthusiasm and their valuable coal, should set out to build a canal, they would find backers. They first obtained permission from the Pennsylvania Legislature in March, 1823, to improve the Lacka-

The Delaware and Hudson Canal

waxen. In the following month the New York Legislature authorized the incorporation of the President, Managers and Company of the Delaware and Hudson Canal Company. The capital was to be $500,000; and when the books were opened, the whole amount was subscribed by 2 P.M. on the same day. Among the incorporators were that graceful and scholarly capitalist, Philip Hone, and several men from Orange and Sullivan Counties, New York—which latter fact indicates that the route of the canal had already been tentatively chosen.

Under the general supervision of Benjamin Wright, two other Erie engineers, Mills and Sullivan, were employed to make a survey from the Hudson River at the mouth of Rondout, up along the trough made by the latter stream and the Neversink River to the latter's confluence with the Delaware; thence up the Delaware and Lackawaxen to a point as near the mines as possible. They figured the cost of a canal from the Hudson to Saw Mill Rift on the Delaware, thence slack-water navigation up the Delaware and Lackawaxen to the foot of the ridge, and a railroad over the ridge, at more than a million dollars.

It being evident that the original estimates had been much too low, the capital stock of the company was in 1824 increased to $1,500,000, of which $500,000 might be used in banking.

Most of the people in New York City then burned wood. It was calculated that 58,000 tons of coal would supply the city for a year; but it was hoped that other towns along the Hudson might become so interested in anthracite as to swell the quantity to 150,000 tons yearly. It was thought that the new canal would give great advantage to the Lackawanna, as the shipments from the Lehigh (then selling coal in Philadelphia at $8.00 per ton) were still being made by arks, which could not be returned.

The corporation was formally organized on March 8, 1825, Philip Hone being elected President. Benjamin

Old Towpaths

Wright was engaged as chief engineer and John B. Jervis, another of the Erie school, as his assistant. Mr. Jervis gradually assumed more and more of the responsibility, and three years later became chief engineer.

Slack-water navigation on the Lackawaxen was soon pronounced impracticable, and it was decided to extend the canal up the Delaware and Lackawaxen to the forks of the latter, from which point a railroad—partly inclined planes—would cross the 850-foot ridge to the mines. The first suggestion had been for wooden locks, but now the engineers declared for stone; for hydraulic cement had been discovered on the lower Rondout, equal to that found and used on the Erie. This was the cement later known as Rosendale, which supported a great industrial district in the Rondout Valley.

On July 13, 1825, a great crowd of people from Ulster, Orange and Sullivan Counties, some of whom had ridden and driven twenty or thirty miles over rough roads and trails, met at the summit of the watershed between what are now the towns of Ellenville and Wurtsboro, and with singing, prayers, speeches and outbursts of enthusiasm, inaugurated the digging of the canal. President Hone made the oration of the day. Later in the year he resigned the Presidency, feeling that his duties as Mayor of New York demanded most of his time. He remained for many years longer, however, as one of the Board of Managers.

In January, 1826, the corporation was legally able to begin its banking business, in a building on Wall Street, New York, soon to become noted as a financial thoroughfare. Work on the canal progressed rapidly, the section from the Delaware to the Hudson, nearly 60 miles in length, being actually in a usable condition in November, 1826, eighteen months after the beginning of the final survey, and sixteen months after the first ground-breaking. But by this time the funds of the company were practically exhausted. Aid was sought from the State, and the Legislature granted a loan

The Delaware and Hudson Canal

of $500,000, taking a mortgage on the property and giving the company the privilege of borrowing $300,000 elsewhere.

With these funds the work was pushed forward vigorously. From motives of economy the canal was ended at Honesdale, seven miles short of the terminus originally planned, and the railroad, 16⅞ miles in length, was surveyed from that point to Carbondale, which was the name of the new town that had sprung up around the mines. Jervis worked out an ingenious scheme of inclined planes for the bringing of the loaded cars to Honesdale—five of them ascending, worked by stationary steam engines, and three descending gravity planes. One of the descending planes had a fall of five hundred feet to the mile, and to prevent too great speed, he equipped the cars with a quaint species of propeller whose blades were of canvas stretched on frames; this was connected with the gearing and revolved so as to exert a backward pull—and thus retarded the speed of the car to four miles an hour.

President Bolton, in a public explanation of the company's policy, defended railroads by declaring that "all were agreed in their great superiority over turnpike roads, and in their near approach to canals in respect to cheapness and facility of transportation." It will be observed that the Delaware and Hudson directors were men of very advanced ideas. Not only did they build a railroad, but they even planned to use that new-fangled contraption, the locomotive, on the two or three lowest levels of their line. But before they could pay for the locomotives or even build the railroad track, they must have more money. We can readily understand the significance of an entry in Hone's diary in November, 1828; "Riding home from Mr. Jones's with Mr. Martin Van Buren, the Governor-elect, I took occasion to interest him in the subject of the Delaware and Hudson Canal, and hope he may be induced to direct, in his inaugural message, the attention of the Legislature to this object."

Genial diplomacy was successful, and the State advanced

another $300,000. With this the canal and railroad were completed. In October, 1828, the first small boat (carrying only 10 tons of coal because the channel was not yet in perfect condition) made its way through the whole canal from Honesdale to tidewater, and was followed a few days later by an impressive procession of ten more boats. A New York news item of December 10, that year, announces that "The sloop 'Toleration' arrived this day from Kingston with a cargo of coal, the first fruits of the Delaware and Hudson Canal."

Until the railroad could be completed, it was necessary to haul coal over the mountain from mines to canal by sled or wagon. Twenty to thirty teams were engaged in this work, pulling loads of one or two tons each. It cost $2.20 per ton to bring coal to the basin by sledge on the snow, or $2.75 by wagon. This made the coal cost $5.25 at tidewater.

Horatio Allen, one of the company's engineers, who had been largely responsible for the decision in favor of locomotives, had been sent to England in the autumn of 1828 to supervise the building of two of the machines. These were delivered at New York during the following spring. Mr. Hone records in his diary that on May 27, 1829, after witnessing the launching of a ship, "I went to Abeel & Dunscomb's foundry to meet a large party of gentlemen who were assembled by invitation to see one of the new locomotive engines in operation."

This engine was the famous "Stourbridge Lion," which is asserted to have been the first practical locomotive to move over a permanent railroad track on the American continent. It was of nine horse power, calculated to draw sixty tons at five miles per hour, and ran on four wheels of oak banded by heavy iron tires. The picture of a lion was painted on the side of the boiler.

The Lion was taken up the Hudson and through the canal to Honesdale where, on August 8, it was given a trial.

Courtesy Delaware and Hudson Company

SUSPENSION AQUEDUCT OF THE DELAWARE AND HUDSON CANAL ACROSS THE DELAWARE RIVER NOW IN USE (AFTER EIGHTY YEARS OF SERVICE) AS A HIGHWAY BRIDGE

The Delaware and Hudson Canal

Grave fears had already developed that the trestle work of the road would not support the engine, which was heavier than had been expected—nearly eight tons in weight, and most of it on one pair of wheels. The rails were only strap iron, laid on none-too-heavy hemlock stringers. But Horatio Allen was daring enough to take the machine on a trial trip; and with him at the throttle, it passed over trestles and around curves with easy motion and no mishaps. Nevertheless, the company was afraid to risk it on the line as constructed, and it was discarded. For years it lay rusting in a shed. Finally it was restored and placed in a museum—but it had had its revenge. It had lived to see the canal killed by the railroad and almost forgotten.

Oddly enough, this canal, which was built primarily to carry anthracite coal, spent its first two or three years of partial operation largely in hauling wood. The New York *Journal of Commerce* in May, 1829, announced that "During the week ending May 18, 110 boats and 106 rafts arrived at Eddyville and 102 cleared. Last season we (New York City) received upwards of 20,000 cords of wood through this channel, which otherwise would not have been brought."

The canal was considered complete from Honesdale to the Hudson in October of that year, and 7,000 tons of coal passed through it before the season closed. It was held back during the following year by the railroad, which could not handle the coal rapidly enough. Its capacity had been estimated in advance at 540 tons per day, or 108,000 tons in a year of 200 working days. But although it was worked to its utmost capacity in 1830, it could deliver only 43,000 tons. Many improvements were necessary before it was adequate to the demands upon it.

The canal itself was too small at first. Its surface width was 28 feet, width at bottom 20 feet and depth 4 feet. The locks would accommodate boats carrying only 25 or 30 tons and were drawn by one horse. In the 106 miles' length of

Old Towpaths

the canal there were 110 locks, overcoming a total grade of 1,073 feet.

Fifty-four thousand three hundred and twenty-eight tons were carried in 1831, and in 1832 the canal hauled ninety thousand tons of coal and three million feet of lumber. The company paid a good dividend that year. It was necessary to build additional boats; locks were operated day and night, and prizes were offered boatmen for quick trips. Mining was continued throughout the winter to increase the next year's output. Where there had been only pine forest five years before on the sites of Carbondale and Honesdale, there were now towns of two thousand and twelve hundred respectively.

But 1833 was a disappointment. There was a business depression over the country during that year and the next; many orders were canceled, sales were slow and an enormous overstock was left on hand at the end of the year. In 1834 only 43,000 tons were forwarded. This depression greatly embarrassed the corporation, and no more dividends were paid until 1839.

John Wurts, a third brother, had been elected President in 1831; he served until 1858. During his administration the company struggled through the Slough of Despond and finally reached the Delectable Mountains. But its path had been hard. It was difficult to widen the market for anthracite as rapidly as production increased. Competition was bitter, the company's rivals even carrying the fight into the financial arena and endeavoring to strike at the banking business. Strikes and other disorders took place among the miners, sometimes fomented from outside. During two seasons epidemics of cholera crippled the operations. Labor was scarce, and the company even sent agents to England and Wales to induce miners to come to the Lackawanna.

Mr. Hone traveled from Albany to New York on a fast day boat in 1840, and wrote in his journal that the boat "burns Lackawanna coal, which answers exceedingly well

The Delaware and Hudson Canal

and costs one-half as much as wood. The use of coal for steam navigation must inevitably become general."

In 1839, dividends of 8 per cent began again, and were continued for many years, with an exception in 1842, when 10 per cent was paid. 148,480 tons of coal were brought down in 1840 and 192,000 in 1841. The enlargement of the canal could be postponed no longer. It was deepened so that 40 to 50 tons could be carried per boat. In 1849-50 it was enlarged again so that boats of 125 tons capacity could be used—and some of them carried as high as 140 tons.

The company's profits were now enormous. Its capital had been doubled, and still from 10 to 24 per cent net was earned per annum. Another great mining corporation, the Pennsylvania Coal Company, was now using the canal. In 1858 the company's railway was extended seven miles farther down the valley of the Lackawanna to reach additional mines. In 1864 the capital stock was raised to $10,000,000, and even on this amount the net earnings of the following year were 31 per cent. It was then dealt what seemed to be a heavy blow when it lost the business of the Pennsylvania Coal Company. But the shock was only temporary. The business of the other coal company had gone to a railroad, and the Delaware and Hudson now began building and buying railroads itself.

The acquisition of the Albany and Susquehanna Railroad, which gave the company a new outlet to the North and East, was the first hint of doom for the canal. But it was still one of the busiest thoroughfares in America. In 1872 it carried its peak load of 2,930,333 tons of coal down to tidewater. But from that time forward, its tonnage slowly yet steadily declined. Railroads were the thing now, and its owners were building and buying more and more of them. Finally the point was reached where the canal was declared to be unnecessary and burdensome.

In 1899 the company asked for the privilege of making a significant change in its corporate name. The word

Old Towpaths

"Canal" was to be dropped, and it was to become merely "The Delaware and Hudson Company." The permission was granted, and also that of abandoning water transportation if the directors found such action desirable. Within a short time afterwards, the few remaining boats stopped, the water was drawn off, and one of the most famous, busiest and most profitable canals in America passed into history.

CHAPTER XX

THE MORRIS CANAL

GEORGE McCULLOCH of Morristown, New Jersey, was fishing at Lake Hopatcong, in the North Jersey hills, one day in the early part of the Nineteenth Century when the idea occurred to him that the overflow of this lake might be turned eastward and westward through an artificial channel which should connect the coal fields of Pennsylvania with New York City and her neighbors. Then and there the Morris Canal was conceived.

The rapidity with which new ideas were taken up by those slow, conservative grandfathers of ours is indicated by the fact that only five years after Josiah White had found it necessary to give public demonstrations of the burning of anthracite coal in Philadelphia, the Morris Canal was begun with the prime object of hauling that coal from the Lehigh River to the seaboard—so greatly had the business grown.

The preliminary surveys had already been made when the company was organized in 1824. A New Jersey legislative committee, investigating the application for a charter, reported that there seemed to be no doubt that stone coal was usable for both manufacturing and domestic purposes. As proof of this they cited the fact that "Within some miles of the various Coal Quarries, farmers go that distance to purchase and draw it, rather than use their own wood. In one instance, an individual living at a distance of 30 miles from the Schuylkill coal, sends his teams for it in preference to Hickory wood, growing within a few hundred yards of his own house."

Old Towpaths

The plan of the promoters to run the canal from the mouth of the Lehigh River to New York harbor was strategically a clever one, especially as the line passed through the iron mining and industrial district of northern New Jersey; but the hilly country made some daring and costly engineering necessary, and because of its wide detours forced the canal to a greater length than desirable. The air-line distance between its termini is about 55 miles; the distance by canal was 102 miles. That fact counted heavily against the Morris when railroad competition began.

The Morris Canal and Banking Company was organized in 1824. Its stock issue of $2,500,000 was quickly sold—that is, it was subscribed for and part payments were made on most of it. Excavations were begun soon after the company was organized, but because of slow collections on stock subscriptions and the difficult nature of the construction, the canal was not completed from Phillipsburg to Newark Bay until 1831.

The Morris was one of the engineering wonders of America. It was the highest climber of all the old canals. Within the distance of 51 miles from tidewater at Newark Bay to the summit level at the tip of Lake Hopatcong the channel climbed 914 feet. Thence it dropped again, 760 feet to the Delaware River at Phillipsburg, opposite Easton—a total rise and fall of 1,674 feet in a trifle over 90 miles. Had locks, with the limited lift of those days, been depended upon for all this, between two and three hundred of them would have been required. This would have been prohibitive.

James Renwick, the English engineer who supervised the building of the canal (he was at that time Professor of Natural and Experimental Philosophy in Columbia College, New York) overcame the difficulty in a spectacular way by building twenty-three inclined planes which took care of the greater part of the grade. Only twenty-three locks were needed to cover the rest.

Courtesy of the American Numismatic Society

CANAL PAPER MONEY.

This Morris Canal bank note pictures at the left a boat ascending one of the famous inclined planes. The portrait is that of Cadwallader D. Colden, First President of the company.

The Morris Canal

Wherever there was a long, steep hill to be surmounted, the canal breasted it boldly, and instead of a series of locks, ascended it by means of one of these inclines, the passage of which consumed but little more time than the passage of a lock. The planes were in reality boat railways. Their usual ascent was somewhere near ten feet for every hundred feet of track. The average lift of the planes was about 63 feet; but the longest one, that at Boonton, surmounted a grade of 80 feet.

In an early report to the stockholders the esthetic as well as the economic features of the canal are touched upon. The President "cannot resist calling attention to the elegance of curve wherever deviation from a straight line is necessary." And it may be added that because of the terrain, the Morris was largely curves.

The Morris directors also assured the stockholders and the public that there need be no apprehension as to the water supply of the canal, for competent engineers had calculated that Lake Hopatcong discharged more than four times as much water as was needed to maintain the whole work, to say nothing of other available lakes and rivers. Such being the case, one wonders why they were so shortsighted as to make the same mistake made by the Union Canal—i.e., build their waterway too small. The fault was of course due in a considerable degree to lack of funds.

On November 1, 1830, a trial was made on the eastern slope of the canal, between Dover and Newark. Five boats loaded with iron and ore left Dover and passed the planes with such ease as to astound every one beyond expression. In these first experiments the operation was performed in as little time as eight minutes. With more experience, it was done in later years even more quickly.

The first boat to pass entirely through the canal to tide level was the *Walk-in-the-Water* which arrived at Newark when the canal was opened on May 20, 1832. Then came two boats loaded with coal from Mauch Chunk. Enthusi-

Old Towpaths

asm ran high in Newark. The prices of coal, wood and some other necessities fell at once, but business in general was stimulated. There was a boom in real estate all along the canal. But it soon became evident that something was wrong. The painful truth was that the canal was too small.

The channel had been made only 31 feet wide at top, 20 at bottom and 4 feet deep. The locks were calculated to accommodate boats of 25 tons capacity. The boats in common use on the Lehigh Canal could not pass through such a lock, and therefore no through traffic from Mauch Chunk could be accomplished until boats sufficiently small could be built by or on the Morris Canal for the purpose. Even then the fact obtruded that a 25-ton boat was not practical, for it required just as many men to operate as a 50- or 75-ton craft.

By way of encouragement to the stockholders, the directors in their annual report for 1833 stated that along the line of the canal between Rockaway and Old Andover there were fifty-six iron forges, of which twenty were in full blast; while the others were shut down because they had exhausted their wood fuel and were merely waiting for the canal to get itself into condition to bring them anthracite coal so that they could resume. This was in effect a confession rather than a boast.

But it seemed impossible just then to find the money wherewith to enlarge the channel. The canal had also found itself hampered by the fact that it touched only the upper end of Newark Bay instead of the actual Bay of New York; and a costly extension across the Bayonne neck to Jersey City, twelve miles in length, had accordingly been begun. This extension was not completed until 1836. And there were other troubles also. The cost of building the canal, estimated in advance at less than $1,000,000, had in actuality mounted to $2,850,000. Of the $2,500,000 in original stock subscriptions, more than half had been forfeited because of

The Morris Canal

failure to pay the balance due; and it was found extremely difficult to resell any of this forfeited stock.

In 1834 so low had the corporation's credit sunk that its stock sold at 50. By the first of the following January the stock had risen to 111, and late in January it reached 142. This was regarded as having been brought about by a dextrous bulling operation, for during the winter the Legislature authorized a large increase in the capital stock, and quantities of the new shares were sold at the inflated price.

With the rising of the great tide of prosperity over the country which reached its culmination in 1836, and the mania of speculation and inflation which accompanied it, the directors of the Morris came to regard their banking privilege as their chief asset, and the canal a mere side line, an encumbrance. Like many another concern in those feverish days, they embarked in financial ventures which were nothing short of criminal. Their bank was a wildcat institution of the worst type. They participated in fake promotion schemes, floated loans on spurious collateral, perpetrated swindles through dummy organizations and divided illegal gains with crooked agents and brokers who were cheating and embezzling from their own employers and clients.

Some of the most reprehensible acts of the Morris organization were those in connection with their purchase of the internal improvement bonds issued by Indiana and Michigan when those young States were struggling desperately to build up systems of transportation for themselves. They got possession of large quantities of Indiana's bonds and of the entire $5,000,000 bond issue of Michigan, and sold these without first going through the formality of paying for them themselves. The gains, legal or illegal, accruing from one speculation they used to stop the hole made by losses in another and to pay for the extension of their canal to Jersey City, as well as the enlargement of its locks and planes which was carried out in 1840–41.

Notwithstanding the large gains resulting from some of

Old Towpaths

their smooth deals, they were compelled to mortgage the canal for $750,000, and finally in 1841 the company itself went down in one of the ugliest bankruptcies of all that unbeautiful period. For three years it lay in a state of suspended animation, while the canal was leased to outside parties for a small annual rental. In 1844 an entirely new Morris Canal and Banking Company was organized with a capitalization of $1,000,000. The new company at once enlarged the canal, and sectional or double boats of 44 tons' capacity, similar to those on the Lehigh, were introduced.

Between 1847 and 1860 the planes were rebuilt and equipped with wire hoisting cable, they having previously used hempen rope. After this change, enlarged boats with a capacity of 60 or 65 and sometimes even of 70 tons were used. These were the few brief palmy days of the canal. The annual tonnage, which had been less than 60,000 in 1845, increased fourfold within four years thereafter, and by 1860 had reached 707,631 tons. Population along the line had increased, the mining industry had developed greatly and new industries had sprung up.

The Morris and Essex Railroad, built in 1835, became a competitor for the hauling of coal to the coast; and when it built its branch to Boonton a few years later it began to get a share also of the iron and ore business. Then came the Lehigh Valley Railroad in 1857 as a strong competitor for the carrying of Lehigh coal. But in spite of all these, the increasing consumption of anthracite and the activity of the North Jersey mines and forges continued for a few years to increase the Morris tonnage.

Boonton and Dover, both on the canal, were the great centers of the North Jersey iron field. In 1860 Boonton had among other things some of the biggest nail factories in the country. In the '50's and '60's many Morris boats went no farther east than Boonton, carrying Lehigh coal to the iron-working plants there. Others carried iron ore from the mines to the furnaces. There were powder mills in the

A Loaded Boat Starting up One of the Inclined Planes on the Morris Canal

Aqueduct of the Morris Canal over the Passaic River at Little Falls as It Appeared in 1924

The Morris Canal

vicinity whose entire product was shipped by canal. The Morris was a purely industrial waterway. It never made a practice of carrying passengers.

The canal reached its high-water mark in 1866 when it carried 900,000 tons and its revenue from all sources amounted to $616,350. But even that year its doom was being written upon the wall. The best possible time that a boat could make between Phillipsburg and Jersey City was three days—and usually it took four or five. By railroad freight train the journey (about 25 miles less in distance than by canal) was accomplished in from five to eight hours, and each car carried almost as much coal as a canal boat. Furthermore, the canal was necessarily closed four or five months every winter; and those who used it in summer learned that they could expect no favors from the railroads when they turned to them for service in winter.

After 1866 the business of the canal slowly but steadily declined. In 1871 it was leased to the Lehigh Valley Railroad for 999 years. When the Central Railroad of New Jersey extended a branch into the Morris County iron field, the canal immediately lost all its remaining business from that district. After 1877 every year showed a loss in operation. In 1902 its total business was only 90,000 tons. The Lehigh Valley Railroad demanded in 1903 that the State take over the property, and after some litigation the transfer was made.

Until 1924 the old waterway remained in the hands of the State, slowly dying. One by one the old freight boats disappeared, and finally no craft were seen along those picturesque curves save canoes and a few motorboats on their way to and from Lake Hopatcong.

Finally the locks and planes became impassable, even for pleasure craft. In 1924 the State decreed that the canal must be eliminated. The banks were cut and the water drained out as best it might be, though this was a difficult task; for the courses of many natural streams had long ago

Old Towpaths

been diverted into it and their former beds were now occupied by buildings. The plane tracks were torn up, locks and buildings removed, and worst of all, the magnificent stone arch aqueduct across the gorge of the Passaic at Little Falls was blown up with dynamite—an act of vandalism which moved every lover of beauty and history to indignation.

CHAPTER XXI

THE LINKED FORTUNES OF THE SCHUYLKILL AND DELAWARE AND RARITAN CANALS

WE have already discussed the building of the Schuylkill Navigation. Its first dividend was declared in 1829. The traffic that year amounted to 134,524 tons. The dividends rose rapidly to 15 per cent in 1835 when half a million tons were carried, and 19 per cent in 1839.

Shares of stock which had originally cost $50 sold in 1842 for $175 to $180. But the lean years following the panic of 1837 finally had their effect, and in the early '40's the company ceased to pay dividends, though it was still in comfortable circumstances.

For the first few years all coal destined for ports beyond Philadelphia was necessarily transferred to other vessels at that city, the Schuylkill canal boats being open and unseaworthy. But in the '30's a new connection for the Schuylkill came into being, and forwarders began experimenting with through traffic. This new line was the Delaware and Raritan Canal, which effected a connection with the Delaware River at Bordentown in 1838.

The proposition to connect New York and Philadelphia by canal was not as old as some other navigation schemes in the country, but it had been talked of before 1800. In 1804 the New Jersey Navigation Company had been chartered for the purpose of opening communication between the tidewater of the Delaware and Raritan Rivers. The incorporators had made no survey when their charter was issued,

Old Towpaths

and so had no idea what capital would be necessary. A survey was made and subscription books were opened at the leading towns between New York and Philadelphia. But at that time neither capital nor enthusiasm for internal improvements were as easy to find in America as they were a few years later. A common objection of the day was the dictum that the country was too young to attempt works so extensive and costly. These things were responsible for the matter's lying stagnant several years longer. In 1816 and again in 1823 the Legislature authorized surveys and appointed commissions to study the matter. It was proven that nearly 60,000 tons of merchandise passed annually between New York and Philadelphia by wagon, and it was believed that all of this would seek the canal, as would also large coal shipments from the Schuylkill and Lehigh and a large volume of traffic from the South.

Sectional jealousy now interfered with the scheme. The only feasible water supply for the western end of the canal was the Delaware River; and the Delaware being a boundary stream, the consent of Pennsylvania was necessary in order to get the use of a certain amount of water from it. This she would not give at the moment. There were other difficulties which the corporation was not able to overcome, and it passed out of existence in 1828.

But the idea had by this time grown more popular. The thousands of wagons hurrying to and fro between the Delaware and New York Harbor gave indication that a canal would pay handsomely. Numerous petitions were sent to the Legislature in favor of the idea; while on the other hand, every one connected with the wagon trade was against it, as were many others.

But the proponents of the scheme prevailed, though an attempt to make it a State project failed. On February 4, 1830, the fifth general act for the canal's construction was passed. Ominously enough, a railroad, the Camden and Amboy, which followed a parallel course, was chartered on

The Schuylkill, Delaware and Raritan Canals

the same day. But the Legislature saw fit to encumber the proposed canal with certain taxes which operated against the sale of stock and made it impossible to secure aid from the National Government. The competing railroad privilege was also a hindrance to stock selling. The managers concluded that public confidence had turned from canals to railroads, and they therefore asked for the privilege of building a railroad along their right of way. But the State replied that such permission could not be given, as it would violate a tacit agreement with the Camden and Amboy. The canal and railroad companies now began negotiating with each other, with the result that a peculiar consolidation was effected in 1831. Under this arrangement, each company retained its own organization and officers, but the two were combined in the matter of expenditures and revenues.

Construction of the canal now began at once. The Camden and Amboy had had no trouble in placing its capital stock, the whole issue of $4,000,000 having been subscribed within ten minutes. When the two companies were first combined, there was a suggestion made that great economy might be effected by building the railroad on the berm bank of the canal. This drew from the New Brunswick *Fredonian* a clever bit of satirical poetry:

> *Canals and railroads moving side by side*
> *Recalls a plan by Newton once applied;*
> *Who had (no doubt the tale you've heard before)*
> *With love of order and proportion smitten,*
> *Two holes cut through the bottom of his door,*
> *A large one for the cat, a small one for the kitten.*

The question that agitated the minds of those who read the skit was, Which was the kitten—the canal or the railroad?

Canvass White, now considered one of the greatest engineers in America, was engaged as chief engineer of the

Old Towpaths

work. With plenty of money behind it, the job went forward so rapidly that the opening of the canal and feeder was celebrated on June 27, 1834. The main canal, extending from tidewater of the Raritan at New Brunswick to Bordentown on the Delaware, is 44 miles long; and there is a feeder 22 miles long beginning at Raven Rock on the Delaware, and joining the main canal at Trenton. The main canal was made 80 feet wide and 8 feet deep; the feeder 60 feet wide and 6 feet deep. This feeder was navigable until very recent years, and was one of the highly important portions of the canal.

This canal should have been one of the greatest successes in the history of internal improvements. It had certain advantages not possessed by any other, not even the Erie. Its original cost of construction had been comparatively low. In its earlier decades it had the largest channel of any canal in the country save the Chesapeake and Delaware. Its general level was low, it was easy to maintain, seldom suffered from freshets, and had few locks. It commanded the trade between the two greatest cities of the country, New York and Philadelphia. It was connected with the trade of the North and West by way of the Hudson River and the Champlain and Erie Canals, and with New England through the coastwise shipping. It was connected with the South by the Chesapeake and Delaware Canal and the two bays which that waterway joined; and finally, it afforded the best of facilities for carrying coal eastward from the fields of Pennsylvania. Because of its larger size and its lesser lockage, it even took a goodly percentage of the Lehigh coal business away from the Morris Canal.

But unfortunately, it was cursed by railroad influence even before it was built. Had it been independent, it might have been one of the most profitable avenues of commerce in America. As it was, it fell into disgrace early with the people because of its being involved in a questionable bargain with the State; and there came a time when it was such a

The Schuylkill, Delaware and Raritan Canals

paying property that its own masters longed to throttle it, and at one stroke deprived it of half its tonnage.

It was a strange situation that obtained in New Jersey— a railroad and a canal company claiming an absolute monopoly of the right to transport freight and passengers across the State between New York and Philadelphia. The charter of the canal provided that no rival work could be built within five miles of its line. The railroad was to pay transit duties to the State similar to those of the canal, and its charter provided that these duties should cease to become obligatory should the State authorize the construction of another road for the transportation of passengers between New York and Philadelphia. In fact, a supplementary act of 1832 provided that no new railroad might be built without the consent of the combined companies.

In consideration for this lucrative privilege the companies handed to the State $200,000 worth of stock in 1831 and 1832; and they agreed that the interest and transit duties paid to the State should not be less than $30,000 annually. The companies in turn then sold monopolies on a royalty basis to certain lines operating between Baltimore and New York, or between the Schuylkill and New York, or carrying coal up the Hudson to Albany. This aroused much bitter criticism, and newspaper and pamphlet wars were waged against the trust; but so firmly entrenched were the companies that they ignored the storm, and did not even make full reports to their own stockholders from 1831 until 1840.

Three sketchy pseudo-reports were issued during the three following years, but these were attacked as being inaccurate; it was asserted that the State was being defrauded, and the Legislature appointed investigating committees now and then, which did nothing but apply whitewash. The Committee of 1849 criticized the methods of the trust, but cleared it of the charge that it had defrauded the State. The Legislature was so well satisfied with this report that in

1854 it extended the companies' monopoly for another fifteen years. Henry V. Poor said in his *Manual of Railroads and Canals* in 1860 that the State had received from the trust over $2,500,000 in graft.

"As the monopoly enjoyed is a very valuable one," he went on, "the Company practices a studious concealment of its affairs as a means for its quiet enjoyment, making only such meagre annual reports as are required by the Legislature. It is consequently impossible to tell what has become of its net income after the payment of dividends." He adds that little information was available on the company's large holdings in other stocks or even as to its equipment. "The Company is the paramount authority in the State, dictating legislature upon all subjects in which it has a real or fancied interest."

The D. and R. did no passenger business; that went to the railroad. It grew so busy with its freight traffic that passengers would have been a nuisance, anyhow. There were some years when it outstripped the Erie in tonnage carried. Its through business was tremendous. In 1854 its feeder was connected with the Delaware River at Lambertville by a lock, and on the opposite shore another lock connected the river with the Delaware Division. Boatloads of coal now came down from the Lehigh through the Delaware Division, crossed the river, entered the feeder and proceeded thence to New York. Boats even came from far up the East and West Branches of the Susquehanna, down to Chesapeake Bay, through the Chesapeake and Delaware Canal, up the Delaware River and through the D. and R. Canal to New York Harbor—a distance of 700 miles or more.

Most important of all was the Schuylkill trade; and in turn, the Delaware and Raritan offered a great opportunity to the Schuylkill boatmen to enlarge their field of operation. In 1839 boats with covered hatches and fitted for coastal use began operating on the Schuylkill. These boats, carrying

Courtesy of the Pennsylvania Railroad Company
THE LAST REMAINING HORSE BOAT ON THE DELAWARE AND RARITAN CANAL

The Schuylkill, Delaware and Raritan Canals

60 tons each, came down to Philadelphia, were towed thence by steam in flotillas of fifteen or twenty to Bordentown, where they entered the D. and R. Canal and were towed through singly to New York Harbor.

There were 800 boats in service on the Schuylkill in 1843, including 278 covered boats adapted to through traffic to New York. Lime-burning was becoming a great industry in the Schuylkill Valley, and most of the product was going down the canal. 119,972 tons of it went by boat through the Schuylkill and D. and R. to New York in 1843.

But the Philadelphia and Reading Railroad was built along the Schuylkill River that same year, and its competition was keenly felt by the Navigation. Nevertheless the latter made arrangements by which the railroad handled coal cars owned by the canal company from the mines to the water's edge. The canal company owned 600 coal cars at this time, which number fifteen years later had increased to 3,400. These were handled not only by the Reading but by other railroads as well, and some of them over the canal company's own tracks.

It was evident in 1843, however, that to keep pace with the railroad the canal must be enlarged again. This was done in 1846. After the enlargement there were 600 boats in the New York trade, and some of them even went to New Haven and New London, Connecticut. Business grew so heavy that in 1858 the company began offering prizes and bonuses for greater speed. Two boats in a race made the trip from Port Carbon to New York and return in a week —which was regarded as marvelous, and really was a remarkable record—too fast, in fact, for the good of the horses. Interest in the speed contests became so great that the time for loading a boat with coal was reduced to eighteen minutes. The rivalry finally became so bitter that the company discontinued the contests.

The canal reached its peak in 1859, when it hauled 1,699,101 tons, of which 1,372,109 were anthracite coal.

Old Towpaths

There were then 1,400 boats in service, nearly all of them of 180 tons' capacity. But the canal was not making any profit. One reason was the heavy cost of the last enlargement. Another was the damage from floods. There were two serious freshets in 1850—in July and September—the last one of which was the most dreadful one that had ever been seen in the Schuylkill Valley. Twenty-three dams were badly injured, and two had to be entirely rebuilt, including one 35 feet high. In all the years from 1855 to 1867 the canal tonnage fell below 1,000,000 in only two years. But the canal could have handled double the business and would have done so had it not been for the competition of the railroad. Tolls were reduced, to hold as much of the traffic as possible; and the heavy expense of enlargement and repairs ate up the rest of the profits.

In 1860, out of more than 1,200,000 tons of *coal* alone (to say nothing of other freight) passing through the Delaware and Raritan, nearly 900,000 tons came from the Schuylkill and 314,237 tons came from the Lehigh. But the Reading Railroad was increasing its business rapidly, and giving very low rates. Even in 1847 it carried more tonnage on its 610 miles of track than the Erie Canal, and at a lower rate. And a goodly portion of its business was taken away from the Schuylkill Navigation.

The year 1869 was a disastrous one for the Schuylkill Canal. For six weeks in May and June a strike of miners almost stopped all shipments of coal. Then came a serious drought, beginning in July. So little water was coming down the Schuylkill that the city of Philadelphia, threatened with a water famine, was compelled to violate its agreement with the Navigation Company, and lowered the water above the Fairmount Dam to such an extent that loaded boats could not pass. The drought continued until September 25, when heavy rains fell and traffic was resumed. But now the rain wouldn't stop! Scarcely more than a week after the resumption of traffic there came the greatest flood the Schuylkill

The Schuylkill, Delaware and Raritan Canals

had ever known, and the works of the Navigation Company were badly wrecked throughout their length.

This was the fatal blow. In the following year the canal was leased by the Philadelphia and Reading for 999 years. It was put in tolerable repair again and business resumed; but now ensued one of those spiteful strokes by one great corporation at another, which hurt innocent parties more than the one at whom the blow is aimed. The Pennsylvania Railroad leased the Camden and Amboy Railroad in May, 1871, and of course were forced to take the Delaware and Raritan Canal also. No sooner had they done this than they refused to permit any coal from the Schuylkill mines—now entirely under the control of the Reading Railroad—to pass through the D. and R. canal. This resulted in a quick decrease of nearly a million tons in the yearly traffic of the Delaware and Raritan, and also in a decided drop in the tonnage of the Schuylkill; for with the through canal route to New York cut off, the Reading now shipped more and more coal to the markets of the North and East by rail.

After passing into the hands of the railroad, the Schuylkill's traffic and its condition steadily declined. Even in the disastrous year of 1869 it had handled 1,100,000 tons. In 1870 this dropped to 879,743 tons. In 1890 only 144,994 tons were carried, and five years later this amount had been cut in half. By 1898 the portion above Port Clinton had been abandoned, leaving only the 90 miles between there and Philadelphia in operation; and by 1904, business traffic on the entire canal had practically ceased. During the past few years almost none but pleasure craft have ever been seen on the beautiful old stream.

Under the dominance of the Pennsylvania Railroad, the Delaware and Raritan Canal also steadily declined, but it was too important to discard as utterly and quickly as the Schuylkill had been discarded. During the twenty years between 1860 and 1880 it averaged more than 2,000,000 tons of freight per year. In 1871 its net earnings were

Old Towpaths

$1,212,429. Even in 1889 it handled more than 1,200,000 tons. But although it is not kept in the best of condition, its upkeep expense is heavy, and for several years past it has lost money for its lessees.

Although it is crumbling in places, it is still a fine canal. It has several miles of paved or riprapped banks, has swing bridges, some of them steam-operated, and steam-operated lock gates. The lessees permitted low permanent bridges to be built across the feeder several years ago, thus stopping all navigation on it; and tolls were recently raised on the main canal, causing the old horse-boat men to complain bitterly that it, too, is being throttled.

Most of the barges that pass through it nowadays are towed by steam or gasoline tugs. In 1924 there were just two horse-boat captains left—each of them operating two boats in one tow, with a team of three horses. In 1926 just one of these ancient outfits survives. Perhaps in another year it, too, will be gone.

The United States Government is now considering the construction of a ship canal through the same territory, but it will not follow the line of the old canal. When the new channel is dug, the old Delaware and Raritan will vanish from the landscape.

CHAPTER XXII

THE JAMES RIVER AND KANAWHA CANAL

IT will be remembered that General Washington was made president of both the Patowmack and James River Companies in 1785. His chief interest was in the former improvement. He did not desire the James River presidency, but the directors were determined to have him. As he was unable to give the company his full attention, Edmund Randolph was appointed acting President.

The James has a good volume of water but is very rough. In early days it was almost the only means of communication between the west-central part of the State and the seaboard. The James River charter specified that the company might collect tolls only on condition that the river be kept navigable in dry seasons for vessels drawing at least one foot of water.

To complete such a navigation it was necessary to build a canal seven miles long from Richmond past the falls of the James up to Westham. This canal was at first planned to run along the south bank of the river, ending in Manchester, opposite Richmond. But a wealthy Scotch merchant of Manchester, believing that the canal would bring too much competition into town against him, employed Patrick Henry at a large fee to combat it. Henry succeeded in diverting the canal to the Richmond side of the river, but the merchant lived to regret his shortsightedness.

This first little waterway was from 25 to 30 feet wide and theoretically 3 feet deep, but did not always maintain that figure. After being aided by a loan from the State in 1795, as described in Chapter II, the company kept a force

Old Towpaths

at work from 1796 to 1801 on the upper river between Lynchburg and Crow's Ferry, 220 miles above Richmond, which was the limit of their operations. Much of the work was done by slaves hired from plantation owners. The time and cost required for doing the work were as usual greater than expected, but the company's bonds did not depreciate in price. The first dividend of 3 per cent was paid in 1801. From that time until 1805 much work was done in the James below Lynchburg, and the Rivanna and North Rivers, important tributaries, were also improved.

In 1805 the company's stock reached par, and thenceforward it was prosperous. It had $210,000 in capital stock outstanding at that time. The James Valley, aided in no small degree by the improved river, was growing in population, production and commerce. In 1808 Gallatin wrote approvingly of the James River Company, then looked upon as one of the most successful internal improvement enterprises in the country. "The natural navigation of the river," said Gallatin, "is considered as better than that of any other Atlantic river above the falls." The dividend paid that year was 8 per cent.

The boats then operating on the river were nearly all the property of planters, and were barges or "batteaux" from 50 to 90 feet long, capable of carrying 75 to 80 barrels of flour or from 8 to 12 hogsheads of tobacco. Boats passing through the canal at Richmond could carry little more than eight tons. The Balcony Falls, above Lynchburg, was the worst impediment on the upper river. Here the water fell 200 feet in four miles; great skill was required and boats were frequently lost. Craft starting from above these rapids seldom attempted to come back, but were usually sold in Richmond. The crews of these boats usually consisted of three negroes—a poleman on either side and a steersman. The trip down from Lynchburg to Richmond occupied about a week, and fully ten days were required for the return.

There was always much dissatisfaction and criticism from

From an old lithograph. Courtesy of the *Virginia State Library.*

THE JAMES RIVER AND THE CANAL, NEAR BALCONY FALLS

The James River and Kanawha Canal

those who used the river, as well as others in no way concerned. There was undoubtedly some ground for the complaints. The company's chief object was the earning of dividends, and there seems little doubt that in some places it did not live up to its charter requirements. On the other hand, complaints against it were at times exaggerated because of the usual dislike of corporations and jealousy over its large earnings. As early as 1805 the General Assembly had threatened to stop its tolls. A legislative committee made an investigation in 1812 and found that the water was sometimes too low, but also that the difficulties under which the company labored were great, the river in some places being very crooked, narrow and dangerous.

About this time there was much discussion (all outside the company) of carrying out the original plan—that is, to connect the James with the Kanawha and thereby make a through route to the West. The commissioners in 1812, leaving the James, had crossed over the divide to the Greenbrier, thence into New River, to the Kanawha and to the Ohio. As a result of that investigating trip, the James River Company was asked if it would undertake the extension. It evaded the issue by suggesting a new corporation for the purpose, in which it would take stock if adequate tolls were assured. No further move was made at the time, but two or three years later the State again broached the subject to the corporation, which now agreed to take over the work, but made such exorbitant stipulations that the Legislature refused to consider them.

Meanwhile there were numerous complaints that while the company was dividing 15 to 20 per cent profit annually, the so-called improvements were in miserable condition, and boats were frequently grounded and lost for this reason. The company issued a pamphlet in defense against these attacks, but made therein some damaging admissions regarding bad locks and the like. It failed entirely to answer the general complaint that it was making large profits and not giving good service. The attacks persisted, and finally the company was put on trial before the Superior Court of Virginia, with intent to nullify its charter. But while this prosecution was pending, the directors made an agreement with the State to surrender the charter and let the enterprise be State-operated. The suit against the corporation was immediately dismissed.

The State, it will be remembered, already owned a considerable portion of the company's stock. It now acquired all rights and equipment, and with the presumption of superiority to economic laws so often evinced by politicians, it guaranteed to the stockholders an annual dividend of 12 per cent up to 1832 and 15 per cent forever after that! The company's stock, which had been selling at 400 just before its indictment, had dropped to 200 while the trial was pending, but soared again when the State made its millennial "guarantee," finally reaching 500.

It was a curious arrangement which was now in force. The State owned all rights and interests formerly held by the corporation; which, however, was still in existence and acting as the agent of the State in administering the river work under the control of the Legislature. The State owned 427 of its 700 shares of outstanding stock. But strangely enough, if users of the river were to be believed, there was little or no improvement in the service. Finally under heavy fire, the company in 1823 admitted its "incapacity to conduct such important concerns" and gave up the job, which was then taken over by State officials.

The talk of further canalization of the river and of extension across the mountains increased in volume. Governor Randolph in 1820 declared the idea entirely practicable. The State in 1824 authorized a short canal around Balcony Falls and an extension of the original canal from Westham up to Maiden's Adventure, 27 miles above Richmond. Benjamin Wright was engaged to assist in new surveys and estimates, and he calculated the cost of the western extension

The James River and Kanawha Canal

at far more than formerly estimated. Work was now ordered to begin on a turnpike across the Allegheny crest and the improvement of the Kanawha River. In 1826 the auditor's report showed that $1,030,000 had been expended on these improvements, and that $4,750,000 would be required to complete a continuous canal up the James as far as Covington.

The Legislature, influenced partly by timidity and partly by sectional jealousy, now halted the work on the river, only completing the short canal at Balcony Falls. Counties not directly within the influence of the movement did not like to see so much money spent on it. A great internal improvement convention, numbering Madison, Monroe and Marshall among its delegates, met at Charlottesville in 1828 and urged the extension of the water route to the Ohio River, but with no effect on the State's lawmakers. The turnpike, however, 200 miles long, across the Alleghenies to the Ohio, was built and for twenty-five years was of great service to westbound emigration.

Several years of argument as to the relative merits of canals and railroads now ensued. It had become evident that the James River improvement under State control was a failure, and it was decided to put the work back again into the hands of a corporation. A charter was obtained for the James River and Kanawha Company in 1832, but not until 1835 was it able to organize. John Marshall took a prominent part in the promotion, and his influence was of great assistance at times when failure seemed imminent. The promoters had a strong argument in their plea that new York, Pennsylvania and Maryland were seizing all the western business with their great canals, while Virginia was being reduced to a minor position among the States.

The State of Virginia took three-fifths of the capital stock; two of the State's leading banks subscribed $500,000 each over the protest of their stockholders, and the cities of Richmond and Lynchburg also bought stock. But the Richmond *Whig* declared that there was a "deep-rooted hostility of the people along the line" to the whole project. It asserted that the existing canal work was unsatisfactory, and urged the company to change its plan. This was a sample of the rancor that pursued the company more or less throughout its entire career.

The new company attacked its task with vigor. There were 1,400 men employed in 1836 and 3,300 in 1837. But almost from the start the company suffered from financial worries. Neither the State nor the cities of Richmond and Lynchburg could pay their subscriptions when due. The capital of the company was nominally $5,000,000, but $1,000,000 of this represented the works of the old company which had been taken over at that valuation, but which the new company had to rebuild entirely, rendering that item almost a total loss. In spite of these handicaps, the 146-mile stretch of canal between Richmond and Lynchburg was completed late in 1840.

The arrival of the first boats at Lynchburg was a noteworthy event. There were evidently some strong partisans on the canal, for the honor of being first to arrive developed into a race between a Democratic boat and a Whig boat. On the morning of December 3, when they were expected to arrive, practically the entire population, including the mayor, the city council, clergy, militia, fire companies and all the town's musicians went down to the landing and remained there most of the day. At last, about four o'clock, the distant sound of a boat's horn was heard far down the river. Excitement rose to a high pitch. The horn was heard again and again. Which boat was ahead? Presently it came into view—horses trotting, covered with foam. It was the Whig entry, the *William Henry Harrison*. Old Rough and Ready had won, just as he did in the November election!

A line of packets was at once installed between Richmond and Lynchburg. The fine boats, *Joseph C. Cabell* and *John Marshall*, left each city three times a week and made the

The James River and Kanawha Canal

trip in thirty hours. Twenty-three years later the *John Marshall* had the melancholy honor of bearing General "Stonewall" Jackson's body home after his death on the field of Chancellorsville, May 2, 1863.

In July, 1842, a flood broke the banks of the canal in 103 places. Four hundred men worked from July until October before it was in condition to use again. Hard upon this backset a hostile Legislature enacted some hampering provisions which injured the company's credit and caused the stoppage of the work above Lynchburg. The Legislature then proceeded to "investigate" the company; but the inquisiting committee disappointed expectations by reporting in its favor. They found no lack of zeal, judgment or honesty in the conduct of the company's affairs, and added that the canal had been built at a smaller cost per mile than either the Chesapeake and Ohio or the Pennsylvania Canals.

The company appealed for aid in 1844, was again investigated and again vindicated. In 1846–47 the State finally granted a loan, and the section from Lynchburg to Buchanan was opened in November, 1851. The distance from Richmond to Buchanan was 196½ miles, of which 159¾ miles were canal and 36¾ slack-water navigation. The work so far had cost $8,259,184. In 1858 the company bought the North River Navigation, extending up that stream to Lexington, some 20 miles, of which half was canal and half pool navigation. This cost the company $273,000 all told, and never paid for itself.

The James River and Kanawha never did as large a business as the more northerly canals. In 1854 there were 195 freight boats operating on it. The traffic was largely agricultural. At distances of a few miles apart there were wharves and warehouses which were the mercantile centers of their neighborhood. The canal was a valuable outlet for some districts far upstream. In 1853, 150,000 bushels of corn and 60,000 gallons of whisky went down it from Rockbridge County alone. The crew of a boat would often tie

Old Towpaths

up alongside a field and help a farmer do his threshing, in order to get the job of handling his wheat crop.

There were three lines of passenger boats out of Richmond in the '50's. The fare between Richmond and Lynchburg, which was $8.00 in 1840, was reduced in later years because of railroad competition to $5.27, or 3.6 cents per mile, including lodging and meals. Because of a great reduction of rates in 1859, passenger business doubled in 1860. Packets began running to Lexington on North River that year. Probably some of the last canal passenger boats in operation in America were on this old waterway.

One advantage which this canal had (and Heaven knows it needed some advantages!) was that it seldom had to suspend operations in winter. From 1840 to 1848 inclusive there was no stoppage on account of ice save for twelve days in 1845. From 1848 to 1868 the suspension averaged only fifteen days per year.

The company would have been far wiser had it relinquished its ambition to build beyond Buchanan. In 1851, when it began work on its extension to Covington, the canal age was declining. The panic of 1857 dealt hardly with the company and stopped work on the extension. Several miles of excavation had been made, a number of locks and aqueducts had been wholly or partly built and one short tunnel and part of a 1,900-foot tunnel had been cut, when the work was halted.

In 1860 the company owed $7,000,000, but it succeeded in making a very excellent bargain with the Legislature. It was permitted to increase its capital stock to $12,400,000, and 72,000 shares of the stock were taken in payment of its debt to the State. This put the company in comparatively easy circumstances, and it planned to borrow money to complete the Covington extension, but the Civil War came on just then and blighted all hopes, just when the company had reached the point where it was the most powerful corporation and the greatest avenue of commerce in the State. In

From "Harper's Weekly"

CONFEDERATE TROOPS IN 1861 GOING VIA THE JAMES RIVER AND KANAWHA CANAL FROM LYNCHBURG TO BUCHANAN ON THEIR WAY TO THE FRONT IN WESTERN VIRGINIA

The James River and Kanawha Canal

1859 its tonnage was more than three times that of the Richmond and Danville, the most important railroad in the State. Interest which it must constantly pay on its heavy loans had, however, prevented its being profitable to its stockholders.

There had been negotiations, beginning in 1859, with a large French syndicate owning 300,000 acres of land in western Virginia which desired to buy the canal and extend it. The Frenchmen planned to organize a new company under the name of the Virginia Canal Company. A charter was actually obtained for the new company on March 29, 1861; but nineteen days later Virginia seceded from the Union, and the project vanished forever.

The business of the canal suffered during the war, but it was valuable as a military adjunct and was kept up by the State until 1864, when so many men had been called into the army that repairs on it were no longer possible. In March, 1865, Sheridan's cavalry spent a week along the canal, cutting its banks and destroying locks, buildings and other works. The company's office and all records were consumed in the great fire in Richmond on April 3, 1865; and its turnpike and Kanawha River improvements were confiscated by West Virginia when that new State came into being.

For years the company begged Virginia and the National Congress for assistance, and its pleas were seconded from many other quarters of the land. The Iowa Legislature in 1868 unanimously voted a memorial to Congress, declaring it to be a work of national importance. Other memorials were sent to Congress from Louisville in 1869; from Ohio, from Iowa again and from Kansas. President Grant mentioned it in his second annual message as an important westward route. Congress authorized a new survey to the Ohio in 1870, and this was made. A board of United States engineers in 1874 declared the project entirely practicable. Its cost was estimated at from fifty to sixty millions and the

Old Towpaths

time required for completion six years. At one time there was talk of a passage through the main Allegheny range by a tunnel nine miles long!

For two years more the company's hopes were at a high pitch. The panic of 1873 gave it some trouble, but by 1875 it was in better condition than it had been since the war. Its debt was small, and its surplus revenue for the year had been $53,729. But its hope for assistance from Congress was vanishing. It now planned to build a railroad from Buchanan to Clifton Forge, where it would connect with a new westbound line. This railroad was well under way when the great flood of November, 1877, on the James and its tributaries occurred. Bridges, aqueducts, locks and towpath were wrecked in scores of places, and the canal was at first thought to be hopelessly ruined; but it was finally repaired after three months' work and the expenditure of two hundred thousand dollars. The unfinished railroad was also badly damaged. Another freshet occurred in 1878. By that time the newly organized Richmond and Allegheny Railroad was negotiating for the purchase of the canal. Perhaps the last trip of a packet boat on it took place when a party of capitalists interested in the new railroad traveled up from Richmond to Lynchburg in November, 1878. The sale to the railroad was consummated in 1880; the track was laid along the canal grade and the old waterway was totally obliterated from the landscape.

CHAPTER XXIII

THE CHESAPEAKE AND DELAWARE CANAL

THE surveys in 1764 and 1769 of a route for a canal between the upper waters of Chesapeake and Delaware Bays have been mentioned in a previous chapter. The American Philosophical Society of Philadelphia was much interested in this project, especially with a view to bringing the country contiguous to Chesapeake Bay more closely in touch with Philadelphia. But when an attempt was made to revive the project in 1784, Pennsylvania found herself unable to interest Maryland and Delaware in the subject, and so considered the matter of building the waterway within her own boundaries. But a corporation chartered for that purpose failed to accomplish anything save to fall into bankruptcy; and in 1799 Pennsylvania again made an effort to interest the sister States.

Favorable resolutions were at length passed by the Legislatures of Maryland and Delaware, though many citizens of Baltimore strenuously objected to their State's giving countenance to the project, for the reason that it was obviously intended to draw the trade of Maryland to Philadelphia and to divert the Susquehanna trade away from Baltimore.

Notwithstanding these considerations, Maryland joined the other two States in chartering a corporation for the building of the canal, and subscription books were opened in 1802. A year later a sufficient sum had been subscribed to enable the company to organize. Four hundred thousand dollars worth of the desired $520,000 capital stock had been taken when engineers were engaged, final surveys made and excavation begun for a feeder. The stockholders now discovered that $100,000 had been expended in surveying, buying water rights and digging on the feeder, but that nothing was yet done on the main canal; and they became alarmed, and refused to pay assessments or balances due on their stock. The company collected some of this money through the courts, but still had not enough to continue its work.

In 1805 it appealed to the three States for aid, but received nothing beyond some kindly wishes and resolutions. It also sent a lengthy memorial to the National Government. Therein the directors pleaded that the canal was a work of national, not merely local importance. It was the beginning of a great system of inland navigation binding together eleven States. The disadvantages of the long detour around Cape Charles when passing from one bay to another were pointed out. One glance at the map, said they, was enough to show that if the Chesapeake and Delaware were dug, another much-talked-of canal would surely be cut across New Jersey between the Delaware and the Raritan. A continuous inland waterway would then be open from Hampton Roads to Narragansett Bay and the headwaters of the Hudson and the Mohawk. Even more than this would come about. The Dismal Swamp Canal would extend its channel to Albemarle Sound and the bays and inlets of South Carolina and a few years would suffice to see the Hudson and Mohawk joined with Lakes Champlain and Ontario.

The economic value of such a work was argued by means of many statistics. Coal was produced along the James River and was needed in the North. Southern tobacco was used everywhere. Flour, wheat, corn and meal from the Middle States and the fish, oils and lumber of New England were wanted in the South. The enormous cost of land transportation and the distance by water hindered this exchange. From the head of Chesapeake Bay to Philadelphia by water the distance was 500 miles, and the journey occupied

Courtesy of "The Explosives Engineer," Wilmington, Delaware
THE OLD DRAWBRIDGE ON THE CHESAPEAKE AND DELAWARE CANAL

Courtesy of "The Explosives Engineer," Wilmington, Delaware
THE DEEP CUT ON THE CHESAPEAKE AND DELAWARE CANAL, ONE OF AMERICA'S EARLY GREAT ENGINEERING WORKS

The Chesapeake and Delaware Canal

a week or ten days. The result was that coal from Liverpool sold in Philadelphia for less than coal from Richmond. A ton of merchandise was frequently brought from Europe for 40 shillings, or about $9.00. But the same sum would not move the same ton thirty miles on land in America. Let the canals be opened, and this hindrance would be removed. By the Chesapeake and Delaware 21 miles of canal would save 500 by sea. By the Delaware and Raritan, 27 miles of canal would save 300 by river and ocean. The vast development of metal-working in England had been brought about by canals which united coal and iron at cheap transportation rates, while in the United States the coal and iron mines might be within ten miles of each other and yet be valueless because of the high expense of transportation.

This eloquent appeal brought no aid from Congress, but it had another effect well worth while. Congress, after glancing at the question now and then for two years, asked the Secretary of the Treasury to look into it. Mr. Gallatin did so, and as a result brought forth his great Report on Roads, Canals, Harbors and Rivers. He recommended aid to the Chesapeake and Delaware—as well as to several other projects for improvement—but the bills for this purpose, introduced into both houses in 1810, were defeated.

In 1822 a movement was made to revive the Chesapeake and Delaware Canal Company, and a new board of directors was elected. A new survey was made, and the cost was now estimated at $1,239,159, more than double the former guess. Benjamin Wright was engaged as permanent engineer of the company. Again the three States were appealed to for help, and particularly effective propaganda was directed at Pennsylvania. That State was now seriously concerned over the menace of the Erie Canal, and although at the very moment planning an enormously expensive internal improvement system of her own, yet she thought it worth while to subscribe $100,000 to the Chesapeake and Delaware project. Maryland took $50,000, Delaware $25,000 and the Federal

Old Towpaths

Government $300,000. Canal enthusiasm now having been aroused in the country, somewhat over half a million was subscribed by individuals, giving the company by the latter part of 1824 $1,000,000 with which to begin work.

Judge Wright being still busily occupied with the Erie, John Randel, Jr., an engineer who had done some of the earlier surveying for the company, was made chief engineer. He opposed the original route chosen on the ground that the water supply was insufficient, and recommended one a little farther south, which was adopted.

Down the center of the neck between the two bays ran a low ridge, through which the canal dug the famous Deep Cut, which was regarded at the time as being "one of the greatest works of human skill and ingenuity in the world." It was more than a mile in length, mostly through solid rock and 90 feet deep at its deepest point. This cut was the one thing which made the cost of the canal so enormous. Not only was the expense of cutting the stone very heavy, but the workers were much troubled by slides of earth from the high banks. On one occasion 375,000 cubic yards of earth slid into the partly completed channel. Such mishaps as this were meat and drink for the croakers and illwishers of the project. "That the canal will never be completed over the present route is now, we believe, generally if not universally admitted," said the Wilmington *Gazette* in 1826.

When the work was in full swing, more than 2,500 men were employed. The eastern section of the canal was in use in 1828, when not more than six or seven miles of it was complete. The elegant packet, *Lady Clinton,* was advertised as being in operation in June of that year. Sloops, heavily laden, were also going in and out of it. "Owing to the depth and expanse of the water," says the company's report, "vessels can easily traverse this splendid canal at from six to seven miles per hour."

Water was turned into the Deep Cut on October 17, 1829, though the canal was not in good condition for use

The Chesapeake and Delaware Canal

until the following year. It was 13⅝ miles long, and had three locks. It had cost $2,250,000, or $165,000 per mile, making it the most expensive waterway of its time in America.

The canal handled only 61,500 tons in 1830, but for forty years thereafter its business steadily increased. It showed rapid improvement after the opening of the Susquehanna and Tidewater Canal, and in 1850, 361,640 tons were handled. Five years later the tonnage had gone above half a million, and in the sixties it passed the million mark, reaching 1,245,928 tons in 1870. Even as late as 1880 it carried 959,146 tons.

The Chesapeake and Delaware was very useful to the Federal Government during the Civil War, and fully demonstrated the value of intracoastal canals in time of national peril. Munitions and supplies were often sent through it by boat which, had they been compelled to make the long journey around Cape Charles, would not only have lost much time, but would frequently have been exposed to the danger of Confederate attack.

The canal's value as a military instrument was demonstrated in the very opening days of the war. On Wednesday, April 17, 1861, Virginia seceded from the Union, and immediately started her troops northward towards Washington. On the 19th the Sixth Massachusetts regiment, on its way to the front, was attacked in Baltimore. That night every bridge on the Philadelphia, Wilmington and Baltimore Railroad between Baltimore and the Susquehanna River was burned, leaving the War Department no means of transporting troops along the seaboard by rail to Washington; land communication was severed.

On the following day, April 20, the Government seized all propeller steamers in the vicinity of Philadelphia that could pass through the Chesapeake and Delaware Canal, and that night they passed down the Delaware River and through the canal. At daybreak they were at Perryville on

Old Towpaths

the north bank of the mouth of the Susquehanna. As the sun rose, the troops which had been rushed to that point by rail were being loaded on to the boats; they steamed down to Annapolis, the troops debarked and went on to Washington by rail the same day.

When those troops reached Washington, the Confederate outposts were threatening the capital; the lower Potomac was closed by a series of batteries and patrolled by a Confederate gunboat. The C. and D. Canal nullified these offensive arrangements and doubtless saved Washington from capture.

In 1871 the proposition was first made that the Chesapeake and Delaware be made a National ship canal. Government engineers were instructed to make surveys and estimates. The stockholders of the company were quite willing and anxious that the Government take over the canal, as its great construction cost precluded its ever being a profitable investment. Certain Maryland promoters, hoping to profit by the agitation for a ship canal, organized the Maryland and Delaware Ship Canal Company in 1872, procured a charter and obtained options on a right of way via the Sassafras River, which they urged as being a superior route to that of the old canal.

For more than forty years—nearly fifty—this company endeavored to have its route adopted; but all in vain. Government engineers made surveys of various routes at intervals, but nothing resulted save elaborate reports. Finally the Chesapeake and Delaware was strongly recommended as being the preferable route. In 1906 a special commission was appointed by Congress to go over the matter again. The commission recommended the old canal as offering a lower cost for rebuilding than the Sassafras route, and also as having military advantages. It was estimated that to enlarge it to ship-canal size would cost more than $21,000,000.

A few of the old horse boats still continued to operate

The Chesapeake and Delaware Canal

through the canal as late as 1902. At that time, and for many years before and after, the annual tonnage was over 700,000 per year, and would have been much larger had the channel been larger. Not until 1919 was the old waterway purchased by the Government for a consideration of $2,500,000. As this book is being written, it is being enlarged and converted into a sea-level ship canal, with a depth of 12 feet at mean low water and a bottom width of 90 feet.

CHAPTER XXIV

THE CHESAPEAKE AND OHIO CANAL

THE Patowmack Company's little canals around the Potomac rapids had been of much assistance to arks and flatboats drawing not more than one foot of water, but they failed to meet the requirements of a rapidly growing country, nor was the company able to fulfill Washington's dream of connecting the Potomac with the Ohio. When work on the Erie Canal was well advanced and Pennsylvania began to talk of a western waterway, Maryland and Virginia grew uneasy at the prospect of being outstripped by the States farther north. In 1820 Virginia sent an engineer to make a rough survey and ascertain whether the Ohio could be united with the Potomac and the Potomac with the Rappahannock. The former possibility was affirmed.

In 1821 a joint commission from Maryland and Virginia reported that the Patowmack Company had failed to comply with the terms of its charter and probably could never do so; that it had spent its capital and tolls, was heavily in debt and seemed likely to remain so. Further aid to it appeared unwise. The only sound procedure would be to cancel its charter and adopt some more effectual means of improving the navigation of the river.

The Patowmack Company signified its willingness to surrender its charter to a new company on liberal terms. In February, 1823, Virginia chartered the new company. In the Maryland Assembly an act was introduced to authorize the corporation under the name of the Potomac Canal Company, but the bill failed to pass. The Assembly, however, called a convention to consider ways and means of

The Chesapeake and Ohio Canal

effecting a connection between the Potomac and Ohio. In response to the call there met at the Capitol in Washington in November, 1823, twenty-six delegates representing Virginia, Maryland, the District of Columbia and one county in Pennsylvania. A letter from Ohio citizens, urging that the canal be built and even extended to Lake Erie, was read. After a three-day discussion, in which there was not much opposition, the convention adopted resolutions strongly favoring the project.

Baltimore had been largely instrumental in defeating the bill in the Legislature. The city was greatly interested in the proposed improvement, but the fact could not be concealed that Baltimore was off its logical route, and many did not believe that the city would benefit largely from it. Therefore they did not like the idea of being taxed to pay for it. Baltimore had only one-fortieth part of the power in the Legislature, but paid one-third of the State's taxes; and as the funds of the State were not sufficient to meet its governmental expenses, Baltimore couldn't grow enthusiastic over the idea of putting up one-third of the State's share in a risky proposition.

A subscription of $2,750,000 to the capital stock of the proposed company had been recommended by the canal convention, to be properly apportioned to Virginia, Maryland, the District and the Federal Government. Ohio was also invited to contribute. Virginia promptly rechartered the company under the new name suggested, the Chesapeake and Ohio Canal Company. The capital stock was set at $6,000,000.

Baltimore could not approve the new project as long as she was not the terminus. Washington, Georgetown and Alexandria were intensely jealous of Baltimore, and Baltimore in turn could not see why Maryland should aid a canal which would terminate outside her boundaries. Baltimore's favorite idea was a branch canal tapping the main waterway far above Georgetown and thus diverting the bulk of the

Old Towpaths

traffic away from the district cities—in effect, making the Baltimore branch the main canal. But a Government engineer who was ordered by the Secretary of War to make surveys for a lateral, reported that it would not be practicable to begin one at any point above Georgetown. He estimated the cost of a canal from there to Baltimore at $2,980,815.

The shock of these figures was as naught compared to that received when General Simon Bernard, the famous French engineer who had been engaged to survey the Chesapeake and Ohio Canal route, gave out his estimates on the canal from Georgetown to Pittsburgh. At the crest of the divide it must climb to 2,754 feet above sea level. General Bernard found the distance to be 341 miles, the number of locks required 398 and the cost $22,000,000! This seemed to make the project impossible, the company's capital being only $6,000,000; and hope sank in the bosoms of many of its friends.

But the leading promoters declared that General Bernard's figures were ridiculously high. James Geddes and Nathan S. Roberts, Erie engineers, were called upon to examine his survey and estimates, with full confidence that they would cut the figures considerably—which they did, proving conclusively that the work could be done for half what Bernard had calculated. Their report was hailed with joy by those who desired to believe something pleasant, but there were still many who could not dispel a fear that after all, Bernard might be the more nearly correct. Probably Geddes and Roberts did not willfully flatter the promoters and people of Maryland; but if the early Erie school of engineers had a fault, it was that of optimism—a tendency to underrate the difficulties and costs of construction; a tendency which after all was due to the general lack of engineering experience in this country.

The enormous potentialities of the great bituminous coal beds around Cumberland, Maryland, were now attracting public notice, and it was decided to make a beginning by

The Chesapeake and Ohio Canal

building the canal that far—184 miles above Washington —and pushing it on to the Ohio a little later when the profits should have made the extension possible. Engineer Roberts gravely announced to the public that the channel would be cut directly through coal beds where the coal would simply be shoveled from the bank right into the boats. Doubtless he believed it.

The cost of construction to Cumberland was at first estimated by Geddes and Roberts at $4,400,000. But the National Government urged that the canal prism be enlarged above its first suggested dimensions, and be made 60 feet wide at the water surface and 6 feet deep. The reason given for this was the belief that in deeper water a boat could be towed or propelled with less power than in shallow. A short section of ditch was tested, and the theory was found to be true. To build the larger channel would add greatly to the cost of the canal, but the company decided to attempt it.

For several years after the first conference it was not fully decided whether the canal would be on the north or south bank of the Potomac west of Harpers Ferry. When the surveys finally indicated that the entire length to Cumberland would be on the Maryland shore, Virginia lost interest in the undertaking and gave it no further support.

Not until June, 1828, was sufficient stock sold to enable the company to organize and accept the charter. By that time $3,608,900 had been subscribed for; of which the national Government had taken $1,000,000, the State of Maryland $500,000, the city of Washington $1,000,000 and Georgetown and Alexandria $250,000 each. Baltimore as a municipality felt no enthusiasm and made no subscription. Instead, her citizens decided in 1827 to attempt a double-track railroad from Baltimore to some point on the Ohio River; and a short time later a charter was obtained therefor.

On August 15, 1828, the Patowmack Company conveyed

to the new corporation all its rights and titles along the river. Work on the new project had already been ceremoniously inaugurated on July 4. No less a personage than President John Quincy Adams was designated to lift the first shovelful of earth and make the chief oration of the day. The ceremony took place at Georgetown in the presence of a great concourse of people.

General Mercer, President of the canal company, made the first address, and President Adams then took the platform. His speech was a triumph of the fulsome rhetoric of the day. He informed his hearers that the canal would be "a conquest over physical nature such as has never yet been achieved by man. The wonders of the ancient world, the Pyramids of Egypt, the Colossus of Rhodes, the Temple of Ephesus, the Mausoleum of Artemisia, the Wall of China, sink into insignificance before it."

If this seems a bit exuberant, one must remember that he was thinking of the full project which contemplated uniting the Potomac not only with the Ohio but with Lake Erie and drawing all the products of the West and Northwest, even to the Rocky Mountains, through its channel. Had the directors had the slightest intimation what the cost would be even as far as Cumberland, they would doubtless have agreed with Mr. Adams in his belittlement of the wonders of the ancient world.

Having led up to the proper climax in his address, the speaker received from General Mercer "the humble instrument of rural labor, the symbol of the favorite occupation of our countrymen," and proceeded to break the sod. But the first thrust struck a root and failed of its purpose. Another stroke, and again he was thwarted. Mr. Adams now dropped the spade, threw off his coat—we search eagerly but in vain for assurance that he also spat on his hands—and with the third stroke plunged the spade into the earth. "The multitude raised a loud and unanimous cheering," and the President then went on with his speech.

Courtesy of the Baltimore & Ohio Railroad Company

AQUEDUCT OF THE CHESAPEAKE AND OHIO CANAL ACROSS THE MONOCACY RIVER

The Chesapeake and Ohio Canal

Mr. Adams, who never fancied himself greatly as an orator, wrote in his diary of this occasion that he "got through awkwardly, but without gross or palpable failure. The incident that chiefly relieved me was the obstacle of the stump which met and resisted the spade, and my casting off my coat to overcome the resistance. It struck the eye and fancy of the spectators more than all the flowers of rhetoric in my speech, and diverted their attention from the stammering and hesitation of a deficient memory."

On the same day and no more than forty miles away, Baltimore with great manifestations of joy was laying the "cornerstone" of the Baltimore and Ohio Railroad. The canal promoters were not in the least perturbed by the coming of the railroad, which could of course carry only passengers and very light freight in its little horse-drawn cars, and was not regarded as in any sense "competition." Instead, ignoring the railroad, the directors talked in large terms of bigger and bigger freight boats, of possible double-decked passenger craft with a speed of seven or eight miles an hour—even of steamboats. But that railroad was destined to plague the canal sorely in later years.

Work proceeded slowly at first. Much trouble was experienced because of the greed of property-owners along the line, and as a result, nearly the whole right of way from Georgetown to Point of Rocks had to be condemned, and 1,300 acres of land purchased, for which the company paid heavily. This caused so much delay that the B. and O. Railroad reached Point of Rocks first with its track. At that place there was not room enough between the cliffs and the river for both railroad and canal, and the railroad secured the right of way. The canal appealed to the courts, and won after a long battle. The railroad thereupon began a survey on the Virginia side of the river, but eventually came to an amicable agreement with the canal company, drove a tunnel for itself through the mountain at Point of Rocks, and they continued up the river side by side.

Old Towpaths

The epidemic of cholera which swept the country in 1832 played havoc with the working force of the canal, and little progress was made. A traveler who made a short packet boat trip on the canal west from Georgetown that year did not believe that the canal would become profitable in half a century. He was the only passenger on the packet, and in traveling thirteen miles he did not meet a single boat. But it must be remembered that the canal at that time was only a few miles in length, and had not yet reached any important town nor any mineral region that could give it business. That lack of way traffic was always a curse to the C. & O.

By 1833 the company had spent all its funds and was in dire straits. The State subscribed for $125,000 of its stock as a temporary relief, and in 1834 loaned it $2,000,000, which was secured by a lien on the revenues of the canal. The company owed almost the whole $2,000,000, so it did not last long. Before a year had passed, they were begging again for relief. The gay, mad days of 1835 had now arrived, and Maryland, in common with many other States, threw discretion to the winds and issued $8,000,000 worth of bonds, of which $3,000,000 worth were turned over to the Chesapeake and Ohio in exchange for preferred stock, and $5,000,000 worth were handed to the other internal improvement companies of the State.

A great many State bonds were going begging in those days, and the C. & O. was compelled to sell some as low as 76. In 1838 the State again assisted the company, this time to the extent of $1,375,000, and took preferred stock in exchange. The State now held $5,000,000 worth of the company's stock, of which $8,359,400 had been issued. Even this much was not sufficient to complete the canal, and the work came to a halt 50 miles from Cumberland, in 1841.

For eight years past the history of the canal had been that of one continuous struggle for ways and means, of begging the State for help, of staving off creditors and trying to meet payrolls. The Irish laborers were frequently in

The Chesapeake and Ohio Canal

revolt because their pay was in arrears, and what with their own civil wars, the working force was often in a turmoil for days and weeks at a stretch. Some of the worst outbreaks in canal history between Corkonians and Fardowns occurred on this canal, armies of 300 to 400 sometimes fighting each other, with numerous deaths and injuries. The militia were frequently called out to suppress these wars.

Pleas were sent to the Legislature to extend more aid to the company, but the State's debt was already so heavy that some were advocating repudiation, and for a time no more loans were possible. The company at length induced the State to waive its claim under the $2,000,000 loan agreement of 1834 to the receipts of the canal, and give a mortgage as security instead. The company now owed, besides its more than $8,000,000 capital stock and the $2,000,000 borrowed from Maryland, $1,174,566 in other debts. But all this must wait. The canal could not become profitable and pay even the interest on its debts until it was completed to Cumberland. All tolls, water power rents and other income were therefore applied to the completion of the few links yet remaining to finish the job. Work began again in 1845, but so slowly did the money dribble in that not until 1850, in the words of the Cumberland *Civilian*, "after undergoing unparalleled vicissitudes of fortune, this great work has been at length consummated."

The whole job had cost $11,071,176, or about $60,000 per mile. From the very beginning, boats of 100 tons burden or more could be used. The canal was fed entirely from the Potomac River. One of its most famous features was the tunnel, 3,118 feet long, by which it cut across a 5-mile bend in the river. Boats going through it lighted their headlights and the drivers carried torches and lanterns.

On June 11, 1850, water was admitted to the channel at Cumberland and a new boat was launched there. The locks below were not ready for use until October. On the 10th of that month the completion was celebrated with much

Old Towpaths

festivity. In nonchalant defiance of the B. and O. a packet line was at once inaugurated from Cumberland. Packets had been running for several years between Williamsport, Harpers Ferry and Georgetown. How and why they did any business when the railroad paralleled their route every foot of the way is a mystery.

From the very beginning of the project, the citizens of Alexandria felt that the importance of their town would not receive proper recognition if they were not reached by an extension of the C. and O. Canal. The canal company had not been able to grant the favor, so Alexandria itself organized a corporation and secured a charter in 1830, authorizing the construction of an aqueduct across the Potomac near Georgetown and a canal thence along the south shore to Alexandria. Congress was compelled to aid the enterprise with a subscription of $100,000 in 1830, and with $300,000 more in 1837. The aqueduct was built of wood, resting on eleven stone piers, and was 1,100 feet long. Work on the canal was begun in 1833, and water was turned in on July 4, 1843.

This was perhaps the most famous aqueduct in American history. When the Civil War crisis arose, the United States Army took possession of the structure on May 23, 1861, drained off the water and converted it into a wagon and foot bridge. Over it passed thousands of troops, artillery and munitions of war. This was the bridge that one finds mentioned so often in descriptions of the defenses of Washington as "the Aqueduct Bridge." Back across it streamed tattered remnants of the defeated Union army retreating from the disastrous field of Bull Run, and forward across it marched many thousands of fresh troops to serve under McClellan and Burnside and Hooker and Grant. At the close of the war the Government surrendered the aqueduct to the canal company, but in such a dilapidated condition that it would not hold water. The company having no funds to spend on it, it was leased and repaired in 1868, but a few years later was abandoned. This canal, costing all told

Courtesy of the Eastman Kodak Company

TYPE OF FREIGHT BOATS IN USE ON THE CHESAPEAKE AND OHIO CANAL IN ITS LAST DAYS, 1923

The Chesapeake and Ohio Canal

$1,150,000, was an unfortunate investment for Alexandria.

The State of Maryland passed an act in 1843 authorizing the sale of the State's interest in all internal improvements, namely, the C. and O. Canal, the B. and O. railroad, the Susquehanna Railroad and the Tidewater Canal, at specified figures; but no reasonable offer was made for any of the shares, and public opinion was against such sale, on the ground that such action would be a violation of a solemn agreement.

The C. and O. Canal was of great value to the Government during the Civil War as a carrier of supplies. The army guarded and assisted in keeping it in repair. Several attempts by Confederate forces to destroy its aqueducts were foiled by the solid character of the masonry, put together with cement made along the line.

For several years the canal did a large business, the revenues reaching almost to $1,000,000 per year. During the '60's, 800 boats were operating on it, and receipts actually began to exceed expenditures. In 1872, 922,177 tons were carried and the net earnings were $253,305. But thereafter business declined. In 1880 the net earnings had fallen to $145,339. In 1888 only 286,813 tons were carried, and net earnings were only $2,700. The profits never did more than pay interest on the debts.

In 1877 a flood on the Potomac did great damage to the canal, and the company was forced to sell $87,000 worth of bonds in order to make the necessary repairs. In May, 1889, the great rainfall which destroyed Johnstown and wrecked the Pennsylvania Canal along the Juniata also struck the upper Potomac, and the Chesapeake and Ohio Canal from end to end was apparently demolished. The company owed (including its capital stock) more than $13,000,000 and was hopelessly insolvent. It seemed that the end had come.

For twenty years railroads had been watching for an

Old Towpaths

opportunity to get possession of the canal. Two railroads in particular had made repeated efforts to obtain control. A new railroad company had been chartered with the expressed purpose of building its line along the towpath. The trustees of the bonds of 1878 hoped to sell to one of these railroads. But the bondholders of 1844 wanted to revive the canal; they agreed to take up the bonds of 1878, and the wreck was turned over to them.

They spent $400,000 in repairing it and put it into perhaps better condition than it had ever known; and after two years of suspended animation, the old waterway revived once more. For several years the canal carried about 250,000 tons annually, nearly all coal; then the tonnage began gradually to decline. In 1904 the State of Maryland sold to the Western Maryland Railroad its interest in the canal for $155,000. In April, 1924, another freshet tore the banks so cruelly that funds sufficient to make repairs were not to be had, and so the old waterway at last gave up the ghost. Considering its dreadful financial difficulties throughout its entire career, it is remarkable that it lived so long.

CHAPTER XXV

THE OHIO CANALS

AMONG the internal improvement ideas which engaged the busy mind of Washington was that one of connecting the Ohio River with Lake Erie by a canal; and even Thomas Jefferson, though he seldom favored anything originated or approved by Washington, thought such a connection highly desirable. It was Thomas Worthington, a senator from Ohio who, when the Chesapeake and Delaware Canal was asking Congress for help, introduced the resolution which brought about Gallatin's Report of 1808.

The first known propaganda for canals in Ohio was put forth by Ethan Allen Brown of Cincinnati, then judge of the Superior Court. In 1816 he corresponded with De Witt Clinton and discussed the matter among his neighbors and political associates. He succeeded in arousing no little interest, and within a few years essays and letters to the newspapers were being written on the subject. When Worthington became Governor he wrote to Secretary of the Treasury Crawford (in 1817), urging the desirability of a canal between the Ohio River and the lake.

Judge Brown was elected Governor in 1818, and in his inaugural address made a strong appeal for canals. The first official mention of the subject occurred in his first message to the Legislature. So fanatical did he appear to the old fogies and to his personal enemies that the whole Ohio canal idea was dubbed by them "Brown's Folly." His first attempt to have a canal commission appointed was thwarted by these opponents, and for a long time nothing could be done.

Old Towpaths

Finally in 1822 he succeeded in getting a commission appointed to study the problem, and the report of these men was a telling argument on his side of the question. It could not be denied that most of the people in Ohio, though dwelling on some of the richest land on the continent, were miserably poor, being held back by lack of transportation. Ohio flour was selling in Cincinnati for $3.50 per barrel; in New York it brought $8.00. With a canal across Ohio, it could be shipped to New York for $1.70, leaving a profit of $2.80. One hundred and thirty thousand barrels of flour were inspected in Cincinnati in 1818–19. If this had all been sold in New York there would have been $364,000 profit for Miami Valley farmers and millers.

New York was in every way a preferable market to New Orleans. Going southward, Ohio boatmen must encounter the dangers of the falls of the Ohio, or else the cost of trans-shipping there—to say nothing of other shoals, snags and so on. Furthermore, the whole Mississippi Valley boated its products down to New Orleans in the spring and early summer, and when the trader from Ohio brought his ark to that port, he often found the market glutted, and might be compelled to wait for weeks to get better prices. "To leave one's property at New Orleans is to abandon it to destruction; to wait for higher prices is to incur the dangers of an unwholesome climate. One must ship his flour or sell at a sacrifice—ofttimes at a price that will not pay the cost of freight and charges."

It was believed that a canal across Ohio would not cost more than $2,500,000, and that its revenue would pay for it in six years. It was also hopefully suggested that the job might be done without extra taxation, as it was thought that the Federal Government would donate public lands on which the necessary funds could be raised by sale or loan.

A survey was authorized, and $6,000 appropriated to pay the expenses of it. James Geddes was called from the Erie, and surveyed 900 miles of lines in eight months. Five

The Ohio Canals

routes were tentatively selected for the lake-to-river canal: via Mahoning and Grand Rivers; Cuyahoga and Muskingum; Scioto and Sandusky; Black and Muskingum; and Maumee and Miami. Any of these was said to be entirely

THE OHIO CANALS

practicable. But now arose the usual clamor from every section of the State, demanding that its interests be considered in selecting the route. It was evident that if the densely populated sections were not favored, their votes would defeat the whole project. At one time the delightful sugges-

Old Towpaths

tion was made that the greatest number of people would be rendered happy by building the canal diagonally across the State from the northeastern corner to the southwestern, terminating it at Cincinnati—a route topographically impracticable.

For three years Ohio studied the subject and made additional surveys. But it must be admitted that in no other State was action brought about so quickly and surely. Less than nine years from the time of Judge Brown's first agitation, only seven years from the time of his first official suggestion, the Legislature passed the canal bill in February, 1825. The route finally chosen was a compromise. It left Lake Erie via the Cuyahoga, touched the Muskingum, then turned west to the Scioto and followed that stream to the Ohio at Portsmouth. This lengthened the line considerably, but served an important territory. Cincinnati and the Miami Valley were influential, and if the line were to be located elsewhere, it was necessary to appease them. So the act also provided for a canal along the Miami-Maumee route from Cincinnati up to Dayton, with the promise that at some future time it should be extended to the Maumee and the Lake.

Considering the frontier condition of Ohio, the task she had undertaken was colossal. The population was not over 700,000. The total taxable valuation of all property, real and personal, in the State in 1826 was $57,982,640; the latest estimate of the cost of the canals was $5,715,203, or nearly 10 per cent of the total property valuation. The figures were staggering, but the majority of the people wanted canals, and the unfortunate experiences of Indiana, Illinois and other States had not yet occurred to serve as a warning.

Above all, Ohio was fortunate in having a wise and honest management of the financing of her canal system. There was a notable scarcity of fraud and scandal in the building of the State works, and no hint of either in the finance department. The two most prominent and able canal

IN EARLY DAYS CORN WAS SOMETIMES HAULED FIFTY MILES TO BE SHIPPED BY THE OHIO AND ERIE CANAL FROM CHILLICOTHE

The Ohio Canals

commissioners were Micajah T. Williams of Cincinnati and Alfred Kelley of Cleveland, leading Fund Commissioner. Kelley left a good law practice from purely patriotic motives to accept the State job, which paid $3.00 a day. He proved to be not only a good executive in the canal work, but a financial wizard as well.

The canal act created a fund which was to consist of such appropriations, grants and donations as might be made by the State and individuals, of moneys raised by the sale of State stock and of the taxes pledged as security for the interest on the stock. The commissioners were authorized to borrow certain specified sums in exchange for which they were to issue certificates of stock redeemable at the pleasure of the State between 1850 and 1875. It was supposed that long before the canals were completed to their full length the tolls on the portions in operation would go far towards paying the cost of building.

The $400,000 worth of State stock issued in 1825 had to be sold at 97½; but thereafter for several years the stock issues sold at par. No time was lost in getting to work at the job. The authorizing act was passed in February, 1825; on July 4 the first excavation was made on the main or Ohio and Erie Canal, at its summit level.

The State was determined to make it a memorable occasion, and so no less a personage than De Witt Clinton was invited to deliver the leading oration and lift the first spadeful of earth. The Erie Canal was then on the verge of completion, and Clinton had become one of the great men of America. He accepted, and reached Cleveland on the last day of June. His progress thence to Newark was one continuous ovation. The ceremony was performed at the Licking summit level, three miles west of Newark, and was attended by a huge crowd. People rode and drove scores of miles to be present, some even coming from the farthest corners of the State. Clinton made an eloquent address, then broke the sod and lifted the first shovelful of

Old Towpaths

earth. Governor Jeremiah Morrow of Ohio lifted the second, and then ensued an almost undignified scuffle among the other prominent men for the honor of lifting the third.

STORAGE.

MIAMI CANAL, Piqua, Ohio:

N. GREENHAM,

Respectfully informs country merchants and all those at a distance, that he will

RECEIVE & FORWARD,

All goods consigned to his care, from Piqua to and from Cincinnati and elsewhere, his warehouse being on the corner of the Basin, more convenient for landing, and unloading free from wharfage to all owners of Boats.

Due care and despatch will be used, and prompt attention paid to all goods which may be placed under his care.

Piqua, July 5, 1837.

Courtesy J. F. Hubbard and John H. Rayner, Piqua, Ohio
A CANAL SHIPPING AGENT'S ADVERTISEMENT, 1837

Distinguished New Yorkers and Ohioans all seized spades and filled the first barrow full of earth, and a militia captain of Chillicothe proudly took the handles, trundled it away

The Ohio Canals

and dumped it over a bank. So happy were the spectators over the thought of their release from poverty that many wept. Caleb Atwater, an early historian of Ohio, will even have it that Clinton wept, too.

Later, Governor Clinton was escorted by a large cavalcade to Columbus, where he was dined and exchanged orations again with Governor Morrow. The two Governors then moved on to Springfield, where there was another dinner and more speaking; then to Middletown, where Clinton broke ground for the Miami Canal on July 21.

Work on the two lines, especially the main canal, went forward with great celerity. David S. Bates of the Erie had been engaged as chief engineer, and Nathan S. Roberts, also from the Erie, was consulting engineer for a time. By November, 2,000 men were at work north of the Licking summit. A village of several dozen shanties was erected for their own use by Irish laborers near the falls of the Cuyahoga; this was the beginning of the present city of Akron. In the following season 3,000 teams of horses were at work on that portion of the canal. While a considerable number of Irish laborers had come from the Erie and some Germans from Pennsylvania, the greater part of those who dug the first Ohio Canals were Anglo-Saxon countrymen, mostly farmers' sons, from the vicinity. They earned from $6 to $10 per month—the standard wage during the first three years was $8 for 26 dry working days, or 30¾ cents for a day lasting from sunrise to sunset. To many of these boys, it was the first opportunity of their lives to earn real money. The work was carried on as nearly as possible the year round. Their pay stopped in bad weather, and it might take all winter to make two months' salary, but the job was regarded as being worth while even at that. Some of them worked on the canal only in their own neighborhood and boarded at home, so that they were able to utilize the bad weather by husking corn and doing other indoor work on their own farms.

Old Towpaths

The men not at home were lodged in rough shanties, and for some time received a regular allowance of whisky as a part of their rations. Some writers assert that the allowance was a "jigger"—a small cup containing not more than a gill—per day; but there seems to be good evidence that in some districts they received no less than four per day—at sunrise, at ten o'clock, at noon and before supper. To say nothing of the evil effects of the liquor, this consumed a great deal of valuable time. Kelley and Williams, the two leading commissioners, finally put a stop to the practice, causing considerable grumbling but a generally higher efficiency.

As always, the difficulties of construction proved to be greater than expected. It cost more to quarry the stone than had been estimated; and the water at first leaked out of the channels in many places through gravelly soil as fast as poured in. There had been sharp competition for contracts on the canals, many eastern contractors making bids at figures which meant a loss; and a few of them tried to get even by using poor material or misappropriating funds. Within a year after the work was begun, several of them absconded, often leaving their workmen's pay far in arrears.

To Twentieth Century readers, the pettiness of some of the contracts of those days seems very quaint and amusing. Many citizens whose regular occupation was farming or storekeeping took contracts to build a section of canal near their homes. A typical example was that of Abram Garfield, father of President Garfield, who had a section about half a mile in length in Tuscarawas County. With his force of twenty men he completed his contract in about a year. The men were housed in shanties similar to those used elsewhere, and Mrs. Garfield, the contractor's wife, furnished them board at the family log cabin. She had a good voice and often entertained the men after supper in the evening with her singing.

Notwithstanding the enthusiasm of the majority in the

The Ohio Canals

State, there were not a few objectors. Of course many not on the canal routes were disgruntled. Some said the State would be forced to borrow so heavily that the debt would never be paid; some railed at the hint of a tax levy to pay interest on the loans; some thought their lands would be damaged and that an undesirable class of people would be brought in by the canals. The antis were actually in the majority in Canton, and when there was talk of bringing the canal through that town, they fought it off. The result was that it passed eight miles west of Canton, where it built up the town of Massillon with a rapidity which caused gnashing of teeth in the now repentant rival village.

Congress granted to Indiana in 1827 a large quantity of land to aid in the building of the Wabash and Erie Canal, and Ohio asked for similar aid. Congress thereupon made a grant in 1828 of 500,000 acres and also donated for the exclusive benefit of the Miami and Erie Canal from Dayton north to the lake, 464,000 acres. Ohio also received some land on account of the Wabash and Erie Canal, 18 miles of which lay within her boundaries and must be built by her. This brought the total of Government land received by the State to more than 1,230,000 acres. The State realized from sales of this land $2,257,487. Individuals and corporations along the route even donated more than $500,000 to the cause.

But meanwhile, costs were rising and work was slowed up. Malaria and other ills disabled many workmen and frightened others away in 1827. The demand for labor on the Pennsylvania Canals and the national road drew more away and began to raise the wage scale. Hundreds of miles of canals were under way in the East and labor was growing scarce. Furthermore, as transportation via the lake and the Erie Canal was improved and as sections of the Ohio canals were completed, the facilities for reaching market were so much better that prices of provisions rose all over Ohio, which added still more to the cost of the public works.

Old Towpaths

Not only this, but not a few citizens learned the knack of demanding exorbitant prices for supplies.

In 1827 the canal boat, *State of Ohio,* of about 45 tons' burden, was launched at Akron, and on July 4 it made the first journey made on an Ohio canal, traveling from that village to Cleveland, 37 miles distant. Even in the few months left of that season the little section of completed canal collected $1,500 in tolls. That same year water was turned into the lower portion of the Miami Canal between Middletown and Hartwell's Basin, near Cincinnati, and some boats passed through. During the following March boats began entering Cincinnati. The first boat reached Dayton in January, 1829. In 1828 the Ohio and Erie collected $4,000 in tolls and the Miami and Erie $8,000. For the following year the figures reached $27,000 and $20,941 respectively.

On August 21, 1830, the first boat arrived at Coshocton and remained there several days, the continuous center of an admiring crowd. In September, 1831, a boat launched at Circleville passed through the 11-mile branch from Lockbourne to Columbus, entering that city amid artillery salutes and wild enthusiasm. On October 7 of that year the channel was open from Cleveland to Chillicothe, 250 miles. Work on the southern portion was delayed by the epidemic of cholera in 1832, but it was declared open to Portsmouth on December 1.

The Ohio and Erie was 308 miles in length, had 1,206 feet of lockage, and had cost $7,904,971. It had 2 summit levels. The Licking summit began 116 miles from Portsmouth and was 413 feet above the level of the Ohio River. Thence the canal descended 160 feet to Dresden Junction, where the Muskingum Canal later began: then it rose again 238 feet to the Portage summit, which was 78 feet higher than the Licking summit. This level, 9 miles long, ended near Akron, and the drop of 395 feet to Lake Erie was accomplished by 41 locks in 35 miles.

From "Picturesque America," by William Cullen Bryant
THE MIAMI AND ERIE CANAL IN CINCINNATI IN THE SEVENTIES, KNOWN AFFECTIONATELY TO OLD CINCINNATIANS AS "THE RHINE"

Courtesy of the Akron Chamber of Commerce
AKRON AND THE PENNSYLVANIA AND OHIO CANAL IN 1865
Main Street now covers the canal right of way, the water of the stream still flowing through a conduit under the pavement

The Ohio Canals

Both the Ohio and Erie and the Miami Canal had been built on a wise plan. The bottom width was never less than 26 feet, nor was the surface width less than 40 feet nor the depth less than 4 feet; but wherever possible without greatly increasing the cost, the channel had been made much larger, often from 50 to 150 feet wide and 5 to 10 feet deep. Thus 60- and 80-ton boats, and even larger, could be accommodated from the very beginning.

The benefits of the canals began to be seen long before they were fully completed. The Ohio and Erie had not yet gotten half way across the State when the price of wheat along its northern portion rose from 25 cents to 75 cents per bushel. In November, 1830, the *Scioto Gazette* of Chillicothe said that the canal "has reduced the price of salt from 87 to 50 cents a bushel, and reduced carriage on every article imported from abroad in a corresponding ratio. It has advanced the price of flour from $3 to $4 per barrel, and wheat from 40 to 65 cents per bushel. It has raised the price of real estate and opened a ready market for it, and has increased the business and hustle of the town fifty percent." Former opponents of the canal, who were nearly all large taxpayers, suddenly found their viewpoint changed. One of the strongest objectors now admitted that his boys with a yoke of oxen and a farm cart hauled enough potatoes to Circleville and sold them at 40 cents a bushel to pay his year's taxes and more.

The agricultural activity of the Miami Valley even at that early day is shown by a report in Niles' Register in 1831 that "In March and April last, about 58,000 barrels of flour, 7,000 do. whiskey, 12,000 do. pork, 18,000 kegs of lard, 750 hhds. of hams and 1,800,000 lbs. bacon passed down the Miami Canal."

The canals were the making of such towns as Akron, Massillon, Newark, Coshocton, Chillicothe, Circleville, Dayton, Hamilton and many others. On the other hand, the leaving of Middlebury, in Summit County, off the route proved the deathblow of that promising village. There were great numbers of freight boats owned by citizens along the line—it is said that almost every town and village owned from one to a hundred—and their profits added to the prosperity of the town. There were 84 boats owned in Chillicothe around 1840, and 420 in the first 100 miles south of Cleveland. Even persons at some distance from the canal owned boats.

In 1832 the income of the Ohio and Erie was $79,982. In the following year, the entire line being open through to Portsmouth, the receipts rose to $136,555. The Miami Canal that year collected over $50,000; and the revenue on both lines steadily increased from year to year. The fact soon became evident that the Ohio and Erie was valuable chiefly for local business. Its indirect course and great length across the State operated against its value for through traffic, and the water supply for the Portage summit level was frequently inadequate.

Meanwhile, with the Miami Canal completed only from Dayton to Cincinnati, large portions of western Ohio were still unprovided with easy communication to the Ohio River and Lake Erie. One result of this condition is seen in the report that wheat was wagoned from farms within 30 or 40 miles of Cincinnati to Chillicothe, because of the better demand at the latter place. The demands of western Ohio were recognized in 1831, when the extension of the Miami to Lake Erie was authorized. Work was not begun, however, until 1833. The canal was theoretically completed as far as the Maumee River in 1836, but it was not in condition to use, and was not open to Toledo until 1843.

In 1835–36 the Legislature was carried away by the general prosperity mania then prevalent throughout the country, and began spending the State's money freely in extensions of the canal system and in assistance to corporations desiring to build other canals, turnpikes and even railroads. There

The Ohio Canals

was some excuse for a feeling of opulence in Ohio, for business was increasing steadily on the main canal, the tolls in 1836 reaching the sum of $211,823. It was reported to Congress that in 1835 there was shipped from Ohio to New York via the Erie Canal 86,000 barrels of flour, 98,000 bushels of wheat, 2,500,000 staves and other products. A considerable portion of this came out of the Ohio and Erie Canal. The Welland Canal was now also giving a fine outlet into Canada for Ohio's products.

Some of the new construction in which the State now invested money seemed at the time highly desirable; the branch to the Hocking Valley coal fields, for example. This vast mineral wealth lay only a comparatively short distance off the main canal. The Hocking shipped its first coal in 1830, when two wagonloads were hauled to Columbus; but little was mined until a canal was built along the valley. A corporation completed a branch canal to Lancaster on the Hocking in 1838; then it was taken over by the State and extended down to Athens, 56 miles in all. This branch would have been a profitable one had it not been frequently torn to pieces by floods.

The Walhonding branch was much more difficult to justify. It started northwest from the main canal near Coshocton, ran 25 miles and reached nowhere in particular. It was of benefit to its territory as a grain carrier, but it lost money persistently for the State.

The canalization of the Muskingum, a much more useful work, was also begun in 1836. Leaving the main canal at Dresden Junction, the navigation continued down the river to its mouth near Marietta. The locks were made 36 feet wide and 180 feet long, for the accommodation of steamboats.

The Warren County Canal was another of the white elephants. A company was chartered in 1830 to connect Lebanon with the Miami Canal at Middletown. The work was still in an unfinished condition in 1836 when the State

Old Towpaths

took it over and finished it, expending in all $217,500. After a few years of unprofitable operation, it was abandoned.

It was in 1836 also that the State began aiding private corporations by subscribing generously to their capital stock. One such company was the Cincinnati and White Water, which was organized to build a canal connecting Cincinnati with Indiana's White Water Canal. From Cincinnati it followed the Ohio River westward for several miles, then turned away from it, crossed the Great Miami River, and joined the White Water Canal above Cleves. This canal was 25 miles long and its cost was $800,000, of which amount Ohio subscribed $150,000 and the City of Cincinnati $40,000. It was completed in November, 1843.

The most ambitious private canal in the State was the Ohio and Pennsylvania. This was talked of as early as 1825. As soon as the Ohio and Erie was located, the suggestion was made that a link was needed, connecting its northerly portion with the Ohio River at or near Pittsburgh. A highway would thus be established from the main Pennsylvania Canal to Lake Erie. Philadelphia merchants were keenly interested in this project, as it would open up northern Ohio to them, and as they believed, give them an equal chance with New York at the business of that territory. It was calculated that by this route Cleveland would be 240 miles nearer to Philadelphia than to New York by the Erie; and there would be a great advantage over the Erie, as the ice left the lake at Cleveland two or three weeks earlier in spring than at Buffalo.

In 1836, while the Ohio Legislature was in its most princely mood, it was induced to subscribe for one-third of the entire stock issue of this canal. With this assistance the company was able to open its channel to Akron, where it connected with the Ohio and Erie, in 1840.

The greatest fiasco among the canals of Ohio was the Sandy and Beaver. It, too, was intended as "a short cut

The Ohio Canals

for eastbound freight," but rather from central than from northern Ohio. It ran from Bolivar on the Ohio Canal, 40 miles south of Akron, directly east to the Ohio River, 40 miles below Pittsburgh. It was begun in 1835, but not completed until 1846, when railroads were already invading Ohio. It was 73 miles in length. It is said that the only boat which ever made the entire passage through it was one sent by the contractors in order that they might collect their pay. The aggregate loss to the stockholders was $2,000,000. Canton wasted several thousand dollars in an attempt to build a branch connecting with the Sandy and Beaver.

Troy and Piqua had a great Fourth of July celebration in 1837, when the first boat reached them on the Miami Canal, bringing as a guest General William Henry Harrison. But the shadow of that year's panic was hanging over all the canals of Ohio, bringing with it the evil results of those wild years, 1835–36. The connection between the Wabash and Erie near Fort Wayne and the unfinished Miami and Erie near Defiance had just been begun, and work was going forward on the latter canal along the Maumee River. In May, 1838, contractors employing thousands of men in this district had received no money from the State for months, some for a year, and were in a desperate condition. The only pay they could give their men was some Michigan wildcat money which they had borrowed, but which rapidly depreciated and became worthless. There was general distress throughout the whole section, and canal work was stopped entirely for a time. The State could afford only meager temporary relief, and thus matters dragged along miserably enough for several years. .To make matters worse, railroads were now coming to threaten the canals' prosperity.

By 1840 Ohio's credit had fallen so low that her canal stock could not be sold in New York, London or anywhere else at any price. In her extremity the State appealed again

Old Towpaths

to Kelley for guidance, and he exhibited patriotism of a high order by undertaking the disagreeable job. Receipts of the Ohio and Erie were still increasing, reaching $452,000 in 1840, while the Miami turned in $74,000 for the same year; but these were not sufficient to pay the current bills. Contractors were clamoring for thousands of dollars long past due; and late in 1841 there were $700,000 in loans and interest to be paid, and no money with which to pay it. Dams were being built for the great supply reservoir of the Miami Canal in Mercer and Auglaize Counties, and the farmers whose lands were about to be overflowed had not yet been paid for their property. There were numerous other debts.

In 1841 Kelley went to New York with the heroic purpose of trying to borrow more money and save the credit of the State. But the country had not yet recovered from the second panic in 1839, and Kelley found the western States in particularly low repute in the East. Indiana, Illinois, Michigan and other States had gotten themselves into a serious pickle on account of their internal improvements. All had defaulted in interest payments and Michigan had repudiated a part of her debt. Fortunately for Ohio, the fund commissioners had striven to keep her paper out of the hands of speculators and in the possession of permanent investors.

By February, 1842, Kelley had succeeded in borrowing sufficient money to carry the State through the crisis, but so low was Ohio's credit sunk that he could not borrow it in the name of the State; it was loaned to him personally, and he pledged his own resources as security. The only expedient left for raising the money was taxation—a bitter pill to citizens who had expected the canals to pay all the expenses of government. It was made still more bitter by the fact that since the collapse of the boom of 1836 wheat had dropped back to 40 and 50 cents a bushel, and other products in the same ratio. But Kelley within a few years

The Ohio Canals

had the satisfaction of seeing Ohio's stocks quoted again at par.

In May, 1843, that portion of the Miami Canal along the Maumee River was completed, also the extension of the Wabash and Erie to the Indiana line, and boats at last began running through from Toledo to Fort Wayne and other Indiana towns. So near was northwestern Ohio still to the primitive that the upper portion of the Miami Canal "was built literally through and amongst Indian villages and wigwams." At the village of White Raccoon, a Miami chief, the log cabin of Cha-pine, the tribal orator, was found to be squarely in the line of the canal. With many regrets, the engineers had the cabin torn down, moved and set up again at the expense of the State, but much to the annoyance of the orator. This Indian background gave old settlers an excuse to declare to tenderfeet in later years that when the canal was first built, "you couldn't git off a boat and take a few steps inter the woods without gittin' shot full of arrers."

That portion of the Miami Canal south from the Maumee to the summit level could not yet be used because the Grand Reservoir which was to supply water for it was not yet completed. This reservoir has already been mentioned as having been begun in 1837. It was formed by two dams, in some places 25 feet high, one two miles, the other nearly four miles in length. The reservoir thus formed was nine miles long and from two to four miles wide, and for many years enjoyed the reputation of being the largest artificial lake in the world. So hastily was the work done that the trees submerged by it were merely girdled and allowed to die standing, while even log cabins and fences were engulfed whole.

The citizens of the neighborhood had always held a grudge against the reservoir, especially those who had been evicted and had been compelled to wait a long time before receiving pay for their lands. Now it was believed that the standing water and decaying wood were causing disease in the vicinity, and for these reasons wide breaches were cut in both dams in 1843. It cost thousands of dollars to repair the damage; but though the rioters were known, no grand jury would find indictments against them.

The lake was finally completed in 1845, and the first boat went through from Toledo to Dayton in June. The canal was 248 miles in length, with 25 miles of navigable feeders. It had cost $8,062,680. Its revenue increased rapidly for several years, being $105,640 in 1843 and $233,527 in 1846.

In 1845, when the Miami was completed, the State owed $4,500,000, which was a serious matter for a young State in those days. However, when one considers that the canals had actually cost more than $16,000,000, the balance of debt remaining in 1845 appears not so bad. The grants of land by the Federal Government and donations by others probably reduced the State's net expenditure on the works to $13,000,000.

Between 1845 and 1857 were the halcyon days of the Ohio canals, though some of the minor lines suffered fearfully from flood damage during that period. Railroads were spreading their webs far and wide, but immigration was filling up the country so rapidly and the prosperity and productivity of the State were increasing so fast that the waterways had not yet begun to feel the railroad competition. In both 1847 and 1848 the total receipts of the State canals were well over $754,000. Packet boats were doing a good business and at high speed—if we are to believe their time tables. An 80-hour schedule was advertised for the 308 miles between Cleveland and Portsmouth; and 24 hours between Columbus and Portsmouth. The Miami was noted for its fast boats. This canal, though 60 miles shorter than the Ohio and Erie, was about to become the more important of the State's two big canals. In 1848 the tolls were $325,-297, and very nearly 4,000 boats cleared from Toledo. Junction, the hamlet where the Wabash and Erie left the

Drawing by courtesy of J. F. Hubbard, Piqua, Ohio

OUTLET LOCK AT ST. MARYS, OHIO, FROM GRAND RESERVOIR INTO FEEDER OF THE MIAMI AND ERIE CANAL.

The Ohio Canals

Miami, became so important that many people moved there from Fort Wayne, believing that it would outstrip the Indiana town in a short time.

The first canal steamboat in the West appeared on the Miami and Erie. In 1847 there was much talk in the newspapers of the remarkably fast travel possible between New York and St. Louis, the trip frequently being made "in the short space of eight days." One went by steamboat from New York to Albany, thence by the railroad cars to Buffalo, from there to Toledo by "one of the floating palaces of Lake Erie," from Toledo to Lafayette "by one of Doyle & Dickey's fine packets," and thence to St. Louis in three days' time "by one of I. & P. Voorhees' fine post coaches."

The portions of the two main canals in southern Ohio were able to keep open as a rule ten months in the year. In 1838 the southern portion of the Ohio and Erie was closed only between January 2 and 23. But there were many happenings not so auspicious. The canals followed the banks of streams throughout the greater part of their courses—streams which were peculiarly liable to disastrous freshets. Occasionally boats were detained by washouts or broken locks for six or seven weeks. At times forty or fifty boats might be seen tied up, waiting for repairs to be made. Some of the minor canals suffered heavily by flood. In 1847 and 1848 the Hocking lateral was put out of commission for weeks by repeated freshets which broke the banks in dozens of places. The Cincinnati and White Water suffered much disaster about the same time. The great flood of December, 1846, on the White Water swept away the feeder dam and about a mile of the canal at Harrison. The channel had scarcely been rebuilt when the trouble was repeated in 1847. The canal thereby lost the better part of two seasons' business.

In 1851 the traffic on the State canals reached its peak. The Ohio and Erie collected $432,711 that year, the Miami and Erie $351,897; and this, with small contributions from

Old Towpaths

the Hocking and Walhonding, brought the total income to $799,024. But that year the Pittsburgh, Fort Wayne and Chicago Railroad was opened across the Ohio and Erie's territory and began to cut into its business. In the following year, what with the loss of traffic and the reduction in tolls, the Ohio and Erie's income was only $208,937, while the Miami's was $308,984. Thereafter the Ohio and Erie never again approached the Miami in revenue.

The decline of the canals was appallingly rapid. Between 1850 and 1860 Ohio surpassed all other States in the building of railroads. There were 375 miles of railroad in the State in 1850; in 1860 there were 2,946. The canals hauled rails and even locomotives for the great mechanism which was destroying them. In 1856 the total revenue of the canals in its rapid decline reached $321,073, while expenditures were $398,378. The breaking out of the Civil War decreased the traffic still more.

Governor Medill in 1856 called attention to the fact that Ohio owned $570,000 in canal corporation stocks and $2,280,796 in stock of railroads and turnpikes. These he advocated selling for whatever they would bring, even if it were no more than $800,000; but no one was willing to offer even that much.

Next came talk among the legislators of abandoning the canals. Up to 1860 they had paid the State $14,000,000 in gross or $7,000,000 in net revenue. They had been the greatest factor in the State's growth during the quarter-century between 1825 and 1850—and that quarter-century was one of the most significant in Ohio's history. Now, however, the waterways had seemingly had their day, and in a mad haste to get rid of them, the Legislature leased them in 1861 to a company which was to pay only $20,075 per year rental. The lease ran for ten years, and was then renewed.

The lessors did not keep the canals in repair, and in 1877 threw up their lease and refused to pay the rent because the

The Ohio Canals

Legislature had permitted the city of Hamilton to fill up part of a basin. Meanwhile, the Legislature had been crippling the canals at other points. In 1863 the outlet of the Miami and Erie in Cincinnati, including ten locks, was given to the city, which promptly passed it on to a railroad company. The railroad built tracks over the canal, turned the water through a conduit to the river, and that portion was forever lost. In the following year several miles of the other end of the canal in Toledo were given up to that city. In 1872 several miles of the Ohio and Erie in Cleveland were granted to the city, to the great detriment of the canal.

Meanwhile the private canals were passing out of existence. In 1854 the controlling interest in the Pennsylvania and Ohio fell into the hands of stockholders in the new Cleveland and Mahoning Railroad, a competitor. Tolls were immediately raised to a rate which killed the business. The canal became dilapidated and noisome, its banks were cut in 1868 and again in 1874, and soon afterwards a portion of it was permanently closed.

The Cincinnati and White Water was killed by the destruction of its Indiana connection, the White Water Canal, and by a railroad built alongside it in the '50's. In 1863 its channel was sold to the Cincinnati and Indianapolis Railroad for their right of way and depot.

The lower portion of the Hocking Canal was practically destroyed by a flood in 1873 and was never repaired. The remainder was abandoned in 1894, as was all but six miles of the Walhonding in 1896. The Muskingum improvements were sold to the National Government in 1887 for $1,500,000.

Although nothing was done to encourage it, the Miami clung to life most tenaciously of all the Ohio Canals. In 1897 its receipts were $97,327, almost as great as in 1843, when the canals were supreme, and greater than it had collected in any year between 1860 and 1879. In 1901 a

Old Towpaths

company was formed to build a track along its bank and tow boats by electric motor. Work was begun that year; but suspicion arose that the company's real object was to acquire the right of way for a railroad, and there was much agitation against it. The Miami was still doing a good business. Its receipts in 1903 were $71,229, those of the Ohio and Erie less than half that amount. Popular opposition was so great that the State refused to give the desired lease to the towing company, and it passed out of existence. But not long afterwards that portion of the canal within the city of Cincinnati was granted to an interurban car line for its track, completely obliterating the southern terminus.

About this time the Legislature made a feeble gesture towards repairing and enlarging the canals, but nothing of consequence was done, and the decay continued. Within a few years more, only isolated sections of the channels contained water, mostly used for power purposes. Many miles have now been totally obliterated.

As in New York, the canals between 1820 and 1860 gave Ohio its greatest impetus towards its present high position in the Union. In 1835 the taxable value of real estate and personal property in the State was given as $94,000,000; in 1859 it was $876,500,000. Between 1820 and 1857 the population of Cincinnati increased from 2,602 to 200,000; of Cleveland from 400 to 60,000; of Dayton from 1,139 to 25,000; of Toledo from 500 to 14,000—all canal towns. The achievements of the canals in building up the State were far beyond all expectations or predictions; but because they did not pay for themselves within a few years and even relieve the State of taxation, they were regarded as a great disappointment, and were grossly neglected. As in other States, the discriminative competition of railroads and the railroad influence in the legislative lobbies were sufficiently powerful to ruin great and useful public works.

CHAPTER XXVI

THE INDIANA CANALS

ONE of Washington's dreams was the connection of the Ohio River with the seaboard—on the one hand via the Potomac River, on the other hand via Lake Erie and the St. Lawrence. He made his usual investigation into the topography of the western country, and in a letter to Secretary of War Knox he mentions the very short portage between the upper waters of the Wabash and the Maumee near the site of Fort Wayne as the most feasible point for water communication between the Ohio and Lake Erie.

One Captain McAfee, who wrote a history of the War of 1812 in the West, spoke of the portage as being only seven or eight miles through a marshy tract whence water flowed towards both streams. "A canal will at some future day unite these rivers," said he. Captain James Riley, a Government engineer sent to survey lands around Fort Wayne in 1818, suggested the importance of a canal, which he thought need not be more than six miles long. He even made a rough survey of the route, but nothing more was done.

Governor Jennings of Indiana in his message of 1818 urged the Legislature to ponder upon a system of roads and canals to facilitate commerce and enhance land values in the State. But not until 1825, when Ohio broke ground for her two great canals, did Indiana begin to exhibit much interest. An Indiana delegate in Congress in 1826 asked for a land grant for internal improvements, but was un-

Old Towpaths

successful. An effort in the Indiana Legislature to procure an appropriation for a canal board and surveys also failed of action.

Meanwhile the White Water Valley in southeastern

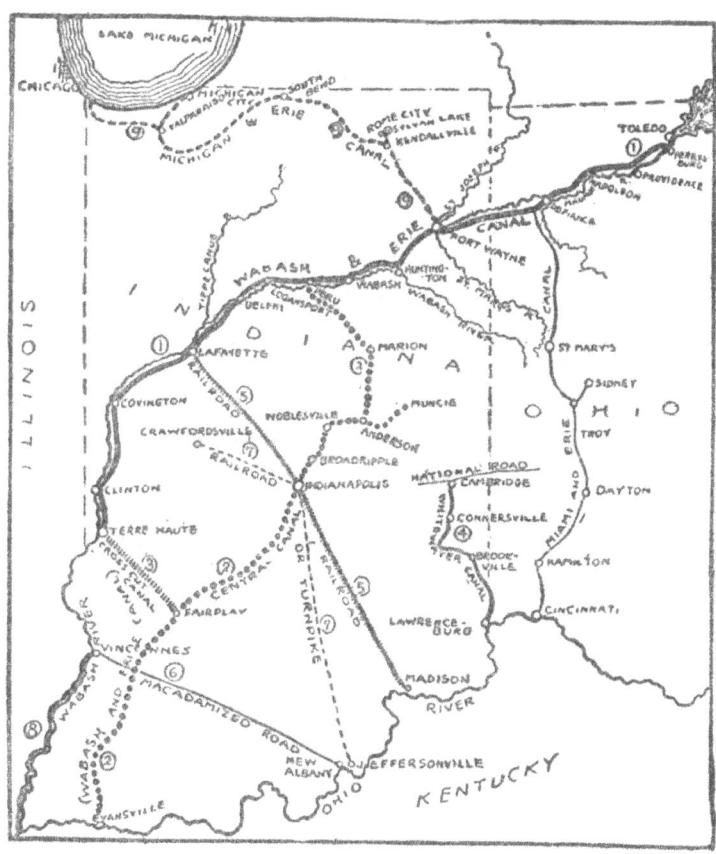

From "History of Fort Wayne" by B. J. Griswold
INDIANA'S GREAT SCHEME OF INTERNAL IMPROVEMENTS

Indiana, the most thickly populated district in the State, was striving for better communication. In 1827 a corporation was chartered to build a canal along the White Water from the Ohio River to Fort Wayne, but accomplished nothing.

The Indiana Canals

In the same year Congress granted to Indiana, to aid in connecting the navigable waters of the Maumee and the Wabash, a strip of land one-half of five sections wide on either side of the proposed canal. Spurred by the upper Wabash settlers, who were kept in poverty by their lack of transportation, the Legislature accepted the grant from the Government and agreed to build the canal. To reach the navigable waters of the two rivers, it must extend down to and past the rapids of the Maumee and down the Wabash at least as far as the mouth of the Tippecanoe.

A board of three canal commissioners was appointed and instructed to employ engineers, locate the canal, select land, lay off town sites and work out a system of financing the job. Indiana's unreadiness for such a project should have been painfully evident, for the State tax levy of the preceding year had brought in all told only $33,000, which barely covered the expenses of Government. But the citizenry cared naught for that. Ohio, New York and everybody else were building successful canals; why should not they? Newspapers and magazines were full of articles about railroads and canals; and Indiana, although poor as poverty itself, was determined to see the job through.

But when the matter of locating the canal came to a focus, no little dissension and petty politics were developed. The southern half of the State could not see how it was going to derive any benefit from the improvement. The White Water country wanted a canal of its own, and threatened obstruction if it did not get one. Another group desired a canal between the Wabash and White River. Governor Ray and others favored railroads. Others called attention to the fact that Ohio was groaning loudly under a burden of taxation as a result of her internal improvement fad.

The upper Wabash citizens became uneasy lest the State forfeit the Government land grant by failure to build the canal within the required time. Indiana had now awakened

Old Towpaths

to the fact that to reach the navigable waters of the Maumee, a portion of the canal must necessarily lie in Ohio. A conference was held between representatives of the two States in Cincinnati in 1829 and an agreement was formulated to the effect that Ohio should build that portion of the canal within her boundary and reimburse herself with the canal lands lying contiguous thereto.

The Indiana Legislature wrestled with the question during 1829 and 1830. There was much sentiment in favor of railroads. But to this propaganda the canal people had a crushing retort; to build railroads would make necessary the buying of rails, locomotives and other material in the East, whereas canals would require only timber and stone, which could be had within the State, and thus their money would be kept at home. The argument was a powerful one, though for the moment it brought about only the ratification of the agreement with Ohio.

During the following winter, sales of canal lands were held at Logansport and Lafayette, but the results were disappointing. Forty-two thousand acres were sold and brought only $75,000, an average of $1.78 per acre, of which one-fourth was cash. Meanwhile Ohio, fearing that the Wabash and Erie would divert much traffic from her own Miami Canal and from Cincinnati, refused for several years to ratify the Cincinnati agreement. She did not finally approve it until 1836, and even then did not begin work. Notwithstanding this fact, a decided canal majority had developed in Indiana, and in 1832 the project was set in motion. An estimate had been prepared, setting the probable cost at $1,081,970. More land was to be sold and the money realized was to be put into the hands of three fund commissioners, who were given power to act. A loan of $200,000 was authorized.

In haste to set the work going, the Board met in Fort Wayne on Washington's Birthday, 1832, and broke ground for the canal amid great rejoicing. The engineering was

The Indiana Canals

entrusted to Jesse L. Williams, who had learned his profession under an Erie engineer, and who had himself built portions of the Ohio canals. At the close of that year 19 miles were under construction, and the Board had $104,673 on hand; but seldom does one find a record of a financial board so incompetent or which performed its functions in so haphazard a manner. Each member collected money and spent it according to his own ideas, often without consulting the others. But the people did not learn of this condition until years later.

Opposition to the canal was disappearing as astounding reports came from New York of the wonderful prosperity brought by the Erie, and in its stead were arising the same desires manifested in New York and Pennsylvania for canals in every unimportant neighborhood.

In 1834 a thousand men were working on the Wabash and Erie, mostly westward from Fort Wayne, Ohio having as yet taken no action towards building the eastern section. The laborers were as usual mostly Irish, divided in about the usual proportion of Corkonians and Ulstermen. A great battle was threatened between these factions at La Gro on one anniversary of the Battle of the Boyne, and the opposing armies were actually on the march when militia reached the scene and dispersed them.

In 1835 the commissioners decided that because of the importance of Lafayette as a steamboat port and commercial center, the canal must be pushed beyond the mouth of the Tippecanoe to that town. During that summer boats reached Huntington from Fort Wayne, but the tolls were still insufficient to pay repair bills, and wooden aqueducts built two or three years were already decaying. Seven hundred and twenty-nine thousand dollars had been spent in construction, and the extension to Lafayette would cost $100,000 more. Had this canal been finished as planned and no other State works attempted, Indiana would have come through in comparative prosperity and happiness. But the

Old Towpaths

great halcyon period of 1835-36 was now upon the land; speculation and promotion were unbalancing the public mind; many sections were demanding improvements, and as sales of public lands were increasing tremendously, there seemed no reason why everybody should not have everything he desired.

Accordingly the Mammoth Internal Improvement Bill was drawn up, with a plum in it for every Jack Horner in the State, and Governor Noble signed it on January 27, 1836. By that mad act Indiana placed her neck in a yoke of debt which was destined to gall her for half a century and to humiliate her in the eyes of the world.

The bill carried appropriations aggregating $13,000,000 —one-sixth of the State's wealth at that time. The Fund Commissioners were instructed to borrow $10,000,000 on twenty-five years' time at 6 per cent—a debt of $20 for every man, woman and child in the State. The following works were authorized:

The White Water Canal; also a canal to connect the White Water with the Central Canal, if practicable; if not, a connecting railroad was to be substituted. For this work $1,400,000 was set aside.

The Central Canal, leaving the Wabash and Erie somewhere between Fort Wayne and Logansport, running via Indianapolis and the forks of White River to Evansville. For this, $3,500,000.

The Wabash and Erie was to be extended from the mouth of Tippecanoe down to Terre Haute and thence via Eel River to the Central Canal. $1,300,000.

A railroad from Madison to Lafayette; a turnpike from New Albany to Vincennes, and a railroad or turnpike from Jeffersonville to Crawfordsville; each to cost $1,300,000. $50,000 was to be spent in improving the Wabash River from its mouth to Vincennes; and finally, a survey was to be made for a canal (if practicable; if not, for a railroad) from the Wabash and Erie near Fort Wayne to Lake

The Indiana Canals

Michigan at Michigan City; this canal to be begun within ten years.

It was freely predicted by Legislators and other orators that within a few years the system would not only pay for itself but that its revenue would take care of all the costs of government and render taxation unnecessary.

The passage of the act was looked upon as virtually bringing on a millennium. In every town which expected any benefit from the improvements, bonfires were built on every street corner and illuminations, bell-ringing, parades,

From "History of Fort Wayne" by B. J. Griswold
WABASH AND ERIE CANAL AQUEDUCT ACROSS ST. MARYS RIVER AT FORT WAYNE

banquets and spread-eagle orations went on for days and even weeks. The whole land rang with praise of the young frontier State. Eastern newspapers made scornful comparisons between her magnificent spirit of enterprise and the somnolence of Massachusetts.

Towns along the canal and railroad routes now joined in the great land speculation mania already prevalent in other parts of the country. Fortunes were made in Evansville and other towns by the shrewd or the lucky gamblers.

The commissioners had been chosen each from a different section of the State, with an eye to securing justice

Old Towpaths

for all; the result now was a scuffle to see who could secure the most and the largest plums for his own district. An engineer-in-chief for the canals and one for the railroads was appointed, and a large corps of minor engineers and surveyors, numbering from seventy-five to a hundred, whose combined salaries ranged from $55,000 to $60,000 yearly. This force later came to be known with bitter humor as "the Eating Brigade."

One of the earliest things done was to send a large surveying party into northern Indiana to settle the question whether a canal or a railroad should be built from Fort Wayne to Lake Michigan. There the party spent months on labor which was perfectly useless to the State. By a general log-rolling agreement among the commissioners, work was begun on small sections of each improvement. No man wanted the other fellow's job any farther advanced than his own. A slight concession was made in favor of the influential White Water Valley. Work was begun on its canal in September, 1836, and in the spring of 1839 a few boats were running as far as Brookville.

With so much jealousy, incompetence and bargaining taking place in the State's business, it is not to be wondered at that discontent and sharp criticism were presently rife among both people and Legislators. There were loud demands that some one line be selected and completed first; but of course it was impossible to agree on which line that should be. Labor was scarce, other States engaged in similar work drawing heavily from the visible supply, and the contractors were keeping conditions unsettled by luring the best hands away from each other. Rumors of enormous expenditures began to reach the people. The report came forth showing that during the first year of the big project $3,827,000 had been spent—and there seemed little to show for it. In 1837 the financial situation grew shaky. Banks were failing in the East, land sales slowed up, money grew scarce. Williams's report in December showed that more

The Indiana Canals

than $1,600,000 had been spent that year. Boats were running on the Wabash and Erie to Peru. Williams now estimated that it would cost $23,000,000 to complete the improvements. The interest on this amount at 5 per cent would be $1,150,000 annually, of which he believed the tolls would supply $475,000; for the rest he suggested a special tax—unpleasant words for the ears of people who had been told only two years ago that the system would pay for itself and even eliminate taxation.

During 1838, $1,693,000 was spent, and in his message to the Legislature in December of that year Governor Wallace, who had been overflowing with optimism a year ago, now grew doleful as he contemplated the State balance sheet. The interest then due was $193,350; the revenue from taxation only $45,000. "If this consideration does not startle us," said he, "it should at least awaken us." The Legislature now contemplated reorganizing the Board and ordering only one line built at a time, but matters had gone so far that even this was futile. Moreover, the panic of 1839 was now upon them. The Fund Commission could not pay their bills, and in August all work was suspended. The facts which the State then had to face were the ugliest in all its history.

"The policy of constructing the work and parts of works simultaneously was so well pursued that no considerable part of any work was completed or fit for use," said the *Tippecanoe Journal* of Lafayette in 1841. "There lies the system still, its unfinished excavations, embankments, locks, culverts, aqueducts and bridges hastening to ruin."

The situation was indeed disheartening. The Wabash and Erie had crept on to and beyond Logansport, but Ohio had not yet built the eastern extension, and without terminals the canal could not pay revenue. The White Water Canal had built the most mileage, but was still incomplete. On the Central Canal 750 men were working when the stop order came. Eight miles of the section from Indianapolis north had been completed, sixteen just south of Indianapolis and

Old Towpaths

nineteen on Pigeon Creek. These, together with the cross cut from Terre Haute to Eel River had cost $1,820,026.

Courtesy Hal C. Phelps, Miami County Historical Society, Peru, Indiana
BILL OF LADING FROM NEW YORK TO PERU, INDIANA, 1843, VIA ERIE AND WABASH AND ERIE CANALS

    Two small pieces of railroad and a few miles of gravel road completed the collection of public works.
    At first the people did not comprehend the extent of the

The Indiana Canals

disaster. They had been so infatuated with the illusion of prosperity that they could not believe that the State was bankrupt. It now began to appear that from the very start of the work in 1832 there had been gross mismanagement in the financial department. The original Fund Commission had been irregular enough in its methods, but the reorganized Commission was far worse. No books had been kept by the Commission, and the State had paid no attention to its operations. Blocks of bonds had been signed and delivered to the several members of the Board, to be disposed of as they saw fit; but the great bulk of them had been handled by Milton Stapp, a Fund Commissioner, and Dr. O. Coe, Secretary of the Commission. These two consulted with and made reports to no one but each other. Coe had his office in New York in order that he might be in closer touch with brokers and men of finance; but he was also enabled thereby to hobnob with his shady pals, the Morris Canal and Banking Company, and to make trades with other crooked bankers which enriched him at the expense of the State of Indiana.

When it developed that Stapp and Coe had put no less than $3,000,000 worth of the State's bonds out on credit, most of them to the Morris concern, which now became bankrupt, an investigation was demanded. A Legislature of very limited ability attempted to probe the tangled affair but could make neither head nor tail of it. Through a session of eighty-five days it wrangled and played at peanut politics, while the chicanery went merrily on. The people of the State lost patience. Cass County petitioned the Legislature to adjourn, charging that it had no capacity for anything other than spending money. The session ended with nothing done.

The record of Coe's knavery is too lengthy to recite here. He was a stockholder in the Morris Canal and Banking Company, and split his illegal gains on State bonds with the company's officials. His method was to make theoretical sales of the bonds to the Morris Company at 88, but in

Old Towpaths

reality to sell them (as if for the Morris) to wildcat banking concerns at 96, being careful to collect sufficient cash to cover the $8.00 per share profit, which he would then divide with the Morris directors. Several of the wildcat bankers failed or absconded without paying the balance due on the bonds. The Morris, when it failed, owed the State of Indiana $2,536,611, to say nothing of having shared in the stealage described. It was totally insolvent. An audit, completed in 1842, showed that $15,000,000 in bonds had been issued, for which the State had received only $8,593,000 in cash and $4,000,000 in worthless securities. More than $2,000,000 had been embezzled by various State officials and agents.

Four or five things were clear; the State owed $13,000,000; the yearly tolls from the canals then in operation were only $5,000 and receipts from the railroads $26,500; the Rothschilds, who had bought some of the State's bonds, were becoming very insistent in their demands for interest; so were the contractors to whom the State owed $1,000,000. Many wild ideas were proposed. Congress was petitioned for aid, but gave none. Some recommended completing the improvements with scrip or paper money. The Legislature favored this idea to such an extent that it passed an act in January, 1840, authorizing the issue of $1,200,000 in treasury notes. The completion of one line at a time was also urged; but the soundest advice seemed to be that the State ought to get rid of most of the works altogether.

A corporation took over the White Water Canal and completed it in 1846. This canal was 76 miles long and was connected with Cincinnati by another waterway. But its valley was too steep and narrow to be safe for it. A freshet in 1847 did $100,000 worth of damage and another the following year $80,000. A railroad paralleled the canal in 1865 and quickly killed its business. The Central Canal fragments were sold to private investors for $2,425. Other unfinished links in the system were either sold or abandoned.

The Indiana Canals

Many felt that work on the Wabash and Erie must go on. The State had accepted Government land on a promise to build it, and upon Indiana's insistence, Ohio was now finishing the eastern link with Lake Erie. Work proceeded in a desultory way on its Indiana end until the Tippecanoe River was reached in 1841; and in 1842 the Legislature authorized its extension to Terre Haute.

The work was now being carried on largely through the use of scrip, which became humorously famous throughout the West through its nicknames. Various issues of it were printed on red, white or blue paper and were called Red Dog, White Dog and Blue Dog. These various scrips were for some time the only circulating medium along the canal. In some towns not yet reached by the canal the merchants agreed to accept the scrip at par in payment for goods until the canal should reach their town. Then the scrip depreciated to forty cents on the dollar, and many merchants were ruined.

In 1843 Ohio completed the eastern end of the canal, and the first boats came through from Lake Erie amid great rejoicing, for now at last there seemed some hope that the enterprise might be made profitable. As construction progressed, more Government land was made available for sale. The country was growing more prosperous, and hopes were high that the work would yet be a success. Since the completion through to Toledo, the line boats were bringing in thousands of new settlers—and there was still plenty of room for them, for one reads of bears being hunted in the vicinity of Knightstown.

But the canal had defects and limitations which augured ill for its future. Sometimes it had too much water, sometimes not enough. The effect of a drought may be seen in an editorial apology in the Fort Wayne *Times* and *People's Press* in August, 1845. "We regret to say exceedingly that it is very uncertain whether we shall be able to issue more than an extra next week. We have the promise

Old Towpaths

... of a supply of paper by the first boat; but that boat is not yet arrived, and when it will, we know not. We learn that the canal between Huntington and La Gro is destitute of water, and that there is not enough in the Wabash to fill it." Neither were the tolls and land sales yet sufficient to pay more than a small portion of the interest due on the State's outstanding bonds. As to retiring the bonds themselves, that seemed almost impossibly remote. For two years the bondholders pressed for some sort of settlement, and finally in 1847 the Legislature simply deeded the canal to them and told them in effect to get what they could out of it. The bondholders, some of whom were poor and had their all invested, made heated protests against this method of settlement, which meant a loss of half their investment, but in vain. To the bondholders, one of the most galling features of the settlement was the fact that they would be compelled to raise $2,225,000 to complete the canal to the Ohio River. Meanwhile the State was left with a debt still of $6,732,880, which would have to be paid slowly by taxation.

Business increased rapidly in the latter '40's. Docks, elevators, warehouses, hotels and mercantile establishments sprang up, and all the towns along the line prospered. Lafayette became such a busy port that the public square was choked with wagons and teams, which often camped there for two or three days while waiting for an opportunity to reach a boat. Packets had been running for several years, and by 1844 the fastest packet service in the country was in operation between Toledo, Fort Wayne and Lafayette. In 1849 the first boats reached Terre Haute. That was an unfortunate season, however. First there was a flood and then an epidemic of cholera which broke up construction gangs, nearly stopped the land sales and reduced the tolls to $135,000—$11,000 less than in the previous year. But 1850 was fairly prosperous. Boats reached Washington

The Indiana Canals

that year, though another outbreak of cholera killed 150 laborers and demoralized the force for a time.

In June, 1852, boats reached Maysville, 392 miles from Toledo. Tolls were lowered 40 per cent that year, and the receipts rose to $193,000—the high-water mark in the canal's history. But the shadows were already closing around it. All the older lock gates, bridges and wooden aqueducts were rotting and frequently breaking. Freshets broke the banks and washed earth and sand into the channel, so that boats were sometimes aground and stranded for weeks. Numerous lawsuits were pending. A flood in 1853 destroyed many aqueducts, and $70,000 was spent on repairs. A railroad was under construction from Evansville to Terre Haute and another along the upper Wabash. The bondholders appealed to the Legislature in a final effort to save their investment, pleading that the State had not proven true to its agreement, but their argument fell upon deaf ears.

The great popular enthusiasm of a few years before for the canal had now changed to contempt with the coming of that new toy, the railroad. There had been numerous complaints that malaria was being caused by the canal supply reservoirs, especially the Birch Creek Reservoir; and the growing scorn for the old ditch, fostered by journalistic sneers, soon led to outrages. One of the aqueducts was fired by a mob in 1855, and men with blackened faces cut the Birch Creek dam, draining the reservoir and leaving a long section of channel dry. The dam was repaired, and was cut again the following year.

The southern end of the canal finally reached Evansville, 452 miles from Toledo, making it the longest canal in America; but at that very moment it was becoming evident that the end was near.

The tolls in 1857 were only $60,000; $40,000 was spent in repairs below Terre Haute alone. Floods broke the banks and destroyed aqueducts in several places. The trustees

Old Towpaths

ordered any portion of the canal not paying expenses to be closed; and all that portion below Terre Haute was closed immediately. The canal was offered on lease to any one who would keep it in repair for its use. Some half-hearted attempts were made to operate it below Terre Haute, but no repairs were made, and that portion closed forever in 1860. The upper half continued to operate fitfully for a few years, but the Wabash Railroad by cutting rates soon drove it out of existence. The last boat which ran through from Lodi, near Terre Haute, to Toledo, was the *Rockey Mountain,* which cleared October 26, 1872. The trustees formally surrendered their trust in 1874. That year the last boat on the canal east of Lafayette was crossing the Deer Creek aqueduct when the decrepit structure gave way, and the mules and negro driver were swept down by the roaring water into the creek below and drowned. As late as November, 1875, a boat managed to get through from Lodi to Lafayette, but by that time the greater part of the old waterway was naught but a muddy, noisome ditch.

The Wabash and Erie would appear to have been the most colossal, the most tragic failure in all canal history, but pitiable as it was, it played a tremendous part in the making of Indiana and the Middle West.

CHAPTER XXVII

THE ILLINOIS AND MICHIGAN CANAL

WE have seen how Louis Joliet in 1673 spoke of the desirability and easy accomplishment of a water connection between the Illinois River and Lake Michigan. For more than a century thereafter the idea lay dormant because the exploring Frenchmen were presently gone, and there were few Anglo-Saxons in the western wilderness to care much about the matter. But after the Revolution people began to move into the territory in greater numbers, and in 1818—though still very scantly populated—the Commonwealth of Illinois became a member of the Union.

Meanwhile the canal proposition had come up again. In 1795 the Illinois Indians were induced to grant a right of way through their territory for such a waterway. Gallatin in his famous Report in 1808 recommended the making of a connection there; in fact, there were few places in America which appeared so appropriate or so well adapted to such a purpose. Congressman Peter B. Porter, the New York canal enthusiast, endeavored (but in vain) in 1810 to enlist Government aid for a system of waterways connecting the Hudson and St. Lawrence Rivers with the Gulf of Mexico via the Illinois and Mississippi Rivers. He pointed out that one of the easiest tasks of the whole scheme would be the cutting of a canal across the Illinois portage.

By a treaty signed in 1816 the Indians gave up a strip of land 20 miles wide along the line of the proposed canal. There was never much doubt as to its route. It was to leave Lake Michigan near Fort Dearborn through a sluggish little

Old Towpaths

stream called the Chicago River, run up that stream a few miles, then cross over to the Des Plaines River, a small feeder of the Illinois, and follow that river and the Illinois down to good boating water. The first Governor of Illinois recommended action on the subject, and in 1822 Congress granted a right of way across the public lands for it, but gave no land to the State to be sold in aid of the project, though strenuous pleas for such a grant were made.

The route of the canal was surveyed in 1824 and the cost estimated at about $700,000. Impatient at the failure to secure Federal aid, the State in January, 1825, granted a charter to a company with a theoretical capital of $1,000,000. There was opposition to this act from those who thought it an outrage upon the people thus to turn over to a corporation so rich a source of revenue. Their anger was futile, for the company never succeeded in selling any stock, and presently gave up the ghost.

In 1827 Congress was at last induced to grant to the State 300,000 acres of land lying along the canal survey. There was great rejoicing among the people with the exception of the old French residents around St. Louis, Kaskaskia, Prairie du Rocher, Cahokia and Peoria, who were bitterly opposed to the improvement because it would make the way much easier for the "Yankees," whether Anglo-Saxon, Dutch, German or Irish, to come in.

At that time Chicago did not exist. In the latter '20's there were only about half a dozen families in the settlement just outside the stockade of Fort Dearborn. Peoria was nothing but a small frontier fort on the outskirts of the settled territory of Illinois. North of it the only settlements were at Fort Dearborn and the village of Galena on the Mississippi. When the newly appointed Board of Canal Commissioners laid out the towns of Chicago and Ottawa in 1829, there were living around the blockhouse at the former place not suite a hundred people, including Indians and half breeds.

WINTER VIEW OF THE AQUEDUCT OF THE ILLINOIS AND MICHIGAN CANAL ACROSS FOX RIVER AT OTTAWA

Courtesy of Horace Hull, Ottawa, Illinois

THE FINAL TRIP OF THE LAST ILLINOIS AND MICHIGAN CANAL PACKET, CARRYING A PICNIC PARTY IN 1885. IT HAD THEN BEEN OUT OF USE AS A PACKET BOAT FOR MANY YEARS

The Illinois and Michigan Canal

The commissioners prepared new plans and estimates for the canal and offered lots for sale in the two new towns; but the results were disappointing. The "boom" spirit was not yet rampant in the country. There were comparatively few people in the West who were able to buy, and these wished to be assured that the canal was a certainty before they invested along its course.

The commissioners tried to borrow money, but failed. For a while it seemed that the canal might not be built; for believers in railroads were increasing in numbers in the State and were making themselves heard. The commissioners were swayed towards the railroad idea by the report of Bucklin, their engineer, after a survey of the situation. Lake Michigan was about 145 feet higher than the point where the canal finally entered the Illinois River; but the summit of the watershed between them was only a few feet higher than the surface of the lake. Bucklin estimated that a lake-level canal, cut deeply enough to permit Lake Michigan to feed it, would cost \$4,107,440.43; that a canal with its summit level eight feet above the lake would cost \$1,601,695.83; while a railroad along the same line would cost only \$1,052,488.19.

The commissioners accordingly told the General Assembly of 1833 that a railroad was the most logical idea; it would cost less to construct, would be open the year round and would be a faster and better mode of transportation than the waterway. Governor Reynolds seconded their report.

But this precipitated a tempest, for canal backers were still numerous in Illinois. As the campaign of 1834 approached, it was evident that this would be the paramount issue. Communication of some sort was becoming an imperative need. Immigrants were pouring in, Chicago had by 1833 become a town of 1,200 people, and the roads from there to the Illinois River were dotted thickly with wagons. It is true that Illinois was somewhat better situated as to

Old Towpaths

transportation than Indiana. From her northeastern corner she had water communication with the Atlantic seaboard, and her port of Chicago saw the arrival in 1834 of 180 vessels, when two years before, said a Chicago newspaper, a dozen would have been considered a lively season's business. Steamboats often came up the Illinois River to Peoria,

Courtesy Charles M. Fish, Joliet, Illinois
CERTIFICATE OF LAND SALE FOR THE BENEFIT OF THE ILLINOIS AND MICHIGAN CANAL

and, save at very low water, could continue to La Salle, the western terminus of the proposed canal. In spite of the heavy cost of wagoning from La Salle to Chicago, this route to New York was cheaper than sending goods east via the Mississippi River and New Orleans. But still the farmers downstate were sorely in need of relief. Wheat was bringing $1.15 to $1.25 in Buffalo, but only 50 cents on the Illinois River. It was calculated that with a canal charging

[282]

The Illinois and Michigan Canal

the same tolls as the Erie, a bushel of wheat could be shipped from the lower Illinois River to Buffalo for 37½ cents—which would allow the farmer a living wage.

In 1834 the voters cast their ballots for a candidate solely because he was for or against the canal. Railroad partisans were still in the minority and Joseph Duncan, a strong believer in the canal, was elected Governor. His dream was a channel large enough to pass steamboats from river to lake. The Legislature in 1835 appointed a new Canal Commission, with power to raise funds and begin work. The sale of lands had not yielded sufficient cash to set the job going, so an emissary was sent east to negotiate a loan of $500,000, which with great difficulty was finally obtained.

Gooding, the new engineer, an alumnus of the Erie school, advocated making the channel larger than at first proposed. Remembering how it had been found necessary to enlarge the Erie shortly after it was built, he wished Illinois to avoid the same mistake. His suggestion was a 60-foot width at the water surface, 36 feet at the bottom and 6-foot depth. He also reported that Bucklin's estimate was much too low, especially since prosperity had brought about higher prices on all commodities. Pork that spring was $20 to $30 a barrel at Chicago; flour $9 to $12; salt $12 to $15; horses $100 each and oxen $80 per yoke. Labor was scarce and could not be had for less than $20 to $30 per month and board. Gooding now estimated the cost of a lake-level canal at $8,654,337—more than double the former figure. But the sprightly contagion of 1836 was in the air, and the commissioners were not men to be frightened by mere figures. They not only adopted the larger channel but the lake level plan as well.

The slighted districts in other parts of the State who had been complaining that they would receive no benefit from the canal now demanded railroads by way of compensation; and thus was brought about the State's reckless

Old Towpaths

attempt at a 1,300-mile rail system which during the next three years was largely responsible for plunging Illinois into a terrible morass of debt.

Ground was broken for the canal with much formality at Canalport on July 4, 1836. The real estate boom was in full swing and it seemed that nothing could stop Illinois. $500,000 worth of her bonds had just been sold with comparative ease in the East, and 375 canal lots in Chicago had been knocked down in June for a total price of $1,355,755. Men were working on the new railroad system at forty or fifty scattered points in the State, and everybody was happy.

The panic of 1837 caused the State bank to suspend specie payments in May, and to prevent a stoppage of the canal work, the Assembly authorized a general suspension of specie payments. The work limped along for another two years and more, though some contractors were forced to quit. In 1839 the commissioners were almost out of money, and a new loan of $4,000,000 was authorized. Blocks of these bonds were sold whenever and wherever they could be placed, but the canal was well-nigh halted for lack of money in 1840 and again in 1841. By that time more than $4,000,000 in canal bonds was outstanding, and $5,000,000 for railroads and other improvements. The State was barely able to scrape together money to pay the interest on its debts on January 1, 1841. Its credit was so low that no new loan could be placed save at a ruinous discount. No resource was left save taxation and the selling of such bonds as were on hand for whatever they would bring. To keep the contractors going the Canal Commission issued scrip; but this soon depreciated, the contractors' orders were worthless, and then work on the canal came to a halt.

The State Bank failed in 1842. The State itself was essentially bankrupt. It owed $14,000,000, and the debt was piling up at the rate of $830,000 a year from interest alone. Illinois was so thoroughly discredited that its bills sold at auction in Chicago in June of that year for $18\frac{1}{4}$ to

The Illinois and Michigan Canal

24 cents on the dollar, while bills of the bankrupt State Bank brought as high as 38¼ cents.

As usual, there were many who advocated repudiation of the State's debts; but others argued that, foolish though it might seem at first glance, the wisest thing to do was to complete the canal. Not to do so would be to waste all the money put into it. Completed, it would be a source of revenue which would at least help to pay interest. It would also build up the country and increase the taxable value of land in all quarters. It would attract many new settlers who would become taxpayers, and would furthermore make the State interesting again to investors. The Administration was impressed by these arguments; but Gooding admitted that to complete the canal on the original plan would cost more than $3,000,000, which was a bit staggering.

The shallow cut idea, with a summit level twelve feet above Lake Michigan, was now adopted again. It was calculated that to finish the job by that plan would cost $1,600,000. More money was borrowed, and work was resumed in 1845. Labor and supplies were now much lower than in 1836; flour had dropped to $3.50, pork to $8.00, and men were willing to work for $16.00 a month. The result was that for once in canal history an estimate was actually bettered, and the work was completed with a further expenditure of only $1,429,606. The total cost had been $6,557,681, not counting interest. By 1871 the sales of canal lands had brought in $5,858,547, so the canal did not cost Illinois so heavily, after all.

The job was finally considered complete on April 19, 1848, and a boat started from each end of the canal and went through to the other with bands playing and champagne corks popping. Chicago had a particularly hilarious celebration—and well she might, for the I. and M. Canal was the chief agency that made her what she is. The Erie had given her a start and continued to assist her; but the I. and M. made her great. She counted 12,088 inhabitants in 1845,

Old Towpaths

when work on the canal was renewed. The promise of completion of the improvement brought a rush of new citizens, and by 1848 she had nearly 20,000. In 1850 her population was 28,269, and by 1854 it was 74,500! Grain brought by the canal made her a great wheat market, and eventually she became the greatest in the country. Cattle and hogs brought by the canal gave her a long start towards becoming the center of America's packing industry. Peoria—and it is needless to say, Joliet, Ottawa, La Salle and other cities along the route—owe their present size and prosperity in no small measure to the old ditch.

The canal trustees in their report for 1848 mention with exultation the fact that sugar and other articles from New Orleans had arrived at Buffalo via the Illinois and Michigan Canal two weeks before the first boat of the season reached that city on the Erie. The Chicago *Tribune* in 1851 said that the canal had changed the course of trade of a large portion of the products of the Illinois River Valley. Previously that region found its only outlet down the Mississippi. "The amount of corn, wheat, pork, lard, beef, tallow and many other articles that have taken the northern route the present season is immense."

The writer had also noticed large consignments of eastern merchandise coming through the lakes destined for St. Louis via the I. and M. "A late number of the St. Louis *Intelligencer* notices the arrival at that place of a canal boat load of Porto Rico sugar, which had been brought from New York. Furs, peltries, wool and the like from the river region south of us are being shipped North and East by the I. and M. and Lakes. Cotton is seeking the eastern market by the same route." Tobacco from the South and beef cattle from the West, going to New York and Boston, were other products which swelled the canal's business.

Passenger traffic on the I. and M. was of comparatively short duration. An excellent line of passenger boats was started as soon as the canal was opened, running through

The Illinois and Michigan Canal

from Chicago to La Salle, where they connected with steam river boats for St. Louis. The fare on the packets was four dollars for the hundred-mile trip, including meals; and the journey was said to be made in twenty-two hours. Business must have been lively at first, for the boats were advertised to leave both Chicago and La Salle morning, noon and evening. With the opening of the Rock Island Railroad in 1854, the packet business was almost obliterated.

Meanwhile Chicago had found that the lake was becoming so polluted by the city's sewage that her water supply was in danger. The project was conceived of making a sewer out of the Illinois and Michigan Canal. Permission for this arrangement was obtained from the State on the understanding that Chicago was to pay for the job herself. By 1871 the city had, at an expense of $3,000,000, reduced the canal to the lake level, and Michigan's waters were sweeping her sewage through it towards the Illinois River.

Because of Chicago's terrible losses in the great fire of 1871, the amount which the city had expended for the rebuilding of the canal was refunded by the State.

For a number of years the canal handled a large volume of traffic. The two best years for tolls were 1865 and 1866, during each of which a little over $300,000 was collected. The tonnage continued to increase after that, however, until it reached its peak in 1882 at 1,011,287 tons. The tolls that year were only $85,947, the rates having been gradually reduced to meet railroad competition. Thenceforward its business declined steadily.

By 1881 the channel had collected so much filth from the city's sewage that it had become putrid and intolerable to every one within several miles of it. The pumping station which had formerly operated at the summit level was set to work again, to rush water through it more rapidly, but this did not give entire satisfaction, and Chicago finally decided to cut a new channel to take the place of the old canal between the Chicago River and the Des Plaines. Thus came

Old Towpaths

about the Chicago Drainage Canal, which was constructed between 1892 and 1900. Meanwhile the old canal was allowed to fill up and fall into disrepair until its traffic practically reached the vanishing point.

Dr. James William Putnam, who has written a monograph on the Illinois and Michigan Canal, concludes his discussion with a paragraph which might well be applied to all the old American waterways:

"The great services of the canal have been in the economic development of the Middle West, particularly of the northern part of Illinois, and in its influence on railroad rates. For the performance of these services, the canal has been worth all it has cost the State."

CHAPTER XXVIII

SHORTER CANALS

PERHAPS the best little piece of canal property in America from a financial point of view has been that two-and-a-half-mile cut around the falls of the Ohio River at Louisville. From the time of the earliest emigrants who floated down the Ohio River, the rapids or "falls" at that point were a nuisance. They could be passed (with good luck) by arks and flatboats during the spring floods, but seldom at other times. The falls really brought about the founding of Louisville. The original village of that name was at the head of the rapids, where boatmen were compelled to debark when the water was low.

As Ohio began to be populated she displayed more annoyance over the falls than its immediate neighbors, Indiana and Kentucky. The first suggestion of a canal came from Cincinnati, where a company was partly formed in 1805 for the purpose of improving the navigation; but the scheme never came to fruition.

One of the first acts of the new State of Indiana in 1816 was the incorporation of the Ohio Canal Company with an authorized capital of $1,000,000. The money supposed to be necessary to build the canal—$100,000—was to be raised by means of a lottery. Work was actually begun in 1819, before the money had been secured. Meanwhile, the commissioners appointed by Ohio, Pennsylvania, Virginia and Kentucky viewed the site and estimated the cost of a canal on the Kentucky side of the river at $400,000, on the Indiana shore at $1,000,000. These were fatal blows to the Indiana company, and it soon passed out of existence.

Old Towpaths

In 1825 the Kentucky Legislature chartered a company, mostly of Philadelphia capitalists, to build a canal. The United States Government subscribed $290,200 to the enterprise. The wagoners of Louisville, who were engaged in portaging goods past the falls, were outraged by the idea and fought it bitterly. How were they to live if it were made possible for boats to go right past the falls without stopping? Many people thought that reducing Louisville to a mere way station would mean its ruin. But as Eddy of the Middlesex had so pathetically remarked, progress could not be stopped.

In 1830 the first steamboats went through the channel, but it was not regarded as finished until the following year. It had cost $750,000. In 1831, 416 steamboats, 46 keel boats and 357 flatboats, in all 76,000 tons, passed through it. The canal had the privilege of levying a toll of 20 cents per ton on steamboats and $4 each on flatboats. If these tolls did not produce a profit of $12\frac{1}{2}$ per cent per annum for the stockholders, the directors were authorized to raise the rates sufficiently to do so. On the other hand, the Legislature reserved the right to reduce the rates if the dividends should exceed 18 per cent per annum. It is evident that they did not exercise this right, though the profits were enormous. On the contrary, the rates were even raised. In the '40's it was calculated that a $25,000 boat of 300 tons plying up and down the river for five years would spend an amount equal to her cost in lockage. In that time the dividends declared were more than the total original investment.

While complaints of extortion were filling the air, another Indiana company secured a charter, but did nothing further. It was found necessary to enlarge the canal in the '50's, and when the matter was first talked of, some super-genius made the brilliant suggestion—which was very respectfully considered by many—that a railroad (of extremely broad gauge, of course) be built around the falls, running into the water at either end; that cars be run under

Modern Lock on the Louisville and Portland (Ohio Falls) Canal.

Shorter Canals

the boats and they be hauled around the obstruction, much more quickly than going by water.

During all the period of western emigration and of the supremacy of the steamboat, this was one of the most important canals in America. It was taken over by the Federal Government in 1872 and is still an important factor in the country's transportation facilities.

The swampy soil of lower Louisiana lends itself readily to the making of canals and (particularly around New Orleans) has also been a reason for digging them; for most of the early ditches were dug either in part or entirely for the purpose of drainage. One such was the Rodriguez Canal, along which a part of Jackson's line was formed during the Battle of New Orleans. A shallow depression marks its course to-day.

The first canal in that region (so far as the records show) used for navigation was mentioned in our Chapter II —that dug by the Spanish Governor Carondelet from the city to Bayou St. John. When the Americans took over Louisiana in 1803 it was practically useless for navigation. An old historian says that "this canal and basin did not last long; the canal got filled up by cattle passing through it." It became so shallow that all the larger vessels bringing farm products, lumber and so on were compelled to stop at St. Johnsburg on the bayou and send their freight into the city by wagon.

In 1805 a corporation took over the canal and spent $375,000 in enlarging it and deepening the bayou. For considerably more than a century the old canal has been bringing its merchandise in from the other side of Lake Pontchartrain and in earlier years from far up the Gulf coast. Until the New Bank or New Basin Canal was dug in 1835 it was the only connection with the parishes across the lake. It has long been known in New Orleans as the Old Basin Canal.

In 1831 the New Orleans Canal and Banking Company

Old Towpaths

was incorporated with $4,000,000 capital to build a canal from the newer or American quarter of New Orleans to Lake Pontchartrain, and incidentally, to do a bit of banking on the side. Simon Cameron, the Pennsylvania statesman, was called to Louisiana to manage the enterprise. The work was much hampered by outbreaks of cholera and yellow fever, but it was finally completed in 1835. The canal, only a little over four miles long, had cost the rather startling sum of $1,226,070. Nevertheless, it has been a very important and prosperous one. Its channel and basin were enlarged as traffic increased; the channel is now 100 feet wide and 10 feet deep. It soon outstripped the old canal, and greatly built up the newer portion of the city.

About 1800 N. N. Destrehan of New Orleans began digging a canal westward from the Mississippi near the city to an arm of Bayou Barataria, about five miles distant. The work was done by slaves when they were not busy with their farm duties, and several years were required to complete it. The channel was at first 12 feet wide and its prime object was plantation drainage. Inland water traveling was done then mostly by luggers and other light craft, and Jean Lafitte, Dominick You and others of the so-called pirates of Barataria found the canal very convenient for their trips to New Orleans. From time to time the channel was enlarged, and began to carry many fish and oyster boats plying between the city, Barataria Bay and the lakes and bayous connected therewith. In 1858 it was dredged to a 60-foot width (later 75) by the Harvey family, who had inherited it, and was lengthened to 13 miles. It has since been known as Harvey's Canal, and has carried during its century of existence enormous quantities of fish, cypress timber and agricultural products.

Another such was the Veret Canal, constructed about 1814 to drain a large plantation. It was about 8 miles long and reached the Mississippi at Algiers, opposite New Orleans. It, too, was much used by fishermen, smugglers

Shorter Canals

and other travelers between New Orleans and the Barataria region, including Lafitte and his confrères. Another canal connecting with the watery labyrinth west of New Orleans is that one now known as "the Company's," leaving the Mississippi at Westwego, a mile or two above Harvey. It is 25 miles in length and 100 feet wide.

It may surprise some to learn that there is in the United States a canal less than two miles in length whose tonnage during many years has surpassed that of the Suez Canal. When the first French voyageurs began to navigate the Great Lakes, they found the rapids in the St. Mary's River, between Lakes Superior and Huron, very troublesome. In 1798 the Hudson Bay Company built a lock on the Canadian side of the river, 38 feet long and with a lift of 9 feet. Oxen pulled the batteaux and schooners through the lock. During the War of 1812 United States troops destroyed these works.

For the next forty years there was no aid to navigation on the St. Mary's. But between 1853 and 1855 the State of Michigan built a canal on the American shore, 5,400 feet long, 100 feet wide at the water surface and 13 feet deep. It had two locks, each 350 by 70 feet, with a lift of 9 feet.

In 1870–71 the United States Government enlarged the old canal and locks, also building a new and larger lock alongside the old ones. In 1880 the State of Michigan turned the canal over to the Federal Government, which a few years later replaced the two old locks with a new one 800 by 100 feet, and 22 feet deep. The canal depth has been increased to 25 feet and its length to 1.6 miles. Since the Government took charge of the canal, no tolls have been levied.

In 1850–51 Texas citizens built the Galveston and Brazos Canal, to connect the bays and inlets along the coast between Galveston and the mouth of the Brazos River. There were 8 miles of artificial channel and 30 miles of slack-water navigation. In 1902 the National Government

Old Towpaths

bought the system for $30,000 and effected a considerable improvement.

A very early project on the Atlantic coast was the Clubfoot and Harlow's Creek Canal in North Carolina, between Pamlico Sound and the coast near Beaufort; first planned in 1797, begun in 1819 and completed in 1830. Recently it has been taken over by Government engineers under a more ambitious scheme and called the New Berne and Beaufort Canal.

A portage often mentioned by early explorers as a desirable place for a canal was that between the Fox and Wisconsin Rivers—the former flowing into Lake Michigan, the latter into the Mississipi. In the '40's the State undertook to improve the navigation of the two rivers and to build a connecting canal across the watershed. The Government granted the State 691,200 acres of land in aid of the project. After expending $400,000 on the job the State gave it up and turned the unfinished work over to a corporation in 1853. The canal at the summit was two miles long. The navigation passed into the hands of the National Government in 1872.

A considerable amount of river canalization was done before the Civil War, some of it by States, some by private interests. In Alabama canals were built on the Tennessee around the Mussel (corrupted for some inscrutable reason in these latter days to Muscle) Shoals and at Huntsville, but both had been abandoned before 1850. Kentucky improved the Kentucky, Green and Barren Rivers with locks and dams in the '40's. Small canals were built around rapids in the Santee and Saluda in South Carolina. In Georgia a water-power canal was built at Augusta and the Congaree and other rivers were improved. The Monongahela and Muskingum River improvements have already been mentioned.

CHAPTER XXIX

CANAL ENGINEERING

"CANALS in 1837," wrote William Dean Howells, "were a greater achievement than railroads are in 1897." One of the most remarkable phases of America's development is the adaptability of the young, untutored nation, and the quickness with which it grasped the secrets of engineering when it began to build canals, and even advanced the science. When the first canals were built, there was not a native-born engineer in America, and almost none of any nationality. The Santee Canal was built by a Swede, the Middlesex and Western Inland Lock Navigation by an Englishman. The South Hadley, Patowmack and Dismal Swamp works were the products of native American talent, and were all skillfully and efficiently done. The Patowmack locks were spoken of with high admiration in Europe, while the inclined plane at South Hadley Falls, built by men who had never seen anything of the sort, was a marvel of Yankee ingenuity.

But most astounding of all was the Erie Canal, the most important transportation line ever built in America because it contributed more to the making of the nation than any other in her history. This mighty work was surveyed and planned and its construction was to a considerable degree superintended by two country lawyers who had done some land surveying, but who could by no stretch of the imagination be called engineers. "Who is this James Geddes and who is this Benjamin Wright that the commissioners have entrusted with this responsibility?" was demanded, scorn-

Old Towpaths

fully, in the legislative halls at Albany. "What canals have they ever constructed? What great public works have they accomplished?"

The only answer that could be given was, "None." But before the canal was completed, Geddes and Wright had fairly earned the degree of engineer. Yet neither they nor any one else connected with the Erie's engineering had ever seen a real canal—none save Canvass White, who, after the Erie was begun, went to England and studied canals by walking 2,000 miles along their banks and towpaths.

Nevertheless, these amateur engineers (including White, who became one of its leading experts) were unterrified by any of the difficulties—frequently great ones—which confronted them. Across the Mohawk and the Genesee they threw great stone aqueducts such as had never yet been dreamed of in this country. They carried the channel through the precipitous gorge of the Mohawk, part of the way blasting a shelf in the face of the cliff (as at the Cohoes falls, where work was done in eighty days which it had been predicted it would take years to accomplish), and in other places building retaining walls up from the bed of the river, but always keeping the channel above flood stage.

One of the features of the Erie which greatly excited the admiration of Captain Basil Hall, and in fact, of all foreign as well as American travelers, was the double flight of five locks, all cut in solid rock, at Lockport—one flight for ascending, and one for descending boats. Each lock had a lift of 12 feet, which was unusual for those days, most of the other locks so far built in the country lifting no more than 5 or 6 feet. These locks were designed by and built under the superintendence of Nathan S. Roberts, engineer of the western section of the canal, a self-taught man who did his first surveying on the Erie right of way in 1816 under Judge Wright. In designing his Lockport triumph he had no advice from others and no assistance save a very meager store of books.

Courtesy of the Delaware and Hudson Company
CABLE ANCHORAGE OF THE REMARKABLE SUSPENSION AQUEDUCT OF THE DELAWARE AND HUDSON CANAL ACROSS THE DELAWARE RIVER

Courtesy of E. W. Drinker, Bethlehem, Pennsylvania
THE "DROP" OR "FALL" GATE FOR LOCKS, A GREAT IMPROVEMENT OVER THE OLD SWINGING GATES

Canal Engineering

"What they did not understand," says Desmond Fitzgerald, President of the American Society of Civil Engineers, "they conquered by diligent study, unwearied zeal and sound common sense." Our versatile pioneer forefathers were accustomed to meeting and surmounting all sorts of knotty problems. Nearly every man had to be a sort of jack of all trades. The backwoods farmer and his wife built their own home and outbuildings, made their own furniture, utensils and most of their tools, made their clothing, hats and shoes, and reared, cooked and preserved practically everything they ate. Our amateur statesmen wrote a Constitution which has been the admiration of the world, and our amateur engineers created the greatest canal of modern times and made it a success.

Some of their first work was experimental, of course, and a small percentage of it had to be corrected or replaced, but most of it functioned as desired; and through their failures the engineers learned more than from their successes. John B. Jervis, who began as an axman on the Erie, and before the canal's completion was being sought elsewhere as an expert engineer, says that the builders scorned no opportunity to acquire information, no matter how humble or inexpert the source might be. "The running of lines and levels," he adds, "was well understood at that time, but the mechanical department of engineering was practically in its infancy. Such matters were freely discussed with intelligent mechanics whose skill was supposed to be useful."

One of the unique features of the great canal was the embankment by which it crossed the valley of the Irondequoit. Geddes conceived this work when he made his first survey; but his scheme was thought so hazardous that the commissioners had decided to bridge the gulf with a high wooden aqueduct. Then it was pointed out that winds sweeping through the gorge would be dangerous to such a structure, and so Geddes's plan was adopted, after all.

Old Towpaths

From rim to rim of this valley, more than 4,950 feet, the canal ran along the crest of a meandering ridge, partly natural, partly artificial. It was made by joining three slender natural ridges by means of two earthen embankments, the first one 1,320 feet long and 50 feet high, the second 231 feet long. The Irondequoit brook passed through a stone culvert, 76 feet below the bed of the canal.

The passage of swamps, such as the Montezuma marshes in the vicinity of the Cayuga River, those encountered on the Chesapeake and Ohio and other canals, was also a serious problem, because of the difficulty of making excavations in muck or wet land, and of building a channel in such soil which should retain its shape and hold water. There was no machinery then for digging, dredging or scooping up dirt, and the whole process must be done laboriously by hand. We have already seen how men worked sometimes up to their waists in mud and water in the Cayuga swamps, how special sharp-edged spades were invented for cutting roots under the muck, how tree- and stump-pulling machines were invented on the spot to fill the needs of the builders. In some cases a swamp could be partially drained; but whether it was or not, a channel to be built across it must be largely built of soil brought from elsewhere—preferably a clay that would be much stiffer and heavier than the spongy vegetable mold of the marsh.

During the year 1825 three hydrostatic weighlocks were built on the Erie, at Troy, Utica and Syracuse, to ascertain the weight of cargoes for toll purposes. These locks were so constructed that the water could be measured with a boat floating in it; then the water was measured without the boat, and the two weights were computed. The difference in weight gave the weight of the boat, according to the law of displacement. The weight of each boat on the canal, empty, was known, and thereby the weight of the cargo was quickly determined.

A little later a more ingenious weighlock was devised,

Courtesy of the Ohio State Department of Public Works

AQUEDUCT OF MIAMI AND ERIE CANAL ACROSS GREAT MIAMI RIVER NEAR DAYTON, COLLAPSED IN 1903. This shows the Howe truss construction, common to all large early aqueducts. They were enclosed, to protect the timber framework from the weather.

Canal Engineering

in which the boat actually rested on a huge steelyard and was weighed like a pound of sugar. "The weight of the boat and cargo on which I saw the operation performed," says Francis Lieber, an admiring German traveler, "was 62 tons, or 136,000 pounds; much heavier cargoes, however, are weighed. When the whole was balanced, I was able literally to move by my little finger 136,000 pounds up and down. . . . The operation of weighing which I witnessed, lasted from the time the boat entered the lock to its sailing out again, nine minutes; but three or four minutes must be deducted, as the weigh master had to fetch a lantern, it having grown dark. He assured me that when the people on board the boat understood the details of the whole operation and no unnecessary delay takes place, he can weigh any boat in four minutes."

Nor must the discovery of American cement be forgotten as one of the great results of canal building in America, and specifically of the building of the Erie. When European cement was so costly that the Erie engineers were trying to build lock walls without it, Canvass White discovered hydraulic cement in Madison County, near the canal. Again, when the Delaware and Hudson was building, the questing engineers discovered the great Rosendale cement field. On the Lehigh, the canal builders found the rock where is now the busy cement manufacturing district of Northampton. The Chesapeake and Ohio and other canals also developed deposits of cement.

"Many of the distinctive characteristics of American engineering," said President Ashbel Welsh of the American Society of Civil Engineers in 1882, "originated with those Erie canal engineers. We practice their methods today. . . . As a class they wrote little. There were then no engineering papers prepared, and no engineering societies to perpetuate them, if they had been prepared. They were not scientific men, but knew by intuition what other men know by calculation. . . . What science they had they knew

Old Towpaths

well how to apply to the best advantage. Few men have ever accomplished so much with so little means."

One by no means wishes to intimate that those early canal builders were infallible. Lacking scientific knowledge and groping for new truths, they sometimes did amusing things. Geddes, for example, who had his own way with the Champlain Canal, built it with many curves "to avoid accumulation of water and its waves by which the bank would be washed. The force of each wave was to be broken against a curved bank of the canal." The result was such slow progress on the part of boats compelled to navigate the snakelike course that William Cullen Bryant, who once made a journey through the canal, records that "a young man belonging to the boat" stepped ashore at one point and rejoined the craft some time later at another place with a basket of very fine strawberries which he had gathered in the neighboring woods while the boat was negotiating the bends.

The Erie has been dwelt upon because it was our first great school of engineering. From it came the men who designed and superintended the building of practically all the canals built during three or four decades thereafter, and the great majority of our early railroads. There was James Geddes, for example, the dean of the Erie corps, who also made the preliminary surveys for the Ohio Canals, the Cumberland and Oxford and the Chesapeake and Ohio, and in 1828 was consulting engineer on the Pennsylvania system.

Benjamin Wright, being a little younger than Geddes, had opportunity to become the best-known canal engineer in America. From 1821 to 1827 he was first consulting and then chief engineer on the New Haven and Northampton Canal; chief on the Blackstone and the Chesapeake and Delaware; between 1824 and 1840 he was first consulting and then chief engineer on the James River and Kanawha. He was also consulting engineer at various times on the Delaware and Hudson and Chesapeake and Ohio. In 1833-34 he worked on the St. Lawrence Ship Canal; and in 1837

Canal Engineering

he was busy with both the Welland and the Illinois and Michigan. In 1834 he was appointed by Governor Marcy of New York to determine a route for the New York and Erie Railroad, and thereafter did much railroad engineering.

Canvass White, probably the greatest genius who sprang from the Erie, was called in 1824 to complete the Union Canal as chief engineer; and while there did an extraordinary amount of other work besides. The city of New York called him into consultation regarding its water supply, and he recommended Rye Pond, and the Bronx and Croton Rivers, all of which were afterwards used. Meanwhile he was consulting engineer on the Schuylkill Navigation and also with Benjamin Wright on the Chesapeake and Delaware. He became chief engineer of the Lehigh Canal in 1827, and after completing that work, built the Delaware and Raritan Canal. When the D. and R. was on the eve of completion, his health failed, and in a few months he died at the untimely age of forty-four.

John B. Jervis was another of the Erie's famous sons. After leaving its service he built the Delaware and Hudson Canal and then turned to railroads, building the Albany and Schenectady and the Schenectady and Saratoga. The State then called him back into the canal service, and he built the Chenango Canal and had much to do with the plans for enlarging the Erie. Next he built New York City's great Croton Dam and Aqueduct, and then took up railroads again, being (among others) chief engineer of the Hudson River, Michigan Southern, Chicago and Rock Island and Pittsburgh, Fort Wayne and Chicago. He engaged in numerous other activities during his long career, dying at the age of ninety.

Nathan S. Roberts was for a time chief engineer of the Pennsylvania Canals and of the Chesapeake and Ohio; bridged the Potomac at Harpers Ferry, made preliminary surveys for the Mussel Shoals Canal, was consulting engineer on the Ohio Canals, and finally returned to serve as chief engineer for the enlargement of the Erie.

David S. Bates, Holmes Hutchinson and David Thomas were other Erie engineers who became famous; the last-named built the Welland Canal. Such canal building between 1825 and 1860 as was not done by Erie engineers was in the majority of cases done by their pupils. After 1825 America no longer looked to Europe for engineering information, but was inclined to think that she knew more about such things than Europe did. Michel Chevalier, a French traveler of the '30's, was astounded to find such technical knowledge in the new States of the West.

"This young State," he wrote of Ohio, "with a population of farmers, not having a single engineer within her limits, and none of whose citizens had ever seen any other canal than those of New York, has thus, with the aid of some second-rate engineers borrowed from that State, constructed a canal longer than any in France. This farming population of Ohio, almost wholly of New England origin, has a business instinct, a practical shrewdness and a readiness to exercise all trades without having learned them. . . .

"The Ohio Canal Commission added to a notable disinterestedness an admirable good sense. . . . They were farmers and lawyers who set themselves about making canals, naturally, easily, and without even a suspicion that in Europe no one dares undertake such a work without long preparation and scientific studies. Now it is no longer an art in that State to plan and construct canals, but a mere trade; the science of canalling is there become quite an affair of the common people. The first-comer in a bar-room will explain to you over his glass of whisky how to feed the summit level and how to construct a lock. All our mysteries of civil engineering are here fallen into the hands of the public, very much as the methods of descriptive geometry are to be found in the workshops, where they have been handed down by tradition."

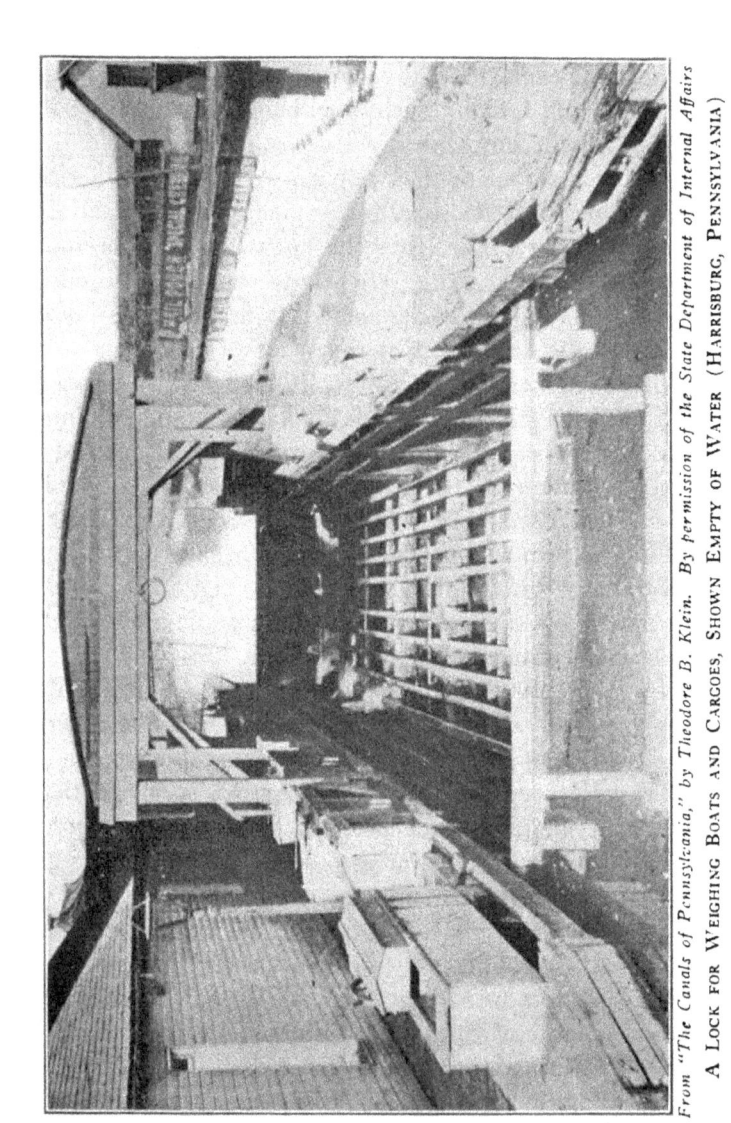

From "The Canals of Pennsylvania," by Theodore B. Klein. By permission of the State Department of Internal Affairs
A LOCK FOR WEIGHING BOATS AND CARGOES, SHOWN EMPTY OF WATER (HARRISBURG, PENNSYLVANIA)

Canal Engineering

One of the chief concerns of the canal engineer—in fact, it might be called the vital consideration—was the water supply. It must be sufficient to keep the channel properly filled, and it should fall by gravity into the canal at the summit or at other levels where needed; any necessity for pumping would greatly increase the operating expense. Supplying the canal with water frequently necessitated the digging of feeder channels, sometimes 20 or 30 miles in length. The bed of the canal must be so carefully pitched that the water would flow through it very slowly and not retard the speed of boats going upstream. The Erie from Buffalo to Lockport had a fall of only one inch to the mile. If there were many locks and heavy traffic, the frequent lockage would use up water more rapidly. The Morris, which worked its twenty-three inclined planes by means of turbine wheels, thereby used more water than some other canals.

One cannot but admire the nerve—though care and skill were back of it, too—with which those fellows often stuck a canal along the side of a hill, sometimes supported on its outer side only by a rip-rapped earthen wall with a slope of perhaps a hundred feet or more below it. And yet by reason of careful construction and close supervision no great disasters or loss of life ever occurred through the breakage of canal banks. There were seldom any accidents to those hillside channels save when a natural stream rose to flood stage and tore away the banks. True, a huge chunk of the Irondequoit embankment 60 feet long and 50 feet deep, crumbled away one spring day in 1830; but no boats were caught, and even on that daring work, no other accident of the sort ever occurred.

The curse of the Union Canal was the difficulty of procuring an adequate water supply for its summit level. The apparatus finally devised to store and pump water to that level was a fine example of the combination of ingenuity and dogged determination which characterized the builders of that day. After the canal was enlarged in 1828 there were

Old Towpaths

three large dams across Swatara Creek, and a dam a mile long and 40 feet high across Cattail Creek. From the Big Dam the water passed into a large power house where there were two great water wheels, each 40 feet high, 10 feet wide and with a head of 6 feet, to which four pumping engines, each of 120 horse power, were hitched. There were also two other buildings containing auxiliary pumps operated by steam.

The water was pumped to the top of a hill 95 feet above the dam, whence it flowed by gravity four miles through an aqueduct of brick and wood. When passing through the ground, the tube was built of wedge-shaped brick laid in cement. Where it passed through the air—and it was sometimes 70 feet above ground—it was a cylinder of white pine staves three inches thick, bound together with heavy iron hoops. Portions of the old brick aqueduct may be found to-day. A few months ago, while engineers were removing the old dam, they uncovered a line of iron pipe used for drainage or overflow purposes, which was still perfectly water-tight. The pipe was made with a very deep "bell" at the end, and the joints were skillfully leaded as in modern practice; but instead of packing the joints with oakum, they had been packed with dried grass, which, due to the careful soldering, was still intact after lying in the ground for the better part of a century.

One of the wonders of America in the early Nineteenth Century was the Morris Canal, with its twenty-three inclined planes. This cannot be claimed as a strictly American device, the planes having been designed by James Renwick, an English engineer, who was at the time, however, a professor in Columbia University. The system was an adaptation of and improvement upon that used in several places in Europe. The planes were in reality boat railways, rising on an average one foot perpendicularly in every ten feet of track. Renwick at first built some of the cars as huge water-tight boxes into which the boats floated through a lock

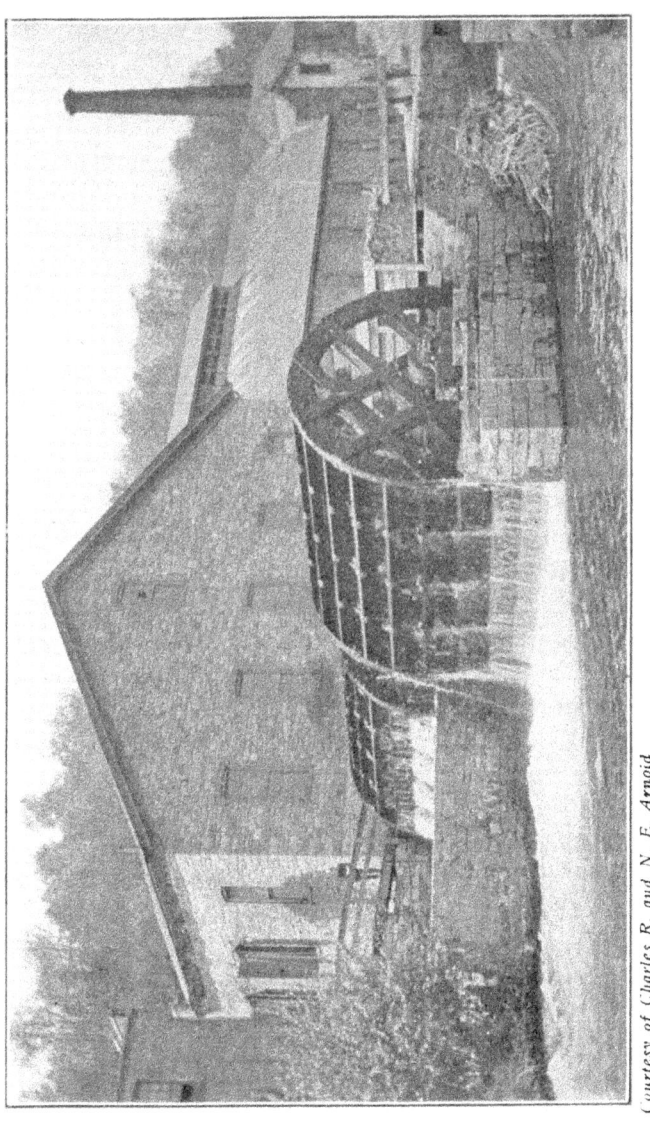

Courtesy of Charles R. and N. E. Arnold

INGENIOUS WATER WHEELS AT NEW HOPE, BY WHICH THE DELAWARE RIVER WAS MADE TO PUMP ITS OWN WATER INTO A FEEDER OF THE DELAWARE DIVISION CANAL

Canal Engineering

gate. The gate of the car was then closed behind the boat, the water was emptied from it through a sluice, the car carried down or up to the other end of the plane, the gates were opened, the car refilled with water and the boat was towed out again.

Then the inventor hit upon a device for making the operation even simpler. The cars were built as merely big skeleton cribs on wheels. At the lower end of the plane the track ran into the water of the canal, so that a car could glide right under a boat—from which the horses had been unhitched. The boat was fastened to the standards of the car, and when the plane machinery was started, the car came out of the water, bringing the boat with it. At the top of the plane, the track ran over a hump—which served to hold the water in the channel on the upper level—thence passed down into the bed of the canal, so that when the boat was unhooked from the standards, it could be floated out of the car, and was ready to go its way.

The water of the canal itself, passing through a flume to a 24-foot water wheel, furnished sufficient power to pull a car containing a loaded boat up the plane. One man conducted the entire operation of the plane, the boatmen moving their own boats into and out of the cars, which was no more difficult than going into and out of a lock. The whole operation of raising or lowering a boat by plane never occupied more than fourteen minutes, and was usually performed in from eight to ten minutes—which was much less time than would have been required to negotiate the same elevation through locks.

The Morris also boasted that its planes cost only $210 per foot of elevation, while the Erie's locks cost $1,100 per foot. Other canals looked askance at the planes and feared to adopt them; but the fact remains that they proved entirely practicable and efficient. They cannot be blamed for the failure of the Morris Canal to achieve great success. That failure was due, firstly, to its channel having been made

Old Towpaths

too small; secondly, to its directors having wasted its substance in riotous speculation; and thirdly, to its being paralleled by railroads. Its locks, planes and channel were increased to more nearly adequate size just as the railroads had begun to take away its business.

The only other example of boat inclined planes on the canals was that of the Portage Railroad in Pennsylvania, already mentioned, when the first experiment of carrying an emigrant's boat over the mountain on the railroad finally resulted in not only the bodily transfer of freight boats, but the remarkable jointed packet boats, which could be cut in halves and carried over the 36-mile, mountain-climbing railroad on cars and set afloat again without seriously disturbing the passengers.

The Delaware and Hudson was notable for a highly original idea—the suspension aqueduct. The canal built two, beginning in 1846, which were the first of their kind in existence. The one crossing the Delaware River was—and is—600 feet in length. The cables rest in cast iron saddles on stone towers 4 by 6 feet in lateral dimensions and rising 6 feet above the towpaths. These aqueducts not only stood until the canal's abandonment without giving away or sagging, but the one which spans the Delaware is in use to-day as a highway bridge; and the opinion was recently expressed that if the canal were to be put in service again, the woodwork of the aqueduct might have to be replaced, but the cables and anchorages are so sound that they would support the weight of the water and boats again, just as they did eighty years ago.

One finds other ingenuities, as for example, the invention at New Hope, Pennsylvania, by which the Delaware River was made to pump its own water into the Delaware Division Canal. Two big wheels were mounted on a single axle. One was an undershot water wheel turned by the river current, which at that point is very swift. The other wheel was encircled with buckets which dipped water out of a

Canal Engineering

more quiet runway, lifted it and dumped it at a higher level into a feeder for the canal.

A few hundred yards above these wheels was another clever bit of originality. An outlet lock had been made from the Delaware Division Canal to the river, while on the other shore there was a similar connection between the river and the Delaware and Raritan feeder. Boats from the Lehigh often came down the Delaware Division and crossed here to the Delaware and Raritan on their way to New York. To propel the boats across the river, the power of the current was again ingeniously utilized. A wooden tower was erected on either shore of the river and a cable stretched between them. Two smaller lines were fastened to two traveling wheels which ran on this cable as on a track. These two lines were of unequal length. The shorter was fastened to the bow of the boat, the longer to a point nearer the stern, so that the boat was held in a diagonal position, with the bow pointing quarter-way upstream. At this angle, the force of the current striking glancingly against the side of the hull, like wind against a sail, simply shoved the boat forward and across the river.

At Millerstown, Pennsylvania, where the Main Line crossed the Juniata, another and no less clever scheme was employed. This was an endless rope running on pulleys mounted on either shore of the river. A towing line was attached to the rope and the boat to the other end of the towing line. A water wheel operated by the river current moved the rope in the desired direction, pulling the boat across. A gear shift operated by a lever enabled the operator to change the direction of the rope's movement, so as to tow the boat towards the north or south shore as desired.

CHAPTER XXX

CANAL OPERATION

ONE of the most difficult things to accomplish when one set out to build a canal was that of constructing and maintaining a channel that would hold water. Light or gravelly soil sometimes caused a canal to leak badly for two or three years (or longer) after building before it seemed to settle and harden. Of course the channel was lined from the very start with a thick layer of stiff clay or "puddle," but even this did not always hold if the soil underneath was very porous.

It has already been mentioned that on the Union and Schuylkill (not to speak of some other canals), in places where the channel was blasted through limestone, the water leaked away so badly through fissures in the stone that boats often grounded unexpectedly. The two companies were finally driven to the extremity of lining the channel with timber.

All the more northerly canals were closed during the worst of the winter, because of the ice; and by the way, not very thick ice was required to stop a blunt-nosed canal boat pulled by one or two horses. Most boats kept going, trying to increase the season's receipts, until all of a sudden there would come a cold night late in November or December, and the canal would freeze and navigation be stopped. If the cold weather continued, many boats were forced to remain where they had been caught until spring—which was often a considerable inconvenience, especially if they had a load of coal or grain or some other commodity. If the canal was drained of its water, as many were during the win-

Canal Operation

ter months, it might be necessary to unload the cargo to avoid damage to the boat.

This sudden stoppage of transportation often worked considerable inconvenience to shippers. Caleb Atwater in February, 1839, to a man who had inquired concerning the possibility of getting a copy of his *History of Ohio,* wrote vexedly that "the second edition is out, but lying frozen up in a canal boat forty miles below here." Think of the anguish to an author of having his work tied up like that, and customers begging for it!

Most of the larger canals, especially the more northerly ones, were drained as soon as they closed for the winter. The feeders would be cut off and all flood gates and sluices opened. Then sand bars and other detritus which had accumulated during the season would be removed, the clay lining of the channel would be renewed and locks and aqueducts repaired. In the spring, the banks and towpaths must be repaired at places where they had eroded during the winter.

The Erie, because of its climate, could not avoid being closed for at least three months, more often four and sometimes five. But some other canals seem not to have drained the channels—at least, it was not done every year. An old citizen of Fort Wayne has told of driving in a sleigh on the ice of the Miami and Wabash and Erie from Defiance, Ohio, to Fort Wayne on the first of April, 1843, "and the ice was as solid as it had been at any time during the winter." In the southern part of Ohio the canals were out of commission as a rule for a very short time in winter. In 1838 the southern end of the Ohio and Erie was closed for only 21 days. The James River and Kanawha in some winters did not close at all; while down in Carolina, on the Santee Canal, conditions were so reversed that July and August, which were dull months, were chosen as the time for shutting down the canal and making repairs.

As years went by the canal beds became so settled and

Old Towpaths

hardened that they held water as the bed of any natural stream, and the clay puddling was no longer necessary. The Lehigh and Delaware Division Canals have had no clay lining applied in several decades, but there is little or no trouble from natural leakage—and the Delaware Division when first built was one of the worst of all canals in this respect.

But if the porous soil no longer bothers the canal superintendent, there are still the muskrats, eels, moles, minks and other fauna which cause leakage by digging holes in the banks or bottom. The Indiana canals suffered much from the boring of crawfish. Muskrats are the most troublesome of all in most sections; and throughout the entire history of the canals there have been standing rewards for them, dead or alive—preferably dead. An old handbill of the Middlesex shows that the reward was higher or lower in proportion as the animal was caught closer to or farther from the canal.

On some canals there were employees whose chief duties were the catching of burrowing animals and the keeping down of weeds and sprouts, all detrimental to the banks. Towpath walkers on the Lehigh in earlier days always carried a number of "whisks" of twisted straw with them. When they saw a tiny whirl in the water, indicating a hole in the bed underneath, they waded in, placed one or two of these wisps of straw in the hole, coiling them and treading them in firmly. The earth soon gathered over them and stopped the leak.

The towpath walker was analogous to the track walker on a railroad. He patrolled a section of the canal every day, observing the waste gates to see whether they were letting out the exact amount of water necessary to keep the canal surface at the proper level, inspecting the aqueducts and other structures for any signs of damage or weakening, watching the erosion of the banks and giving prompt notice of repairs needed. In stormy weather, when freshets were

Courtesy of I. M. Church, Superintendent of the Lehigh Coal and Navigation Company

TESTING ELECTRIC TRACTION ON THE LEHIGH CANAL

The heavy wash caused by boats moving at high speed was very detrimental to American canal banks

Courtesy of E. W. Drinker, Bethlehem, Pennsylvania

FOR CANALS WITH EARTHEN BANKS, NO TRACTIVE POWER SUPERIOR TO THE MULE HAS YET BEEN FOUND

Canal Operation

likely, he must be particularly vigilant, and often had to make temporary repairs himself. He was apt to be called from his bed in the night to help in the search for some person—adult or child—supposed to be drowned. One such employee had in charge a section of the Morris Canal ten miles long between Newark and a point three miles above the Bloomfield inclined plane, and walked over that stretch of towpath every day for nearly fifty years.

If a break in the bank was discovered, news was sent to repair headquarters by the quickest means possible, usually by a man on a fast horse, and the wrecking crew hastened to the scene on a boat whose horses were put to their best speed. The boat carried clay, straw, stakes, rope, pile planking, plenty of picks and shovels and a force of expert repair men. If a culvert or flood gate was broken, they shut off the water on either side of it by driving pile planking across the canal. This heavy pile planking was tongue-and-grooved, and was the ancestor of the modern steel coffer-dam piling, with the added advantage that when wet it swelled and made a water-tight barrier. Score another one for Grandfather!

If the break was in the bank of the canal, the repair crew drove down two rows of stakes across the breach, the rows being a foot or so apart. They wattled these with rope, and if the breach was deep, other stakes were driven obliquely beside the hurdles thus made to act as struts or props. The space between the hurdles was then filled with straw, well trodden down from the sides to the center. This slowed up the water—in fact, nearly stopped it. A row of pile planking was now driven, which stopped the water entirely, and then the breach was built up again with earth and stone.

The majority of canals followed the courses of rivers and creeks more or less closely, and for that reason often suffered terribly from the freshets in the natural streams. A canal whose banks had been badly broken by a flood presented one of the most disheartening sights imaginable. In

Old Towpaths

places the entire towpath, which was almost invariably on the outer or supporting bank, would be torn away for hundreds of feet in length, and sometimes to a depth of twenty or thirty feet. Such disasters meant destruction or serious damage to many boats. The great floods of 1862 on the Lehigh and Delaware Division, of 1869 on the Schuylkill, and of 1889 on the various Pennsylvania and Chesapeake and Ohio Canals destroyed and partly wrecked great numbers of boats; in the last-named year the number ran up into the hundreds. Many were washed out into cornfields or up into creek gulches and lay there until they decayed and disintegrated.

One is apt to think of canal navigation as being smooth and free from the dangers and annoyances caused by irregularities of the channel, but in those canals which used a river's slack-water pools for a portion of their course, the captain certainly had to mind his p's and q's. The Schuylkill Navigation was so complex a problem that a guidebook was written for it, telling masters of vessels just how to negotiate it in either direction.

The author certifies that "The Schuylkill Canal is considered very difficult without an experienced navigator or proper directions; especially the lower section from Reading to Philadelphia, occasioned by rocks, points and bars." As a sample, here are the instructions for completing a downstream voyage below Manayunk:

"Descending—from Manayunk direct from the locks (after taking on the horse) to the opposite shore, that you might land at the *lower wharf*—pass down near the other side by pushing with the poles—pass to the left of the *four bold rocks*—pass round them, keeping about 12 feet off to avoid the rocks on the left hand side of the river—Pass down near the middle of the river till you come near the piers of the *Falls bridge*—keep to the right of the *big rock* above the middle pier—land at *Young's wharf* and take off the horse, then tow till you pass the *island,* keeping out about

Canal Operation

30 feet—unhitch the horse and row for the other side—keep down half a mile—make for the tow-path side again at the point—hitch again, then tow to the locks, avoiding the stumps and rocks." Fancy packet-passengers enduring all that knocking about!

Thus the matter runs regarding the whole voyage save the part between Reading and Mount Carbon, of which he declares enthusiastically that "It is in such complete order that it may be passed without danger, only—" ah, here comes the rub!— "only observing to keep out from the tow-path about 10 or 12 feet from the dams—by going farther out there is danger of sticking on rocks or stumps in the canal—keep in the middle."

Even on the larger canals certain maneuvers were sometimes difficult and apt to get one into trouble. From the diary of Philip Hone one learns of the dilemma of a captain who tried to turn around in the canal. While traversing the Pennsylvania Canal in 1847, "this morning at sunrise," he writes, "the 'Commet,' a huge canal boat, had the bad manners to get stuck across the canal (what better could be expected from a fellow who spells Comet with two m's?). Here I witnessed a gallant exploit of our Captain, the raising a swell, which is thus performed; he puts six horses on the tow lines, backs the boat, and then lashing on with the fury of the horses in the hippodrome, raises a swell like the waves at Rockaway. The first onset removed the 'Commet' a little from her orbit, and the second carried us triumphantly through the obstacle. The sight of this spirited display of canal tactics compensated for the delay."

It was easy to raise a swell with an old canal boat, because some of them were as square in the bow as a packing case, while others—on the Erie, for instance—though quite as blunt, were rounded so that they received the nickname of "ball-head" boats, which eventually was corrupted to bullhead. Because of the necessity for speed, the packets had to be made a little more trim in their lines.

Old Towpaths

There were boats of many types on the various canals. You hear of counter-sterns, toothpicks, scows, lake boats, store boats and so on. Certain boatyards or towns often gave their name to a type. On the Lehigh Canal there were "chunkers" and "flickers," the former obviously named from Mauch Chunk. When the double boats were introduced on the Pennsylvania Canal, they were nicknamed snappers.

There was a great deal of rafting of timber on the canals, especially in the earlier years when timber was more plentiful. The rafts would float down the rivers or creeks to the canal, and thence be towed through by horses, though in some cases on the Middlesex oxen were used. Rafts were always built in sections of just the proper size to fit into one of the canal locks. These sections were called "bands" or "shots" on the Middlesex, and "cribs" farther west. From six to ten of them would be linked together in a single raft. A crew of four or five men would handle such a raft, sleeping in a rough board shelter built on one of the sections. Not much steering was needed, as the rafts trailed fairly well, only an occasional push with a pole being necessary to keep them in line. Other boats kept to the outside when passing rafts, and the timber crew carried the boats' towlines over the raft. On the Erie, where traffic was heavy, if a raft and a number of boats were waiting at a lock, the tender would pass one crib of the raft through, then a boat, then another crib, another boat and so on.

Horses were hitched to the boats by towlines 70 to 90 yards in length, according to circumstances or according to the captain's theories regarding the laws of physics. Upstream boats had the right of way at locks and elsewhere. When two boats met, the downstream boat's team stepped to the outside of the towpath and stopped, so that the towline lay on the ground and sank into the water; meanwhile the boat steered to the opposite side of the canal, away from the towpath. The upstream boat and team passed between

Canal Operation

the other boat and its team, the mules stepping over the other's towline, and the boat passing over it in the water. A similar procedure took place when one boat passed another going in the same direction, as packets did the slower freight boats. Boats of the same class often tried to pass each other, not only packets but freight boats—which brought on some tortoiselike races, and in the case of freight boats, not infrequently fights. The Middlesex sternly forbade any boat to pass another of the same class going in the same direction, thus taking all the joy out of racing. But it flourished on other canals, sometimes to a pernicious degree.

Long iron-tipped poles were carried by most boats to use in releasing the craft from rocks and sand bars, getting into locks, and the like, though many canals forbade their use in the ordinary channel, for the reason that a hole punched in the clay lining with a pole might be almost as bad as if it had been dug by a muskrat. There were fines assessed for entering a lock so clumsily as to bump the gates at the other end, which might damage both boat and gates. On some canals, boat crews were forbidden to have any fishing tackle aboard.

There were rules against "parking" in the open canal or within 150 feet of a lock, unless in a basin. On those canals whose locks were closed during the latter part of the night, these rules did not apply to boats gathered at the locks at night, waiting for the gates to open next morning. In early days the Middlesex forbade any traffic after dark because of possible damage to the locks and banks. "Dark" was specified as 7 P.M. in spring and autumn and 9 P.M. in summer. On moonlit nights, boats might pass until 10 P.M., but not after that nor before daybreak at any time. But on the Erie and Pennsylvania, and at times on other canals, traffic continued all night. On most of the waterways, the length of the day's operation was apparently gauged by the limit of the lock tender's physical endurance—which meant that it comprehended about eighteen hours.

Old Towpaths

In Bloomfield, on the Morris Canal, were an inclined plane and a lock, about a mile apart. An old man who tended the plane for many years says that during the busy days of the canal, there would often be boats tied up at night as closely as they could snuggle for a mile above the plane, all the way from the plane to the lock, and for a mile below the lock. "We'd begin putting 'em through the plane at the first peep of dawn in the morning," says he, "which meant four o'clock or ealier in midsummer. We'd keep it up till seven, and get most of the fellows from above through by that time; then we'd knock off an hour for breakfast, and the rest of the boats had to wait. At eight when we got started again, there'd be another bunch from above added to the crowd—the fellows who'd stayed overnight at Centerville, and started at dawn. By the time we got them through, the crowd who'd spent the night at Paterson would be coming in, and from below, the boats that had been overnight at Newark and Jersey City. And so it went all day long, until ten o'clock at night. Late in the evening some fellows would be coming up who had gone down to Newark in the morning, unloaded and were going back light. Long hours? Yes, but no one thought of making a serious kick about such a thing in those days."

Canal boat cargoes of a century ago included many items which sound strange and trivial to-day—ashes, for example. One frequently finds a boat carrying two or three hundred barrels of ashes. They were much in demand for use in manufacturing lye, potash, soap and other alkaline products. Another quaint item was firewood, of which immense quantities were handled. It must be remembered that coal, even bituminous coal, was little used in this country until the Nineteenth Century had gotten well on its way. Poor people hovered about the docks where wood was being loaded or unloaded, picking up the bark and broken fagots, just as they search the railroad yards now for scattered lumps of coal.

The pride of a captain and crew in their boats was often

Canal Operation

enhanced by the gorgeous coloring of the boat's exterior and the glittering trappings of the teams. A basin full of boats,

BOUNTY
ON
Musquashes and Mink,
TAKEN ON THE
Middlesex Canal.

If within two rods of the Canal, 50 cents a head; quarter of a mile, 30 cents; half a mile, 10 cents; one mile, 5 cents.

Application to be made either to Mr. Cyrus Baldwin, Mr. Nathan Mears, Col. Hopkins, Mr. Isaac Johnson, Mr. Elijah Peirce, Mr. Samuel Gardner, or Mr. Joseph Church, whichever of them lives nearest the place where the animal may be taken.

If the person applied to is satisfied of the facts, his certificate or verbal declaration thereof to the subscriber will entitle the applicant to the bounty. The applicant must produce the Musquash or Mink entire, to one of the above-named persons. He may then take his skin.

J. L. SULLIVAN.

MARCH, 1809.

Courtesy Public Library of Woburn, Massachusetts
HANDBILL OF THE MIDDLESEX CANAL, OFFERING A REWARD FOR MUSKRAT AND MINK

especially on the Erie or the Pennsylvania Main Line, when the packets were in their glory, inevitably exhibited not only

Old Towpaths

the seven colors of the spectrum but symphonies in crimson, maroon, brown, pink, lilac, magenta, yellowish-green, and any other mongrel shade that an experimental mixer of paints might chance to hit upon. Bright brass and sometimes nickel or silver mountings and bangles on the harness were distinguishing features of some outfits. One popular packet on the Wabash and Erie, the Silver Bell, was drawn by three gray mules who were said to have worn real silver-mounted harness and had silver bells tinkling at their throats.

The crew of a boat was intensely loyal to it, as a rule—any man who wasn't loyal wasn't wanted—and would fight for it on the slightest provocation. Fighting was one of the besetting sins of the canallers. Look into canal rules and regulations—here are those of the Wabash and Erie, for example—and you will find that one section reads something like this: "If, on the arrival of any two or more floats at or near any lock, a question shall arise between their respective masters as to which shall be first entitled to pass, such question shall be determined by the lockkeeper or superintendent having charge of such lock," etc.

But any canal man could tell you that this was not the manner in which the question was settled. The boat first through the lock was the boat whose crew could lick the other crew. On the Wabash and Erie and in some other places posts were set at short distances above and below the locks, and the first boat into this "block" had first right to the lock. But even this didn't always check the pugnacity of a crew who had determined to be first, whether right or wrong.

Captains often chose men for their fighting record rather than for their skill in navigation. Two crews which had had an argument about lockage or other question, when they met again, sometimes tied up to the bank and began fighting again. When one side cried "enough," they separated and went on their way as if nothing had happened. There were canal bullies who lorded it over all less pugnacious boatmen, and when two of these met each other, the occasion was

Canal Operation

historic. One of the great days in Erie history was that when Ben Streeter, the Rochester bully and one of the noted fighters of the canal, fought the bully of Buffalo for one hour in the old Rochester Arcade, and licked him. The police, we are told, "dared not interfere."

It must be set down to the credit of the canallers that they usually fought with nothing more deadly than their fists. There were occasional mêlées, however, which were of a more serious tone. We read of a collision of two boats; a quarrel arose instantly, and the crews of two other boats were drawn into it. A missionary happened to come upon the scene and found that stones had already been thrown, the towrope of one boat had been cut, and the crews of the four boats were moving upon each other, armed with clubs and pike poles, one man having a knife drawn. At the risk of his life the missionary rushed between them, and by an eloquent appeal calmed the fury of the warriors and averted bloodshed.

Every one familiar with the life stories of our great men will remember that President Garfield was a canal boat driver in his youth. As a matter of fact, his experience in that capacity was brief, being cut short by malaria. He was only sixteen when he secured a job as driver from his kinsman, Captain Amos Letcher, of the freighter *Evening Star*, on the Ohio and Erie Canal. In a document which may or may not have been produced during a political campaign, Captain Letcher tells how, on Jim's first trip, they approached the first of the twenty-one locks of Akron and came into conflict with another boat which appeared to have an equal if not a better claim to first chance at the lock.

"Every man from both boats was on hand, ready for a field fight," says the Captain. "Jim Garfield tapped me on the shoulder and asked, 'Does that lock belong to us?' 'I suppose according to law it does not. But we will have it, anyhow.' 'No, we will not!' 'Why?' said I. 'Why!'— with a look of indignation which I shall never forget. 'Why,

Old Towpaths

because it doesn't belong to us.' Said I, 'Boys, let them have it.'

"Next morning one of the hands accused Jim of being a coward because he would not fight for his rights. Said I, 'Boys, don't be hard on Jim. I was mad last night, but I have got over it. Jim may be a coward for aught I know, but if he is, he is the first one of his name that I ever knew that was. His father was no coward. He helped dig this canal and weighed over 200 pounds and could take a barrel of whisky by the chime and drink out of the bung-hole, and no man dared call him a coward. You'll alter your mind about Jim before fall.'"

How vividly it all reminds us of Parson Weems's original anecdote of little George Washington and the cherry tree! The spectacle of the sixteen-year-old boy lecturing and cowing a hard-boiled canal boat captain and crew must be preserved; it is too delicious to be lost from our traditions. But great man and good citizen though General Garfield became, there will inevitably be low-minded readers who will insist that the youthful scion of a husky pioneer who could stand flat-footed and h'ist a barrel of whisky to drink out of the bung-hole would never have yielded a lock so tamely in those fighting days.

Come to think of it, let us compare the above narrative with the following, told by Captain Parkhurst of the boat *Blue Bird* of Circleville, who must have been a veracious man, because he always tied his boat up on Sunday, though such was not the common practice. Captain Parkhurst tells of witnessing a fight "at Lock No. 1, Akron, between a boatman and a heavy-set, muscular boy, the driver of the canal boat, *Evening Star*, on the side-cut canal. The former's boat reached the lock first and a taunting remark by a member of the crew caused the boy driver to take the black-snake whip from around his neck and pitch it at the fellow, knocking him down, with the result that the boy's boat entered the lock first. This boy was afterwards President Garfield."

Courtesy of the Bucks County Historical Society, Doylestown, Pennsylvania
CANAL BOATS WRECKED BY A FLOOD IN THE ADJACENT RIVER AND PILED IN THE BED OF THE RUINED CANAL; DELAWARE DIVISION, NEAR NEW HOPE, PENNSYLVANIA, 1903

Courtesy of I. M. Church, Superintendent of Lehigh Coal and Navigation Company
REPAIRING A CANAL WHOSE BANKS HAVE BEEN BROKEN BY A FLOOD

Canal Operation

The reader may select the story he likes best.

Somebody was always trying to cipher out a way to get rid of the canal mule. They even gave oxen a severe test on the Middlesex. An ox can pull more than any other draft animal save an elephant. One yoke of oxen drew on the Middlesex a raft of timber calculated to weigh 800 tons. But oxen are also the slowest of four-footed animals, their rate of progress being no more than one mile per hour. At that speed the experts decided that "steers" wouldn't pay.

Probably the first steamboat ever run on a canal was the one which appeared on the Middlesex in 1818. This boat was the third seen in Massachusetts waters, and was built on the canal, probably in the shipyard at Medford. She was between 50 and 60 feet long and about 10 feet wide, with a single paddle wheel which was said to be "within the stern." The boat did not remain long on the canal, possibly because of detriment to the banks.

A steamboat passed through the Schuylkill Canal in 1826, but did not repeat the trip, and steam was not used on the Schuylkill again for twenty years. In 1827 a Mr. Costell of Philadelphia planned a steam vessel "calculated for canal navigation, being so constructed as not to injure the banks." The *Ariel* in 1828 mentioned "a small steam canal boat, an experiment, which passed Weedsport on the Erie Canal recently. She proceeded with great velocity and threw very little water upon the banks."

Experiments were made with steam on the Chesapeake and Delaware in 1834, and it was declared entirely practicable. But the C. and D. was larger than other canals and not so apt to be injured by the swell. It had very little traffic of its own, being rather a sort of strait or connecting link between two large bodies of water, used by craft whose termini were far distant from its own.

Meanwhile, other experimenters were trying to increase the speed with horse power. The report that the Ardrossan or Paisley Canal in Scotland operated fast passenger boats

Old Towpaths

at 9 or 10 miles an hour aroused much envy in this country, and many vain attempts to equal or surpass it. Our canals were too narrow and too cheaply built to withstand the erosion caused by such a speed. We were just beginning to comprehend that on a narrow canal with earthen banks, a speed of more than 3½ miles per hour is highly detrimental to the waterway.

From Old Residents' Historical Association Publications, Lowell, Massachusetts
A "SHOT" OR "CRIB" OF TIMBER GOING THROUGH A LOCK

Striving to do away with the towline and make the boat self-contained, one Burke of Pennsylvania invented a propeller boat operated by a horse walking a treadmill. In this boat, as in most others first designed for the canals, the propeller was placed at the bow with the idea that it would there exert a less serious wash on the banks than if it were at the stern.

Mellen Battel in 1840 patented a boat with "combined ground and paddle wheel so as to run upon the bottom of the canal and to propel the boat by the friction of the crossbars and runs alone, and when raised from the bottom to effect the propelling by the buckets or paddles." John I. Weeks had a similar idea save that his wheel was toothed to take hold of the canal bed. A scientific committee which examined Weeks' boat believed that it would "perform the duty required of it" and did not think it would injure the bed

Canal Operation

of the canal. The driving wheel of another inventor's boat was perfectly smooth and was supposed to take hold of the canal bed by mere friction, as the driving wheel of a locomotive does the rail.

So far, all the "propellers" which beat upon the water alone were mere paddle wheels. Ericsson, the Swedish-American inventor, is credited with having invented the screw propeller. His experiments first began to attract attention about 1836, and he brought his device to a practical stage about 1840–41. But Frank J. Kingsbury, a bank

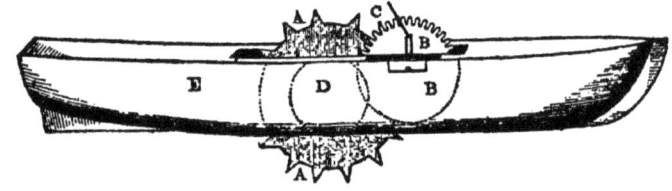

JOHN I. WEEKS'S DESIGN FOR A CANAL TOWBOAT

president of Waterbury, Connecticut, writing in the *Connecticut Magazine* some time ago, said that a man named Benjamin D. Beecher had antedated Ericsson by several years, though Ericsson was probably unaware of Beecher's experiments.

Beecher was an ingenious mechanic and inventor who began experimenting with the idea of a screw propeller in 1831, and after a few years had completed a working model. The boat to which it was attached was hauled by oxen three or four miles to the New Haven and Northampton Canal and launched, and there Mr. Kingsbury saw it in use in the middle '30's. A small steam engine operated the propeller, which again was located at the bow. But the inventor was poor and did not know how to get his idea before the public. Probably he did not realize what a tremendous part it was to play in the navigation of the future.

Inventions came thick and fast in those days. The

Old Towpaths

Logansport, Indiana, *Telegraph* in 1840 reported a canal boat invented by "an ingenious mechanic of this city" to operate by steam without injury to the banks. Time and again this great discovery was announced, but always it came to naught. Steam cargo and packet boats were actually built and used, however, on several canals before the Civil War. The steam packet *Niagara* was built on the Miami Canal in 1845. It cost $10,000 and was not a financial

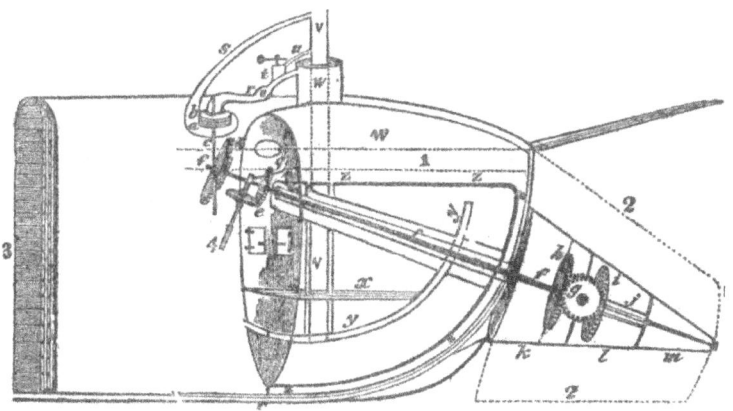

From the "Connecticut Magazine"
PROPELLER INVENTED BY BENJAMIN D. BEECHER ON THE NEW HAVEN AND NORTHAMPTON CANAL, CLAIMED TO ANTEDATE ERICSSON'S BY SEVERAL YEARS

success. The *Scarecrow*, a freight boat which appeared on the Miami in 1859, did better. It had a propeller three feet in diameter at the stern, to which power was communicated by a belt from the flywheel on the engine, located nearer amidships. The Miami being larger than some other canals, a great speed was permissible, but not enough to render its first cost and operating expense worth while.

Steam packets with iron hulls were built on the Schuylkill in 1846–47, but did not operate long. Two steamboats made a trip through the Chesapeake and Ohio in 1855, but did not repeat the experiment. In 1860 another was built and tried on the Ohio and Erie. That year also a steam towboat

Canal Operation

appeared on the Susquehanna and Tidewater, which was large enough to accommodate such craft more comfortably than some other waterways. The managers exultantly announced that the introduction of steam "must inaugurate a new era in the history of our canals," and that it would be "a useless waste of means on the part of railroad companies controlling parallel lines to carry on a competition for the through trade." The foolhardy railroad companies nevertheless went right on doing that very thing.

The continued prosperity of the Erie Canal after the Civil War led to many experiments with mechanical towage. But now the striving was not for high speed, but merely to attain three miles per hour, which was twice as fast as the horse's average when drawing a freight boat. One of the methods tried on the Erie was that known as the Belgian System, which had been successfully operated on foreign canals. Under this system a chain or steel cable—preferably the cable—was laid along the bottom of the canal, being fastened only at its termini. The tug, which was capable of pulling several boats, had an engine amidships with a clip driving wheel. The cable was lifted from the bottom of the canal and placed in the groove on the rim of the drive-wheel. The engine was then started, and the drive-wheel took hold of the cable with sufficient grip to move the boat forward.

A cable was laid under this system in a portion of the canal, but did not gain favor because the canal authorities were becoming more and more interested in self-operated boats—which inevitably meant steamboats. Bonuses were being offered for steam craft to operate successfully at three miles per hour, and in 1874 three men were granted concessions for operating such boats. So slowly did steam get a foothold, however, that in 1883, out of 4,000 boats on the canal, only 92 were steam-propelled.

Electric haulage was tried on both the Miami and Erie and the Lehigh Canals. The story of the Miami and Erie

Old Towpaths

fiasco has already been told. On the Lehigh in 1907 a determined effort was made to find a better method of towage. An ordinary electric mine locomotive running on a two-rail track was given a test and of course hauled several boats with ease; that was to be expected. But the device which created most enthusiasm was a monorail electric "mule," which some hailed as having "revolutionized" canal navigation. "The knell of the canal mule has been sounded," wrote several editors. "Our old, braying, long-eared friends will soon be in the discard." But they spoke too soon. The old objection to mechanical towage was found to be still valid. If boats were moved at much greater speed than the mule's walk, the damage to the banks of the canal nullified the benefits derived from the change. The net result was that no knells were sounded for the long-eared friends, who still continued to dawdle along the towpaths as of yore.

CHAPTER XXXI

LIFE ON THE CANAL

THERE was a wide variety in the sort of boats seen on a canal. Every canal being a public highway, anybody who desired and would pay the tolls could build and own boats thereon. In the early days of the Erie and some of the other canals, many farmers and other producers built each his own boat and carried his own products to market with the assistance of one or two hands. It is said that some of these jerry-made products of men who had never before done any boat-building in their lives had an unfortunate habit of sinking every night while they were tied up, and must be raised and pumped out every morning before they could proceed. Later the carrying business fell more into the hands of professional boatmen—either captains who owned their boats and made that their sole business, or companies owning a number of boats.

They tell of a farmer on the banks of the Susquehanna who, drawn by the lure of the seafaring life, built a boat and set sail to do general hauling, with his two farm hands as crew. They knew nothing of the country outside of their own neighborhood. One night on their first trip, they tied up at a town which bears the mellifluous name of Shickshinny. Here, while they snored peacefully in their berths, certain jokers among the regular boatmen turned their craft around so that it was headed in the opposite direction. Next morning, never noting the trick, the crew hooked up and plodded back over the very ground from whence they had come; but as they were passing through Beach Haven, eight

Old Towpaths

miles distant, the driver, who had been looking about him uneasily, exclaimed, "W'y, dang it, this looks jest like a town we come through yistiddy!"

The crew of a boat ranged in number all the way from two to six men. If the boat was a large one and ran night and day, as they did on the busier canals such as the Erie and Pennsylvania, there were usually two drivers, two steersmen and a cook. Often there was a "bowsman," though the word didn't mean anything, the bowsman being merely a sort of general deck hand. Some have guessed that the word was in reality a metamorphosed form of "boatswain."

Before the Civil War, bowsmen and steersmen were contented with $20 per month wages. Adult drivers were paid $12 and boy drivers in the East $10, while on some of the western canals they drew as low as $8. Of course it must be remembered that the employee also received his board and lodging on the boat while in service. Wages became much higher after the war.

The drivers of the freight boats, especially those employed in earlier days and by individual boat owners, were often mere children. In a missionary report of 1848 it was estimated (with how much accuracy it is difficult to say) that there were 10,000 boys working on the New York canals. Many of them led a pretty hard life. Their $10 a month wages were seldom paid to them until the end of the season, when they would have $70 or $80 due them. If paid earlier, they often drank and gambled it all away. On the other hand, brutal and unscrupulous captains not infrequently cheated them out of the whole season's wages.

The missionary report says that there were "some awfully precocious specimens of depravity among them." No doubt there were. Herbert Quick in *Vandemark's Folly* pictures vividly some of the temptations to which they were subjected. But it must be remembered that the missionaries' code was exceedingly strict. One feels a tendency to think less harshly of the boys when one reads of a case

Courtesy of the Baltimore & Ohio Railroad Company
MORE OR LESS PERMANENT HOUSEBOAT LIFE ON THE CANAL

From "Harper's Magazine"
BOY OVERBOARD!

Life on the Canal

of infant depravity reported by a missionary on the New Jersey canals:

"One Sabbath morning, as I was going around, distributing tracts," he says, "I observed two boys, drivers on the Canal, in a small boat in which they had been out on the River on an excursion of pleasure. I expostulated with them on the awful effects of desecrating a day ordained expressly for the worship of the Creator. . . . I soon perceived that one of them was deeply affected, while the other was apparently inexorable; threatening that he would go out on the River again, and making use of every effort to get his companion with him." It is pleasant to record that the missionary was finally able to melt the conscience of this hardened sinner.

But if the boys were bad, what shall be said of the men—that jolly, roistering, hard-swearing, hard-drinking, hard-fighting lot who gave the missionaries sent to them by the Seamen's Friend and the American Bethel Societies many an hour of despair?

Deacon Mason, who began his work as a missionary on the Erie in the early '40's, when its working population was about 25,000, said afterwards that he did not suppose there was another place in the world where there was as much iniquity. He declared that it was difficult for youth or man from the canal to obtain employment over the winter because of his supposed depravity as a boatman. Canal life was bad enough, in all conscience, but let us not forget that as in the case of the Sabbath-breaking driver boys, the missionaries of that day had sins entered in their catalogue which would be considered quite venial now.

Some of the canallers themselves seemed to regard their spiritual condition as hopeless. "Many seem to think," wrote a missionary, "and do actually assert, that religion and boating are incompatible—that a boatman cannot be a consistent Christian. The assertion, of course, has no foundation in fact." The writer admitted, however, that "Boat-

Old Towpaths

men, from the very nature of their business, are liable to become careless and wicked. Their occupation withdraws them from the salutary influences of the sanctuary and the restraints of female society, and brings them in daily contact with men who are perhaps more careless and wicked than themselves." Among the tools which were used in the struggle to pluck the souls of the reckless canallers from the burning were tracts with such titles as "The Swearer's Prayer" and "Esau; or, the Ruinous Bargain." But let us not smile too broadly at those old missionaries. They saved many a man from disgrace and ruin, and played a noble and self-sacrificing part in upholding law, order, decency and righteousness.

"It is a sad sight," says another report, "to see the evils of rum among the boatmen. . . . They not only drink it by the glass at the rum-shop, but in some instances they carry it on their boats. The rum sellers, when conversed with on the subject, were willing to admit that the sale of rum produced vice, poverty and wretchedness. Yet they are unwilling to discontinue the vile traffic whilst it continues to be profitable."

Small wonder if the boatman drank when liquor was almost cheap as water. Good whisky could be bought for a "fip" (6¼ cents) the half pint in Pennsylvania small towns in the early days of the canals, and similarly low prices prevailed everywhere. One hears of whisky and applejack at 25 cents the gallon in Ohio in the '20's. At almost every lock or group of locks there was a tavern, often kept by the locktender; and at the horse stations there were others. Here the crews of all the boats which lay overnight in the vicinity would gather, and the squawk of the fiddle and wail of the accor-deen would mingle on the evening air with the rasp of rugged voices raised in song.

"Flip was the high-toned beverage in New England," says Lorin L. Dame, "but black strap (rum and molasses) at three cents per glass was the favorite drink of boatmen.

Life on the Canal

In the smaller taverns a barrel of old Medford and a pitcher of molasses invited patrons to draw and mix at will." Drunkenness? "Bless your heart, no!" said Uncle Joe, an old salt of the Middlesex Canal, to Dr. Dame. "Mr. Eddy"

From "Harper's Magazine"
A MORRIS CANAL CAPTAIN OF 1860

(Caleb Eddy, the canal manager) "didn't put up with no drunkenness on the canal. They could drink all night, sir, and be steady as an eight-day clock in the morning." The testimony of other witnesses does not always agree with Uncle Joe's as to the iron heads of the boatmen; but it

Old Towpaths

must be admitted that most of them carried their liquor remarkably well.

J. L. Ringwalt, in his *Development of the Transportation System in the United States,* reports a conversation which he held with a driver on the Erie in 1883, which gives a fair idea of salaries and conditions during the two decades following the Civil War:

"How do the drivers work? By the trip or by the day?"

"Both ways. A man can git a dollar a day or he can hire out by the trip and git about twenty dollars a month. But when he works by the day, he gits nothin' while a boat unloads, and workin' by the trip, his pay goes right on. So it makes it even."

"How long does it take to make a trip from Buffalo to Albany and return?"

"Depends on the load. About three weeks, on an average. The current goes east, so it's easier goin' to Albany than comin' back."

"How many trips can a boat make in a season?"

"About nine or ten."

"Is pulling a canal boat very hard work for the mules?"

"A mule kin stand it better'n a hoss. Take a hoss, and it only takes a few seasons to wear him out. Now you mayn't believe it, but that off mule has been pullin' a boat twenty-three years."

"But isn't a mule harder to drive?"

"Wal, yas; they git kinder rambunctious sometimes. . . . Something curi's about them mules. You can ca'c'late their age pretty close every time by the way they wobble their ears. Take a young mule, and he twists 'em all shapes all the time; when he gits old he quiets down and holds 'em kinder steady. They're mighty good for tellin' the weather, too; when a mule keeps his ears pricked up, it's a sure sign of rain."

"How many months of a year does a driver work?"

Life on the Canal

"Oh, eight or nine months is fair. Sometimes nine or ten, when the weather's good."

"And what do you do winters?"

"Haul up at either end and git what you can. Sometimes you can git work on the railroad, and sometimes nothin' at all."

"How many men are there on a boat?"

"Five, generally. There's two drivers, two steersmen and the captain."

"The steersman of course gets higher wages than the driver?"

"Oh, yes; a steersman can git about $40 a month. That's the place the driver is allus fishin' for. It takes about four or five years drivin' to git there, though."

Captains at this time, if on salary, drew $50 or $60, rarely $70 a month.

The drivers for companies which owned a number of boats worked—somewhat like the horses—in stages of only fifteen or twenty miles, and made their headquarters at the horse stations. The vast traffic brought about the introduction of a public horse-and-driver service, by means of which any captain who had no horses or drivers of his own could arrange to have changes of teams and drivers promptly supplied to him at every station of the service company through the canal's length. Such horse stations were busier places even than the street-car barns of a later day.

Even to the end of the horse traffic days on the Erie, some captains continued to own and carry with them their own horses. Clifton Johnson describes a boat on which he rode in 1900 which had seven horses, three working in one team and four in another. Each team had six hours on and six off. After reaching Albany, the horses had a vacation while they rode down to New York and back in the stable in the bow of the boat. This gave a welcome rest to their sore shoulders, from which affliction canal horses often suffered severely. Horses were often dreadfully abused in

Old Towpaths

early days. Niles in 1827 hoped that the time was not far distant when steam would supplant horses, "for it is a fact noticed by those conversant with canal navigation that horses engaged in drawing canal boats, either from the nature of the duties imposed or from bad treatment, exhibit the most disgusting spectacles."

Horses (and the generic term "horses" must always be understood to include mules) suffered other vicissitudes as well. They were often caught by fouled towlines and thrown into the canal. The same disaster was apt to befall them if the boat collided with another or was caught against a bridge. Wherever the canal was enclosed by perpendicular walls, as was the Erie at Lockport and on the Mohawk, there were occasional ramps or runways leading up from the water by which horses might be brought back to the towpath after falling in.

In the beginning all boats save packets tied up on Sunday. Then as business became more brisk, a few captains began running on the Sabbath, and presently the practice became general. But there were some Sunday regulations. The Middlesex ran no freight boats on that day, but passenger traffic was permitted "in consideration of the distance from home at which those persons using it generally are." However, "it may be reasonably expected that they should not disturb those places of public worship near which they pass, nor occasion any noise to interrupt the tranquillity of the day. Therefore it is established that no *Signal-Horn* shall be used or blown on Sunday."

In Albany in 1827 John Dows and others complained of "the blowing of horns and bugles in the evening, and prayed that such might be prohibited between 7 and 10 P.M." "Those gondoliers," said a newspaper writer, "seem to be possessed with an unaccountable furore for bugles and French horns, and the whole country is serenaded by them to a painful extent."

We find no record of an abatement of this nuisance;

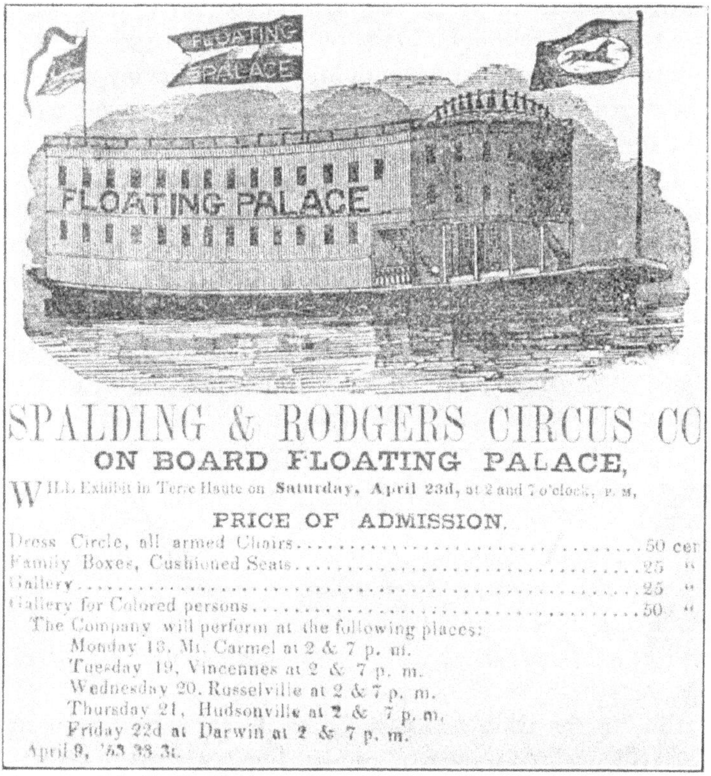

Courtesy of the Emeline Fairbanks Memorial Library, Terre Haute, Indiana

A FLOATING CIRCUS OF ANTE-BELLUM DAYS WHICH ONCE TOURED FOR SOME DISTANCE ALONG THE WABASH AND ERIE CANAL

From "Harper's Magazine"

A DRIVER AND TEAM OF 1860

Life on the Canal

but the town of Rochester very firmly prohibited the blowing of canal horns within its limits on Sunday. In fact, a great agitation arose against Sabbath-breaking, and many thought that even the boats should be halted. Mass meetings were held for both sides of the question, and some attempt was made to boycott the boats operating on Sunday. Three citizens sought to damage the business of the Sabbath-disregarding boats by starting a line of packets which did not run on Sunday. But they gave up the struggle after they had lost $60,000. Even in that early day there were "antis," and the "friends of liberal principles and equal rights" held counter meetings for some time and protested against "blue laws" and "Sabbatarian regulation."

A Schenectady newspaper in 1852 observed a great improvement in the moral tone of the Erie. "We have noticed," said the editor, "during this season of navigation that many boats tie up on Sunday. This is a gratifying sight to every good citizen. In this respect, as well as in the decrease of crimes and fights, abundant proof is found that the Erie Canal boatmen of this day are a more moral class of men than their predecessors of fifteen years ago."

But on the Ohio and Erie Canal, Captain Parkhurst of Circleville, who refused to run on Sunday, was so unique that his fame spread to the uttermost corners of the State, and his craft was known everywhere as "the Sunday boat."

The Delaware and Hudson was unique in that it was a strict Sabbath-keeping canal. At midnight between Saturday and Sunday the locks were closed, and under no circumstances were they operated again until Monday morning. The missionaries said that although twenty-five or fifty boats often spent Sunday at the same place, yet the men were quieter and of better behavior than those on any other canal.

Ministers when traveling in those days usually left the packets and coaches at some inn on Saturday night, refusing to travel on Sunday. But two clergymen who were once traversing the Pennsylvania Canal were asked by the captain

Old Towpaths

and passengers to remain on board and hold service on Sunday. We are told that "after mature deliberation, the clergymen, from all the circumstances of the case, decided it their duty to change their original purpose of leaving the packet on Saturday evening and to remain on board for the purpose of conducting divine worship on Sunday. . . . The whole day wore the aspect of solemnity. The sound of the horn and the hammer and other instruments ordinarily employed in conducting the packet onward ceased, and the day was quiet." There were 140 passengers on board, and it must have been a severe strain to maintain an aspect of solemnity and quiet all day long in such close quarters.

Canal-boat nomenclature is an interesting study. Hero worship, intense pride in their craft, and effervescent American humor were the three characteristics most clearly revealed by the boatmen's names for their craft. There were rules on all canals regarding the naming of boats. No two might bear the same name (though some names such as George Washington were common to all the canals, and there might be some slight confusion when such a boat visited another waterway); all boat names must be duly registered and must be painted in letters of a certain size on the stern of the boat.

Every American hero was honored, including all the Presidents up to date, commanders of the Revolution and War of 1812, *De Witt Clinton, Poor Richard, John Jay, Rip van Winkle, Major Jack Downing* and hordes of others. There were, of course, numerous *Andrew Jacksons* and *Old Hickorys,* properly balanced by *Daniel Websters* and *Henry Clays.* Among foreign notables *Napoleon, Julius Cæsar, Kosciusko, Lord Byron, Robert Bruce, Queen Anne, Cleopatra,* and *Bolivar* were among those honored. The captain's family furnished many of the names, which were apt to be doubled—as, *Hattie and Mattie, Cynthia and Sarah, John and Annie, Ida and Virginia.* Doubtless also in delicate tribute to kinsmen and friends were such names as *Two*

Life on the Canal

Sisters, Four Boys, Three Partners, Two Annies, Four Friends and *Eleven Brothers.*

Most of earth's fauna were remembered, from *Lion, Elephant, Whale, Elk, Eagle* and *Sea Lion* down to *Bee, Rat, Fly* and *Flea.*

On the other hand, can anyone fancy a canal boat living up to the name of *Splendid?* or *Fame?* or *Fashion?* or *Palace?* There seems to be a vaunt of honest dealing in such names as *Good Intent, Fair Play, Good Return, Fair Chance, Honest Farmer, Fair American, Fair Trader* and *Honest Quaker.* Possibly these phrases were put into practice, but there is something irresistibly comic in such names as *Greyhound, Swiftsure, Racer, Meteor, Lightning, Locomotive, Lady Lightfoot, Express* and *Whirlwind,* applied to vehicles whose maximum speed was four miles an hour, and who—many of them being freight boats—seldom did half that well.

They tell in Pennsylvania of a man who named his boat *To and Fro* and was quite happy in his originality until one night when a joker crept up on him while his craft lay moored to the bank and added certain letters to the name on the stern. Next day he had gone placidly on his way for many a mile before the laughter of observers caused him to discover that his boat was now sailing under the appellation of *Toads and Frogs.*

Among other names, whimsical, poetic and what not, found on the Erie were *Coat of Mail, Post Boy, Corn Planter, Young Lion of the West, May Fly, Octoroon, Columbia's Son, Extenuate, Unexpected, Ado, Tea Plant, Anticipation, Humility, Farmer's Daughter* and *Holland Purchase.* Names on the Morris had a devil-may-care swagger of their own: *Jolly Boatman, Bluddy Pirate, Bridge Smasher, Lager Bier, Wild Irishman* and *Sarsey Fanney.* On the Pennsylvania Canals there were such gems as *Yankee Spy, Green Branch, E Pluribus Unum, Sylvan Stream, Two Guns, Bondage Free, The Wooden Child, May Flour* (sic),

Old Towpaths

Ladies' Friend, Local Option, Sabbath Rest, Here I Am and *Ubydam*.

On the Ohio canals the play of fancy was, if possible, even wilder and more polysyllabic. There one finds *The Ark, Black Strap, Darby Ram, Corn Crib, Flying Cloud, Blooming Youth, Floating Artist, Queen City of the Valley, Pride of the Hocking, Ocean Queen, Saloon of Yellow Bud, Saw Log, Shadow Catcher* and *Wild Horse of Mill Creek*.

Let nothing hereinbefore said cause the impression to get abroad that there were not many worthy men among the canallers—sometimes a bit rough coated, perhaps, but decent and orderly citizens. Among them were those whose freight boats were the floating homes of their captain-owners. Some captains' families remained at home, usually in a village along the line of the canal, where they were apt to tend a thriving truck patch or perhaps even run a little store. Other families spent some seasons aboard the husband's vessel and some ashore. In the heyday of the canals, a village man was sometimes able to rent a boat for a season, upon which he would close up his little home on shore and he and his family would take to the water.

The incredibly small cabin at the stern was usually as neat as a new pin if a woman was on board. There would be colored curtains at the tiny windows, perhaps a red geranium growing in a tin can on the sill. On some canals, such as the Lehigh, Morris and Delaware Division, where the boats were narrow and the cargo space almost crowded the cabin space out of existence, the cooking was usually done on a stove standing on the open deck at the "hinges," where the double hulls were joined together by turnbuckles. The reason for this location was that the deck was lower there than at either bow or stern, giving more headroom for the stove under the bridges.

On the three canals mentioned, the crew not infrequently consisted of two men only, each of whom took turns at driving while the other steered. The man who was steering at

Life on the Canal

mealtime did the cooking. He would lift the potlid and take a look at the beans, run about forty feet to the stern and give the rudder a twist, trot forward to the stove, put on the coffee and break an egg into it, run back and give the tiller another swing, possibly take out the tiller handle until a bridge was passed, put it in place again and dash forward to snatch off the coffee pot, which was boiling over. When he had gulped down his hasty meal, he would leap to the towpath and drive while the other man ate. One old-timer tells us that "if it rained, an umbrella must be held over the stove," but how the steersman could do this under the circumstances described, it is hard to guess.

While waiting their turns at loading or unloading points or awaiting repairs on a broken lock or towpath, sometimes fifty or a hundred boats might collect and lie together for days or weeks, while their crews fraternized, and occasionally fought. Fishing, wrestling, foot racing, excursions into the neighboring city or country, card playing, smoking and swapping yarns filled most of these days of waiting for the men, while women sewed, visited and traded gossip and household lore. Old Pennsylvania boatmen laugh yet over the story of Mrs. Captain Jenkins, who was visiting Mrs. Captain Jones while their boats lay in a large fleet in New York Harbor, and was so absorbed in conversation with her crony that she paid no attention when a tug picked up the Jones boat's towline and started with it towards the Raritan, unintentionally removing her from the bosom of her family for nearly a week.

Even sixty to ninety years ago one finds those queer seminomads, the shanty-boat folk, on the canals. Sometimes high and dry on the bank, sometimes tied up at a wide place in the channel, the boat might drowse for months or years; then all of a sudden a bony old horse, either bought or borrowed, would be hooked up, and the clumsy old craft would go stumbling away along the canal, seeking some vague, indefinable advantage, good fortune or new vista beyond the horizon.

Old Towpaths

There were floating saloons and boats of entertainment on the canals, too. One finds in Indiana newspapers advertisements of a "floating palace," in which a "circus" performed along the Wabash River and Wabash and Erie Canal in the '50's. On the Pennsylvania canals a showman who must have been a free thinker had a fleet of three boats named Volney, Voltaire and Tom Paine which were of such ingenious construction that when lashed alongside each other the sides of each could be taken out, thus throwing the three into one large auditorium, in which was given, we are told, a wonderful performance consisting of "Minstrels, Ledgerdemain, and acts by trained dogs, monkies and white mice." As may be imagined, his troupe was vastly popular and was eagerly looked for everywhere along the canal. After operating his show for some years, the owner sold two of the boats and converted the other into a traveling grocery store.

The canals were favorite swimming places, both for the boating and land population. An aqueduct was a desirable spot because of the flat bottom and uniform depth of the channel, and because the smooth, elevated towpaths furnished a nice diving platform. The shade of the covered wooden aqueducts found on some canals was particularly welcome on scorching summer days to little boys who swam entirely "in the buff." Moving canal boats gave opportunity for many stunts by the youngsters. An empty boat draws only eight or ten inches of water, and daring mermen showed their prowess by passing under such a boat from side to side. A favorite diversion (when permitted) was "stemming"—lying on the back with feet against the prow of a moving boat, which thus propelled one headfirst through the water in a seemingly rapid, effortless glide. If the captain or steersman would permit it, there might be two or three other small, pink barnacles trailing in the water from the blade of the rudder.

One of the most exclusive organizations in America is

Life on the Canal

the "Old Aqueduct Club" of Fort Wayne, Indiana. It is composed of men who swam in the Wabash and Erie Canal aqueduct across the St. Mary's River in that city in their boyhood. To be a member of the club, one must have been born before 1867, and have lived west of a certain street before 1872, in which year the top and sides were torn off the old structure, never to be replaced. At the present writing, therefore, no one is eligible who is not at least 60 years old. The membership includes prominent business and professional men not only in Fort Wayne, but scattered all over America.

Many children were born and nursed in the tiny cabins on those old canal boats; as they grew up, the decks and towpaths were their playgrounds. One of their favorite games was of course "playing boat" with chips pulled by string on the water; and when there was a collision, they carried out the imitation by fighting and swearing just like their elders. As the boys grew older, some of them became drivers, then steersmen, then perchance captains; while the girls learned to cook and steer and finally married men along the canals.

Many who were boatmen born outlived the canal age as did Uncle Joe, saw their occupation gone and were compelled to turn to other fields for a livelihood. But there were in New York, New Jersey, Pennsylvania, Maryland and Ohio canal workers in a single family through sometimes four or five generations; and in some generations whole families followed the canal—Charles Miles of Harrisburg, Pennsylvania, and his ten sons, for example, to say nothing of Reuben Armstrong, also of Pennsylvania and his five sons, all boatmen, and his seven daughters, every one of whom married a canal man. In spite of the hard work, the long hours and the exposure, there was a fascination, a sort of freedom, a tinge of vagabondry about the life which not only bound a man to it for all his days, but drew his sons and daughters after him as well.

CHAPTER XXXII

TRAVELING BY CANAL

PERHAPS the earliest American passenger vessels on inland waters were some boats propelled by oars on the Mohawk River between Utica and Schenectady, which were in operation by or before 1800. They were covered, said to have been "tastefully curtained," and were calculated to carry twenty passengers. Christian Schultz, who traveled on the river in 1807, wrote, "Believe me, nothing could be more charming than sailing on the Mohawk."

The earliest canal passenger boats were those on the Middlesex Canal between Boston and Lowell. The cabins had upholstered seats but no beds, as the 27-mile trip was made entirely by daylight.

The Erie Canal had scarcely reached Syracuse when passenger boats began to ply between that city and Utica, extending their routes as the canal was extended. Some of these boats began by carrying half a dozen passengers and much freight; then as the demand grew for high-class passenger accommodations, the freight space was decreased and finally eliminated, save on the "line boats"—of which, more later. On June 1, 1820, the Erie Canal Navigation Company announced passenger service over 100 miles of the canal. Boats left Utica on Monday and Thursday at 9 P.M. and arrived at Canastota at 7 P.M.; price of passage $4.00, including board. In 1823 the company announced four new, spacious and beautiful boats, making regular trips between Utica and Rochester in 48 hours.

Traveling by Canal

When the canal was completed to Buffalo, packets began running through from Schenectady. No packets went any farther east than Schenectady, because the numerous locks between that place and Albany made the journey so slow and tedious that the 17-mile distance could be covered more quickly and pleasantly by stagecoach. Passengers often went to Schenectady in the evening and spent the night at Givens's Hotel. Shortly before 8 A.M. and 7 P.M. (and later, as packets became more numerous, at other hours as well) two blasts on a horn gave warning that the Buffalo packet was about to start.

As the "lines" became more numerous, rivalry among their runners reached a high pitch. A traveler through New York in 1829, writing anonymously in the *Ariel* magazine, says:

"We arrived at Schenectady about 1 P.M. As soon as the stage stopped at the Hotel, even before the driver could undo the door, up stept a large, muscular fellow and bawled out at the highest pitch of polite etiquette, 'Gentlemen, do you go to the West?' 'We do,' was the reply. 'The packet starts at 2 o'clock, gentlemen; you had better take your passage and secure your berths; only 3½ cents per mile, gentlemen, and two shillings a meal, with best accommodations and a very superior boat, gentlemen.' 'Hang his boat, gentlemen, don't take passage in her!' said a second fellow. 'I'll take you for less than half the money in a devilish fine boat, and charge you but a shilling a meal.' By this time there were at least a half dozen more, all anxious for us to engage our passage with them at almost any price we pleased." So bitter did competition become that fights often took place between runners and boat crews, especially those of the emigrant or line boats. One strip of canal bank in Schenectady came to be known as "the Battleground" because of the shindies over passenger business.

A newspaper scribe of the '20's, when the first passenger boats were put in service on the Erie, wrote that

Old Towpaths

"The new boats are built in the best manner, and fitted up in a style of magnificence that could hardly be anticipated in the infancy of canal navigation in this country." If we could see one of those boats, 75 or 80 feet long and only 11 feet wide, with its very primitive concessions to comfort and sanitation, we would marvel at the writer's idea of magnificence. Dickens's statement that it was barely possible for a man of middle height to walk to and fro in the cabin

DAILY LINE OF OHIO CANAL PACKETS

Between Cleveland & Portsmouth.

DISTANCE 309 MILES—THROUGH IN 80 HOURS.

A Packet of this Line leaves Cleveland every day at 4 o'clock P. M. and Portsmouth every day at 9 o'clock A. M.

T. INGRAHAM, *Office foot of Superior street, Cleveland,*
OTIS & CURTIS, *General Stage Office,* do. } Agents.
G. J. LEET, ... *Portsmouth,*

NEIL, MOORE & CO.'S Line of Stages leaves Cleveland daily for Columbus, via Wooster and Hebron.
OTIS & CURTIS' Line of Stages leaves Cleveland daily for Pittsburgh, Buffalo, Detroit and Wellsville.

Courtesy Western Reserve Historical Society
POSTER ADVERTISING OHIO CANAL PACKETS

"without making bald places on his head by scraping it on the roof," must have had a bit of truth in it, for the whole height of the boat from keel to roof was seldom more than eight feet. Some of the magnificence was on the brightly painted exterior. The *Indiana,* the first packet to reach Pittsburgh over the Pennsylvania Canal, had a red and black underbody, white upper cabin, green shutters on the twenty little windows along the sides, and red curtains, an inevitable item in the color scheme.

"The boats are ingeniously and well constructed," says

Traveling by Canal

a Travelers' Guide of 1824 in speaking of the Erie packets, "have accommodations for about thirty passengers, furnish good tables and a wholesome and rich fare." Some travelers have registered exceptions to the words "accommodations," "wholesome" and "rich," in the case of certain boat lines. There must have been plenty to eat on Pennsylvania canal boats in 1842, for Dickens lists the everyday menu as being, for breakfast and supper, tea, coffee, bread, butter, salmon, shad, liver, steaks, potatoes, pickles, ham, chops, black-puddings and sausages. Midday dinner was precisely the same, only minus the tea and coffee. One should certainly not have gone hungry there; but a passenger on a Wabash and Erie packet in 1854, when their prosperity was declining, says that "Captain Davis looked very black if any asked to be helped a second time."

The Travelers' Guide describes the canal boat as "a very pleasant, cheap and expeditious (!) mode of traveling, where you have regular meals, pretty quiet rest after a little experience, say of the first night, and find the time pleasantly employed in conversation and the variety of incidents, new topics, stories and the constantly changing scenery. The bustle of new comers and departing passengers, with all the greetings and adieus, help to diversify the scene."

Notwithstanding all these advantages Mrs. Trollope, after one voyage on the Erie, remarks in her genial way that "I can hardly imagine any motive of convenience powerful enough to induce me again to imprison myself in a canal boat under ordinary circumstances."

The packet boats are described by an observer as resembling a small Noah's Ark—a houseboat whose only deck was on the roof. Those used in the East were all of similar design. Right in the bow, carefully cut off from the rest of the boat, was a tiny cuddy for the crew. Next back of this came the ladies' dressing room and cabin, sometimes a separate room, sometimes cut off from the main cabin only by a red curtain. Next was the main cabin, 36 to 45 feet long,

Old Towpaths

which was saloon and dining room by day and men's dormitory by night. Back of this was the bar, and finally, at the very stern, was the kitchen, almost always presided over by a negro cook, who was usually the bartender also. He was kept busy fifteen or eighteen hours per day. The other members of the crew on the early Erie packets were the captain, two drivers and two steersmen, one each for the night and day trick.

At nine o'clock in the evening two or three members of the crew began carrying the adjustable berths, sheets, pillows, curtains, and so forth into the main cabin, and the passengers must go out on the upper deck or huddle themselves in the center of the room while the berths were made up. Each berth was a narrow wooden or metal frame with a strip of canvas fastened over it. It was held in position at one side by two projecting iron rods which fitted into two holes in the wall of the cabin; and on the other or front side by two ropes attached to the edge of the frame and suspended from hooks in the ceiling. There were at least three beds in a tier, one above another—sometimes four; and all fastened to the same rope. The tiers were set as closely together as possible all around the cabin, which thus furnished beds for from thirty-six to forty-two people. But the boats were frequently overcrowded, seventy-five and even a hundred or more people being jammed into a single cabin. In fact, a *soi-disant* "Traveler's Guide" unblushingly stated that a certain boat on the Pennsylvania Canal had "accommodations" for one hundred and fifty. It seems incredible that so many people could have lain down in the limited space on one of those boats, even with the floor and tables entirely covered with them. In such cases the passengers' hand baggage (usually limited to sixty pounds or less) must be stacked on the roof or upper deck under tarpaulins. Of course large trunks were not to be thought of for canal travel.

As for the berths which lined the walls by night, Mrs. Harriet Beecher Stowe declares—let us hope, with a femi-

Courtesy of the Dayton Chamber of Commerce and National Cash Register Company
TYPE OF CARGO BOATS IN USE ON THE OHIO CANALS

Courtesy of the Virginia State Library
THE OLD PACKET BOAT "JOHN MARSHALL," ON THE JAMES RIVER AND KANAWHA CANAL, ON WHICH GENERAL "STONEWALL" JACKSON'S BODY WAS CARRIED FROM LYNCHBURG TO HIS HOME IN LEXINGTON AFTER HIS DEATH AT CHANCELLORSVILLE, MAY 2, 1863 (AS IT APPEARED IN 1910)

Traveling by Canal

nine ineptitude for figures—that they were only a foot wide; but indeed, Dickens backs her up by saying that when he went below at ten o'clock he found "suspended on either side of the cabin three long tiers of hanging book shelves designed apparently for volumes of the small octavo size. Looking with greater attention at these contrivances (wondering to find such literary preparations in such a place) I descried on each shelf a sort of microscopic sheet and blanket; then I began dimly to comprehend that the passengers were the library, and that they were to be arranged edgewise on these shelves till morning."

Dickens neglects to mention the "mattress"—a thin, flat, lumpy pad of straw encased in blue canvas—which was used in the best packets. On some lines it would appear that the mattresses were omitted.

The method of assigning berths varied on different lines. Wilkie, a Scotch traveler on the Erie in 1836, says, "Our berths were allotted to us by precedence as the names were placed in the way-bill. When each cognomen was sung out by the captain, the individual doffed boots, coat and vest and hoisted himself into his place."

On other boats, as for example, in Pennsylvania, the choice was by lot. Dickens saw "some of the passengers gathered around the master of the boat at one of the tables, drawing lots with all the anxieties and passions of gamesters depicted in their countenances; while others with small pieces of cardboard in their hands were groping among the shelves in search of numbers corresponding with those they had drawn. As soon as any gentleman found his number he took possession of it immediately by undressing himself and crawling into bed. The rapidity with which an agitated gambler subsided into a snoring slumberer was one of the most singular effects I have ever witnessed. As to the ladies, they were already abed behind the red curtain, which was carefully drawn and pinned up the centre; though as every cough or sneeze or whisper behind the curtain was perfectly

Old Towpaths

audible before it, we had still a lively consciousness of their presence.

"The politeness of the person in authority had secured to me a shelf in a nook near the red curtain, in some degree removed from the great body of sleepers. . . . I found it, on after measurement, just the width of an ordinary sheet of Bath post letter-paper; and I was at first in some uncertainty as to the best means of getting into it. But the shelf being a bottom one, I finally determined on lying upon the floor, rolling gently in, stopping immediately I reached the mattress and remaining for the night with that side uppermost, whatever it might be. Luckily, I came upon my back at exactly the right moment. I was much alarmed on looking upward to see, by the shape of his half-yard of sacking (which his weight had bent into an exceedingly tight bag) that there was a very heavy gentleman above me, whom the slender cords seemed quite incapable of holding; and I could not help reflecting upon the grief of my wife and family in the event of his coming down in the night. But as I could not have got up again without a severe bodily struggle; and as I had nowhere else to go, even if I had; I shut my eyes upon the danger and remained there."

It was fortunate, both for the great novelist's comfort and for America's sensibilities that Dickens did not happen to board one of those crowded boats. Had his luck chanced to be like that of J. Richard Beste, another Englishman who voyaged over the Wabash and Erie and Miami Canals a few years later, there is no telling what other scathing things might have been written about America. "I never saw people packed so close as they were that night in the men's saloon," says Beste of his experience on the Miami Canal. "Mattresses completely covered the floor, on which people lay as close as possible. The dinner table was covered with sleeping humanity more thickly than Captain Davis ever strewed it with beefsteaks; and those who lay under the

Traveling by Canal

table thought themselves favored, inasmuch as they could not be trodden upon."

Bernhard, Duke of Saxe-Weimar-Eisenach, who traveled in America in 1825-26, says of a night on the Erie: "As there was a want of births, the beds were placed upon benches, and as I was the tallest person, mine was put in the centre upon the longest bench, with a chair as supplement. It had the appearance of a hereditary sepulchre, in which I lay as father of the family. I spent an uncomfortable night on account of my constrained posture, the insects which annoyed me and the steersman, who always played an agreeable tune upon his bugle whenever we approached a lock. . . ."

When berths, table and floor were all occupied by sleepers, it became necessary to string clotheslines across the cabin for the discarded garments of the passengers, giving the room a tenement-district effect. But, as Mr. Wilkie has indicated, no one took off all his clothes on a canal boat. Most men removed their shoes, hats, coats and waistcoats, some their collars and cravats, while a few fastidious nincompoops even took off their trousers; but they were exceptions. The problem of a passenger who desired to disembark at a way landing during the night without being garroted in the pitch darkness by a clothesline or stepping on his fellow passengers and getting into a fracas is enough to make one shudder at the thought.

A vivid picture of a night on a canal boat is drawn by that mellow old Virginia writer, George W. Bagby, in telling of a boyhood journey over the "Jeems and Kanawhy Canell" between Richmond and Lynchburg.

"Great was the desire of the men," says he, "not to be consigned to the 'upper.' Being light as cork, I rose naturally to the top, clambering thither by the leathern straps with the agility of a monkey, and enjoying as best I might the trampling overhead whenever we approached a lock. I didn't mind this much, but when the fellow who

Old Towpaths

had snubbed the boat jumped down about four feet, right on my head as it were, it was pretty severe. Still, I slept the sleep of youth. . . .

"The lamp shed a dim light over the sleepers, and all went well until some one—and there was always some one—began to snore. *Sn-a-a-aw—aw—poof!* They would turn uneasily and try to compose themselves to slumber again. No use. *Sn-a-a-aw—poof!* 'D—— that fellow! Chuck him in the ribs, somebody, and make him turn over! Is this thing to go on forever? Gentlemen, are you going to stand this all night? If you are, I am not. I am going to get up and dress. Who is he, anyhow? No gentleman would or could snore in that way!'

"After a while silence would be restored, and all would drop off to sleep again except the little fellow in the upper berth who, lying there, would listen to the *trahn-ahn-ahn-ahn* of the packet-horn as we drew nigh the locks. How mournfully it sounded in the night! . . . To this day you have only to say within my hearing, *trahn-ahn-ahn*, to bring back the canal epoch."

One of the hazards of canal travel touched upon by Dickens is further pictured by Frederick Gerstaecker, a German tourist of the '30's. Lying in his berth on the Erie Canal one night, "I awoke," says he, "with a dreadful feeling of suffocation; cold perspiration stood on my forehead and I could hardly draw my breath; there was a weight like lead on my stomach and chest. I attempted to cry out—in vain; I lay almost without consciousness. The weight remained immovable; above me was a noise like distant thunder; it was my companion of the upper story, who lay snoring over my head; and that the weight which pressed on my chest was caused by his body no longer remained a doubtful point. I endeavored to move the Colossus—impossible. I tried to push, to cry out—in vain. He lay like a rock on my chest and seemed to have no more feeling. I bethought me of my breastpin, which luckily I had not

Traveling by Canal

taken out of my cravat the night before; with great difficulty I succeeded in reaching the pin, which I pressed with a firm hand into the mass above me. There was a sudden movement, which procured me momentary relief; but the movement soon subsided, the weight was growing more insupportable, and to prevent being utterly crushed, I was obliged to reapply the pin. 'What's that? Murder! Help!' cried a deep bass voice above me. Feeling myself free, I slipped like an eel from under the weight and saw by the dim light of the lamp a sight of no common occurrence. A stout, heavy man who slept in the upper frame without mattress was too much for the well-worn canvas; during his sleep it had given way under the weightiest part of his form, which descended till it found support on my chest. The thrust of my breastpin caused his body to jerk upward, allowing me to escape. As he returned to his former position with greater force, the support being gone, the canvas split still wider, and more than half asleep, he was sitting on my bed, while his head and feet remained in his own. He continued calling out, 'Help! Murder!' Everybody started up to see what was the matter and to laugh heartily at the extraordinary attitude of this stout gentleman."

Philip Hone wrote in his diary in 1835, after a journey on the Erie: "The boat was not crowded, the weather was cool and pleasant, the accommodations good, the Captain polite, our fellow-passengers well-behaved, and altogether, I do not remember to have ever had so pleasant a ride on the Canal. My hammock, to be sure, was rather narrow and not very soft and my neighbor overhead was packed close upon my stomach, but I slept sound as a ploughman and did not wake until tapped on the shoulder by the boy and told to 'clear out.'"

But in 1847, when he was twelve years older, he wrote: "This canal traveling is pleasant enough by day time, but the sleeping is awful. . . . The sleepers are packed away on narrow shelves fastened to the side of the boat, like dead pigs in a Cincinnati pork warehouse. We go to bed at 9 o'clock, and get up when we are told."

"Between five and six in the morning," says Dickens, "we got up, and some of us went on deck to give them an opportunity of taking the shelves down; while others, the morning being very cold, crowded around the rusty stove, cherishing the newly kindled fire. . . . The washing accommodations were primitive. There was a tin ladle chained to the deck, with which every gentleman who thought it necessary to cleanse himself fished the dirty water out of the canal and poured it into a tin basin, secured in like manner. And hanging up before a little looking glass in the bar, in the immediate vicinity of the bread and cheese and biscuits, was a public comb and brush."

Fancy the atmosphere—but no, it can't be fancied!—in a packet cabin on a summer night. The historian Lossing, after a night on a little Champlain Canal packet, speaks of the "Turkish bath" of a packet cabin. A rainy day was almost as bad. In the early morning, says Dickens, the odors of the breakfast food mingled with those of gin, whisky, brandy and rum from the bar, with "a decided seasoning of stale tobacco. . . . Nor was the atmosphere quite free from zephyr whisperings of the thirty beds which had just been cleared away, and of which we were further and more pressingly reminded by the occasional appearance on the tablecloth of a kind of Game not mentioned in the Bill of Fare."

Harriet Martineau says of her trip on the Erie that besides "the heat and noise, the known vicinity of a compressed crowd lying packed like herrings in a barrel, the bumping against the sides of the locks . . . we suffered under an additional annoyance in the presence of sixteen Presbyterian clergymen—some of the most unprepossessing of their class. If there be a duty more obvious than another on board a canal boat, it is to walk on the bank occasionally in fair weather or at least remain outside in order to air

Reproduced by permission of the Philadelphia Commercial Museum

ONE OF LEECH & COMPANY'S FAST PENNSYLVANIA PACKETS, WITH THE HORSES IN A TROT, PASSING A FREIGHT BOAT NOT FAR FROM THE PORTAGE RAILWAY

Traveling by Canal

the cabin (close enough at best) and get rid of the scents of the table before the unhappy passengers are shut up there. These sixteen gentlemen on their way to a Convention at Utica could not wait till they got there to begin their devotions. . . . They were not satisfied with saying an almost interminable grace before and after each meal, but shut up the cabin for prayers before dinner; for missionary conversation in the afternoon and for scripture reading and prayers quite late into the night." One of the other passengers assured her that these preachers were so strict that they wouldn't drink water out of the Brandywine River—and Miss Martineau seems to have believed it. It might have been true, at that.

"I would never advise ladies to travel by canal," says Miss Martineau, "unless the boats are quite new and clean; or at least, far better kept than any that I saw or heard of on this canal." But many ladies did travel by packet at times, as is evinced by Mrs. Harriet Beecher Stowe's picture of a night on a canal boat, written for *Godey's Lady's Book* in 1841. It was evident as the swarms of passengers descended on the eastbound boat at Pittsburgh that it was going to be dreadfully overcrowded.

Going down into the cabin, they are appalled to discover that the space allotted to the ladies is, Mrs. Stowe declares, only ten feet long and six high, and that thirty ladies and several children must sleep in it. "The state of feeling becomes perfectly desperate. Darkness gathers on all faces. 'We shall be smothered!' 'We shall be crowded to death!—we *can't* stay here!' are heard faintly from one and another, and yet they do live and bear it in spite of protestations to the contrary."

But when, at nine o'clock, the attendants put the berths in position, the chorus rises again. " 'What, sleep up there?—*I* won't sleep on one of those two top shelves, I know. The cords will certainly break.' The chambermaid here takes up the conversation and solemnly assures them that such an

Old Towpaths

accident is not to be thought of at all, that it is a natural impossibility. . . . Points of location being after a while adjusted, comes the last struggle. Everybody wants to take off their bonnet, to look for their shawl, to find their cloak, to get their carpet-bag, and all set about it with such zeal that nothing can be done. 'Ma'am, you're on my foot,' says one. 'Will you please to move, ma'am,' says somebody who is gasping and struggling behind you. 'Move!' you echo. 'Indeed, I should be very glad to, but I don't see much prospect of it.' 'Chambermaid!' calls a lady who is struggling among a heap of carpet bags and children at one end of the cabin. 'Ma'am!' echoes the poor chambermaid, who is wedged fast in a similar position at the other. 'Where's my cloak, chambermaid?' 'I'd find it, ma'am, if I could move.' 'Chambermaid, my basket!' 'Chambermaid, my parasol!' 'Chambermaid, a glass of water!' 'Mamma, they push me so!' 'Hush, child, crawl under there and lie still till I can undress you.'

"At last, however, the various distresses are over, the babies sunk to sleep, and even that much-enduring being, the chambermaid, seeks out some corner for repose. Tired and drowsy, you are just sinking into a dose, when bang! goes the boat against the sides of a lock, ropes scrape, men run and shout, and up fly the heads of all the top-shelf-ites, who are generally the more juvenile and airy part of the company.

" 'What's that? What's that?' flies from mouth to mouth, and forthwith they proceed to awaken their respective relations. 'Mother—Aunt Hannah!—do wake up—What is this awful noise?' 'Oh, only a lock!' 'Pray, be still!' groan out the sleepy members from below.

" 'A lock!' exclaim the vivacious ones, ever on the alert for information. 'And what is a lock, pray?'

" 'Don't you know what a lock is, you silly creatures? Do lie down and go to sleep!'

" 'But say, there a'n't any danger in a lock, is there?' respond the querists. 'Danger!' exclaims a deaf old lady, poking up her head. 'What's the matter? There ha'n't

Traveling by Canal

nothin' burst, has there?' 'No, no, no!' exclaim the provoked and despairing opposition party, who find that there is no such thing as sleep till they have made all understand exactly the philosophy of a lock. After a while the conversation again subsides. Again all is still—you hear only the trampling of the horses, the rippling of the rope in the water, and sleep again is stealing over you. You dose, you dream, and all of a sudden you are startled by a cry, 'Chambermaid! Wake up the lady that wants to be set ashore!'

"Up jumps chambermaid and up jumps the lady and two children, and forthwith form a committee of inquiry as to ways and means. 'Where's my bonnet?' says the lady, half awake and fumbling among the various articles of the name. 'I thought I hung it up behind the door.' 'Can't you find it?' says poor chambermaid, yawning and rubbing her eyes. 'Oh, yes, here it is,' says the lady, and then her cloak, the shawl, the gloves, the shoes, receive each a separate discussion. At last all seems ready and they begin to move off, when lo! Peter's cap is missing. 'Now, where can it be?' soliloquizes the lady. 'I put it right here by the table leg—maybe it got into some of the births.' At this bright suggestion the chambermaid takes the candle and goes round deliberately to every birth, poking the light directly in the face of every sleeper. 'Here it is, perhaps,' she exclaims, pulling at something black under a pillow. 'No, indeed, those are my shoes,' says the vexed sleeper. 'Maybe it's here,' she resumes, darting upon something dark in another birth. 'No, that's my habit,' responds the occupant. The chambermaid then proceeds to turn over all the children on the floor to see if it isn't under them, in the course of which they are all most agreeably waked up and enlivened; and when everybody is broad awake and uncharitably wishing the cap and Peter, too, at the bottom of the canal, the good lady exclaims, 'Well, if this isn't lucky!—here I had it safe in my basket all the time.'—and she departs amid the—what shall I say? —execrations?—of the whole company, ladies though they be.

Old Towpaths

"Well, after this follows a hushing up and wiping up among the juvenile population, and a conversation commences from the various shelves, of a very edifying and instructive tendency. . . ." This goes on, the writer declares and as we can very well believe, until would-be sleepers are driven almost to madness. "At last, however, voice after voice drops off—you fall into a most refreshing slumber—it seems that you sleep about a quarter of an hour, when the chambermaid pulls you by the sleeve. 'Will you please to get up, ma'am; we want to make the beds.' You start and stare—Sure enough, the night is gone! So much for sleeping on a canal boat."

"I like travelling by the canal boats very much," wrote Frances Anne Butler (Fanny Kemble), the actress. She compliments the beautiful scenery, the quiet, the placid gliding of the boat, but a few moments later she is reviling "the horrible hen-coop allotted to the female passengers," and the necessity for undressing in public. James Stuart, the Scotch traveler, going west from Albany, was so disgusted by the frequent cries of "Bridge! Low bridge!" that he and his family left the boat at Utica and pursued the rest of the journey by coach.

The elder Tyrone Power, the great Irish actor, had an unfortunate experience in that he struck the Erie during the great heat wave of the summer of 1834. Incidentally, he was delightfully "spoofed" by a steersman regarding the swamps and the mosquitoes, though it is probable that Mr. Power didn't swallow as much of the misinformation as one might think.

"All this day," says he on the second torrid evening out from Buffalo, "the air stood absolutely still. At our places of halt we were joined by men who had left the stages in consequence of those vehicles not being able to travel. Our pace was reduced considerably; and the cattle, although in excellent condition. were terribly distressed. At Lockport

Courtesy of the Pennsylvania Railroad Company

SECTIONAL PACKET BOAT LEAVING STOCK EXCHANGE CORNER, PHILADELPHIA, FOR PITTSBURGH ABOUT 1840
The boats were carried eighty-one miles to Columbia by rail before entering the canal.

Traveling by Canal

we found business nearly at a standstill; the thermometer was at 110 degrees Fahrenheit. We passed several horses dead upon the banks of the canal, and were compelled to leave one or two of our own in a dying state. Here more persons joined than we could well accommodate, and I found positively that all movement by the stage route was at an end, forty horses having fallen on the line the day previous. . . .

"This night I found it impossible to look in upon the cabin; I therefore made a request to the captain that I might be permitted to have a mattress on deck; but this, he told me, could not be; there was a regulation which positively forbade sleeping upon the deck of a canal packet; indeed, he assured me that this could only be done at the peril of life. . . . I appeared to submit to his well-meant arguments; but inwardly resolved, *coute qui coute,* not to sleep within the den below.

"I got my cloak up, filled my hat with cigars and, planting myself about the center of the deck, here resolved, *malgre* dews and musquitoes, to weather it through the night.

"'What is the name of the country we are now passing?' I inquired of one of the boatmen who joined me about the first hour of the morning.

"'Why, sir, this is called the Cedar Swamp,' answered the man, to whom I handed a cigar, in order to retain his society and create more smoke against the hungry swarms surrounding us on all sides.

"'We have not much more of this Cedar Swamp to get through, I hope,' inquired I, seeking for some consolatory information.

"'About fifty miles more, I guess,' was the reply of my companion, accompanying each word with a sharp slap on the back of his hand, or on his cheek or forehead.

"'Thank Heaven!' I involuntarily exclaimed, drawing my cloak closer about me, although the heat was killing;

Old Towpaths

'we shall after that escape in some sort, I hope, from these legions of musquitoes?'

" 'I guess not quite,' replied the man; 'they are as thick, if not thicker, in the Long Swamp.'

" 'The Long Swamp!' I repeated: 'What a horrible name for a country! Does the canal run far through it?'

" 'No, not so far, only about eighty miles.'

" 'We've then done with swamps, I hope, my friend?' I inquired, as he kept puffing and slapping with unwearied constancy.

" 'Why, yes, there's not a heap more swamp, that is to say, not close to the line, till we come to within about forty miles of Utica.'

" 'And is that one as much infested with these infernal insects as are the Long and Cedar Swamps?'

" 'I guess *that* is *the* place above all for musquitoes,' replied the man, grinning. 'Thim's the real gallinippers, emigrating north for the summer all the way from the Balize and the Red River. Let a man go to sleep with his head in a cast-iron kettle among thim chaps, and if their bills don't make a watering-pot of it before morning, I'm d——d. They're strong enough to lift the boat out of the canal, if they could only get underneath her.' . . ."

"And yet despite these oddities," says Dickens, after describing some of his own trials, "and even they had, for me, at least, a humor of their own—there was much in this mode of traveling which I heartily enjoyed at the time and look back upon with great pleasure. Even the running up, bare-necked, at five o'clock in the morning, from the tainted cabin to the dirty deck, scooping up the icy water, plunging one's head into it and drawing it out, all fresh and glowing with the cold, was a good thing. The fast, brisk walk upon the towing path, between that time and breakfast, when every vein and artery seemed to tingle with health; the exquisite beauty of the opening day, when light came glancing off from everything; the gliding on at night so noiselessly, past frown-

Traveling by Canal

ing hills sullen with dark trees and sometimes angry in one red, burning spot high up, where unseen men lay crouching round a fire; the shining out of the bright stars undisturbed by any noise of wheels or steam or any other sound than the limpid rippling of the water as the boat went on; all these were pure delights."

A canal trip in mild weather when the boat was not crowded must really have been a rather pleasant adventure. And a moonlit evening on deck was a bit of the most beautiful tranquillity in life. All the sounds were pleasant—the soft whisper of the water as it purled away from the bow, the cheeping of tree toads, which Dickens said "sounded as if a million of fairy teams with bells were traveling through the air and keeping pace with us," the distant cry of a night bird or bark of a farmhouse dog, and by way of contrast, the murmur of voices and laughter from the cabin below. Many of the packets had a small organ in the cabin, and the passengers would gather round it and sing some old stave like "Come Haste to the Wedding" or one of those delightfully lugubrious things so popular in those days; something starting off, for example, like this:

> *The livelong day, alas! in pain and grief I pass,*
> *And e'en at even I am weeping,*
> *When out upon the night I turn my weary sight,*
> *My grief's unceasing,*
> *My tears increasing,* etc., etc.

"The bar was small, but vigorous and healthy," says Bagby. ". . . Mr. Mallock's pregnant question, 'Is life worth living?' was answered very satisfactorily, methought, as I watched the Virginians at their juleps: 'Gentlemen, your very good health'; 'Colonel, my respects to you'; 'My regards, Judge. When shall I see you again at my house? Can't you stop now and stay a little while, even if it is only a week or two?' 'Sam,' (to the barkeeper), 'duplicate those drinks.'"

Old Towpaths

One must not forget the sundry dangers connected with travel by canal. There were very remote possibilities of accident which could cause a boat to sink—in which case you might get wet up to your middle and be laid up with influenza. There is a thrilling narrative in an old magazine describing how the *Sarsey Fanny* on the Morris Canal hove to alongside the ancient tramp freighter, *Rip van Winkle*, which had sprung a leak and was going down. All hands turned to and by superhuman efforts saved the stove, table, bedding, dishes, kitchenware, feed boxes, furniture and personal effects of the captain's family, taking off the final articles just as the ill-fated craft staggered and made her last awful plunge into four feet of water.

Then there was a rare possibility of the boat's catching fire, which might force the passengers to wade ashore, though this was not probable, as the craft was always close to the bank. One might be careless about the low bridges and get a cracked head or even lose one's life. The writer in the *Ariel*, already quoted, says that a boat captain on the Erie "informs me that six persons have lost their lives by being crushed under the bridges, which is a greater number than have been killed during the same time by the bursting of steam engines in the waters of the middle or eastern States." And you were particularly cautioned not to poke your head out of a window while the boat was in a lock, lest it—your head, that is—be smashed between the boat and the lock wall.

The *Ariel* tourist traveled on a line boat, and says he fared well. These boats have already been mentioned as being considerably patronized by westbound emigrants. Their rates were usually 1½ cents per mile, with an extra charge for meals, or the passenger could take his own food with him; while the packets charged 4 to 5 cents per mile, including meals. The line boats had poorer horses and ran only about 40 miles a day, as against the packets' 80 or 90. The line boats' accommodations were poorer; Colonel Stone, palpably a rock-ribbed Whig, was compelled to ride on one

Traveling by Canal

of them from Weed's Basin to Lyons, and reported that the cabins were too small to turn around in, the beds dirty, fleas and bedbugs numerous, "and the passengers . . . all Jackson men, as the color of their shirt collars abundantly attested." Wilkie remarks that the slow progress of his line boat permitted the passengers "to make detours into the adjoining forest or villages on the banks, for the several purposes, among others, of shooting squirrels, drinking grog and buying tobacco."

At first the four-cents-a-mile rate for through passengers on the packets applied also to way or local passengers; but there presently appeared a species of dead beat who jumped aboard just at mealtime, guzzled down about a dollar's worth of food while the boat was traversing a mile, and then handed the captain a nickel as he stepped off again. So the boats presently fixed a minimum fare of fifteen or twenty-five cents, no matter how short the distance traveled; and some lines made a rate to way passengers of three cents per mile, with additional charges of 37½ cents for dinner, 25 cents each for supper and breakfast and 12½ cents for lodging.

There were few of the old canals of any consequence that did not have a packet service at one time or another. On most of them the packets were set in operation as soon as the canal or a part of it was opened. On the Pennsylvania Main Line, Leech began operating packets over the completed portion between Harrisburg and Huntingdon in 1832. They were 79 feet long and intended to carry 25 passengers and 30 tons of freight.

These of course were line boats. Traveling accommodations advanced rapidly in elegance on the Pennsylvania Canals and culminated in such craft as the Pittsburgh, the one advertised to have "accommodations for 150 passengers." This boat carried a crew of nine. It left Pittsburgh at 9 P.M. and made the difficult run to Johnstown, 103 miles, in 28 hours, using thirteen changes of horses en route.

Old Towpaths

An advertisement of the New Haven and Northampton Canal in 1829 indicates that commencement at Yale in early days took place in the autumn. The New Haven *Chronicle* of September 2 says that "the elegant Canal Packet New England will, for the purpose of accommodating Commencement passengers, leave Farmington on Tuesday before Commencement, which takes place on Wednesday, the 9th inst."

In 1825 packet boats began operating on the Schuylkill, carrying passengers between Reading and Philadelphia in one day. To do this, it was necessary to start at 3 A.M. Fairmount Locks would be reached at 8 P.M., whence a coach took passengers downtown to the White Swan. As the boats were not out overnight, they had no berths. Some passengers found the trip a bit strenuous, and one of the boats was therefore scheduled to break the trip at Pottsgrove. By 1832 anthracite traffic had become so heavy that passenger craft were crowded off the canal. In the latter '40's steam packets were tried on the Schuylkill, but did not last long.

The numerous changes made by travelers of the old days would have made a long journey simply unbearable to the modern American. Reverend B. W. Chidlaw, who traveled from New York to Cincinnati in 1839 lists his various stages and the costs as follows. Of course he used line boats:

	Fare
New York to Albany, 160 miles (steamboat)	$2.00
Albany to Utica, 110 miles (stage and canal)	1.50
Utica to Buffalo, 254 miles (canal)	3.75
Buffalo to Cleveland, 193 miles (steamboat)	2.50
Cleveland to Newark, 171 miles (canal)	2.00
Newark to Columbus, 40 miles (canal)	.75
Columbus to Portsmouth, 82 miles (canal)	1.25
Portsmouth to Cincinnati, 100 miles (steamboat)	1.00
Entire journey, 1,110 miles	$14.75

Traveling by Canal

And the time occupied probably not much less than a month!

One of the strangest vehicles of travel ever seen was that placed upon the main Pennsylvania Canal about 1840. The passengers had hitherto been subjected to many transfers; Philadelphia to Columbia by rail, including two inclined planes, thence to Hollidaysburg by canal, then by Portage Railroad over the mountain, with ten planes to negotiate, and finally, 103 miles by canal to Pittsburgh.

All this was obviated after John Dougherty had conceived the idea of hauling the emigrant's boat bodily over the mountain on the Portage Railway. The next step was to build full-length boats in two halves, so that they could be taken apart and mounted on cars of moderate size. These half-boats were brought on the railroad all the way into downtown Philadelphia. There the passengers took their seats, the halves were hauled by rail to Columbia, where the cars were run down into the water until the boats were afloat. Then the halves were locked together into one boat and pursued their way to Hollidaysburg; were divided and hauled over the mountain on adjoining cars, united again at Johnstown and floated thence to Pittsburgh as a unit. The traveler thus made his journey through "without change."

The Wabash and Erie began running packets on its completed sections in 1835; but not until 1843 was the eastern section completed to Toledo, so that boats could run through from Lake Erie to Lafayette. The first packets ran on no scheduled time. The boats started whenever they got a full load of passengers, and arrived whenever they conveniently could. Passengers sometimes got their meals at farmhouses along the way. But within a year they had a packet service organized over that route which was probably the fastest in the country—if it lived up to its schedule. The Erie and Pennsylvania Canals boasted of their fast four-mile-an-hour boats, covering 80 to 90 and sometimes 100 miles a day. Passengers went from Schenectady to Buffalo,

Old Towpaths

346 miles, in four days, and from Philadelphia to Pittsburgh, nearly 400 miles, in five days. But on the Wabash and Erie we are assured that boats ran regularly from Toledo to Lafayette, 242 miles, in two days and eight hours, or at the rate of nearly 104 miles per day. The opportunity for speed was better there, the traffic being much lighter than on the Eastern canals.

In order to maintain fast passenger service, it was found necessary to change horses every eight or ten miles. Racing was a common practice. A canal law on the Erie fixed a fine of $10 for "speeding" at more than four miles per hour because of the resulting damage to the banks. So racing captains would jump off at the collector's office and throw down a $10 bill when presenting their clearance to be signed. This was considered as settling their fine, and averted arrest and delay of the boat. Such a practice, however, ran the bill up to a considerable figure, as there were collectors' offices in every large town; but the passengers, who became quite as enthusiastic over a race as the crew, often contributed to help pay these fines. They would cheer their boat and captain enthusiastically, and if the boat got into a jam, male passengers would leap ashore, seize the towline and assist the horses. There was at times some heavy betting on the results of races. As for the crews, they stopped at nothing in their efforts to win. Sometimes in the heat of a race, an opposing boat's towline would be cut, which almost invariably brought on a fight. Other canals, lacking the great number of passenger boats, never saw as much of this bitter rivalry as did the Erie.

One of the most distinguished passengers that the old canals ever had was former President John Quincy Adams. He crossed the State of Ohio by canal packet in 1843, and from his journal we learn the astonishing fact that the packets in Ohio did not get relays of horses at stations along the way, but carried the extra horses with them on the boat!

Traveling by Canal

He embarked on the packet, *Rob Roy,* at Akron on November 2, 1843. "The boat," he says, "is 83 feet long, 15 feet wide and has about 25 passengers. It is divided in six compartments; the first in the bow with two settee beds for the ladies, separated by a curtain from a parlor bed-chamber with an iron stove in the center and side settees on which four of us slept, feet to feet; then a bulging stable for four horses, two and two by turns, and a narrow passage with a side settee for one passenger to sleep on, leading to the third compartment, a dining hall and dormitory for thirty persons; and lastly a kitchen and cooking apparatus, with sleeping room for cook, steward and crew, and necessary conveniences. So much humanity crowded into such a compass was a trial such as I had never before experienced, and my heart sunk within me when squeezing into this pillory, I reflected that I am to pass three nights and four days in it. We were obliged to keep the windows of the cabin closed against the driving snow, and the stoves, heated with billets of wood, made the rooms uncomfortably warm. It was a comfortless evening; but before its close I found that our fellow travelers who shared the after cabin with us were well bred persons and pleasant companions."

In a boat with a stable squarely in the middle of it, no matter how carefully partitioned away from the rest, it is probably fortunate, notwithstanding his asthma, that Mr. Adams made the trip in November rather than in midsummer. It is explained that the packet men on the Ohio and Erie had tried keeping their horses at relay stations, but had been unable to make any profit. They had to overwork their horses, often keeping them on duty for forty-eight hours at a stretch, which wore them out rapidly. They finally tried carrying the extra horses on the boats and found that they not only kept them in better condition, but greatly reduced the cost of towage.

Lafayette was another distinguished canal passenger. During his last visit to America in 1824–25 he made two

Old Towpaths

journeys on the then uncompleted Erie Canal. On his final voyage eastward he went by carriage from Buffalo to Lockport, where he was greeted by the acclamations of a large crowd and some tremendous blasts fired by the workmen who were quarrying the canal bed at that place. The Marquis and party embarked for the East on a canal boat in the evening, and next morning were called on deck to find themselves in the midst of the aqueduct across the Genesee at Rochester and a great crowd assembled. A stage had been erected over the canal at the center of the aqueduct, and from there Colonel William B. Rochester delivered the address of welcome.

The arrival of a packet boat in a small town, especially in thinly settled Ohio, Indiana and Illinois, was the great event of the day or week, and the entire population turned out to meet it. It brought the mail and all the news from the outer world and gave glimpses of travelers from far distant parts, perhaps even from another State. It did not always handle the mail efficiently, as one learns from the diatribe of an editor in Peru, Indiana, who declares that it is "a common occurrence for the mail to be carried by this point to Lafayette or Fort Wayne, and returned two days after the time it should have arrived."

William Dean Howells, in his boyhood at Hamilton, Ohio, was always on hand to see the arrival of the packet. He tells us how it came in grandly, the deck thronged with people, the three horses in a trot, the driver sitting on the rearmost horse and doing expert things with his whip. The captain stood on deck, and as the horses were changed at Hamilton, he had his foot on the spring catch which held the towrope, a recent and much-admired invention. Just before reaching the landing he pressed the catch and the rope was released. "The driver kept on to the stable with unslackened speed and the line followed him, swishing and skating over the water, while the steersman put his helm hard aport and the packet rounded to and swam softly and

Courtesy of the Dayton Chamber of Commerce and National Cash Register Company

PACKET BOAT "ST. LOUIS" ON THE MIAMI AND ERIE CANAL

Traveling by Canal

slowly up to her moorings. No steamship arrives from Europe now with such thrilling majesty."

"The boat captain," says Richard Smith Elliott, "outshone any driver that had ever held rein or sounded his brass horn as he swept proudly round on a high trot to the tavern door. . . . No more the expectant gatherings at the tavern portals. They were down at the canal to greet the packet."

"The consequential captain" of his boat on the Erie Canal rather jangled the nerves of Captain Marryat, the writer. "The boat was a very small affair," says he, "about 50 feet long and 8 feet wide. The captain of her was, however, in his opinion, no small affair; he puffed and swelled until he looked larger than his boat." Could this be professional envy?

"And when Henry Clay came along on his way to Washington," says Elliott, speaking of his boyhood on the Pennsylvania Main Line, "what a chance for the village orator to speak at him and all of us to hear him in response as we sailed from one set of locks to another! No hurried hand-shake on a platform or speech from the tail of a car (with the engine bell petulant) can reach the sublime in trip oratory. Only the calm interior of the canal packet or steamboat cabin can assure us this. And oh, the generous pride we felt when our own orator, Lawyer Fisher, made the best speech on the whole line!"

Whenever a railroad paralleled a canal, the increased speed offered by the locomotive quickly put the packet boats out of business. The history of transportation was epitomized in the story of a forgotten little rate war in the Genesee Valley many decades ago. When the Genesee Canal was built from Rochester towards Cuba and Olean and packet boats began running, a stage line which traversed the valley made war on the boats by cutting fares. The boats promptly retaliated in kind. Again and again the rates were slashed, until finally the coaches were offering

Old Towpaths

to haul passengers free. But the boats still held a trump card—they now offered not only free passage but free meals as well. The stage could not meet this, and soon gave up the ghost. The triumph of the packets was short-lived. Within a few years a railroad was built down the valley, and the packets in turn were compelled to bow to a stronger competitor and pass out of the picture.

It is an astonishing thing that packets continued to operate on the Erie for several years after it had been paralleled from end to end by railroads. On January 1, 1848, there were still sixty-two packets on the canal, and they did not disappear entirely until after 1850. On some of the branch canals they continued for several years after that. Records are wanting to show when the last canal passenger service operated in America; but the packets on the upper Lehigh continued until 1862, when a flood destroyed the canal between Mauch Chunk and White Haven, and there were undoubtedly a few boats operated on the upper James River and Kanawha system for a short time after that.

CHAPTER XXXIII

CANAL LOTTERIES

AN interesting picture of the gradual mutation of ethical standards in America is afforded by a study of the history of lotteries. In the Eighteenth Century, although a few inveighed against them, lotteries were looked upon by the great majority of folk as entirely respectable. National, State and city governments did not scruple to operate them and everybody, even ministers of the gospel, bought tickets. They were the favorite method of raising large sums of money for public, charitable, educational and religious purposes.

The United States Government distributed an early issue of bonds by a lottery scheme, and in 1793 the Commissioners of the District of Columbia raised money by lottery for the improvement of the city of Washington. Many a turnpike, bridge or public building was erected by city or county with funds derived from a lottery scheme. Colleges used them; Harvard ran a prosperous lottery for several years, and Williams, Yale, Dartmouth and others also profited by the idea. States built up their educational systems with profits from lotteries. Did a church need a new organ, a new bell or a new building, it was no uncommon thing for the necessary cash to be raised through a lottery device. The Patowmack Company, which had built the short canals along the Potomac, tried a lottery in 1811, but with no very great success.

As nearly all the early canal projects in America were at one time or another (and some of them continuously)

Old Towpaths

in straitened circumstances, it is not to be wondered at that many of them resorted to one of the most popular forms of indoor amusement as a means of mending their financial condition. Perhaps the first of these lottery schemes was that of the Santee Canal, which was set in motion about 1797, when the company was struggling hard against rising costs of construction. It could not have been a very successful one, for we observe that assessments continued to be laid upon the long-suffering stockholders.

In 1802 the South Hadley Canal, unable to make ends meet, petitioned the Legislature of Massachusetts for relief, and obtained the right to raise $20,000 by a lottery. With the funds thus obtained, the bed of the canal was lowered and several feet taken off the dam. The famous incline was also removed and five locks substituted.

Most of the canal lottery managements, as might have been expected of gambling concerns, were shot through and through with crookedness. The canal companies seldom handled the lottery arrangements themselves, but turned the whole thing over to a professional manager or subsidiary concern. The result was that few of the canal companies received anywhere near the money they should have received from their lotteries, and there were many scandals, lawsuits and recriminations and much bad blood.

One of the smaller instances of this chicanery may be found in the story of the mile-long canal around the Amoskeag Falls in the Merrimac River, New Hampshire. A lottery scheme was carried on for the benefit of the canal, and a serious dispute arose between Judge Blodgett, one of the leading promoters of the canal, and the lottery managers. The Judge charged that the lottery drawings had been unfairly managed, and that the money paid over to the canal company was only a small part of the proceeds. The lottery managers retorted that a goodly portion of the money paid over to Judge Blodgett had been illegally used by him in the construction of a handsome mansion alongside

Canal Lotteries

"He's a Screamer!"
Col. Wildfire.

As *Tom* and *Jemmy* were one morning passing HECKMAN'S LOTTERY Office, Says Tom to Jemmy—"Let's just drop intil his offus, and try our luck, if ye'r a-mind to, Jemmy?" "I'm ye'r chap," answered Jemmy, and in they went. Jem says to Heckman, "Just let your wee son draw out a ☞ Quarter, and we'll be after going halves." And the child, without ever thinking, slapped down its paw, and pulled out one. Heckman exclaimed, "Good luck to ye, my chap!" And so it was. A few days elapsed, and Tom and Jemmy called again to ascertain the luck of their ticket, that the wee child scarce five years old, selected for them, and upon examination, they found it had struck a prize of **$500!** "Look here, now, Tommy; see what a child will do nor a Lottery." "Yes, but, I'm not at all, at all astonished," answered Tom. "you seen how Heckman paraded the ticket; it was giving the child a big chance. But Heckman's the man for us till go to get prizes. Jemmy, sure, jist jug up the same chap, and we'll be after trying 4 quarters in the next class, and if the wee child again should be lucky, we'll jist kape him pulling out all the while. This Lottery is aqual to a sand blast; for, och, by the powers of mud, it makes the money fly in every direction. Jemmy, just greaso your eyes with a look underneath:"

UNION CANAL LOTTERY.

CLASS NO. 23, FOR 1831.

To be drawn on Saturday the 19th of November inst., when the following brilliant Prizes will be distributed:

SCHEME.

1	Prize of	$30,000	is $30,000
1	do	20,000	20,000
1	do.	10,000	10,000
1	do.	3,160	3,140

LOTTERY ADVERTISEMENT IN AN EASTON, PENNSYLVANIA, NEWSPAPER, 1831

the canal. Blodgett claimed that the house was built from his own private purse—which local historians say was probably true. But however that may be, the canal profited little from the lottery.

Not a few canal lotteries were carried on for the benefit of projects on which work had not begun; and on some of them work never did begin. The second attempt (in 1819) to build a canal around the falls of the Ohio at Louisville was to be financed by a lottery; but though the lottery managers realized some gains thereby, the canal could not be built. A lottery privilege was granted in 1823 to raise $50,000 for the building of the projected Cumberland and Oxford Canal; but in this case the canal was actually constructed.

Quite different was the "Union Canal Lottery" which was carried on in Massachusetts, beginning about 1814; not the Union Canal Lottery of Pennsylvania, but evidently named with intent to do a little trading upon the reputation of the well-known Pennsylvania concern. Its purpose is best described by one of its newspaper advertisements:

UNION CANAL LOTTERY

First Class—Twenty-Five Thousand Dollars

It rarely happens that the object of a Lottery is interesting to the whole Community. To save the *Metropolis of New England* from declining in its commerce and consequence . . . to open its internal resources, to unite New Hampshire and Vermont to Massachusetts by bonds of mutual benefit as permanent as the rivers and canals by which their intercourse will be carried on—to make Boston advance like New York, supported by a populous, extensive and productive back country, are *considerations* into which every reflecting man, every merchant and every owner of real estate, must enter and must feel.

Canal Lotteries

When the Erie Canal was nearing completion and Boston grew enthusiastic over the idea of a canal to the Hudson at Albany, this lottery was ostensibly diverted to that purpose; but as a matter of fact, it never benefited any cause or anybody save the men who operated it.

Courtesy Historical Society of Pennsylvania
LEHIGH NAVIGATION LOTTERY TICKET

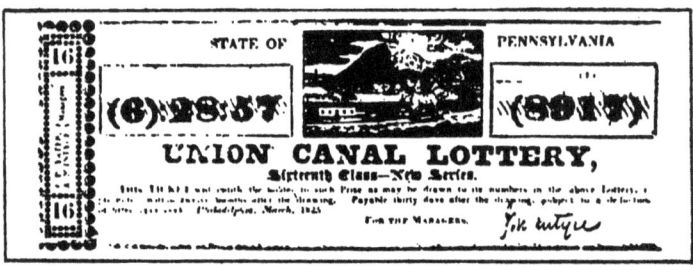

Courtesy Historical Society of Pennsylvania
UNION CANAL LOTTERY TICKET
This was the greatest of all Canal Lotteries

By far the greatest of all canal lotteries was that of the Union Canal of Pennsylvania, which may be traced back to a grant by the Legislature on April 17, 1795, of a lottery privilege to the Schuylkill and Susquehanna and Delaware and Schuylkill Canal companies. They were given permis-

Old Towpaths

sion to raise $400,000 by a lottery, of which the Schuylkill and Susquehanna was to receive two-thirds and the Delaware and Schuylkill one-third. They began issuing tickets shortly thereafter, and continued to do so for fifteen years with very little profit. Up to 1810 the total net earnings had been only about $60,000, which sum was of course inconsequential for canal-building purposes. The companies then petitioned the State for relief. They confessed abjectly that their affairs had "fallen into disorder and embarrassment; that they were covered with reproach and ridicule," and that the public confidence in their efforts was impaired.

The Legislature coöperated by permitting the two companies to unite in 1811 under the name of the Union Canal Company, and by granting a renewal of the lottery privilege, to continue until the profits should complete the amount of $400,000 authorized by the act of 1795—in other words, $340,000 might be raised. As the companies had not made a success of running the lottery themselves, the new corporation was empowered to sell or assign its lottery rights to any persons it might select. Under this arrangement the lottery, in the years that followed, became enormously successful—that is, for the managers. The canal company got little out of it.

During the ten years between 1811 and 1821 a number of large lottery schemes were completed by the managers, but the canal company did not realize enough profit from these to enable them even to begin excavation. Another petition to the Legislature in 1821 brought permission to continue the privilege for twenty-five years, raising enough each year to enable the company to pay 6 per cent annually on its stock. Increased stock sales that year had enabled the company to begin work on its canal, and the Act provided that as tolls increased, the profits from the lottery should decrease. It was hoped and confidently expected that the tolls would be sufficient in a few years to meet the annual

Canal Lotteries

dividend payments. Between 1811 and December, 1833, this company, or its managers, conducted fully fifty lottery schemes and awarded in prizes more than $33,000,000. In the year 1832 alone the prizes amounted to $5,216,240. But because of the numerous irregularities it seems evident that the canal company did not receive more than 5 per cent of the money realized from the sale of tickets. In a report to the Legislature they asserted that the managers had made millions, whereas the canal company had actually received all told only $269,210.40. The wrangles and scandals over the matter flamed up at frequent intervals throughout more than twenty years.

In 1798 the Lehigh Navigation Company secured the right to operate a lottery whereby to raise money for the completion of certain improvements in the Lehigh River. In 1832 tickets in no less than 420 lottery schemes were sold in Pennsylvania.

The drawings of the Union Canal Lottery were held at stated times from a landing on the stairway leading to an upper floor of the State House in Harrisburg, and were attended by great crowds of people who packed the floors below, groaning, cursing or rejoicing as their numbers proved unlucky or lucky. One reads now and then in the newspapers of the period of cases of insanity, suicide, embezzlement or other crime following the drawings. The odds were very heavy against ticket-holders in those old lotteries, but that did not deter them from buying.

The Union Canal Lottery was one of the best known in our history. Its tickets were sold by agents in all parts of the United States. Often several brokers in the same town would advertise its tickets in the same newspapers. As a sample of one of its schemes, an advertisement from the Albany (New York) *Argus* of November 8, 1826, may be quoted:

Old Towpaths

$20,000 FOR $5!—UNION CANAL LOTTERY
To be drawn on the 15th of November.

60 NUMBER COMBINATIONS	8 BALLOTS TO BE DRAWN
1 Prize of $20,000	10 Prizes of $1,000
1 " " 10,000	20 " " 500
1 " " 4,000	20 " " 200
1 " " 2,000	52 " " 100
1 " " 1,500	52 " " 50
1 " " 1,020	1,352 " " 10

10,608 Prizes of $5

Whole Ticket $5, halves $2.50, quarters $1.25, eighths $0.63

Tickets in a variety of numbers may be had at the Lucky Office of

S. & M. ALLEN & CO.

Harmony Row, 443 So. Market St.

Premium for Gold. Uncurrent bank notes discounted at the lowest rates.

Of course there was keen competition among the brokers, and they struggled hard to produce the most seductive advertising possible. They gave their offices such titles as "Waite's Truly Fortunate Lottery and Exchange Office," "Allen's Truly Lucky Office," and "Carson's Old Gold Mint." Their advertising bore such catch lines as "A speedy cure for broken fortunes." "Nothing venture, nothing have," "Now is the time to fill your bags," "Money made easy," "Try your luck these hard times."

Much doggerel verse was composed for lottery advertising. "Latshaw's Lucky Office," of Lancaster, Pennsylvania, was rather proud of its seventeen-line poem whose conclusion ran thus:

If once Dame Fortune lets you draw
You'll find her faithful ever.
Her only agent is Latshaw,
And he'll forget you never.

Canal Lotteries

A Boston office began its poem of half a dozen long stanzas with this choice bit of metaphor:

In the fish pond of fortune men angle always.
Some angle for titles, some angle for praise;
Some angle for favor, some angle for wives,
And some angle for nought all the days of their lives.
Ye who'd angle for Wealth and would Fortune obtain
Get your hooks baited by KIDDER, GILBERT & DEAN.

A bit of crude verse in an Easton, Pennsylvania, newspaper of 1829 will give a hint of the great number of lottery-ticket brokers in a single small town:

Come, let us hitch the pony up to our little cutter,
And ride to town and buy a prize of Christian Jacob Hutter.
And if we cannot suit ourselves, we'll pass by Jacob Hutter,
And down we'll go that pretty walk to Michael Odenwelder's.

And if we find no prizes there, we'll be as stiff as sawyers,
We'll crack our whip, away we'll go across to Davy Moyer's.
If Davy won't insure a prize, we will no longer bother,
We'll keep the money in our purse and then we'll try another.

We will then cut it down the street and call on Harry Hammon,
But not a prize we found at all, nor nothing of that gammon—
The one reply'd, we'll have to go, 'tis nearly time for dinner,
You know we'll have to stop once more and call on Tommy Gwinner.

"It is impossible to tell upon whom the GOLDEN SHOWER will fall!" exclaims an advertisement of the South Hadley Canal Lottery, which is headed by a favorite stock design showing a blindfolded lady, presumably the goddess Fortuna, poised on one toe upon the rim of a wheel, recklessly emptying a cornucopiaful of money, which is being caught in

Old Towpaths

the hat of a youth apparently too poor to possess any other clothing. "Ye that have the least relish," the announcement proceeds, "to obtain 8,000 dollars for a trifling sum, be *'up and doing!'* The third class of Hadley Lottery will commence drawing the 15th of June.

"*Remark*—The object of this Lottery is of great public utility—that of improving SOUTH HADLEY CANAL in order to make it permanent and beneficial to the public—and the Proprietors in this arduous undertaking have to cut through an entire mass of rocks for *three* miles! Laudable and praise-worthy perseverance!"

It was a sign of the changing times when in 1833 the Pennsylvania Legislature suppressed all lotteries in the State. Even then the lawmakers felt so conscience-stricken over the injury they were inflicting upon the Union Canal Company that as a compensation they gave the State's subscription for a thousand shares of the canal company's stock.

CHAPTER XXXIV

THE LAST OF THEIR RACE

THERE is just one tiny district in the United States—you could cover it with a bent finger on the maps—where you may see the old canal transportation being carried on almost precisely as it was a hundred years ago. This district consists of a little ribbon of water in New Jersey and another in eastern Pennsylvania, the two touching each other at Trenton.

The Delaware and Raritan, laziest of all northern canals because of its gentle slope and few locks, now operates only from New Brunswick, at the Raritan tidewater, over to Trenton on the Delaware; the short extension from Trenton to Bordentown was abandoned long ago. Most of the navigation on the canal—and there is no great amount, it must be admitted—is now carried on by steam; but there is still one horse outfit which toils to and fro, bringing Pennsylvania coal from Trenton to New Brunswick, and for the return trip getting a cargo of whatever may be found. In another year or two it, too, may be gone. One calls it an outfit because there seems to be no other word which precisely fits the case. It consists of two full-sized boats, drawn one behind the other—scarcely sufficient to be called a fleet. Three horses are used, and when once under way, the team seems to draw the load rather handily through the almost static water of the canal. The steering of such a flotilla is very easily done. The rudders of both boats are connected by cables running along the gunwales of the rear boat. The rearmost itself—or perhaps we should say herself, for her name is *Mollie Bowles*—acts as a rudder when negotiating the bends, as well as being the flagship. In the little stern

Old Towpaths

cabin may be found the Captain's family—a sturdy wife, three or four children and, of course, a dog.

Here is family life such as one saw on the old canals fifty years and more agone. The cabin stands higher above the deck than on the Lehigh and Morris boats, for there are no low bridges to dodge on the D. and R.; they all rise or swing aside for you. This makes it possible, too, to rig clotheslines on deck and dress the old boat with a flapping array of multicolored cloth, like a warship at a gala review.

"I used to be up on the Champlain Canal," explains the Captain; "up there fifteen years. Then they began to enlarge it and cut out the horse boats, and I come down here. It's better here, anyhow, in one way. You can get in at least one or two months' more work in a season. The canal usually opens here in March, but up there it was lucky to get started by the middle of April, and sometimes it was May.

"But I don't think the old Raritan's goin' to last much longer. They're tryin' to kill it. They've raised the tolls again; they've built low bridges across the feeder so it can't be used, and they're not keepin' up repairs like they oughter. Some day there'll be a lot of breaks in the banks, and it'll never be repaired."

One finds this pessimism everywhere on the few canals that are left. Reaching Trenton we cross the Delaware River to Morrisville, in Pennsylvania, and find a still older, slightly smaller and more primitive waterway—the Delaware Division, Pennsylvania Canals.

Cottage homes are ranged along both banks of the placid little stream as we walk northward along the towpath, cut with thousands of small hoof-marks; but presently we sight a big building around which are grouped boats in the water and trucks on the shore; and the building, with a great iron hand, is clawing coal rapidly out of the boats and transferring it to the trucks. Some of the boats stop here, some go on ten miles farther to the mouth of the canal at Bristol.

Never a bit of steam is used on this canal. The boats

The Last of Their Race

are all of one pattern—nearly a hundred feet in length, and looking just as if a single long boat had been sawed in halves, the sawed ends covered, and then the two halves joined together with iron rods so that they are only a foot apart. This obviates the strain to which a single long, narrow boat would be subjected with a hundred tons of coal in it. When loading or unloading, the two halves or "boxes" are uncoupled, so that the laden one may be deep in the water while the other stands high in air, resting on the surface like a dry leaf.

The Lehigh and the Delaware Division are now operated as one canal, and are under the control of the great anthracite company at Mauch Chunk which supplies most of their cargo, and with very few exceptions owns all the boats. The company's boats are merely loaned to the captains, who furnish the horses, rope and other equipment, and receive pay by the ton for hauling the coal.

We ask a captain whose boat is just about to be unloaded whether he expects to go up to-morrow or next day.

"If they can git me unloaded by four o'clock to-day, I'll start," he says.

"But you couldn't get very far before night, could you?"

"We don't usually stop when it gits dark, mister. We'll run to New Hope, anyhow—that's about fourteen miles; may take us till ten o'clock to-night. If we could git started a little earlier, we might make it to Center Bridge, four miles farther."

You wonder how the captains induce modern boatmen to work through such long days until you learn that these men are also paid by the ton, and therefore, the more they haul, the more wages they receive.

Presently a boat is emptied and we start up the canal. One man walks with the team, the other steers. Suburban Morrisville trails a long way up the canal, but after we pass the lock at Yardley, we are in the beautiful countryside of the Delaware Valley. No wonder Dickens and other travelers,

Old Towpaths

to say nothing of the old boatmen, found canal travel so delightful. It is the most soothing experience in the world. Nothing else that I know of embodies such pure placidity. There is no throb nor clatter of machinery, no straining of oars, no jerking, no rocking, not even the slap of waves against the hull. Save at the locks, where it is momentarily churned by side cuts and restless gates, this old stream is utterly at peace. We might almost be floating in a pool of air. An occasional twig or leaf on the surface of the clear brown water, slowly drowsing its way southward, the soft tinkle of the bells at the throats of the mules, eighty yards distant—these contribute calm to the spirit. In the fields, farmers are opening long, clean brown furrows—for it is late April—and their clucks and low-toned commands to their horses come clearly to us across a quarter of a mile of fallow.

We pass a boat going southward with only one man aboard, and he necessarily at the tiller. The two gray mules are taking their own sweet time, perfectly well aware that the captain's occasional threatening yells do about as much harm to them as the small lumps of coal which he throws now and then, and which miss their targets far more often than they hit.

"I see Whitman's lost his crew," remarks our captain. "Mighty hard to keep men nowadays, workin' these long hours, even if they git more money. Oh, yes, he'll maybe pick up a hand goin' back. Makes it tough on a feller, doin' all the work himself."

An old canal like this has long since lost its appearance of artificiality and seems like a natural stream—a stream which has lost its youthful impetuosity and drifted into the tranquillity of age. There are no longer any raw gashes in earth or stone—the banks are covered with verdure down to the brim. Violets and dandelions bloom along the towpath, and rhododendron and ferns dip their feet in water on the other shore. Trees arch overhead from either side

Courtesy of the New York State Bureau of Canals

A MODERN CANAL SHIP, 258 FEET LONG, TRAVERSING THE GREAT LAKES, THE NEW YORK STATE BARGE CANAL AND EVEN THE OCEAN, IF NECESSARY

Courtesy of the New York State Bureau of Canals

THE OLD AND THE NEW AT LOCKPORT—FIVE LOCKS OF THE OLD ERIE CANAL AT THE RIGHT AND TWO LOCKS OF THE NEW BARGE CANAL AT THE LEFT

The Last of Their Race

until at times their wind-blown bough tips caress each other. Even the walls which support the towpath when the river comes close underneath it are masked with vines, and the locks and aqueducts are so weathered and so covered with moss that one can easily fancy they have been there always.

At every few yards along the towpath we hear a "queek!" and a plop in the water as some little frog makes a nose-dive. Whenever the stream is widened by a shallow inlet on its upper or bermbank side, there are apt to be rushes growing there, and among the stems a few big, green-backed, yellow-bellied bullfrogs who sit with two knobby eyes barely poking above the water and now and then "twang a loose, low string on their bass viols." Occasionally one catches a glimpse of a muskrat slipping silently into the water, and once we see a badger scurrying away among the weeds on the opposite shore.

Even the buildings along the Delaware are hoary with age. This is Bucks County, Pennsylvania, where Daniel Boone was born, where some of the first iron foundering in America was done, where the Seckel pear originated, whence spring many other ancient memories. Old, old stone and brick farmhouses slumber amid exquisite settings. We pass the farm among the hills where Washington and his little army hid for several December days just before he made his dash for Trenton. The big stone farmhouse is deserted now; down in the edge of a thicket is a painter sketching it. Artists swarm in these parts; you may see one with his outfit under his arm at every turn.

We ride several miles with Captain John Minder, a jolly old soul who has been on the canal forty-five years. "I dunno as you'll git much out of him," said a lock tender. "He's mighty nigh as deef as a post." He is very deaf, indeed, but one of the sweetest and liveliest of spirits, and gave us much information. He shouts jokes at friends on shore as he passes, regardless of the fact that he can seldom catch the full flavor of the reply.

Old Towpaths

At New Hope there are four locks. Two which closely adjoin each other are both tended by a tall man with a bitter countenance and with one leg cut off at the hip. Still he manages to handle the job well, hopping furiously to and fro, poor fellow, on a single crutch. At New Hope also we see the great wheels which pumped water from the river into the canal, and still swinging across the river is the great cable by means of which boats crossed from the Delaware Division to enter the Delaware and Raritan feeder on the opposite shore.

The two boatmen take turns at driving and steering, sometimes changing jobs at the locks, or when in a long level like that between New Hope and Yardley, making a quick swap without stopping the boat. The steersman brings her around until near the stern she is fairly brushing the bank; he drops lightly to the towpath, and the other man, seizing the ladder, a series of cleats nailed to the side of the hull at the stern, clambers aboard.

The high hill, almost a mountain, at our left is casting deep shadows across the canal as we come in sight of the little shoestring of houses called Lumberville, the spot most beloved of artists along the Delaware. As we pass almost under the balcony of the little hotel perched on the rip-rapped bank twenty feet above us, Captain Minder calls the lock tender with long, mournful blasts of his conch shell, an instrument used by all the Lehigh and Delaware boatmen.

Slipping through the lock, we creep on another mile and a quarter to Lower Black Eddy, which is at the beginning of Point Pleasant, another attenuated, one-street hamlet at the mountain's foot. We leave the boat at the Eddy lock to spend the night at a little inn near by. Dusk is falling, tree frogs are peeping and the crew is lighting the "night-hawker" or headlight as we turn away. The night-hawker is a lantern hung against a sort of paddle-shaped board whose large, rounded end—always gaily decorated with a star or some such device—acts as a reflector. The night-

The Last of Their Race

hawker of earlier days was a big, boxlike affair about twelve inches square, with glass on three sides, and burning camphine.

Captain Minder and his crew are going to push on to their home village, Upper Black Eddy, fully ten miles farther, in order that they may spend at least a portion of the night under their own roofs; but as they will hardly reach there before eleven and will be under way again by dawn, one somehow cannot feel that their night at home will be a very great privilege. This being Wednesday night, however, they are hoping to reach the loading station at Slate Dam on the Lehigh, take on a load and get back to Upper Black Eddy for the week-end.

We are dressing next morning when we hear the tinkle of canal bells and looking out, see a boat with a gray mule team approaching the lock just below our windows. It is Whitman, and he is still without a crew. Our breakfast is not yet ready, and we are so delayed that he gets an hour's start of us; but after walking seven miles through another glorious April morning we catch up with him, and at the lock at Uhlertown we board his boat. The Captain is very grateful when we offer to steer.

He steps off to the towpath, and the mules suddenly become ambitious. We have the honor of steering the boat into one of the old "single-width" locks, and find that the job of fitting a big, clumsy hull 10 feet, 6 inches in width into a stone chamber only 11 feet wide is not so easy as might be supposed. Some of the locks on the canal are just twice as wide; we wish they all were.

The canal mule may be leisurely, but the service at the locks is far from slow. The layman who for the first time sees a boat locked through is astonished at the quickness with which the job is done. One is reminded of Captain Marryat's notes upon the subject after his trip through the Erie Canal:

"The locks did not deter us long—they never lose time in

Old Towpaths

America. When the boat had entered the lock and the gate was closed upon her, the water was let off with a rapidity which considerably affected her level, and her bows pointed downward. I timed one lock with a fall of fifteen feet. From the time the gate was closed behind us until the lower one was opened for our egress, was exactly one minute and a quarter; and the boat sunk down so rapidly in the lock as to give you the idea that she was scuttled and sinking."

A few of the locks on the Lehigh and Delaware Canals are still closed at both ends by the old-fashioned mitre gates, one swinging out from each side and meeting in the middle; but they have long since discarded the ponderous timber beams extending from the gates and pivoted so as to balance their weight. All the double-width locks are closed at the upper end by a new, ingenious device which on various canals has been nicknamed the "fall," "drop" or "tumble" gate. It is a single gate extending across the lock, and instead of swinging horizontally, it opens by sinking down into the bottom of the channel. It is weighted with iron on its upstream side, but is held upright when the lock is empty by the pressure of the water of the canal against its upper face; held so firmly that the beam along its top is used as a footpath. Now close the lower gates of the lock, open the wickets under the fall gate and let the water fill the lock. Just as soon as the water in the lock reaches the level of the water above the gate, that gate sinks quietly beneath the surface, even to the bottom of the channel, and the boat passes over it.

Slowly we toiled, upstream that day, past the Narrows of Nockamixon, where huge cliffs three hundred feet in air fairly overhang the canal; past Kintnersville Lock, alongside which is an ancient mill, one of whose earliest duties was the grinding of cement for the locks, bridges and aqueducts of the canal; past Durham, which gave its name to the Durham boats and where lie the ruins of perhaps the oldest iron furnace in America—one which doubtless cast cannon balls for

The Last of Their Race

Washington's army; and finally reach Easton, where the Lehigh Canal ends and our Delaware Division begins. At intervals we passed more loaded boats headed southward. On one of them was another captain handling his job alone. He was a true Pennsylvania German, and as he passed us, he told us of his troubles with the labor turnover.

"Dey don't vant to vork! I pick up a man dis veek—his shoes vas about wore out and he vas mighty nigh nekkid. I bought him some clo'es—I bought him some shoes—I loaned him a tollar—and next day he vas gone! Tam it, dey don't vant to vork!"

At Easton we meet the Superintendent of the canals, and board another boat. "Now, Pete," says the Boss, "show us some speed. We want to get up to Bethlehem or Siegfried's in time to catch that evening train up to Chunk."

Thus exhorted, Pete and his crew put the mules to their best efforts, Pete not failing to call our attention frequently to our high velocity. The trip up the Lehigh is in its way quite as fascinating as that along the Delaware, though vastly different. Here we are sometimes in an enclosed canal, sometimes skimming along the edge of a broad pool in the river. The scenery grows more rugged and grand as we go upward; but everywhere are towns and factories, everywhere the smoke and roar of industry. The forty-seven miles from Easton to Mauch Chunk, where once Josiah White and Erskine Hazard lay out in the woods at night for lack of human habitation to shelter them, are to-day one vast, unbroken workshop. Now we pass through a belt of iron furnaces and forges, now through a cement district, where all the houses are covered and the air is cloudy with the gray powder, now through a belt of slate quarries, now through a zone of zinc mines and smelters, and finally into the anthracite region. Intermingled with these are many other industries. Allentown, for example, a city of some 75,000 population, is full of silk mills. Literally dozens of railroad tracks parallel the canal and river; and

Old Towpaths

as long freight trains thunder by us and sometimes over us, the engineers and firemen, seeing passengers on our boat, lean from their windows and make derisive gestures, reflecting upon our speed; but our boatmen, calloused by years of endurance, gaze at and through these contumelious ones with magnificently unseeing eyes.

A little later we are passing a great steel plant, half a mile long, on our left, while on our right the tombs of an old Moravian cemetery look over the edge of the bank above us. Bethlehem! We have covered the twelve miles from Easton in four hours flat. We gather that it is almost a record on the Lehigh. Pete is frankly proud of it, but slightly apologetic for his hard driving. "I don't usually push them mules that way," he explains, "but you folks was in such a hurry—"

Canal navigation really ends at Slate Dam or Siegfried's Bridge, twenty-three miles above Easton—which means that one half of the canal between Easton and Mauch Chunk is virtually abandoned. A century's accumulation of coal dust in the river and upper canal had become so troublesome to navigation that in 1923 a new loading station was installed at Slate Dam, and the large boats are now all loaded there, the coal being brought down to that point by rail. The canal farther up is kept in tolerable condition and a few small boats operate, but not regularly. Dredges are busy scooping up the coal dust—173,000 tons were taken out in 1924—and after being washed, it is sold. The Boss insists that some day the river and canal will be so cleaned up that they can be used again, but most of the boatmen are skeptical. "Never again!" they say. "The old canal is dying. Even the oldest of us may live to see the end of it."

We have spent a happy week on the old canals and we turn away from them with poignant regret. Probably nowhere else in all the neurotic whirl of our present-day business and social life may we find so real a motion picture of America as it was a century ago. We yearn to hear a good

The Last of Their Race

reason why canals should be so rare in America and so numerous and so widely used in Europe. Yet even as we ask the question we know the answer. The reason is the same as that which prompts an American spender, even though he be in no great hurry, to take a taxicab for a journey of three blocks, rather than walk.

There are a few—just a few—wise shippers in America who realize the economy of water transportation. Consider the operations of the Standard Oil Company, for example, on the New York State Barge Canal. This great corporation was quick to grasp the advantages of the new waterway. Beginning with tug-towed barges, it then began to build self-propelled vessels which became larger and larger at every experiment. The latest model is a tanker 260 feet in length, 40 feet in the beam and 14 feet in depth of hold. It carries 705,000 gallons of oil and has propelling engines of 700 horse power.

The company finds the canal so useful and economical that practically the entire distribution of Standard Oil products for the State of New York is now carried on by water. There are at least two other companies owning "ships" which pass through the Hudson, the Canal and the Great Lakes, carrying freight all the way between New York City, Buffalo, Cleveland, Detroit and Duluth. Some of them have even gone down the Atlantic coast, through the Gulf of Mexico and the Panama Canal and up to California. It has been proven that immense quantities of goods can be handled simultaneously and speedily on the Barge Canal; as for example, 500 tons of steel rails and 60 automobiles in one tow. Goods are frequently carried through the canal in quicker time than by the railroad. And yet so neglectful has the public in general been that the canal is used to not more than a tenth of its capacity, and there are not lacking citizens of New York who advocate its abandonment. The "imagination is led captive" still by the fancied advantages of speed.

We built more than 4,400 miles of canals before the

Old Towpaths

Civil War, costing over $200,000,000; "and then," says Herbert Quick, "we went railroad-mad and left our waterways to ruin and neglect." Water transportation has always been, is yet and probably will be for a long time to come, cheaper than any other method of carriage. Europe, always forced by necessity to economize, gives her heavy merchandise a little more time for its passage and sends it by water. Although disorganized by the War, her transportation tools are still highly efficient and the cheapest in the world. Belgium, with an area less than that of Massachusetts and Connecticut, has more than 1,200 miles of waterways, all in active service. France is still building canals—just the other day the newspapers told us of the completion of a tunnel seven kilometers long on a new canal in the southern part of that country.

With the recklessness engendered by our wealth, we would rather pay higher freight charges and move the goods faster. We would rather wait until the last minute and then send merchandise by what we believe to be the swiftest carrier; it tickles our craving for speed and our belief in our own superior efficiency. Perhaps not until our land shall have become much more densely populated than now, our natural resources much more nearly exhausted and our wealth begins to flow towards newer Midases, will we think of economy in such little matters as transportation.

"Once a really valuable though premature canal system was in working order," says Seymour Dunbar in his *History of Travel,* "it would not have been allowed to disintegrate in large part had there been a general or governmental appreciation of the future needs of the country, coupled with a popular sense of business morality sufficiently strong to resist those blandishments which finally resulted in the crippling or outright abandonment of important, costly and useful public improvements. . . . America has not developed beyond the era of canals, but is on the contrary apparently still to enter upon it."

BIBLIOGRAPHY

GENERAL

THE AMERICAN: WHICH CONTAINS NOTES OF A JOURNEY FROM THE OHIO VALLEY TO WALES; A VIEW OF THE STATE OF OHIO, ETC., by Rev. B. W. Chidlaw, A.M. (Llanrwst, Wales, 1840), reprint in Historical and Philosophical Society of Ohio Quarterly, Cincinnati, 1911.
THE AMERICAN CENTENARY, by Benson J. Lossing, Philadelphia, 1876.
AMERICAN SCENERY, by N. P. Willis, illustrated by W. H. Bartlett, London, 1840.
A BOOK FOR ALL TRAVELERS, by George Conclin, Cincinnati, 1855.
THE CANAL AND THE RAILROAD FROM 1861 TO 1865, by Emerson D. Fite, in *Yale Review*, New Haven, 1907.
COLTON'S TRAVELER'S AND TOURIST'S GUIDE BOOK THROUGH THE NORTHEASTERN AND MIDDLE STATES AND THE CANADAS, published by J. H. Colton, New York, 1850-1852.
COLTON'S WESTERN TOURIST OR EMIGRANT'S GUIDE THROUGH THE STATES OF OHIO, MICHIGAN, INDIANA, ILLINOIS, AND THE TERRITORIES OF WISCONSIN AND IOWA, published by J. H. Colton, New York, 1844-1847.
COMPENDIUM OF THE INTERNAL IMPROVEMENTS OF THE UNITED STATES, by Samuel Augustus Mitchell, Philadelphia, 1835.
A CONNECTED VIEW OF THE WHOLE INTERNAL NAVIGATION OF THE UNITED STATES, by a citizen of the United States (G. Armroyd), Philadelphia, 1830.
A DESCRIPTION OF THE CANALS AND RAILROADS OF THE UNITED STATES, by H. S. Tanner, New York, 1840.
DEVELOPMENT OF THE TRANSPORTATION SYSTEM IN THE UNITED STATES, by J. L. Ringwalt, Philadelphia, 1888.
DISTURNELL'S GUIDE THROUGH THE MIDDLE, NORTHERN AND EASTERN STATES, published by J. Disturnell, New York, 1847-1850.
DOCUMENTS TENDING TO PROVE THE SUPERIOR ADVANTAGES OF RAILWAYS AND STEAM CARRIAGES OVER CANAL NAVIGATION, by John Stevens, New York, 1812.
ECONOMIC HISTORY OF THE ANTHRACITE-TIDEWATER CANALS, by Chester Lloyd Jones, Publications of the University of Pennsylvania, Philadelphia, 1908.

Old Towpaths

JOURNAL OF A RESIDENCE AND TOUR IN THE UNITED STATES OF AMERICA FROM APRIL, 1833 TO OCTOBER, 1834, by E. S. Abdy, London, 1835.
JOURNAL OF THE FRANKLIN INSTITUTE OF THE STATE OF PENNSYLVANIA, Philadelphia, 1826—.
HISTORIC HIGHWAYS OF AMERICA, by Archer Butler Hulbert, Cleveland, 1904.
A HISTORY OF THE PEOPLE OF THE UNITED STATES, by John Bach McMaster, 8 volumes, New York, 1883-1913.
HISTORY OF THE RAILROADS AND CANALS OF THE UNITED STATES OF AMERICA, by Henry V. Poor, New York, 1860.
HISTORY OF TRANSPORTATION IN THE UNITED STATES UP TO 1860, by Caroline E. McGill and collaborators. Edited by Balthasar Henry Meyer, Carnegie Institute of Washington, D. C., 1917.
A HISTORY OF TRAVEL IN AMERICA, by Seymour Dunbar, Indianapolis, (1915).
LETTERS ON THE INTERNAL IMPROVEMENT AND COMMERCE OF THE WEST, by Henry A. S. Dearborn, Boston, 1839.
MEMORIES OF A HUNDRED YEARS, by Edward Everett Hale, New York, 1902.
NAVIGATION AUX ETATS-UNIS, par H. Vetillart, Paris, 1892.
NILES'S NATIONAL REGISTER, Baltimore, 1812-1849.
ORPHAN CANAL BOYS, in *Sailor's Magazine and Naval Journal*, New York, 1846.
OUR COUNTRY, by Benson J. Lossing, New York, 1876.
PICTURESQUE AMERICA, by William Cullen Bryant, New York, 1874.
THE RAMBLER IN AMERICA, by Charles Joseph Latrobe, New York, 1833.
RAMBLES IN THE PATH OF THE STEAM HORSE, by Eli Bowen, Philadelphia, 1855.
REGISTER OF PENNSYLVANIA. edited by Samuel Hazard, Philadelphia, 1828-1835.
REPORT OF THE AMERICAN BETHEL SOCIETY, New York, 1848.
REPORT OF THE SECRETARY OF THE TREASURY ON THE SUBJECT OF PUBLIC ROADS AND CANALS, MADE IN PURSUANCE OF A RESOLUTION OF SENATE OF MARCH 2, 1807, Washington, 1808.
THE RISE OF THE NEW WEST, by Frederick Jackson Turner, New York, 1906.
SOCIETY, MANNERS AND POLITICS IN THE UNITED STATES, by Michel Chevalier, Boston, 1839.
THE TOURIST: OR, POCKET MANUAL FOR TRAVELERS ON THE HUDSON RIVER, THE WESTERN CANAL, ETC., (R. J. Vandewater), New York, 1830, 1834, 1835, 1838.
TRANSPORTATION IN THE EASTERN COTTON BELT UP TO 1860, by Ulrich Bonnell Phillips, New York, 1908.

Bibliography

TRAVELS IN NEW ENGLAND AND NEW YORK, by Timothy Dwight, S.T.D., LL.D., New Haven, 1821-22.
A TREATISE ON THE IMPROVEMENT OF CANAL NAVIGATION: EXHIBITING THE NUMEROUS ADVANTAGES TO BE DERIVED FROM SMALL CANALS, by R. Fulton, London, 1796.
THE WORLD ON WHEELS AND OTHER SKETCHES, by Benjamin F. Taylor, Chicago, 1874.
THE WRITINGS OF GEORGE WASHINGTON, collected and edited by W. C. Ford, New York, 1889-1891.

ILLINOIS

THE CHICAGO DRAINAGE CANAL AND ITS FOREBEAR, THE ILLINOIS AND MICHIGAN CANAL, by Alexander Jones, publications of the Illinois State Historical Society, Springfield, 1906.
THE ECONOMIC HISTORY OF THE ILLINOIS AND MICHIGAN CANAL, by James W. Putnam, Chicago, 1909.
FORTY YEARS AGO! A CONTRIBUTION TO THE EARLY HISTORY OF JOLIET AND WILL COUNTY, by George H. Woodruff, Joliet, Ill., 1874.
HISTORIC ILLINOIS: THE ROMANCE OF THE EARLIER DAYS, by Randall Parrish, Chicago, 1905.
A HISTORY OF ILLINOIS FROM ITS COMMENCEMENT AS A STATE IN 1818 TO 1847, by Thomas Ford, Chicago, 1854.
THE ILLINOIS AND MICHIGAN CANAL, by James W. Putnam, Chicago, 1918.
PUBLICATIONS OF THE CHICAGO HISTORICAL SOCIETY.
PUBLICATIONS OF THE ILLINOIS STATE HISTORICAL SOCIETY.

INDIANA

HISTORY OF CANALS IN INDIANA, by Howard Payne Comstock in *Indiana Magazine of History*, Indianapolis, 1911.
HISTORY OF VIGO COUNTY, INDIANA, by H. C. Bradsby, Chicago, 1891.
HISTORY OF WABASH COUNTY, INDIANA, by Thomas B. Helm, Chicago, 1884.
INDIANA GAZETTEER OR TOPOGRAPHICAL DICTIONARY OF THE STATE OF INDIANA, published by E. Chamberlain, Indianapolis, 1850.
INTERNAL IMPROVEMENTS IN EARLY INDIANA, by Logan Esarey, Indiana Historical Society Publications, Indianapolis, 1912.
THE PICTORIAL HISTORY OF FORT WAYNE, by B. J. Griswold, Chicago, 1917.
PUBLICATIONS OF THE INDIANA HISTORICAL SOCIETY.
THE WABASH: OR ADVENTURES OF AN ENGLISH GENTLEMAN'S FAMILY IN THE INTERIOR OF INDIANA, by J. Richard Beste, London, 1855.

Old Towpaths

THE WABASH TRADE ROUTE IN THE DEVELOPMENT OF THE OLD NORTH-WEST, by Elbert J. Benton, Johns Hopkins University Studies, Baltimore, 1903.

KENTUCKY

CANAL AROUND THE FALLS OF THE OHIO, by William J. Ball, Cincinnati, 1850.

MARYLAND

CHESAPEAKE AND DELAWARE CANAL COMPANY PUBLICATIONS, edited by Joshua Gilpin, Philadelphia, 1809.
CHRONICLES OF GEORGETOWN, by Richard P. Jackson, Washington, 1878.
EARLY CHAPTERS IN THE DEVELOPMENT OF THE POTOMAC ROUTE TO THE WEST, by Mrs. Corra Bacon Foster, Washington, 1912.
EARLY DEVELOPMENT OF THE CHESAPEAKE AND OHIO CANAL PROJECT, by George Washington Ward, Johns Hopkins University Studies, Baltimore, 1899.
HISTORY OF CECIL COUNTY, MARYLAND, by George Johnson, Elkton, Md., 1881.
HISTORY OF CUMBERLAND, MARYLAND, by Will H. Lowdermilk, Washington, 1876.
HISTORY OF DELAWARE, 1609–1888, John Thomas Scharf, Philadelphia, 1888.
HISTORY OF MARYLAND FROM THE EARLIEST PERIOD TO THE PRESENT DAY, by John Thomas Scharf, Baltimore, 1879.
HISTORY OF WASHINGTON COUNTY, MARYLAND, by Thomas J. C. Williams, Hagerstown, 1906.
A NEW CHAPTER IN THE EARLY LIFE OF WASHINGTON, by John Pickell, New York, 1856.
PICTURES OF THE CITY OF WASHINGTON IN THE PAST, by Samuel C. Busey, Washington, 1899.
THE (MARYLAND) STATE CONVENTION ON INTERNAL IMPROVEMENTS, CONTAINING THE RESOLUTIONS, ETC., by Thomas Phenix, Assistant Secretary to the Convention, Baltimore, 1825.

NEW ENGLAND

AN ACCOUNT OF THE FARMINGTON CANAL COMPANY, OF THE HAMPSHIRE AND HAMPDEN CANAL COMPANY, AND OF THE NEW HAVEN AND NORTHAMPTON COMPANY, New Haven, 1850.
THE CAPE COD CANAL, by William Barclay Parsons, in Annals of American Academy of Political and Social Science, 1908.
A DOWN EAST YANKEE, by Windsor Daggett, Portland, Me., 1920.

Bibliography

FROM STAGE COACH TO RAILROAD TRAIN AND STREET CAR, by George Glover Crocker, Boston, 1900.
HISTORICAL SKETCH OF THE MIDDLESEX CANAL: WITH REMARKS FOR THE CONSIDERATION OF THE PROPRIETORS, by Caleb Eddy, Boston, 1843.
HISTORY AND ANTIQUITIES OF NEW HAVEN, CONNECTICUT, FROM ITS EARLIEST SETTLEMENT TO THE PRESENT TIME, by John W. Barber and Lemual S. Penderson, New Haven, 1870.
HISTORY OF CHELMSFORD, by Rev. Wilson Waters, Lowell, 1917.
HISTORY OF THE CONNECTICUT VALLEY IN MASSACHUSETTS, by Nathaniel Bartlett Sylvester, Philadelphia, 1879.
HISTORY OF NORTHAMPTON, MASSACHUSETTS, by James Russell Trumbull, Northampton, 1902.
HISTORY OF PORTLAND (Maine), by William Willis, Portland, 1865.
HISTORY OF WESTERN MASSACHUSETTS; THE COUNTIES OF HAMPDEN, HAMPSHIRE, FRANKLIN AND BERKSHIRE, by Josiah Gilbert Holland, Springfield, 1885.
HISTORY OF WORCESTER, MASSACHUSETTS, edited by D. Hamilton Hurd, Philadelphia, 1889.
HISTORY OF WORCESTER, MASSACHUSETTS, FROM ITS EARLIEST SETTLEMENT TO SEPTEMBER, 1836, by William Lincoln, Worcester, 1837.
MEDFORD HISTORICAL REGISTER, Medford (Mass.) Historical Society.
MEMORIAL HISTORY OF BOSTON, edited by Justin Winsor, Boston, 1881.
THE MIDDLESEX CANAL, THE MERRIMAC RIVER, by Lorin L. Dame and George Stark, Old Residents' Historical Association Contributions, Lowell, Mass., 1886.
PUBLICATIONS OF THE CONNECTICUT HISTORICAL SOCIETY.
PUBLICATIONS OF THE MASSACHUSETTS HISTORICAL SOCIETY.
PUBLICATIONS OF THE RHODE ISLAND HISTORICAL SOCIETY.
PUBLICATIONS OF THE WORCESTER HISTORICAL SOCIETY.
WESTFIELD AND ITS HISTORIC INFLUENCES, by Rev. John H. Lockwood, Westfield, Mass., 1922.

NEW JERSEY

AMONG THE NAIL MAKERS, *Harper's Magazine*, New York, 1860.
APPEAL TO THE PEOPLE OF NEW JERSEY IN RELATION TO THE EXISTING CONTRACTS BETWEEN THE STATE OF NEW JERSEY AND THE UNITED DELAWARE AND RARITAN CANAL AND CAMDEN AND AMBOY RAILROAD COMPANIES, by Robert F. Stockton, Princeton, 1849.
BEAUTIES OF THE MONOPOLY SYSTEM IN NEW JERSEY, by a citizen of Burlington (Henry C. Carey), Philadelphia, 1848.

Old Towpaths

An Exposition of the Character and Management of the New Jersey Joint Monopolies, the Camden and Amboy Railroad and Transportation Company, the Delaware and Raritan Canal Company and their Appendages, by George H. Tathorn, Philadelphia, 1852.
Historical Collections of New Jersey, edited by John W. Barber and Henry Howe, New Haven, Conn., 1868.
History of Essex and Hudson Counties, New Jersey, compiled by William H. Shaw, Philadelphia, 1884.
History of Hunterdon and Somerset Counties, New Jersey, by James P. Snell, Philadelphia, 1881.
An Investigation into the Affairs of the Delaware and Raritan Canal and Camden and Amboy Railroad and Transportation Companies, in Reference to Certain Charges by "A Citizen of Burlington," Newark, 1849.
Letters and Extracts Relative to the New Jersey Canal, by John Rutherford, (1822?).
The Lorist, papers in Newark (N. J.) *Evening News*, by Rev. Joseph Folsom.
New Brunswick in History, by William H. Benedict, New York, 1925.
Report of the Commissioners Appointed to Invesigate Charges Made Against the Directors of the Delaware and Raritan Canal and Camden and Amboy Railroad and Transportation Companies, Trenton, 1850.

NEW YORK

The Advantages of the Proposed Canal from Lake Erie to Hudson's River, Fully Illustrated in a Correspondence Between the Honorable Gouverneur Morris and Robert Fulton, Esq.,(1814?).
Annals of Albany, compiled by Joel Munsell, Albany, 1850–1859.
Appeal to the People of New York and Their Representatives in the Legislature in Favor of Constructing the Genesee and Allegany Canal, New York, 1833.
Atticus to the Citizens of New York, by De Witt Clinton, 1812.
The Autobiography of Thurlow Weed, edited by Harriet A. Weed, Boston, 1883–84.
A Brief Autobiography of My Life, by Chester Burbank, Albany, 1888.
Buffalo Historical Society Publications, especially Vols. 12, 13, 14, 16 and 22.

Bibliography

COLLECTIONS OF THE HISTORY OF ALBANY FROM ITS DISCOVERY TO THE PRESENT TIME, compiled by Joel Munsell, Albany, 1865-1867.
CONSIDERATIONS ON THE GREAT WESTERN CANAL, FROM THE HUDSON TO LAKE ERIE; WITH A VIEW OF ITS EXPENSE, ADVANTAGES AND PROGRESS, by Charles Glidden Haines, 1818.
CONSTITUTIONAL HISTORY OF NEW YORK FROM THE BEGINNING OF THE COLONIAL PERIOD TO THE YEAR 1905, by Charles Z. Lincoln, Rochester, 1906.
A DIARY IN AMERICA, by Captain (Frederick) Marryat, C.B., New York, 1839.
DISTURNELL'S TRAVELER'S GUIDE THROUGH THE STATE OF NEW YORK, CANADA, ETC., New York, 1836.
DOCUMENTARY SKETCH OF THE NEW YORK STATE CANALS, by S. H. Sweet, Albany, 1863.
DOMESTIC MANNERS OF THE AMERICANS, by Mrs. (Frances M.) Trollope, London, 1832.
THE EMPIRE STATE, by Benson J. Lossing, Hartford, 1888.
THE ERIE CANAL AND THE SETTLEMENT OF THE WEST, by Lois Kimball Mathews, Buffalo Historical Society Publications, Buffalo, 1910.
FIVE YEARS ON THE ERIE CANAL, by M. Eaton, Utica, 1845.
HISTORICAL COLLECTIONS OF THE STATE OF NEW YORK, by John W. Barber, New York. 1851.
HISTORICAL REVIEW OF WATERWAYS AND CANALS CONSTRUCTED IN NEW YORK STATE, by Henry Wayland Hill, Buffalo Historical Society, Buffalo, 1908.
HISTORY OF ALLEGANY COUNTY, NEW YORK, by John S. Minard and Mrs. Georgia Drew Merrill, Alfred, N. Y., 1896.
HISTORY OF THE CANAL SYSTEM OF THE STATE OF NEW YORK, by Noble E. Whitford, Albany, 1905.
HISTORY OF DETROIT, by Silas Farmer, Detroit, 1884.
HISTORY OF THE MOHAWK VALLEY, by Nelson Greene, Chicago, 1925.
HISTORY OF MONROE COUNTY, NEW YORK, by Prof. W. H. McIntosh, Philadelphia, 1877.
HISTORY OF MONTGOMERY AND FULTON COUNTIES, NEW YORK, published by F. W. Beers & Co., New York, 1878.
HISTORY OF ONEIDA COUNTY, NEW YORK, by S. W. Durant, Philadelphia, 1878.
HISTORY OF ONONDAGA COUNTY, NEW YORK, by Prof. W. W. Clayton, Syracuse, 1878.
HISTORY OF ORANGE COUNTY, NEW YORK, by Edward Manning Ruttenber, Philadelphia, 1881.
HISTORY OF ROCHESTER AND MONROE COUNTY, NEW YORK, by William F. Peck, New York and Chicago, 1908.

Old Towpaths

HISTORY OF THE RISE, PROGRESS AND EXISTING CONDITIONS OF THE WESTERN CANALS IN THE STATE OF NEW YORK, by Elkanah Watson, Albany, 1820.
HISTORY OF SARATOGA COUNTY, NEW YORK, by Nathaniel Bartlett Sylvester, Philadelphia, 1878.
HISTORY OF SULLIVAN COUNTY, NEW YORK, by James Eldridge Quinlan, Liberty, N. Y., 1873.
HISTORY OF ULSTER COUNTY, NEW YORK, edited by A. T. Clearwater, Kingston, N. Y., 1907.
IMPRESSIONS OF AMERICA, by Tyrone Power, London, 1836.
INTERNAL IMPROVEMENTS IN THE STATE OF NEW YORK, by Azariah C. Flagg, (1851).
JOURNAL, by Frances Anne Butler (Fanny Kemble), London, 1835.
JOURNAL OF A TOUR FROM NEW YORK TO NIAGARA, by William Leete Stone, Buffalo Historical Society Publications, 1910.
JOURNAL OF A TOUR IN THE STATE OF NEW YORK IN THE YEAR 1830, by John Fowler, London, 1831.
LAFAYETTE IN AMERICA IN 1824 AND 1825; OR, JOURNAL OF A VOYAGE TO THE UNITED STATES, by A. Levasseur, secretary to General Lafayette during the journey, Philadelphia, 1829.
LAWS OF THE STATE OF NEW YORK IN RELATION TO THE ERIE AND CHAMPLAIN CANALS, ETC., Albany, 1825.
LETTERS OF A TRAVELER; OR, NOTES OF THINGS SEEN IN EUROPE AND AMERICA, by William Cullen Bryant, New York, 1871.
LETTERS TO A GENTLEMAN IN GERMANY, WRITTEN AFTER A TRIP FROM PHILADELPHIA TO NIAGARA, by Francis Lieber, Philadelphia, 1834.
LIFE AND LETTERS OF JOSEPH STORY, edited by his son, William W. Story, Boston, 1851.
LIFE AND TIMES OF PHILIP SCHUYLER, by Benson J. Lossing, New York, 1860.
LIFE AND WRITINGS OF DE WITT CLINTON, by William W. Campbell, New York, 1849.
LIFE OF DE WITT CLINTON, by James Renwick, New York, 1854.
LIFE OF GENERAL PHILIP SCHUYLER, 1733-1804, by Bayard Tuckerman, New York, 1903.
LIFE OF GOUVERNEUR MORRIS, by Jared Sparks, Boston, 1832.
MARCO PAUL'S TRAVELS AND ADVENTURES IN THE PURSUIT OF KNOWLEDGE; ON THE ERIE CANAL, by Jacob Abbott, Boston, 1848.
MEMOIR OF DE WITT CLINTON, by David Hosack, M.D., New York, 1829.
MEMOIR PREPARED AT A REQUEST OF A COMMITTEE OF THE COMMON COUNCIL OF THE CITY OF NEW YORK AND PRESENTED TO THE MAYOR OF THE CITY AT THE CELEBRATION OF THE COMPLETION OF THE NEW YORK CANALS, by Cadwallader D. Colden (New York), 1825.

Bibliography

THE MOHAWK VALLEY, by W. Max Reid, New York, 1901.
THE NORTHERN TRAVELER, published by A. T. Goodrich, New York, 1826.
THE OLD MOHAWK TURNPIKE BOOK, by Nelson Greene, Fort Plain, N. Y., 1924.
OLD STEAMBOAT DAYS ON THE HUDSON RIVER, by David Lear Buckman, New York, 1909.
OLDE ULSTER (Magazine), Kingston, N. Y., 1905-.
ONONDAGA'S CENTENNIAL, edited by Dwight H. Bruce, Boston, 1896.
THE ORIGIN OF THE ERIE CANAL, by M. S. Hawley, Buffalo, 1866.
THE ORIGIN OF THE ERIE CANAL, by Benjamin H. Wright, Rome, 1870.
ORIGIN AND HISTORY OF THE MEASURES THAT LED TO THE CONSTRUCTION OF THE ERIE CANAL, by G. Geddes, Syracuse, 1866.
OUR COUNTY AND ITS PEOPLE, edited by Daniel E. Wager, Boston, 1896.
PIONEER HISTORY OF THE HOLLAND PURCHASE OF WESTERN NEW YORK, by O. Turner, Buffalo, 1850.
A POCKET GUIDE FOR THE TOURIST AND TRAVELER ALONG THE LINE OF THE CANALS AND THE INTERIOR COMMERCE OF THE STATE OF NEW YORK, by Horatio Gates Spafford, New York, 1824.
PROCEEDINGS OF THE NEW YORK STATE CONVENTIONS FOR RESCUING THE CANALS FROM THE RUIN WITH WHICH THEY ARE THREATENED BY EXPOSING AND RESISTING THE RAILROAD CONSPIRACY, ETC., New York, 1859.
PROPOSALS OF THE SPEEDY SETTLEMENT OF THE WASTE AND UNAPPROPRIATED LANDS ON THE WESTERN FRONTIER OF THE STATE OF NEW YORK AND FOR THE IMPROVEMENT OF THE INLAND NAVIGATION, ETC., by Christopher Colles, New York, 1785.
REPORT OF A COMMITTEE APPOINTED TO EXPLORE THE WESTERN WATERS, . . . FOR THE PURPOSE OF PROSECUTING THE INLAND LOCK NAVIGATION, Albany, 1792.
RETROSPECT OF WESTERN TRAVEL, by Harriet Martineau, London, 1838.
ROCHESTER AND ITS EARLY CANAL DAYS, by Captain H. P. Marsh, Rochester, 1914.
SETTLEMENT IN THE WEST, SKETCHES OF ROCHESTER, by Henry O'Rielly, Rochester, 1838.
SKETCHES OF A SUMMER TRIP TO NEW YORK AND THE CANADAS, by D. Wilkie, Edinburgh, 1837.
STEAM ON THE CANAL IN 1872 AND 1873, by D. P. Dobbins, Buffalo, 1873.
A SUBALTERN'S FURLOUGH, by E. T. Coke, New York, 1833.
THREE YEARS IN NORTH AMERICA, by James Stuart, Edinburgh, 1833.
TRAVELS IN NORTH AMERICA, by Captain Basil Hall, London. 1859.
TRAVELS THROUGH AMERICA IN THE YEARS 1825 AND 1826, by Bernhard, Duke of Saxe-Weimar-Eisenach, Philadelphia, 1828.

Old Towpaths

A VIEW OF THE GRAND CANAL FROM LAKE ERIE TO THE HUDSON RIVER, by John Law, New York, 1825.
WILD SPORTS IN THE FAR WEST, by Frederick Gerstaecker, Boston and Chicago, 1870.

OHIO

A BRIEF HISTORY OF OHIO'S INTERNAL IMPROVEMENTS, by William D. Gallagher, in Hesperian or Western Monthly Magazine, 1838.
FIFTY YEARS AND OVER OF AKRON AND SUMMIT COUNTY, by Samuel A. Lane, Akron, 1892.
HISTORICAL COLLECTIONS OF OHIO, edited by Henry Howe, Cincinnati. 1848, 1850, 1852, Norwalk, 1896.
HISTORY OF BUTLER COUNTY, OHIO, Cincinnati, 1882.
HISTORY OF COSHOCTON COUNTY, OHIO, 1740-1881, by N. H. Hill, Jr., Newark, O., 1881.
HISTORY OF FRANKLIN AND PICKAWAY COUNTIES, OHIO, published by Williams Bros., Cleveland, 1882.
HISTORY OF HOCKING VALLEY, Interstate Publishing Co., Chicago, 1883.
HISTORY OF LICKING COUNTY, OHIO Compiled by N. H. Hill, Jr., Newark, O., 1881.
HISTORY OF NORTHWEST OHIO, by Nevin Otto Winter, Chicago, 1917.
HISTORY OF OHIO, by Caleb Atwater, Cincinnati, 1838.
HISTORY OF OHIO, by Emilius O. Randall and D. J. Ryan, New York, 1912.
HISTORY OF THE OHIO CANALS by C. P. McClelland and C. C. Huntington, Ohio Archaelogical and Historical Society, Columbus, 1905.
HISTORY OF ROSS COUNTY, OHIO, edited by Lyle S. Evans, Chicago and New York, 1917.
HISTORY OF SCIOTO COUNTY, OHIO, by Nelson W. Evans, Portsmouth, 1903.
HISTORY OF STARK COUNTY, OHIO, edited by William Henry Perrin, Chicago, 1881.
HISTORY OF SUMMIT COUNTY, OHIO, by Baskin and Battey, Chicago, 1881.
HISTORY OF TRUMBULL AND MAHONING COUNTIES, OHIO, Cleveland, 1882.
HISTORY OF TUSCARAWAS COUNTY, OHIO, compiled by J. B. Mansfield, Chicago, 1884.
HISTORY OF WARREN COUNTY, OHIO, Chicago, 1882.
INTERNAL IMPROVEMENTS IN OHIO, 1825-1850, by Charles N. Morris, in American Historical Association Papers, 1889.
LIFE AND REMINISCENCES OF HON. JAMES EMMITT, AS REVISED BY HIMSELF, edited by M. J. Carrigan, Chillicothe, 1888.
MEMOIRS OF JOHN QUINCY ADAMS, edited by Charles Francis Adams, Philadelphia, 1874-1877.
MEMOIRS OF THE MIAMI VALLEY, OHIO, edited by John C. Hover and others, Chicago, 1919-1920.

Bibliography

OLD LANDMARKS OF CANTON AND STARK COUNTY, OHIO, by John Danner, Logansport, Ind., 1904.
PUBLIC DOCUMENTS CONCERNING THE OHIO CANALS, ETC., compiled by John Kilbourn, Columbus, 1832.
RECOLLECTIONS OF LIFE IN OHIO FROM 1813 TO 1840, by William Cooper Howells, Cincinnati, 1895.
STORIES OF OHIO, by William Dean Howells, New York, 1897.
YEARS OF MY YOUTH, by William Dean Howells, New York, 1916.

PENNSYLVANIA

ACCOUNT OF THE CONEWAGO CANAL ON THE RIVER SUSQUEHANNA; TO WHICH IS PREFIXED THE ACT FOR INCORPORATING THE COMPANY, Philadelphia, 1798.
AMERICAN NOTES FOR GENERAL CIRCULATION, by Charles Dickens, London, 1842.
BUCKS COUNTY HISTORICAL SOCIETY PAPERS, Easton, Pa., 1917.
THE CANAL BOAT, Mrs. Harriet Beecher Stowe, in *Godey's Lady's Book*, Philadelphia, 1841.
CANAL LORE, by Edwin Charles, in Snyder County Historical Society Bulletin, Middleburg, Pa., 1922.
THE CANALS OF PENNSYLVANIA AND THE SYSTEM OF INTERNAL IMPROVEMENTS, by Theodore B. Klein, Harrisburg, 1901.
CORRUPT PRACTICES CONNECTED WITH THE BUILDING AND OPERATION OF THE STATE WORKS OF PENNSYLVANIA, by Avard L. Bishop, in *Yale Review*, New Haven, 1907.
DESCRIPTIVE AND HISTORICAL MEMORIALS OF HEILMAN DALE, by Rev. U. Henry Heilman, in Lebanon County Historical Society Papers, Lebanon, 1909.
FACTS AND ARGUMENTS IN FAVOUR OF ADOPTING RAILWAYS IN PREFERENCE TO CANALS IN THE STATE OF PENNSYLVANIA, ETC., Philadelphia, 1825.
A GEOGRAPHY OF PENNSYLVANIA, by Charles B. Trego, Philadelphia, 1843.
HISTORICAL ACCOUNT OF THE RISE, PROGRESS AND PRESENT STATE OF THE CANAL NAVIGATION IN PENNSYLVANIA, Philadelphia, 1795.
HISTORICAL COLLECTIONS OF THE STATE OF PENNSYLVANIA, by Sherman Day, Philadelphia, 1843.
HISTORICAL SOCIETY OF MONTGOMERY COUNTY, Sketches, Norristown, 1895–1910.
HISTORICAL SOCIETY OF SCHUYLKILL COUNTY, PUBLICATIONS, Pottsville, 1905–1910.
HISTORY OF BERKS COUNTY IN PENNSYLVANIA, by Morton L. Montgomery, Philadelphia, 1886.

Old Towpaths

HISTORY OF BERKS AND LEBANON COUNTIES, by I. Daniel Rupp, Lancaster, 1844.
HISTORY OF THE COUNTIES OF DAUPHIN AND LEBANON IN THE COMMONWEALTH OF PENNSYLVANIA, by William H. Egle, Philadelphia, 1883.
HISTORY OF THE EARLY SETTLEMENT OF THE JUNIATA VALLEY, by U. J. Jones, Philadelphia, 1856.
HISTORY OF LEHIGH COUNTY, PENNSYLVANIA, by Charles Rhoads Roberts, Rev. John Baer Stoudt, Rev. Thomas H. Krick and William J. Dietrich, Allentown, 1914.
HISTORY OF LYCOMING COUNTY, Published by D. J. Stewart, Philadelphia, 1876.
HISTORY OF MONTGOMERY COUNTY, edited by Theodore W. Bean, Philadelphia, 1884.
HISTORY OF NORTHAMPTON, LEHIGH, MONROE, SCHUYLKILL AND CARBON COUNTIES, by I. Daniel Rupp, Harrisburg, 1845.
HISTORY OF THE PENNSYLVANIA RAILROAD, by William Bender Wilson, Philadelphia, 1899.
HISTORY OF PHILADELPHIA, 1609-1884, by J. Thomas Scharf and Thomson Westcott, Philadelphia, 1884.
HISTORY OF SCHUYLKILL COUNTY, PENNSYLVANIA, edited by Adolf W. Schalk and Hon. D. C. Henning, State Historical Society, 1907.
HISTORY OF THE SCHUYLKILL NAVIGATION, by Jay V. Hare, in *The Pilot* (Reading Railroad Magazine), Philadelphia, 1912–13.
HISTORY AND TOPOGRAPHY OF DAUPHIN, CUMBERLAND, FRANKLIN, BEDFORD, ADAMS, PERRY, SOMERSET, CAMBRIA and INDIANA COUNTIES, I. Daniel Rupp, Compiler, Lancaster City, Pa., 1846.
HISTORY OF WAYNE, PIKE AND MONROE COUNTIES, by Alfred Matthews, Philadelphia, 1886.
HISTORY OF YORK COUNTY, edited by John Gibson, Chicago, 1886.
AN ILLUSTRATED HISTORY OF THE COMMONWEALTH OF PENNSYLVANIA, by William H. Egle, Harrisburg, 1877.
JOSIAH WHITE'S STORY, GIVEN BY HIMSELF, Philadelphia, 1910.
LEBANON COUNTY HISTORICAL SOCIETY PAPERS, Lebanon, 1898–1919.
LETTERS ADDRESSED TO THE PEOPLE OF PENNSYLVANIA, RESPECTING THE INTERNAL IMPROVEMENT OF THE COMMONWEALTH BY MEANS OF ROADS AND CANALS, by William J. Duane, Philadelphia, 1811.
LOTTERIES IN PENNSYLVANIA PRIOR TO 1833, by Asa Earl Martin, in *Pennsylvania Magazine of History and Biography*, Philadelphia, 1924.
NOTES TAKEN IN SIXTY YEARS, by Richard Smith Elliott, St. Louis, 1883.
OLD SCHUYLKILL TALES, by Mrs. Ella Zerbey Elliott, Pottsville, 1906.
PICTURE SKETCH BOOK OF PENNSYLVANIA, by Eli C. Bowen, Philadelphia, 1853.

Bibliography

REPORTS ON CANALS, ROADS AND OTHER SUBJECTS, MADE TO THE PENN-
SYLVANIA SOCIETY FOR THE PROMOTION OF INTERNAL IMPROVEMENTS,
by William Strickland, Philadelphia, 1826.
THE SCHUYLKILL CANAL NAVIGATOR, by S. Alspach, Philadelphia, 1827.
THE SCHUYLKILL NAVIGATION, by Edwin F. Smith, in Schuylkill County
Historical Society Publications, Pottsville, 1910.
A SHOT FROM A BACKWOODS MARKSMAN, MOST RESPECTFULLY ADDRESSED
TO THE PEOPLE OF PENNSYLVANIA BY THEIR HUMBLE SERVANT, A
SHINGLE MAKER, Philadelphia, original, 1832, reprint, 1911.
THE WYOMING VALLEY, UPPER WATERS OF THE SUSQUEHANNA AND
LACKAWANNA COAL REGION, by J. A. Clark, Scranton, 1875.

SOUTH CAROLINA

HISTORY OF THE SANTEE CANAL, by F. A. Porcher, South Carolina Historical Society, Charleston, 1903.

VIRGINIA

CENTRAL WATER LINE FROM THE OHIO RIVER TO THE VIRGINIA CAPES,
James River and Kanawha Company, Richmond, 1868.
CORRESPONDENCE OF THE PRESIDENT OF THE JAMES RIVER AND KANAWHA
COMPANY WITH AN ASSOCIATION OF FRENCH CAPITALISTS, Richmond,
1860.
HISTORY OF THE JAMES RIVER AND KANAWHA COMPANY, by Wayland
Fuller Dunaway, New York, 1922.
HISTORY OF NORFOLK COUNTY, by Col. William H. Stewart, Chicago, 1902.
HISTORY OF ROCKBRIDGE COUNTY, by Oren F. Morton, Staunton, Va.,
1920.
LYNCHBURG AND ITS PEOPLE, by W. Asbury Christian, Lynchburg, 1900.
THE OLD VIRGINIA GENTLEMAN AND OTHER SKETCHES, by George W.
Bagby, New York, 1910.
REPORT OF THE COMMITTEE APPOINTED BY THE VIRGINIA LEGISLATURE IN
THE SESSION OF 1811-12 TO CONSIDER THE NAVIGATION OF THE
JAMES RIVER (1812).
RICHMOND IN BYGONE DAYS, by S. Mordecai, Richmond, 1856-1860.

This bibliography does not pretend to be complete. There are other works which touch more or less remotely upon canal history; and among the well-defined canal material there are hundreds of argumentative pamphlets, petitions, charters, reports of managers, engineers, boards of directors, stockholders' committees, legislative and Congressional committees, governors' messages, canal rules and regulations, etc.

Much valuable material is also contained in the newspapers and magazines of the period.

www.ingramcontent.com/pod-product-compliance
Lightning Source LLC
Chambersburg PA
CBHW070525090426
42735CB00013B/2864